Chain of Title

HOW THREE ORDINARY AMERICANS UNCOVERED
WALL STREET'S GREAT FORECLOSURE FRAUD

David Dayen

THE NEW PRESS

NEW YORK
LONDON

Requests for permission to reproduce selections from this book should be made through our website: https://thenewpress.com/contact.

This paperback edition published by The New Press, 2017
Distributed by Two Rivers Distribution

978-1-62097-158-1 (hc)
978-1-62097-159-8 (e-book)
978-1-62097-350-9 (pb)
CIP data available

The New Press publishes books that promote and enrich public discussion
and understanding of the issues vital to our democracy and to a more equitable world. These
books are made possible by the enthusiasm of our readers; the support of a committed group
of donors, large and small; the collaboration of our many partners in the independent media
and the not-for-profit sector; booksellers, who often hand-sell New Press books; librarians;
and above all by our authors.

www.thenewpress.com

Composition by Westchester Publishing Services
This book was set in Minion

Printed in the United States of America

CONTENTS

PREFACE

There is a rot at the heart of our democracy, rooted in a nagging mystery that has yet to be unraveled. It gnaws at people, occupies their thoughts, leaves them searching for answers in the chill of the night. Americans want to know why no high-ranking Wall Street executive has gone to jail for the conduct that precipitated the financial crisis.

The oddest thing about the predominance of the question is that everyone already assumes they know the answer. They believe that too many politicians, regulators, and law enforcement officials, bought off with campaign contributions or the promise of a future job, simply allowed banker miscreants to annihilate the law in pursuit of profit. But they must not like the explanation very much, because they keep asking why, as if they want to be proven wrong, to be given a different story.

Maybe they don't like the implications of a government that lets Wall Street walk. It does too much violence to the conception of the country they have in their mind, with its ideals of justice and fairness. It explains the disempowerment people feel in the face of a rigged economic and political system, with differing standards of treatment depending on wealth and power. It engenders a loss of faith in core institutions, turning our democracy into a sideshow, where the real action happens offstage. It inspires people to don tricornered hats and protest crony capitalism, or pitch camp at the base of Wall Street and refuse to move. It generates a profound anxiety, for if bankers can bring the economy to the point of ruin and get away with it, what's to stop them from doing it again? It makes our economy seem too fragile, our laws too impotent.

Or maybe people just want the details filled in, to confirm their suspicions, so they can point fingers at those who created this two-tiered system of accountability. There must be a set of facts that prove we're living in a new Gilded Age, where holders of prodigious wealth guide government policy the way a string guides a marionette. There must be a smoking gun.

Those details are available, but not where most chroniclers of the financial crisis have ever cared to look. They usually take a ten-thousand-foot view, recounting stories of the hubris of bank CEOs or tracking the swashbuckling, without-a-net exploits of those tasked with stanching the bleeding. But few have offered the perspective of millions of ordinary Americans, the ones who never visited a Wall Street office tower or a Washington conference suite, and who endured most of the suffering that resulted from the crash. At ground level, the crisis was not a cautionary tale of greed or an adventure plot: it was a tragedy, too casually hidden from view.

Starting in 2009—as the crisis raged—three of these ordinary Americans decided to take on this mystery for themselves, to fill in those details, to understand what Wall Street perpetrated and why. In so doing, they played a significant role in uncovering the largest consumer fraud in American history.

They didn't work in government or law enforcement. They were not experts in real estate law. They had no history of anti-corporate activism or community organizing. They had no resources or institutional knowledge. They were a cancer nurse, a car salesman, and an insurance fraud specialist, and they were all foreclosure victims. While struggling with the shame and dislocation and financial stress that foreclosure causes, they did something extraordinary: they read their mortgage documents. Wall Street's scheme was not hidden but readily apparent in millions of pieces of documentary evidence, and to be a whistleblower, you just had to pay attention.

All whistleblowers are a little bit crazy. They obsess over things most people overlook. They see grand conspiracies where others see only shadows. In this case, these whistleblowers, armed with only a few websites and a hunger for the truth, found that the mortgage industry fundamentally ruptured a centuries-old system of U.S. property law; that millions of documents generated to foreclose on people's homes were phony; and that all those purchasing a mortgage in America were taking a gamble that they would be tossed onto the street with nothing, even if they made every payment and played by the rules. Virtually everyone to whom they presented this information reacted the same way: "That can't be true." Right up until the day the banks admitted it.

These three—Lisa Epstein, Michael Redman, and Lynn Szymoniak—unearthed another layer of the mystery, too. After they exposed foreclosure fraud and forced the nation's leading mortgage companies to stop repossessing homes, they saw firsthand the unwillingness of our government to deliver any consequences. In fact, walk into any courtroom today and you will see the same false documents, the same ones Lisa, Michael, and Lynn exposed, used to foreclose on homeowners.

As America searches for understanding amid the perversity of the financial crisis, they should know that there were a few determined people, far from the corridors of power, who tried to write an alternative history, one where the perpetrators of fraud get rounded up and put away. But the same democracy that allows ordinary Americans to collaborate and organize and build a movement allows their deep-pocketed opponents to use the tools of entrenched power to counteract it. And we have to reckon with the fact that, in our current system of justice, who you are matters more than what you did.

Michael Redman, one of these whistleblowers, sat next to me one night as he told me his story, and said over and over again, "I don't believe your book. I lived through it, and I don't believe it." I will forgive readers their skepticism, as even a protagonist in the tale shares it. It is unbelievable. That doesn't make it untrue.

1

A KNOCK AT THE DOOR

As a man is said to have a right to his property, he may be equally said to have a property in his rights.

—James Madison, *National Gazette*, March 29, 1792

February 17, 2009

The sun crept down over the Intracoastal Waterway, separating Palm Beach from its companion cities to the west. With the proper nautical chops, you could navigate from Norfolk, Virginia, to Key West through this shore-hugging water highway bordering open ocean, down through the Great Dismal Swamp, under the Hobucken Bridge, across the marshy lowlands of South Carolina and Georgia, and through the Mosquito Lagoon Aquatic Preserve, on the Indian River near the city of Edgewater. Eventually you would hit Palm Beach, located on a sixteen-mile-long barrier island of manicured lawns, ritzy mansions, and precisely fashioned grains of sand, a place where American ingenuity and truckloads of money summoned paradise out of the Atlantic. A few miles inland, amid vacationers and part-time snowbirds seeking refuge from winter winds up north, a car motored down Route 80 to tell Lisa and Alan Epstein that their bank wanted to take their home away.

Florida felt the worst of the Great Recession's force, a financial hurricane that spared almost nobody, not even in paradise. This was one of the "sand states," warm-weather regions of the country with economies disproportionately based on real estate. Home prices in Florida, Arizona, California, and Nevada surged more than 264 percent from 1998 to 2006. Over half of all subprime mortgages written in 2006 were issued in these four states. "Sand states" turned out to be an accurate description of the market's feeble foundations, as prices crumbled and industries that supported and sustained the bubble washed out.

In fact, Florida suffered two waves of foreclosures. The first engulfed those who purchased or refinanced mortgages at the height of the bubble, in 2004, 2005, and 2006. While tagged as "irresponsible," these homeowners actually suffered from inadvertent timing and susceptibility to predatory lending. When prices sank, borrowers went "underwater"—owing more on the mortgage than the homes were worth. They couldn't sell or refinance to escape, and many couldn't afford the payments to begin with. This led to defaults, even in Palm Beach. Then came the second wave, relentless ripple effects from unemployment in real estate, construction, and pretty soon everything else, swallowing those who paid their mortgages effortlessly for years. Suddenly hundreds of thousands of Floridians needed help, and help was slow to come.

So it was not uncommon to find cars like the four-door sedan motoring past West Palm Beach's shiny subdivisions. Process servers contracted by "foreclosure mill" law firms, so named because they pumped out foreclosures the way a textile mill would fabrics, made their daily rounds here, unsmilingly handing homeowners legal documents and informing them that as a result of their failure to pay their mortgage promptly, their lender would place them into foreclosure.

By early 2009, one in twenty-two Florida homeowners had received some sort of filing like this, such as a notice of default, court summons, auction sale, or foreclosure judgment—nine times the historical average. Local sheriff's deputies used to deliver the papers, but there were now too many to handle. So the foreclosure mills had to hire private contractors; it represented one of the few recession-era growth industries in the state.

Nobody on either side of the transaction felt particularly good about it. The process servers greeted eyes filled with tears, faces lined with desperation. The full force of post-recession fury at Wall Street malfeasance and personal tragedy refracted onto them. Though business boomed, it was shit work, the misery beat. In fact, you can almost understand why some contractors ducked the emotional tumult by resorting to "sewer service"—a popular scam where they would simply throw envelopes in front of the home, technically fulfilling their obligations while ensuring that the homeowner would not see the complaint or know to show up for court. This was illegal, but it also carried the benefit of being way faster than actually knocking on the door, increasing volume—and profits.

Sensing opportunity, some process servers and foreclosure mills even invented fake recipients of foreclosure papers. In Pasco County, Judge Susan Gardner found numerous charges for serving papers to "unknown spouses" and "unidentified tenants." One process server in Miami listed forty-six defendants on a single property, racking up $5,000 in fees. He claimed he had to serve everyone in the state with the same name as the homeowner, in case one of them was the real defendant. Every two-bit business in Florida had its own way of skirting the edges of the law to get ahead; this was a particularly crude one.

As for the homeowners, news of foreclosure tore through their front door like a wrecking ball. Taking a family's house involved taking their spirit and snuffing it out like a candle, the bright light fading into smoke. Millions of Americans who thought they gained a foothold in the middle class, a clear pathway to wealth and economic security, absorbed the collateral damage of a fatal miscalculation on Wall Street.

This evening's pageant of process serving would come to rest at 607 Gazetta Way, in an unincorporated area near West Palm Beach, a classic post-boom development of oversized properties on small lots. Built in 2006, the three-bedroom, two-bathroom, one-story home with a clay tile roof and yellow siding was wedged between a collection of larger properties all painted the same, as if the builder decided yellow was the optimal color to convince buyers to take the leap. Inside the house, the Epstein family had no warning of their impending visitor.

Lisa Epstein sat on a ledge in the master bathroom, hospital scrubs rolled to her knees, her daughter Jenna kept upright in the bathtub by a reclining baby seat. Lisa's brown hair was pulled back with her trademark multicolored scarf, the kind you would see in the 1970s, maybe on *Rhoda* or *The Bob Newhart Show*. She had blue eyes, soft features, and a laugh you could hear across a crowded room. When she got excited she got very loud. But at the moment she focused on her daughter in the tub.

Blond-haired, big-eyed Jenna had been born with a mild form of spina bifida. Her spinal cord was tethered at the base, something that could generate motor control problems as she grew. The child would turn two in March; surgery had been scheduled for April. And Lisa could think of practically nothing else, ministering to Jenna at nearly every waking moment. As a cancer nurse, she worked with families coping with the stress of a sick child. Now she was experiencing the same emotions: consumed by the same yearning to keep her daughter comfortable, and at stray moments wondering how this beautiful creature could be marked for affliction.

Lisa was forty-three, a nurse, a wife, and a new mother. She had only lived in the house two years. And her life was about to change forever.

KNOCK KNOCK KNOCK!

She did not hesitate for a second. "That's about the house, Alan!" she yelled out to her husband. "They're from the bank, and it's not good news!"

Lisa Epstein dreamed of following her father, a pediatrician, into medicine. After earning a nursing degree from George Mason University in 1988, she bounced around the mid-Atlantic from one job to the next: the pediatric intensive care unit at D.C. Children's Hospital; an OR in Rehoboth Beach, Delaware; an endocrinology unit at the National Institutes of Health. Soon she started her own business as a freelancer in Columbia, Maryland, working with terminally ill patients in home care, while filling in for nurses across the Washington Beltway.

Lisa chose to enter an area of nursing that involved long-term, one-on-one collaboration with people who were at the end of their lives and often aware of their own mortality. There were daily duties, techniques to make patients comfortable and free of pain. And she loved the perpetual motion of the job, marking her ability in the eyes of her patients. But to Lisa, the real appeal was the challenge of being the last new person these terminally ill people would ever connect with, a confidant amid an atmosphere of grieving. Lisa would make her patients laugh, hear their stories, pray with them, cry with them, and give them strength when needed. Building intimacy and trust helped keep people alive, too.

Part of the job involved knowing when and how to tell patients, "It may be time for you to videotape yourself reading bedtime stories to your grandchild. I'm not saying you won't be there to read to them, but with this new information from your scan, it would be nice for your family to have that." Even doctors flinched at such naked honesty. Everyone in the medical system, on both sides of the desk, clings to the faintest possibility of recovery. If treatments A, B, C, D, E, F, and G don't work, let's try treatment H. But someone has to stress the importance of organizing thoughts, of compensating loved ones with the word "goodbye." In those darkest moments of loss and depression, the truth can be an odd comfort. It took as much skill as knowing how to connect an IV or read an EKG.

Over nine years in the D.C. area, Lisa built her freelance nursing business, helping patients balance hopes of recovery with the realities of the life cycle. She had lived in the region since early childhood, and while she wasn't too interested in politics, she grew accustomed to the dynamic, politically charged environment. Plus D.C. had another side: a storehouse of experts with accumulated wisdom on virtually every topic. Whenever she found herself in the District, Lisa would find a lecture on something she knew nothing about. Away from the stress of caretaking, it was nice to decompress and enter an unknown world.

But these were also restless years for Lisa. Every fall, when the leaves changed color and the clouds rolled in, she would feel a powerful rush of sadness, bursting into tears for no reason. These days they call it seasonal affective disorder, but Lisa never gave it a name. She just recognized the need for a change of scenery. So in 1997 Lisa decided to head to Florida for the winter. The state had three renewable resources: alligators, palmetto bugs, and the elderly, and the last meant that nurses never had trouble finding work.

After writing a few letters, Lisa got offered a temp job at a chemotherapy infusion center at Good Samaritan Medical Center in downtown West Palm Beach. The work sounded grueling, but Lisa focused on three syllables: Flo-ri-da. She packed a bag, locked up her apartment in Maryland, and drove down I-95.

A week or so after taking the job, Lisa strolled outside the cancer center on her lunch break, and under a cloudless sky she sat on a seawall in front of the Intracoastal Waterway. Palm trees lined the waterfront; the view seemed to go on for miles. Lisa felt the sun on her face and listened to the dull hum of the water cresting against the barricades. Her legs dangled below the seawall, her head raised to meet the light.

She never left Florida again.

Nearly every day that first year, Lisa would come home from work (the temp job soon became permanent), change into a bathing suit, and stroll along the beach, the spray from the Atlantic Ocean hitting her bare toes. She

missed the fast-paced lifestyle in D.C.—she even subscribed to the Sunday
Washington Post to keep up with the news. But the sun and the sand provided ample reimbursement.

Lisa initially stayed with family—her mother's parents lived in the
area—then rented a townhouse recommended by a patient. Within a
couple of years she wanted to put down roots, a major decision. Lisa had always been conservative with money. She stashed away her paychecks,
clipped coupons, and skipped extravagances. Her hobbies included such
inexpensive pursuits as reading and walking. This gave her sterling credit
and plenty of savings for a down payment. While Lisa hesitated at the
commitment attached to homeownership, she determined that Florida
was where she wanted to be.

Real estate agents routinely tried to upsell Lisa. She gave them a price
range, and they would show her houses 25 percent above it. So Lisa cut her
price range by 25 percent and was then shown places within her limits. That
meant a lot of condos and a lot of junk. Lisa had two non-negotiables: a balcony and a view of the water. "I don't care what it looks like on the inside,"
she'd tell the agents. They'd smile and show her a snappy two-bedroom
with granite countertops, where if you stood in the corner of the balcony
and leaned out far enough to the left, you could maybe spot a tiny lake. The
foray into home buying just wasn't working out.

Then Lisa read in the newspaper about a 700-square-foot one-bedroom,
owned by a retired couple who loved the place but wanted to move from the
fifth floor to the second to make things easier. Lisa went out to see the 1960s-
era white building, known as the Royal Saxon, at the southern tip of Palm
Beach. The interior resembled an old hotel just past its prime, and the apartment was definitely small. But the balcony looked directly onto the Intracoastal Waterway, with swaying palm trees and the bridge to Lake Worth
on one side and boats tied up on a little dock below. Though she would be
the youngest tenant in the building by about thirty years, Lisa instantly pic-
tured herself there.

There was one problem. The apartment was a New York City–style co-op.
Instead of obtaining a mortgage, purchasers take out loans to buy shares
in a corporation that owns the entire building, enabling them to occupy one
of the units. These "share loans" include the cost of maintenance and up-
keep, much like a homeowners association fee. Tenants don't own their res-

idence when they complete the mortgage payments, but they own a stake in the property, which they can sell at the market rate.

Share loans are often cheaper than traditional mortgages, but because of their uncertainty—for example, defaults by one resident can force others to carry their costs—lenders steer clear of them, particularly in places like Florida, where they aren't widely used. That's what happened to Lisa, whose preapproved financing collapsed.

The retired couple liked Lisa. Or maybe they liked the idea of adding some youth to the building. So they financed the property themselves. In December 1998 Lisa put down $25,000 cash and signed a private, fifteen-year fixed mortgage with her neighbors for $56,000. Every month she would walk down three flights of stairs and slide her payment under the door. She never dealt with a mortgage company and never had to take out a separate homeowner's insurance policy, as her neighbors bundled it with the monthly payment. Lisa's local "banker" lived in her building, and they agreed to a mutually beneficial private deal. No hidden fees, no adjustable-rate mortgages, none of the innovations of the past forty years of financial services. There were maybe a dozen mortgages like this left in America.

Lisa had backed into a nice little life: a job she enjoyed, the respect and appreciation of her patients, the view of the water. And then she met Alan in an America Online chat room. Both Alan and Lisa were middle-class Jews raised in the Northeast, reinventing themselves amid the sunshine. Lisa introduced Alan to her brother, who ran a business reselling mobile phones and equipment, and Alan began to work with him. A closeness soon blossomed between Lisa and Alan, and they quickly fell in love.

Very early into the relationship, while not explicitly trying to have a child, Lisa and Alan stopped trying to prevent it. The tug of motherhood pulled Lisa into her life's next phase. In the fall of 2002 she became pregnant. The couple made plans to marry and beamed with joy. But twelve weeks into the pregnancy, Lisa was at work when she found a pink spot on her clothing. Hours later, at the hospital, the obstetrician couldn't locate the baby's heartbeat. It took surgery to extract the fetus; Lisa's body wouldn't let go.

Despite their profound grief, Lisa and Alan did marry. And it took three years—a period of much heartache, guarded hopefulness, and expensive fertility treatments—before they conceived a second time. After enduring so much, Lisa was thrilled to have life growing inside her again. She was forty-one and knew this would be her final pregnancy. She smiled every time the baby kicked and when she got to see her little arms and legs on the sonogram.

And then Alan tried to sell Lisa on moving.

Lisa and Alan lived in Lisa's one-bedroom co-op. The place could barely fit two people; Alan considered three out of the question. He started telling Lisa he wanted their daughter to grow up in a typical American home, with her own room. Lisa felt like the motivation wasn't simply greater comfort but a sense of duty, what you could call "white picket fence syndrome." People get married and have a child and move into a big house. Society dictated that, and everyone had to play by the rules.

"For people all over this world, this would be paradise," Lisa argued, pointing out how families lived in New York with two kids and a dog in a studio apartment. Maybe in a couple of years, after the baby started walking, after they built up more equity, it would make sense to move, but not now. Lisa had her view of the water, and she didn't want to give it up. But Alan was insistent.

It was early 2007 when Lisa and Alan started looking for a new place. Whatever Lisa remembered about the housing market when she bought her apartment did not correspond. Stories about real estate mania were legendary in Florida. Turn on the radio or television, pass by a bus stop, and the messages bombarded you: *New homes! Great opportunity! Buy now!* One day Lisa drove by a row of people in tents, lined up in front of a trailer on an empty tract of land. These were prospective buyers, camped out for two or three days to pick their preferred spot on a grid of new construction. In Florida during the housing bubble, every day was Black Friday.

As Lisa and Alan began their search, however, things were a little less frenzied. Where advertisements once stressed urgency (*Don't miss out!*), now they highlighted deals (*Was $400K, now $350K!*). The professionals pitched it as a moment for bargain hunting, "a great time to buy." Lisa wondered if they would ever consider it a *bad* time.

In truth, the housing bubble had begun its long decline. If you scanned the back of the business pages, you knew it. Ameriquest, one of the biggest mortgage lenders in the country, abruptly closed all its retail branches in the middle of 2006. New Century Financial, another giant, faced a huge cash shortfall that summer, and would go bankrupt the following spring. Homeowners felt the crunch as well; foreclosure rates doubled within three years. For most ordinary Americans, even prospective home buyers, these warning signs stayed far in the background. And you could still find optimists among economic analysts. As Federal Reserve chair Ben Bernanke testified to the Joint Economic Committee in early 2007, "The impact on the broader economy and financial markets of the problems in the subprime market seems likely to be contained." In other words, there would only be one foreclosure wave, not two, flushing out only those who bought too much house and borrowed too much money. Young families with steady incomes, like Lisa and Alan, didn't have to worry.

But while Ben Bernanke didn't foresee a crisis, Florida home builders knew the machine that had sustained profits for the last decade was seizing up. They needed to dump their remaining homes before the market collapsed. Subdivisions halfway through construction suddenly listed all their properties for sale. Developers hired landscapers and quickly poured asphalt for streets. They cut prices to reel in shoppers and flush inventory off their books. Those looking for homes thought they were smartly buying low, but they were actually the last unsuspecting souls lured into the housing bubble's trap. Lisa didn't pay much attention. She was pregnant, still working full-time, and low on energy.

One day Alan asked Lisa to stop by a house on Gazetta Way, in a brand-new gated community built by D.R. Horton, one of America's largest developers. She made the trip to the development, twenty minutes west of the Atlantic Ocean, down one of the wide boulevards that seemed to stretch endlessly through south Florida. The homes inside the gate looked gargantuan, dwarfing the tiny, just-planted palm trees scattered about. To the left was a standard item in Florida subdivisions: the giant, purposeless man-made lake, with a fountain shooting water skyward. Lisa called Alan and asked if he was sure the house was on Gazetta Way. "These look like college dorms, not homes!" Alan assured her she was in the right place.

The model Alan picked out was the most affordable on the block. But Lisa frowned before walking inside. Despite the relative modesty— neighbors' homes towered close on either side—the house was almost three times the size of her co-op. The front door opened to a giant room with high ceilings that Lisa found pointless. Mazelike corridors spilled into bedrooms split between opposite sides of the house. Lisa hated the idea of having to walk through the giant unusable room to attend to her child in the night. The kitchen had no windows, but the bedroom windows looked directly into the neighbor's property, with zero space in between. Lisa thought she could reach out her hand and actually touch the neighbor's house, at least if the windows would open.

Lisa stepped outside to a tiny backyard patio bracketed by two saplings, and a few feet beyond that was a thin canal containing something resembling a liquid substance. It hardly compared to Lisa's view of the water. Everything about the house seemed rushed and slapped together. She had no interest in the place. But Alan did, and so did his parents, who encouraged the house hunt. Lisa felt outnumbered and exhausted, so she just went along.

They made a plan to buy the house and then sell the condo. Lisa was eight years into a fifteen-year mortgage, and thanks to sometimes paying extra principal, she only owed about $25,000. Meanwhile, the value of the condo had shot up. They figured they could get at least $250,000 for it and put the proceeds toward the new house, with a small mortgage left over. It wasn't a reckless idea; growing families stepping up into bigger homes had used the same strategy for decades. And the bubble-era price spike would theoretically work in their favor on the condo.

To lock in the house, however, they had to close the deal first. So on February 23, 2007, Lisa and Alan sat down at DHI Mortgage, D.R. Horton's financing subsidiary, to sign the closing papers. They put $17,000 down for the house on Gazetta Way, 5 percent of the purchase price, and took out a mortgage for the remaining $313,000. Because Alan's phone reseller business had unpredictable revenue, the couple decided to use Lisa's superior credit score—803 at the time—and put the loan in her name. And Lisa, eight months pregnant, told the loan officer, much to his surprise, that she would read every page of the mortgage before signing it.

The problem was that she had to pee. A lot.

The closing agent, representatives from the builder, and Alan had to wait while Lisa perused the mortgage, line by line, in between trips to the bathroom. She could get through about five pages at a time before excusing herself.

Lisa's only experience with mortgages was the private one with her neighbors. That was a simple fifteen-year fixed-rate deal; this was much more complicated. Despite her perfect credit, DHI Mortgage put Lisa into a loan reserved for subprime rather than prime borrowers. To keep initial payments low, it was interest-only for the first ten years. After that, not only would principal payments get added and the mortgage reamortized over the final twenty years, but the interest rate would adjust upward. The monthly payment would end up hundreds if not thousands of dollars higher. Financially speaking, it was a time bomb set to explode in ten years, by which time DHI Mortgage would have made plenty of money.

The interest-only terms meant the couple would build no equity for a decade, beyond the 5 percent down payment. Once closing costs were factored in, a small decline in home value, maybe 3 percent, would put them underwater. That would create a precarious situation if they experienced any financial disruption. As prominent financial analyst Josh Rosner said back in 2001 when these types of mortgage products started coming out, "A home without equity is just a rental with debt." But Lisa wasn't aware of these downsides. Reading through the mortgage was more of a formality, a way to appear responsible. She didn't have the background to decipher it all, and in the back of her mind she gave herself an out: Lisa was planning to sell the apartment and use the money to pay down the mortgage significantly. So whatever those pieces of paper said wouldn't apply. When she reached the last page of the mortgage, she signed it.

Only later would Lisa and Alan realize their mistake. They could not sell the co-op, whose value would eventually drop by more than 60 percent. Every week Lisa would call the listing agent, and every week she'd hear the same thing: no bidders. Lisa slid the mortgage payment under her neighbors' door at the Royal Saxon once a month, then came back to write a check for the house. The couple had enough savings to handle two mortgage payments for a little while, but not forever.

In March Jenna was born, and Lisa considered all the hardship of bringing her into the world worth it. But when she was eighteen months old a new pediatrician found a birth defect on Jenna's lower spine, something her old doctor had dismissed as nothing important. The new doctor requested an MRI, which led to the diagnosis of spina bifida. Her vertebrae were tethered to the bottom of the spinal cord, pulled tight as a rubber band. Without treatment, the stretching would aggravate over time. The barrage of tests and doctor's visits took Lisa out of work periodically. Jenna's doctors recommended surgery to correct the malady, and between that and aftercare, Lisa and Alan were looking at thousands of dollars in medical bills. At the same time, as the housing bubble popped, businesses throughout Florida failed, including the cell phone reseller. Alan lost his job.

The cascade of financial and emotional pressures overwhelmed the young couple, their relationship suffering the collateral consequences of the mounting pile of debt. Compounding this was the fact that Lisa and Alan dared not tell family or friends about their money troubles. Anybody in Florida in 2007 could recognize a foreclosure crisis if they paid attention—a moving truck in the driveway, packed boxes on the curb with a crude sign attached reading "Free"—but you'd almost never hear about it in public. Neighbors who lost their homes drove down property values, which led to more foreclosures and more drops in home prices. So people had powerful reasons to keep to themselves, to try to solve their problems in isolation, lest they be identified as the source of the community's downward spiral. As a result, the foreclosure wave swept through Florida practically in silence.

In January 2008 Lisa made some calculations and determined she could pay the mortgages on the house and the condo for nine more months. After that she would need financial help for the first time in her life. She called her mortgage company, hoping it could modify the payment or work something out. Though Lisa had taken out the loan with DHI Mortgage, early on she was advised to mail payments to Chase Home Finance, a division of JPMorgan Chase, one of America's biggest banks. The whole thing always seemed a little suspicious. But JPMorgan Chase's stature encouraged Lisa about the prospects for assistance. The company boasted of its "fortress" balance sheet. When the investment bank Bear Stearns failed in March 2008, government officials solicited Chase to buy it. Lisa read about other banks failing left and right, but Chase seemed secure. Surely it had some smart people who could make this all work.

She talked to a Chase Home Finance representative. "I have nine months to work something out," she said. "We have plenty of time, I have a perfect credit score, and I've never paid anything late. What can we do?" The representative told her to fax in financial documents and they would get back to her. Lisa did what she was told but never heard anything. She called back the next week. And the next week. And the next.

Lisa never talked to the same person and would constantly have to explain her story from scratch. They always requested new copies of the documents, claiming to have lost the previous ones. Lisa spent a fortune in copy and fax charges; it was as though the documents she sent drifted into a black hole. And there didn't seem to be any consistency from one Chase representative to the next. Someone would tell Lisa she was days away from approval, and the next employee would have no record of her application, forcing her to start over. The ordeal took enough time and effort to become a second job.

At the cancer center, Lisa increasingly found herself enmeshed in her patients' financial crises, just as she struggled to deal with her own. It was customary for patients to ask for a doctor's signature confirming their diagnosis so they could present it to creditors and secure financial relief. But patients would come back multiple times to Lisa, asking for another doctor's note, and then another. The mortgage companies were obviously losing the notes. Lisa understood what was happening but never revealed her own secret of financial suffering. Patients would even ask Lisa to call their mortgage company to confirm their medical condition. But that only brought her face-to-face with the same crushing bureaucracy she personally encountered. Lisa's frustration compounded as she haggled with other people's mortgage companies by day and her own at night.

At one point a Chase representative told Lisa, "Well, you're calling us, but on loans like this we answer to Wells Fargo, and they're blocking all modifications." Lisa had never walked into a Wells Fargo bank or had any dealings with them at all. What interest did they have in her mortgage? She called Wells Fargo and asked why it was blocking her modification, but nobody there had any record of a Lisa Epstein. Since Chase representatives gave her different information every day, she figured Wells Fargo agents might as well. She added them to her roster of weekly calls. But nobody at Wells ever recognized her as a customer.

The runaround used up Lisa's entire buffer of savings. Instead of being able to act prudently in January, she was now desperate in September, after wasting months calling, faxing, pleading, and begging. Finally someone at Chase offered advice. The bank had enough problems assisting borrowers who had already defaulted; it would never go out of its way for someone current on her loan. And while no agent ever said explicitly, *You must skip a few payments to earn our attention,* the implication was clear: Lisa should stop paying her mortgage for ninety days, trigger a formal default, and then call back. Only then would Chase offer help.

Lisa had never missed a payment on anything in her life—not her mortgage, not her car loan, not her utility bills, nothing. Something inside her associated delinquency with shame, with inadequacy, with a betrayal of her most cherished obligations. "I'm a good person because I have a good credit score," she would tell herself. But like millions of Americans on the wrong side of the housing collapse, she was desperate. Her marriage was breaking apart, her daughter required medical attention, and her savings were nearly depleted. If not paying the mortgage could lead her out of this mess, though it went against every impulse in her body, she would do it.

At the end of October 2008, the same month banks like Chase received hundreds of billions of dollars in a government bailout, Lisa Epstein didn't turn in her monthly mortgage payment. The day she became a delinquent homeowner, she vomited. And she did the same thing almost every day for three months. Lisa checked each day off on a wall-mounted calendar, and by the end she must have lost twenty pounds. It wasn't about losing the house: after all, she considered it a monstrosity. It was more about losing her self-worth, her mark of accomplishment, those numbers on a page that size you up as a net contributor to society or a burden.

Around this time Lisa had a dream. It was nighttime in the big house, amid a deluge of rain that was pouring down the windows in sheets. Lisa held her daughter to comfort her during the clatter. The walls filled up with water, giant pulsing bulges swelling against the furniture, expanding and expanding. Finally the walls popped and water burst through, flooding the home. Lisa grabbed her child and ran out into the street, away from this underwater home that threatened to submerge her and her family. She didn't need to consult a psychiatrist to interpret the dream's meaning.

The ninety days were up, and Lisa called Chase again. "Okay, it's been three months," Lisa said. The rep said Chase would send something right out to her, just hang on, not to worry.

A couple weeks later, she got the knock at the door. And she just knew.

"They're from the bank and it's not good news!"

Alan trudged to the bathroom with the bundle of documents and put it in Lisa's hands. She steadied herself and tore open the envelope.

In Florida, when lenders wanted to foreclose on a delinquent borrower, they had to file a lawsuit. So this was a copy of a complaint from Florida Default Law Group, a leading foreclosure mill, holding Lisa liable for violating the terms of her mortgage, accompanied by a court summons and a bevy of legal notices. She had twenty days to file a written response.

Lisa found a surprise atop the summons. The name Chase Home Finance didn't appear. Neither did Wells Fargo. Lisa ran her finger along the section that named the plaintiff: "U.S. Bank NA as trustee for JPMorgan Mortgage Trust 2007-S2."

Lisa already had no idea how Wells Fargo fit into her mortgage. Now here was U.S. Bank—which to her sounded fictional, like the name of a bank in a movie—listed as the lead plaintiff in the foreclosure. And what was a trustee? Or a trust?

What did any of this mean?

2

THE DARK SIDE OF THE AMERICAN DREAM

Lisa Epstein drove down Highway A1A, along the Intracoastal Waterway, back to her old apartment in Palm Beach. At her side was Jenna, in a car seat; atop the dashboard was an envelope containing the monthly payment on the unsold co-op. Though her house was in foreclosure, Lisa always paid the mortgage on the apartment, her fallback in case of eviction.

Lisa gazed at the water out the window. She never wanted to miss mortgage payments; Chase told her to do it and promised assistance afterward, but then put her into foreclosure. The delinquency triggered late fees, penalties, and notifications to national credit bureaus. A damaged credit score affected a mortgage company's decision to grant loan relief, which hinged on the ability to pay. Even if Lisa managed to finally sell the apartment, even if she could satisfy the debt on the house, the injury from this "advice" would stick with her for years. Chase Home Finance never mentioned the additional consequences, emphasizing only the possibility of aid. The advice was at best faulty, at worst a deliberate effort to seize the home. Lisa spent a lifetime living within her means, guarding against financial catastrophe. Now Chase Home Finance obliterated this carefully constructed reputation. She felt tricked.

America has a name for people who miss their mortgage payments: deadbeats. Responsible taxpayers who repay their debts shouldn't have to "subsidize the losers' mortgages," CNBC host Rick Santelli shouted from the floor of the Chicago Board of Trade on February 19, 2009, two days after Lisa got her foreclosure papers. "This is America! How many of you people want to pay for your neighbor's mortgage, that has an extra bathroom and can't pay their bills, raise your hand!" The floor traders in Chicago, between buying and selling commodity futures, hooted. This rant would later be credited as the founding moment of the Tea Party. And it signified a certain posture toward delinquent homeowners, a cultural bias that equated missing the mortgage payment with failing the duties of citizenship. The indignation didn't account for mortgage companies *driving* customers into default. However, lenders welcomed anything that humiliated deadbeats into blaming themselves. In most cases it worked: in the twenty-three states that required judicial sign-off for foreclosures, around 95 percent of the cases went uncontested.

But Lisa had an inquisitive mind. Before she would acquiesce, she wanted to understand the circumstances that led to this lawsuit from U.S. Bank, an entity she had never encountered before seeing it listed as the plaintiff. She had three questions: who was this bank, why did it have a relationship with her, and why was it trying to take her house?

As it happens, U.S. Bank *is* real. It's the fifth-largest bank in the country, with more than three thousand branches, mainly in the Midwest and the Pacific Coast, not in Florida. Lisa learned all this through a cursory Google search. U.S. Bank also had a toll-free customer service number. But just like Wells Fargo, U.S. Bank's reps had no record of a Lisa Epstein. "Look, you're suing *me*. How could you not know who I am if you're suing me?" Lisa implored. She gave U.S. Bank her Social Security number, her address, all her mortgage information. Nothing turned up.

Lisa kept every document from the closing in an old canvas bag from a nursing conference. She read the mortgage documents line by line, the way she had while eight months pregnant and sitting in the offices of DHI Mortgage. There was no mention of U.S. Bank, Wells Fargo, or even Chase, where she sent mortgage payments for a couple of years. Lisa made the deal with DHI Mortgage. How did these other banks get into the picture?

Lisa had a bit more luck when she Googled "U.S. Bank NA as trustee for JPMorgan Mortgage Trust 2007-S2," the name of the plaintiff on her foreclosure documents. This sent her to the website of the Securities and Exchange Commission, specifically an investor report (known as an 8-K form) for the JPMorgan Mortgage Trust. One paragraph included every party she had become familiar with over the past several months:

> J. P. Morgan Acceptance Corporation I (the "Company") entered into a Pooling and Servicing Agreement dated as of May 1, 2007 (the "Pooling and Servicing Agreement"), by and among the Company, as depositor, Wells Fargo Bank, N.A., as master servicer (in such capacity, the "Master Servicer") and securities administrator (in such capacity, the "Securities Administrator") and U.S. Bank National Association, as trustee (the "Trustee"), providing for the issuance of J. P. Morgan Mortgage Trust 2007-S2 Mortgage Pass-Through Certificates.

Most homeowners had as much chance of decoding this as they did of learning Mandarin Chinese. Lisa had no background in real estate, economics, or high finance. The only time she dealt with anything Wall Street–related was when she chose funds for her 401(k) upon starting a new job. It took years of study to master nursing; nobody offered her a class in pooling and servicing agreements, or mortgage pass-through certificates. However, everything that transformed the mortgage market, everything that layered risk and drove the housing bubble, everything that made buying a home in 2007 infinitely more dangerous than it should ever be, was contained in that innocuous-sounding paragraph.

One thousand families. That's how many Americans lost their homes each *day* at the height of the Great Depression. Franklin Roosevelt's response to this relentless destruction created the most successful housing finance system in the world, a key to America's political stability and emergence as an economic powerhouse.

To stop foreclosures, the Home Owner's Loan Corporation (HOLC) bought defaulted mortgages from financial institutions at a discount and sold them back to homeowners. Beginning in 1933, HOLC acquired one million mortgages—one out of five in the country at that time. Eighty percent of HOLC clients saved their homes when they otherwise might have lost them. And once every mortgage was paid off and the program closed, HOLC even turned a small profit.

HOLC gave borrowers a twenty-year mortgage with a fixed interest rate, allowing them to gradually pay off the principal over the life of the loan, a process known as amortization. At the time very few Americans had long-term mortgages. The most common product lasted two to five years; borrowers would pay interest each month and then either make a "bullet" payment of principal at the end or roll over into a new loan. When bullet payments came due during the Depression, there was no way for out-of-work homeowners to find the cash. And mortgage holders, saddled with their own funding problems, refused to renegotiate contracts and seized the homes. This only accelerated the housing collapse, putting more homes on the market when nobody could afford to buy. The HOLC solution was intended to attenuate this downward cycle. But it also eliminated the volatility of the bullet payment, which magnified periods of economic hardship. HOLC generated confidence in the long-term, fully amortized mortgage, which previously was seen as a scam unscrupulous door-to-door salesmen used to rob lower-class laborers of down payments.

The government did not want to hold HOLC mortgages, and investors feared buying them, since the families making payments had previously defaulted. So in 1934 Roosevelt established the Federal Housing Administration to provide mortgage insurance on HOLC loans. Borrowers paid a small FHA premium, and investors would be guaranteed their share of principal and interest payments. The FHA would eventually offer protection to loans made by private lenders as long as they issued mortgages with a 20 percent down payment and terms of at least twenty years. In 1938 the Federal National Mortgage Administration, commonly known as Fannie Mae, enabled this by purchasing government-insured mortgages, injecting additional capital into the lending industry.

More than anything, the system delivered security. Families could make one affordable monthly payment for two or three decades, and glory in the dignity of homeownership. Builders supported the desire by constructing developments of detached single-family homes outside of metropolitan centers. The interstate highway system connected suburbs to the cities. Subdivisions sprang up everywhere, and millions of Americans sought long-term fixed-rate loans to secure their spot in them. The FHA loosened standards and granted insurance on thirty-year loans with as little as 5 percent down for new construction. The GI Bill for returning World War II servicemembers further guaranteed low-rate loans through the Veterans Administration. In 1940, 15 million families owned their own homes; by 1960 that number jumped to 33 million. Buying a place in the suburbs became part of growing up, like college graduation or a wedding, the epitome of the promise of the middle class from the country that claimed to have invented it. It was a utopia of white picket fences, modern kitchens, and freshly cut grass.

Private lenders filled the demand for these loans, particularly the savings and loan industry, which had been around since the 1830s (known back then as the building and loan). The biggest problem for companies lending long is the funding: there's money to be made, but lenders need large amounts of cheap up-front capital. Savings and loans found the formula by funding home mortgages with customer deposits. Government-supplied deposit insurance made ordinary Americans confident that they could put money into a bank and have it protected. The S&Ls benefited further when Congress granted them an interest rate advantage over commercial banks. This nudged depositors into S&Ls, increasing the funding available for mortgage finance.

S&Ls typically paid a healthy 3 to 4 percent rate of interest on accounts and charged between 5 and 6 percent on mortgages. That small float on hundreds of billions of dollars in loans added up. The system was mutually beneficial, and everyone had a stake in a successful outcome. State laws initially restricted savings and loans to issuing residential mortgages within fifty to a hundred miles of their headquarters. So the S&Ls needed communities to prosper to increase deposits and subsequently increase loans. S&L presidents became local leaders, sponsoring local golf tournaments or Little League baseball teams.

When families encountered trouble—unemployment, medical bills, untimely death—and could no longer pay the mortgage, lenders worked with them to prevent foreclosure, because it was in their financial interest. They made more money keeping the borrower in the home, even with a reduced payment, than having to sell at a discount in foreclosure. This incentive maintained stability and kept home values rising. The annual foreclosure rate from 1950 to 1997 never rose above 1 percent of all loans and was often far lower.

By 1980 there was more money sloshing around the mortgage market—about $1.5 trillion—than in the stock market. And Wall Street investment banks looked at all that cash the way Wile E. Coyote looked at the Road Runner. They wanted a piece of the action.

Lew Ranieri took over the mortgage trading desk for Salomon Brothers in 1978. He was fat, unkempt, and owned four suits, all of them polyester. In the Wall Street memoir *Liar's Poker*, Michael Lewis describes Ranieri as "the wild and woolly genius, the Salomon legend who began in the mailroom, worked his way onto the trading floor, and created a market in America for mortgage bonds." But he didn't issue the first mortgage-backed securities; the federal government did.

Faced with a budget deficit during the Vietnam War, in 1968 Lyndon Johnson split up Fannie Mae to push its liabilities off the books. A redesigned Government National Mortgage Company (Ginnie Mae) continued to buy government-insured mortgages. But the new Fannie Mae and its counterpart, the Federal Home Loan Mortgage Corporation (Freddie Mac), became quasi-private, quasi-public companies (officially government-sponsored entities, or GSEs), which could purchase conventional mortgages not insured by the government, provided they met certain guidelines— usually thirty-year fixed-rate mortgages carefully underwritten to ensure that the borrower would pay them back. The GSEs would pool hundreds of these loans together and create bonds; they called it securitization. Revenue streams were created from the monthly mortgage payments, with each investor entitled to a proportional piece. For a small fee, GSEs guaranteed payments to investors, and because investors believed the government would never let the GSEs default, they happily bought the bonds. Investor cash built additional capital for mortgage financing, allowing more people to purchase a home.

Investment banks assisted Freddie Mac with the initial securitizations in 1971 but were only paid a small retainer. Salomon Brothers and Bank of America (BofA) attempted to bypass Fannie and Freddie with a private-label securitization in 1977, packaging BofA-originated loans into a bond. But government regulations prohibited the largest investors, like pension funds, from buying the securities. Others were too spooked by the uncertainty of whether the underlying loans would fail. And thirty-five states blocked mortgages from being sold into a private market. Despite this, Robert Dall, the Salomon trader who brokered the Bank of America deal, believed investment banks would profit from trading U.S. home mortgages, the biggest market in the world. They just needed creativity and some regulatory relief.

Ranieri took over at Salomon just as the savings and loans grew desperate, battered by the twin diseases of high inflation and Federal Reserve chairman Paul Volcker's remedy, high interest rates. This hurt S&Ls on every level. Nobody wanted to borrow money at 20 percent to buy a home, nobody wanted to save when prices could soar next week or next month, and nobody wanted to keep money in a rate-capped S&L when they could get better returns from a money market fund or Treasury bill.

In 1981 Congress gave the S&Ls a huge tax break that allowed them to hide losses, helping to keep them afloat. But to take advantage of the tax relief, they needed to move assets off their books. Ranieri stepped into this void, buying mortgages from one S&L and selling them to another, profiting from the markup. It revealed the possibilities of Wall Street involvement in the mortgage market, and Salomon made a killing. Ranieri then got Freddie Mac to help with a bond deal that packaged older loans from a D.C.-area S&L called Perpetual Savings. Freddie's involvement eliminated regulatory restrictions that prevented nationwide sales of mortgage-backed securities. But to attract institutional investors with the most cash, Ranieri redesigned the bond.

Big investors didn't like the uncertainty in mortgages: you never knew when homeowners would pay them off, so you never knew the length of the loan and the projected profit on interest. So in 1983 Ranieri and his counterpart at First Boston, Larry Fink, created the collateralized mortgage obligation (CMO), the basic securitization structure used during the housing bubble.

Instead of investors buying bonds backed by mortgages and getting a proportional share of monthly payments, CMOs created different classes for investors with different risk profiles. Typically there were three tranches: the senior tranche, the mezzanine, and the equity tranche. When mortgage payments came in, the senior tranche would get paid first. Whatever was left over went first to the mezzanine and then to the equity tranche. Lower tranches received higher interest payments on the bond to accommodate their higher risk. Investors buying senior tranches had confidence they would get paid off within a short time frame, usually five years. They didn't have to worry whether each individual borrower could afford the payments; by selling a pool of thousands of mortgages, the odd default here or there wouldn't matter. The higher-risk tranches had longer terms, from twelve to thirty years, and stronger payoffs. These more complex securitizations converted the mortgage, a hyperlocal, idiosyncratic, individual instrument, into a bond, a defined security that investors could buy and sell with confidence.

The initial CMOs needed Freddie Mac: it was still the only way to get them sold nationwide. But once the securitization structure was in place, Ranieri went to work legalizing it. As a trader told Michael Lewis about Ranieri, "If Lewie didn't like a law, he'd just have it changed." In 1984 Congress passed the Secondary Mortgage Market Enhancement Act (SMMEA), which eliminated the ban on private banks selling mortgage-backed securities without a government guarantee. SMMEA also preempted state restrictions on privately issued mortgage-backed securities; no longer did investment banks have to register with each state to sell them.

The most important part of SMMEA involved the rating agencies, companies that assessed the risk of various bonds. Under SMMEA, institutional investors who previously were barred from making dangerous investments could purchase mortgage-backed securities as long as they had a high rating from a nationally recognized statistical rating organization. Investors could outsource their due diligence to the rating agencies; they didn't have to examine the salary of some home buyer in Albuquerque in order to buy an interest in his loan. President Reagan signed SMMEA in October; Ranieri showed up for the ceremony.

Next Ranieri secured a tax exemption for pools of mortgages held in a special investment vehicle known as a real estate mortgage investment conduit (REMIC). The REMIC operated like a trust, able to acquire mortgages and pass income to investors without paying taxes. Investors would pay taxes only on the bond gains, not on the purchase of the mortgages. The Tax Reform Act of 1986 legalized the REMIC structure and made mortgage bonds more desirable.

The mortgage-backed securities market reached $150 billion in 1986. It probably accelerated the demise of the S&L industry, which finally imploded in the late 1980s. The money used for making mortgage loans, instead of coming from depositors, now came from investors all over the world. Ranieri and his allies insisted the goal was to free up more funding for mortgages. He was a dream salesman who just wanted to give every American a piece of something better, a nice house for their families. But homeownership rates rose nearly twenty points from the 1940s to the 1960s under the old system. From 1970 to 1990, during the handover of mortgage finance to Wall Street, rates only went up two points.

While Wall Street did well with securitization, it could not dislodge the GSEs from their market dominance. The GSEs still had that implicit backstop of a government rescue. Investors valued that and bought most of their mortgage bonds from Fannie and Freddie. As long as banks tried to compete on a level playing field, packaging carefully underwritten thirty-year fixed-rate loans, they couldn't win.

Salomon Brothers fired Lew Ranieri in 1987. He was a victim of his own success. When the mortgage business standardized, Wall Street investment banks staffed up with Ranieri's old traders. Another generation would crack the code and beat Fannie and Freddie, finding a new set of mortgage products to slice and dice. Ranieri, who started his own firm, never saw that coming. As he would later tell *Fortune* magazine, "I wasn't out to invent the biggest floating craps game of all time, but that's what happened."

Once she understood the securitization structure, Lisa Epstein could identify all the component companies and their involvement in her mortgage. DHI Mortgage was the originator that sold Lisa her loan. DHI immediately flipped it to JPMorgan Chase, which became the "depositor," in industry parlance. JPMorgan acquired thousands of loans like Lisa's, pooling them into a mortgage-backed security to sell to investors. To securitize the loans, JPMorgan placed them into a trust (JPMorgan Mortgage Trust 2007-S2), which qualified for REMIC status and its significant tax advantages. The REMIC forced JPMorgan to add an additional link in the securitization chain—in this case, U.S. Bank, trustee for all the assets in the trust. U.S. Bank hired a servicer, Chase Home Finance, to collect monthly payments, handle day-to-day contact with borrowers, and funnel payments to investors through the trust. So Chase had one link in the chain as a depositor and a separate link as a servicer, basically a glorified accounts receivable department.

Investors in the trust get their portion of the monthly mortgage payments, but under the law they're merely creditors, holders of JPMorgan Mortgage Trust 2007-S2 pass-through certificates; the trustee, the entity passing payments through to investors, owns the loan. That's why U.S. Bank, not JPMorgan Chase, sued Lisa. JPMorgan Chase gets its proceeds from the sale of the mortgage bonds and walks away. U.S. Bank earns a fee for administering the trust. For performing day-to-day operations on the loans, the servicer, Chase Home Finance, gets a small percentage of the unpaid principal balance, along with any fees generated from servicing. This securitization added an additional wrinkle: the inclusion of Wells Fargo as the securities administrator, with the function of calculating interest and principal payments to the investors. As this involved scrutinizing cash flow from the servicer, it also made Wells Fargo the "master servicer" on the loan. When Chase Home Finance informed Lisa that Wells Fargo was blocking mortgage modifications, it probably had to do with this master servicer role.

At no time was it made clear to Lisa that when she sent in her mortgage payment to Chase Home Finance, somebody at Wells Fargo crunched the numbers on it and told a colleague at Chase to send the money through U.S. Bank to investors, whether a Norwegian sovereign wealth fund or an Indiana public employee retirement plan. Heck, nobody told Lisa that DHI Mortgage would grant her a loan and immediately sell it off to a *different* division of JPMorgan Chase from the one she'd been paying all these years. This idea of banks trading mortgage payments like they would baseball cards didn't sit well. And it made it all the more galling to Lisa that Chase Home Finance would tell her to stop paying: according to the securitization chain, they didn't even own the mortgage. Maybe they profited so much off late fees, they *wanted* to push people into foreclosure.

But while this was all critical information for Lisa to know, it only raised more questions. She had to understand why securitization translated into suffering for so many homeowners, especially in her backyard. By 2009, one out of every four Floridians with a mortgage was either behind on payments or in foreclosure. How was that even possible? It wasn't like someone detonated a bomb in Miami and Orlando to wipe out businesses. No plague triggered all the state's crops to rot in the fields. Depressions like this—and

Florida was experiencing a depression, in Lisa's eyes—didn't happen spontaneously. Who put this in motion? Who prospered from the pain?

A week after receiving her foreclosure notice, Lisa stumbled across a blog called *Living Lies*. Neil Garfield was a former trial attorney in Fort Lauderdale, and in his biography he also claimed to be an economist, accountant, securitization expert, and former "Wall Street insider." He had striking features, big eyebrows, and a perfectly cropped, jet-black beard. He looked like a character actor in a 1970s cop movie. Garfield started *Living Lies* in October 2007. The site featured day-to-day commentary on the mortgage crisis, a large volume of legal resources, and a mission statement: "I believe that the mortgage crisis has produced manifest evil and injustice in our society. . . . Living Lies is the vehicle for a collaborative movement to provide homeowners with sufficient resources to combat bloated banks who are flooding the political market with money."

It didn't take much digging to see that Garfield was running a business. He sold manuals on how lawyers and laypeople could defend themselves from foreclosure. He conducted paid seminars across the country. He had an ad for something called "securitization audits." Many people presenting themselves as lawyers descended on homeowners at this time, making optimistic yet vague promises that they held the secret to saving homes from foreclosure. State and federal authorities warned homeowners to proceed cautiously with "foreclosure rescue" specialists, especially in Florida, where white-collar scams were a local specialty, even an economic growth engine.

But Garfield had attracted a following. He told NBC News in early 2009 that the site had jumped from 1,000 hits per month a year earlier to 67,000 per month. And he did pull together the loose threads Lisa craved to comprehend: how securitization drove people into foreclosure, who profited from the outcome, and whether their financial machinations violated the law. More important, Garfield maintained an open comment section, so everyone in the then-small community of people willing to talk about their foreclosures online could share stories and swap information. It was like two parallel websites existing in the same space: Garfield on top, and the rabble of dispossessed homeowners underneath.

They included Andrew Delany, known online as Ace, a licensed carpenter from Ashburnham, Massachusetts, who lost his income due to a spinal disorder. Alina Virani (Alina), a paralegal from Orlando, her lender told her she couldn't refinance, and when she called to complain, she discovered they went out of business. James Chambers (Jim C), of Clearwater, saw his business devastated by the downturn, and faced bankruptcy. These stories were familiar to Lisa: personal misery combined with underhanded behavior. James Chambers said Chase sued him but Washington Mutual owned his loan. Alina Virani got some help from an attorney in Ohio, who found that her lender violated federal consumer protection laws. Ace never could find out who owned his mortgage.

There was no support group for foreclosure victims; nobody wanted to even talk about it. It reminded Lisa of when everyone called cancer "the big C," not daring to utter the word. But the commenters at *Living Lies* represented the stirrings of a community, all focused on solving the same problem, like a distributed network. Lisa bookmarked the site and returned to it daily. There was a spirit there, the opposite of the shame and humiliation everyone assumed foreclosure victims should feel. These people were ready to fight. And as Lisa read on, the schemes they related sounded less like the sober processes of modern finance and more like a crime spree.

Michael Winston, a new executive at Countrywide Financial Corporation, pulled into the company parking lot one day in 2006 and read the vanity license plate on the next car over: "FUND-EM." Winston asked the man getting out of the car what that meant.

"That's [CEO Angelo] Mozilo's growth strategy. We fund all loans."

"What if the borrower has no job?" Winston asked.

"Fund 'em."

"What if they have no assets?"

"Fund 'em."

"No income?"

"If they can fog a mirror, we'll give them a loan."

Countrywide, which came out of nowhere to become the nation's largest mortgage originator, was part of a new system of mortgage financing that realized Lew Ranieri's master plan for Wall Street domination of the residential housing market. Congress shepherded the industry down this path, eliminating roadblocks so lenders could issue mortgages to people with bad credit.

The Depository Institutions Deregulation and Monetary Control Act (DIDMCA) of 1980 preempted state anti-usury caps, which limited the interest rate lenders could charge borrowers. Two years later, the Garn–St. Germain Depository Institutions Act eliminated mortgage down payment requirements for federally chartered banks. Embedded in Garn–St. Germain was the Alternative Mortgage Transaction Parity Act. This also tossed out state restrictions on mortgages, allowing all lenders, federal or state, to offer adjustable-rate mortgages with steep resets, where the interest rate went up sharply after the initial "teaser" rate. It also permitted interest-only or even "negative amortization" loans, where principal increased in successive payments.

Congress was trying to save the savings and loan industry by making mortgages more profitable, effectively legalizing consumer abuse to aid a class of financial institutions. That didn't work: S&Ls blew up by the end of the 1980s. But without the elimination of these anti-predatory lending laws, argued Jennifer Taub of Vermont Law School in her book *Other People's Houses,* "subprime lending could not have flourished."

Wall Street figured out how to outflank Fannie Mae and Freddie Mac by securitizing alternative loans, which didn't conform to GSE standards. Investment banks made the securities attractive with "credit enhancements," guarantees to investors in the form of insurance or letters of credit. With these enhancements, even packages of the worst mortgages could achieve super-safe credit ratings. Riskier mortgages were more lucrative for Wall Street, because these "subprime" loans reeled in higher interest rates over the thirty-year terms. In other words, subprime loans were prized precisely because they gouged the borrower more. And as long as investors received assurances of risk-free profits, they would buy the bonds.

Investment banks began to offer lightly regulated nonbank mortgage originators, who specialized in marketing to poor borrowers, warehouse lines of credit, or defined funding for their mortgages. In exchange, the banks would purchase all the originator's loans and package them into private-label securities (PLS), separate from Fannie and Freddie's mortgage-backed securities on conforming loans. The originators knew what the big banks wanted: subprime mortgages, and lots of them. Brokers were given "yield spread premiums," bonus payments for every high-rate mortgage they sold.

Lenders perversely described exotic loans as "affordability products." After a teaser period of one to two years, monthly payments would increase by thousands of dollars. If borrowers ever showed concern about this (and typically they didn't, as disclosures were written in such byzantine legalese that virtually no one could decipher it), brokers told them not to worry: they could always refinance again. Every refinance away from the payment shock added closing costs—profit for the lender—and built up unpaid balance on the loan. It was not uncommon for homeowners to refinance five or six times in a few years, taking on more debt each time.

Another industry creation was the cash-out refinance, giving borrowers with equity in their homes a new loan with a lower starting payment, along with some cash to cover other expenses. This was an attractive option for newly targeted low-income families of color. Since the 1930s African Americans and Hispanics were locked out of the housing market, with government maps "redlining" designated tracts of land (indicating them as off-limits to nonwhite buyers) and banks shunning their business. Now old women in inner-city Detroit or Cleveland got knocks on their door from pitchmen promising to make their financial hardships disappear. It was redlining in reverse. For decades the problem had been that black people couldn't get loans; now the problem was that they could.

Nonbank lenders Option One, New Century, and First Alliance started in the mid-1990s, joining Countrywide and Long Beach Mortgage, which would eventually become Ameriquest. Federal Reserve statistics show that subprime lending increased fourfold from 1994 to 2000, to 13.4 percent of all mortgages. Brokers were under significant strain to pump out subprime loans with high interest rates or else lose their warehouse lines of credit. So lending standards flew out the window. Practically no applicants were rejected.

That these loans were harmful concerned nobody. The Clinton administration wanted to increase homeownership rates, which had fallen amid the S&L collapse. It wasn't likely to crack down on irresponsible lending practices if they served that goal. Anyway, the Federal Reserve held responsibility over consumer protection for mortgages, and Alan Greenspan viewed regulations the way an exterminator viewed termites.

Investment banks also got more sophisticated about the securities. Mathematicians fresh out of college—quantitative analysts, or "quants"—

spent their working hours converting risky subprime loans into something that could secure a coveted AAA rating, guaranteeing sale into the capital markets. For example, banks had no problem selling high-rated tranches of their mortgage-backed securities, but the lower-rated mezzanine and equity tranches were more of a puzzle. To solve this problem, they built something called a collateralized debt obligation (CDO), using the same tranching mechanism, squeezing AAA ratings out of low-rated junk. Then they would make CDOs out of the unsold portions of CDOs, creating what was known as a "CDO-squared," and so on. Investors knew they were buying securities backed by mortgages; they didn't know they were getting repackaged leftovers of the worst bits, julienned through financial alchemy into something "safe."

CDO sales increased exponentially after market deregulation through the Commodity Futures Modernization Act in December 2000, in one of President Clinton's last official acts. You didn't even have to own the mortgages to wager on whether they would go up or down. "Synthetic" CDOs just tracked the price of certain mortgage securities, with investors taking up either side of the bet. This multiplied the amount of money on the line well beyond the value of the mortgages and turned the whole thing into gambling.

The securitization machine resembled the children's game of hot potato. Everyone stopped caring whether the borrower could pay back the loan, because everyone passed the default risk up the chain. The lenders didn't care because they sold the loans to Wall Street banks; the banks didn't care because they passed them on to investors; and the investors didn't care because Wall Street's financial wizards lied to them. Investors were assured that the loans were of high quality; furthermore, they were told that even if a few failed, slicing and dicing thousands of loans from all over the country into bonds would make up for the delinquencies and eliminate the risk. The geographic diversity of the bonds would insulate investors from a regional market collapse, and everyone knew that mortgage markets were regional; you never saw a broad-based price decline. The credit rating agencies, paid by banks to rate the securitizations, blessed the whole scheme, either out of ignorance or to make sure they grew their businesses.

In the late 1990s, amid the Asian financial crisis, Wall Street pulled back on warehouse funding for nonbank lenders. Subprime lending momentarily stopped, and some lenders went out of business. But this was only a blip. Though consumer lawsuits exploded during this period, complaining of predatory practices, the Federal Reserve and other regulators showed no interest. When the smoke cleared, the remaining subprime lenders and their Wall Street funders started up the machines again. The second wave of subprime mortgages dwarfed the first wave.

The entire industry was assembled on a mountain of fraud, starting from the first contact with a prospective home buyer. Many brokers over-inflated home appraisals to increase the loan balance. Some pushed borrow-ers into "no income, no asset, no job" (NINJA) loans by telling them they would get better deals if they falsely inflated their income. These were also called "liar's loans." If loan officers demanded income verification, brokers would sometimes even use Wite-Out and replace the numbers on W-2 forms, or construct fake tax returns with a photocopier, to get them through underwriting. In his book *The Monster*, Michael W. Hudson describes one loan sent to underwriting that claimed a man coordinating dances at a Mexican restaurant made well over $100,000 a year. The dance coordi-nator got the loan.

The typical borrower too easily fell prey to this routinized deceit. Some lenders took borrowers eligible for prime-rate loans—people with perfect credit, like Lisa Epstein—and gave them subprime ones. Others forged bor-rowers' signatures on disclosure forms that would have actually explained how much in interest and fees they were paying. Some brokers used light-boards or even a bright Coke vending machine to trace signatures and en-able the forgery. Others presented borrowers with a loan at closing whose first few pages looked like a fixed-rate loan, masking the toxic mortgage underneath. When the borrower signed all the papers, the broker ripped those first pages off.

The fraud continued up the chain as well. The Financial Crisis Inquiry Commission found that a third-party firm called Clayton Holdings, brought in to reunderwrite samples of loans backing subprime mortgage securities for twenty major banks, consistently found defects in half the loans in the samples. Clayton relayed its findings to the banks, who promptly used them to negotiate after-the-fact discounts on the full loan pools from originators. Those discounts never got passed on to bond investors, who remained ignorant about the defects. In such cases, the securitizers knowingly sold defective products to investors without disclosure, and took extra profits based on how defective they were. It was clear securities fraud.

Many investment banks knew about, and indeed drove, the poor quality of the loans. Internal documents later uncovered in a lawsuit against Morgan Stanley, the largest buyer of mortgages from subprime lender New Century, showed the bank demanding that 85 percent of the loans they purchase consist of adjustable-rate mortgages. When a low-ranking due diligence official told his supervisor about the litany of problems associated with New Century loans, she responded, "Good find on the fraud :). Unfortunately, I don't think we will be able to utilize you or any other third party individual in the valuation department any longer." In other words, finding the fraud got people fired.

In September 2004 the FBI's Criminal Division formally warned of a mortgage fraud "epidemic," with more than twelve thousand cases of suspicious activity. "If fraudulent practices become systemic within the mortgage industry," said Chris Swecker, assistant director of the FBI unit, "it will ultimately place financial institutions at risk and have adverse effects on the stock market." Despite this awareness, almost no effort was put into stamping out the fraud. In fact, when Georgia tried to protect borrowers with a strong anti-predatory lending law in 2002, every participant in the mortgage industry, public and private, bore down on them. Ameriquest pulled all business from the state. Two rating agencies, Moody's and Standard and Poor's, said they would not rate securities backed by loans from Georgia, cutting off the state from the primary mode of funding mortgages. And the Office of the Comptroller of the Currency, which regulated national banks, told the institutions that they were exempt from Georgia law. Georgia eventually backed down and replaced the regulations, rendered moot by an unholy alliance of the industry and the people who regulated them.

Banks issued $1 trillion in nonprime mortgage bonds every year during the bubble's peak. Subprime mortgages made up nearly half of all loan originations in America in 2006. Total mortgage debt in America doubled from 1999 to 2007. There was so much money in mortgages that loan brokers right out of college made $400,000 a year. Traders on Wall Street made even more.

Home prices appreciated rather slowly for fifty years, but between 2002 and 2007 they shot up in a straight line. In several states, *annual* price increases hit 25 percent. Since this boosted property values, boosted the economy, and made the industry more profitable, few politicians or regulators raised alarms. Even Fannie Mae and Freddie Mac, locked into buying "conforming loans" for their securities, lowered their standards and bought subprime loans once they started to lose market share to the private sector. Everyone mimicked industry claims that the market transformation was good for homeowners, and for a little while it was: even amid rising prices, homeownership rates rose over this period to an all-time high of 69.2 percent. Nobody wanted to stop the merry-go-round while the song was still playing.

At the end of 2006 the song stopped, and homeowners used to refinancing out of trouble were stuck. Even before this point, you could see warning signs in skyrocketing early payment defaults—people missing their very first mortgage payment. Foreclosures started to occur in large enough numbers—they nearly doubled in 2007, and again in 2008—that mortgage-backed securities, even the senior tranches that were supposed to be infallible, took losses. Investors tried to dump the securities, and banks stopped issuing new ones. Brokers suddenly had no money to make new loans; by 2008, all of them were either out of business or, in the case of Countrywide, sold to Bank of America. The entire system, which soared along with home prices, crashed when those prices dropped. And because the system had been replicated multiple times, in CDOs and other credit derivatives, failures cascaded through Wall Street investments and led to a catastrophic financial crisis.

Lisa read about all this and internalized it; after a couple of weeks of intense study, she could cite chapter and verse on previously unknown financial industry machinations. She started to daydream while working, her mind filled with theories about mortgage-backed securities and what caused the crash. At work or at home, it became hard for Lisa to concentrate on anything else.

Of all the websites she sought out, none deconstructed securitization and Wall Street malfeasance like *Living Lies*. Neil Garfield went much deeper than the surface layer of fraud in the subprime scam. He viewed the originators as straw lenders, because they immediately sold the loan and did not care about its quality. To Garfield, this violated modest federal mortgage laws such as the Truth in Lending Act. Garfield called such originators "pretender lenders" and thought the fact that they relinquished their interest in the loan by having investors pay it off in full could form the basis of a legal challenge.

More interesting to Lisa were Garfield's contentions about promissory notes, mortgage assignments, and pooling and servicing agreements. "The reality is that nearly all securitized mortgage loans are worthless and unenforceable," Garfield wrote in one post. "The ONLY parties seeking foreclosures . . . do not possess ANY financial interest in the loan nor any authority to foreclose, collect, modify or do anything else," he wrote in another. He quoted a bankruptcy attorney in Missouri, who added, "Democracy is not supposed to be efficient—because in the tangle of inefficient rules lies the safety and security of popular rights. The judge is not there to clear the sand from the gears of the machine—the judge is the sand." Lisa didn't understand Garfield's line of argument at first, but a lot of *Living Lies* commenters were agitated about it, talking about document fraud and broken chain of title. And the discussion refreshed Lisa's memory about something in her court summons.

Count II in the complaint was entitled "Re-establishment of Lost Note." Lisa needed more information about what that actually meant—what was the difference between the note and the mortgage?—but it surprised her that the plaintiff admitted that it lost a key document and was trying to reestablish it in some manner. Others at *Living Lies* had note problems; for example, Andrew "Ace" Delany's lender could never supply the note, although he asked for it every week. What was with this epidemic of lost notes? Where did they go? And how did that impact foreclosure cases?

As the twenty-day deadline for responding to the summons loomed, Lisa wanted to find out.

3

SECURITIZATION FAIL; OR, CIRILO CODRINGTON AND THE PANAMA DOC SHOP

None of Lisa Epstein's options for dealing with her foreclosure seemed very attractive. She could try the Home Affordable Modification Program, or HAMP, which President Obama announced from Mesa, Arizona, on February 18, 2009, the day after Lisa was served. She pulled the speech up at the White House website. The idea was that the Treasury Department would give mortgage servicers incentive payments to modify delinquent loans. In the speech, Obama kept stressing borrower responsibilities more than the responsibilities of fraudulent lenders or securitizing banks. Did he not understand how this crisis happened? Plus HAMP involved applying through Chase Home Finance, Lisa's servicer, which spent nine months losing her paperwork, ignoring her requests for help, and driving her into foreclosure by advising her to miss payments. Common sense dictated they wouldn't be much better at administering a new program, no matter how many inducements the government gave them.

Lisa could fight it out in court, but the handful of lawyers taking foreclosure cases in Palm Beach County wanted retainers of up to $5,000, and $340 an hour in consultation fees. If Lisa had that kind of money, she probably wouldn't be in foreclosure to begin with. Legal aid societies and pro bono lawyers working for free were overloaded and unavailable for someone with a decent job, like Lisa. Banks knew troubled homeowners didn't have the resources to fight foreclosures; that's why everyone told her most cases never got challenged. Besides, anytime Lisa would meet with a lawyer—and she talked to several, even drove an hour down to Broward County once—she'd explain her operatic theories about the housing crash, and the attorneys would stare at her like she sprouted horns. They all told her there wasn't much she could do if she didn't pay. But Lisa pleaded, "You don't understand. The bank suing me says they have no relationship with me. How could I just give up?"

Without hope of a last-minute intervention, and without funds for legal representation, Lisa had a third option: fight the foreclosure herself, as a *pro se* litigant. This sounded crazy to her. She had no legal training, picking up bits and pieces in late-night cram sessions. The saying went that anyone who represents herself as a lawyer has a fool for a client. But Lisa's motivations went far beyond whether or not she would keep that misbegotten house on Gazetta Way.

Something had gone horribly awry at the highest levels of the economy, causing the largest destruction of wealth in eighty years. Wall Street recklessness played the signature role, and Lisa wanted to challenge that in her small way. Maybe she could unearth some novel strategy, share her knowledge, and help spare other unsuspecting Americans from her pain. It would be difficult, no doubt, maybe impossible, maybe preposterous to even try. But Lisa didn't think it worth her personal comfort to stay silent. Something about the magnitude of the crisis and the constancy of voices tagging foreclosure victims like her as irresolute deadbeats made her more determined to prove everyone wrong, to keep searching until she found something she could call justice.

While running through all this, Lisa kept coming back to Count II, the "Re-establishment of Lost Note."

A mortgage has two parts. There's the promissory note, the IOU from borrower to lender, and the mortgage, which creates the lien on the home in case of default. Foreclosure laws vary from state to state and evolve with every court decision, but in the simplest terms, to be able to foreclose, a financial institution must hold the mortgage, the note, or both. This gives you standing, as it would in most judicial contexts: if you accuse someone of stealing your car, you'd need to establish that you actually owned it in the first place.

During securitization, mortgages were transferred from the originator through a series of intermediaries and then to the trustee, who administers the mortgage-backed trust. Lisa's case featured three parties in all— DHI Mortgage (originator), JPMorgan Chase (depositor), and U.S. Bank (trustee)—but sometimes these deals had as many as seven or eight transfers. The securitizations included intermediaries mostly to reassure investors that they would still get payments if the originator went out of business, which actually happened quite a bit. This desire for "bankruptcy remoteness" drove securitization transfers, and it didn't hurt that every transfer generated another fee.

At each stage there would have to be documented evidence of transfer, like links in a chain—a chain of title, which lays out the different transactions. You can't skip a link: the chain must show evidence of transfers from originator to depositor to trustee, and everyone in between, in precise order. Mortgages are assigned with a signed piece of paper affirming the transaction. Notes are endorsed the same way you would endorse the back of a check. Theoretically, the originator could endorse the note "in blank," so that anyone in possession of the note could enforce it. But that theory ran up against the reality of the securitization agreements.

When Lisa finally found copies of the rules governing securitizations, known as the pooling and servicing agreements (PSAs), they all had roughly the same language about transfers. This comes from the prospectus of Soundview Home Loan Trust 2006-OPT2:

> On the Closing Date, the Depositor will transfer to the Trust all of its right, title and interest in and to each Mortgage Loan, the related mortgage note, Mortgage, assignment of mortgage in recordable form in blank or to the Trustee and other related documents received from the Originator pursuant to the Master Agreement (collectively, the "Related Documents")....
>
> The Pooling Agreement will require that, within the time period specified therein, the Depositor will deliver or cause to be delivered to the Trustee (or a custodian on behalf of the Trustee) the mortgage notes endorsed to the Trustee on behalf of the Certificateholders and the Related Documents.

The mortgage and the note had to be physically conveyed into the trust and delivered to the document custodian, with the mortgages assigned and the notes endorsed with a wet-ink signature at every step along the way, culminating in assignments and endorsements to the trustee. And this had

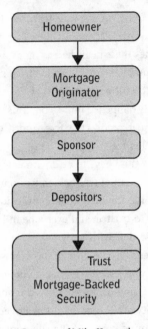

Courtesy of Mike Konczal.

to be done within ninety days of the transaction, with no grace period beyond that closing date. Only then would you have a "true sale" of the loans from originator to trustee.

Most trusts were created under New York State trust law, which is unbelievably clear. It stipulates that the pooling and servicing agreements are the governing documents. Any transaction that doesn't comply with the PSA is void. Failure to convey mortgages and notes would result in noncompliance. That means the trust would be unfunded and effectively *not exist*. Ownership would revert back to the last verifiable owner in the chain. And under New York law, there was no mechanism to transfer mortgages and notes after the closing date.

There are tax consequences associated with this failure as well. All securitization trusts were set up as REMICs. If the trust closed without the key documents conveyed over, those assets would not qualify for the REMIC tax exemption. They could not be added later, especially in the middle of foreclosure, because REMICs cannot acquire nonperforming assets. As a result, any income derived from the assets would get taxed, under the law, at *100 percent.*

Those were the rules, spelled out in governing documents agreed to by all parties. And the *Living Lies* chatterers were convinced that nobody in the mortgage industry bothered to follow them. If this theory was correct, it would turn mortgage-backed securities into non-mortgage-backed securities. And the trustee, in Lisa's case U.S. Bank, would not have the right to collect on the promissory note or use the mortgage lien to foreclose on the borrower. As Neil Garfield put it, "There is an 18-minute Nixonian gap in the record that cannot be cured." Activists took to calling it "securitization FAIL."

The prevalence of "lost" notes, including Lisa's, created more suspicion. If the notes were safely stowed away by the trustee's document custodian, losing them could never be an issue. One study hinted that the losses could be systemic. Neil Garfield originally got interested in securitization FAIL after reading a November 2007 report by law professor Katherine Porter, then of the University of Iowa. Porter examined public court records in 1,733 bankruptcy cases filed in 2006. She found near-universal disagreement between borrowers and mortgage servicers over amounts owed, with multiple instances of illegally imposed fees, including charging homeowners for ordinary office activities like delivering faxes or creating payoff statements. But one passage leaped out at Garfield: in a majority of cases, servicers lacked one or more pieces of documentation needed to establish the validity of the debt. That included the note, which was missing over 40 percent of the time.

Bankruptcy cases and foreclosure cases are different. But in two out of every five in the study, mortgage companies simply didn't comply with the rules to verify standing. The fact that, according to Porter's paper, bankruptcy courts would routinely let cases advance even without critical documents didn't bode well for those who wanted to fight the system. But thinking about all these different links in the chain and how fast financial institutions were swapping mortgages during the bubble, Lisa was convinced that the companies involved didn't comply with the law. And she couldn't stay quiet about that.

Under Florida law, plaintiffs didn't necessarily have to present the original promissory note at trial. But they did need to give an explanation and show proof of underlying ownership. This was the "Re-establishment of Lost Note" count in Lisa's complaint: U.S. Bank was announcing its intention to submit evidence that, despite losing the note, it indeed had the right to foreclose.

So on March 9, 2009, just a few weeks after being served with foreclosure papers, Lisa, acting in her own defense as a *pro se* litigant, filed a motion to dismiss for lack of standing. She cribbed from a couple of sample legal templates at *Living Lies*, arguing that U.S. Bank had no interest in her loan and therefore could not foreclose. The motion was meant to provoke a reaction, to get whatever the bank saw as their proof submitted into the court records. U.S. Bank filed a motion for extension. They weren't prepared to actually make a case.

Shortly after filing her motion, Lisa entered what she would later call her "sleepless phase": staying up until three in the morning, taking a catnap, and waking up at six. She spent every night reading and researching and learning. She analyzed lists of securitizations, read foreclosure defense strategies, and devoured every article on *Living Lies*. Every morning she would run to the computer to see if she missed anything. It was like going to college for an intense, self-administered degree in high finance. It lasted over three years.

This further strained her relationship with Alan, which had already taken more shots than most marriages could endure. Lisa was spending her nights outside the marriage bed, sitting in that big useless room glued to the home computer, while Alan tossed and turned. The couple barely spoke.

Lisa doesn't quite remember when she moved out of the house. One day, at a light on the outskirts of downtown West Palm Beach, instead of taking a left, she took a right, to the co-op by the Intracoastal. With so much disorder in her life, she longed for the simple pleasures of sitting on the balcony, hearing the water hit the seawall. She'd spend a day at the house and a day at the apartment, consumed by the fantasy that if she just spent more and more time at the condo, maybe Alan wouldn't notice she left. The marriage could dissolve of its own accord, without conflict or even discussion. Lisa gradually gathered her possessions, a couple of things a day, until she had everything out of the house. She didn't care if Alan stayed there, provided they still owned it. She chuckled at the irony of spending most of her waking hours trying to prevent foreclosure on a house she no longer even lived in.

At the end of April, Jenna had surgery at Miami Children's Hospital, to release the tethered spine and relieve pressure on the vertebrae. Alan came to Miami, staying in a local Ronald McDonald House. Lisa bunked in the hospital room, never leaving Jenna's side. The surgery went well, though afterward Jenna couldn't move for a couple of weeks, confined to lying still on her back. Lisa would lie beside her, breastfeeding or staring at the ceiling, which the hospital used for immobile patients as a projection screen. Lisa would point out the objects or colors that flashed against the ceiling, and Jenna loved it. Dogs and clowns and play pals would come by every day, activities known inside the hospital as "child life." Sometimes nurses would put Jenna in a wagon and ride her around the corridors.

Loaded up with drugs to relieve the pain, Jenna would also sleep for hours and hours, and Lisa could only wait out the slumber. But Children's Hospital did have an Internet connection. Lisa brought an old Acer laptop, sat by her daughter's bedside, and day and night continued her research. There were moments when Lisa was the only person awake in all of Children's Hospital, the blue light of the computer screen illuminating her face, eyes darting from article to article.

The family returned to Palm Beach for months of recovery, Lisa staying home with Jenna for a few weeks. Finally, on June 3, 2009, Florida Default Law Group (FDLG), the foreclosure mill law firm litigating on behalf of U.S. Bank, responded to the motion to dismiss. Count II, the "Re-establishment of Lost Note," had been removed. FDLG now maintained that its client found the note and the assignment of mortgage. They submitted them, along with a bundle of other affidavits and documents. Lisa finally possessed the raw materials to assess U.S. Bank's case. And she got right to it.

The newly found note was not endorsed in blank but directly endorsed from DHI Mortgage to JPMorgan Chase Bank. Kathy Harman, an assistant secretary at DHI Mortgage, signed the endorsement. In Lisa's view, U.S. Bank had to receive the endorsed note under the pooling and servicing agreement. But the chain of title stopped at Chase. The wrong entity was foreclosing. Furthermore, the mortgage assignment went directly from the assignor, "Mortgage Electronic Registration Systems, incorporated as Nominee for DHI Mortgage Company," to the assignee, U.S. Bank. Lisa made a mental note to Google "Mortgage Electronic Registration Systems" later, but she knew enough to see a fatal error. The assignment skipped a link in the chain. It should have gone from DHI Mortgage to JPMorgan Chase, with an additional assignment from JPMorgan Chase to U.S. Bank. But that was not what this assignment showed. It looked like whoever put these things together had no idea which entity belonged in which spot. One affidavit had asterisks wherever the name U.S. Bank appeared, and a handwritten footnote, "**Chase Home Finance LLC as-attorney-in-fact-for."

U.S. Bank's address was listed on the assignment as 3415 Vision Drive, Columbus, Ohio. Googling the address revealed it was actually the headquarters of Chase Home Finance, her mortgage servicer. How did two banks fit in the same headquarters? Then there was the date on the assignment: "Assignor has executed and delivered this Instrument on May 21, 2009." That was three months *after* Lisa Epstein was served with foreclosure papers. According to this document, U.S. Bank had not yet been assigned the mortgage at the time they sued Lisa.

Here in Lisa's hands was clear evidence of securitization FAIL, documented proof that the transactions on her mortgage were either improperly done or not done at all, with the assignment mocked up after the fact. Lisa rechecked the pooling and servicing agreement for her trust; like all of them, it stipulated that JPMorgan Chase had a ninety-day closing window back in 2007 to deposit the mortgage and note into the hands of U.S. Bank. The documents showed that U.S. Bank never got assigned the mortgage in time, meaning the securities based on her loan were invalid and unenforceable. And this poorly drafted cover-up was presented to a court, entered into the public record for everyone to see. Lisa laughed out loud for what felt like the first time in months.

Lisa also finally had actual names of people involved in these transactions. For example, there was Kathy Harman at DHI Mortgage, who endorsed her note to JPMorgan Chase. Lisa found a number for DHI Mortgage and tracked down Harman. "Hi, Kathy, my name is Lisa Epstein. I bought a mortgage from your company a couple years ago. I don't know what's going on here—I'm being sued by a bank. I don't even know anything about U.S. Bank."

"Mm-hmm."

"I just got a copy of the note, and your name is on it. I'm just trying to get to the bottom of this—can you send me what you have in your file about me?"

Kathy Harman may have never received a call like this before. But after the initial bewilderment, she offered to fax Lisa all the information she could find on her mortgage, including screenshots from the computer system. "I hope this can help you," Kathy said.

One screenshot showed that DHI Mortgage shipped the loan out to something called "Chase Alt-A Bulk" right after Lisa signed it ("Alt-A" is industry shorthand for a below-prime mortgage that isn't quite a subprime loan). JPMorgan Chase "table-funded" the loan, supplying the funding up front and taking possession of the mortgage and note thereafter. Under Department of Housing and Urban Development regulations, table funding actually had to be disclosed; Lisa never received any disclosure. More important, nothing in Kathy Harman's file included any reference to U.S. Bank, whose law firm managed to doctor up the assignment but not the promissory note, which was—by its own evidence—held by a different party.

The mortgage assignment, dated three months after the foreclosure filing, also had a bunch of names on it. Christina Trowbridge was listed as vice president and Whitney Cook as assistant secretary of the mysterious company known as Mortgage Electronic Registration Systems. The assignment included two witnesses, Zaher Gerges and Vladimir Buskarov. After their signatures came a statement from a notary public from Franklin County, Ohio, named Jennifer Jacoby, who attested that Christina Trowbridge and Whitney Cook "personally appeared" before her and "acknowledged that they executed the foregoing as its duly authorized officers." Underneath, in small type, there was this little notation: "Recording requested, prepared by and return to: Cirilo Codrington."

Of all the names on the assignment, Lisa figured she'd have the easiest time finding the real Cirilo Codrington, since that name was so unusual. Plus he wasn't just a witness; he prepared the incorrect, after-the-fact document. Maybe he could shed some light on its origins. So Lisa went to where presumably all private investigators start missing-persons searches these days: Facebook. When she typed in Cirilo Codrington, only one profile came up. The location: Panama City, Panama. Lisa sent Cirilo a friend request, not knowing whether someone in Panama would notice an unknown lady from Palm Beach, or what she would even do about it if he did. But Cirilo quickly replied with a confirmation. He then sent Lisa a private message: "Who are u?"

Before panic set in, Lisa pulled together a cover story. "Your name looks so familiar," she wrote back. "I was searching for someone else and saw your profile and something was triggered in my memory. Have you ever been to Florida or Washington D.C. area (VA and/or MD)?"

Fortunately for Lisa, she cast her net wide enough to find a connection. "Washington dc my dad used to live over there, his name is bruce antonio codrington. I live in Panama and my aunts live in landover hills Maryland."

"I used to live all over Wash. DC!" Lisa replied. "In No. VA and in Kensington, MD and Columbia, MD. Now I'm in Florida. Do you ever go by Cirilo besides here on Facebook?"

Lisa didn't get a response right away, so a few days later, she tried to pump more info out of her new Panamanian friend. "Hi Cirilo, by any chance did you used to work doing mortgage stuff? I'm just starting to work in the industry and I saw your name on a document and wondered if that was you! I mean, how many people have the same name as you do? Small world! How's life in Panama these days? Lisa."

Thirteen minutes later, Cirilo messaged back. "Sure I work for Firm Solutions Panama it has to do with foreclosures I am the training manager."

Maybe private detective work was Lisa's calling, not nursing. She later tried to get Cirilo interested in an interview about mortgage documents with a local paper; she would be the interviewer, of course. Cirilo replied, "I will let u know promptly," but never followed up.

But Firm Solutions Panama was enough of a lead. The company billed itself as "the premier legal and financial support services provider in Panama." They seemed to work directly with foreclosure mills, providing and processing documents. Like outsourcing in American manufacturing, law firms apparently outsourced document creation, which would go from the doc shop in Panama to wherever the documents needed to be signed. Lisa found one Facebook page where Firm Solutions and Florida Default Law Group, the firm in her case, were connected.

Why would a law firm employ an offshore document processor in Panama unless the documents had never been created initially? These were basic forms, to be completed for any mortgage transfer. It was obvious to Lisa that this was all a weak attempt to paper over inattention to proper procedure during the go-go housing bubble. Mortgage originators sold $1.9 million worth of loans *every minute* in the peak bubble years; they had no time or inclination for paperwork. These fabrications covered up the original sin: nobody established the chain of title properly, on perhaps millions of mortgages.

Cirilo seemed nice enough to Lisa. She figured he was just a cog in the Great Foreclosure Machine, a line worker, someone told what to do and when to do it. If it wasn't so sad it would be comical: day by day, unsuspecting Central Americans put on ties and dress slacks, went to the office, and nonchalantly manufactured the raw materials in U.S. foreclosure cases, unaware of their central role in what increasingly looked to Lisa like a criminal enterprise. How many families were thrown onto the street every day because of what someone in Panama did for a living?

Lisa had one more question. What was Mortgage Electronic Registration Systems?

Several different entities had a connection to Lisa's loan: DHI Mortgage, JPMorgan Chase Bank, Chase Home Finance, Wells Fargo, U.S. Bank. But this new company, Mortgage Electronic Registration Systems, seemed to play no role in the securitization chain. The assignment called it the nominee for DHI Mortgage. But the note said DHI sold the originated loan to JPMorgan Chase. How was Mortgage Electronic Registration Systems the nominee for the mortgage but not the note? How did they fit into the picture?

The answer can be found in hundreds of obscure county offices all over America. In Palm Beach County they call the lead administrator at this office the "clerk of courts." Elsewhere they are called "county recorders" or "registers of deeds." Whatever the title, public servants have managed these offices since before the American Revolution. They track and record property transfers on every piece of land in the United States. You could walk into a county recording office and trace the history of your property for as long as it existed.

Property recordation is based on old English common law. After the feudal period, when the monarchy owned all land, statutes governing privately owned real estate gradually developed. The need for standardized property laws intensified during the Crusades, when landowners would travel to fight and leave their properties in the care of trusted colleagues. Often, when the landowners returned, the colleagues proved to not be so trustworthy, as they would refuse to give the properties back.

The Statute of Frauds, passed in England in 1677, required that all agreements related to land, from leases to conveyances of transfer, had to be recorded in writing, signed and dated by all parties involved in the transaction. Later, notarizations, the ultimate assurance that the proper person signed a document on a specific date and in a particular place, were added. Contracts without written evidence would be unenforceable. The purpose of the Statute of Frauds, laid out in its preamble, was "For prevention of many fraudulent Practices which are commonly endeavoured to be upheld by Perjury and Subornation of Perjury." It allowed courts to fairly adjudicate disputes over property, and it gave land a specific value, turning it into a tradable and insurable instrument. If anyone could claim property without consequence, nobody would have confidence to buy or sell real estate. In *The Mystery of Capital*, Peruvian economist Hernando de Soto identifies accurate property records as what separates undeveloped countries from developed ones. "What creates capital," de Soto writes, "is an implicit process buried in the intricacies of its formal property systems. The formal property system is capital's hydroelectric plant. This is where capital is born."

Without a landed gentry in America, colonists frequently bought and sold property, prompting the need for a system to codify transfers in law. The Massachusetts Plymouth Bay Colony established a recording law in 1636, mandating public acknowledgment to the governor for all home and land sales. Other colonies followed, legalizing the recording statutes used today. They created land registration offices, typically at the county level, to track property transfers and hold evidence of legal title. These offices designated what instruments needed to be recorded and preserved, along with penalties for failure to record. The information was indexed and available to the public, so mortgage lenders could confirm ownership before they issued loans, tracking the chain of title back to the original owner and ensuring the lack of defects in that chain. All transfers included a nominal fee to the public recording office to cover administrative costs. Like any pen-

and-paper system subject to human error, it wasn't without its occasional rough spots. But it worked pretty well for three hundred years.

When banks started securitizing mortgages on a wide scale in the 1980s, they viewed recording offices as a problem to be overcome. The nominal recording fee, typically between $25 and $50, barely registered on a mortgage costing several hundred thousand dollars. But to create the bankruptcy-remote trusts used in mortgage-backed securities, banks needed to transfer mortgages multiple times. Under the old system, that would trigger a recording fee and document creation at every step. With millions of mortgages expected to enter securitization, suddenly recording fees represented a drain on profits.

In October 1993, at the Mortgage Bankers Association annual convention, a white paper suggested the creation of a private electronic database to track mortgage transfers. A subsequent accounting study by Ernst & Young identified hundreds of millions of dollars in savings by avoiding recording fees, leading to the incorporation in 1995 of the Mortgage Electronic Registration Systems (MERS), backed by funding from several major financial institutions, Fannie Mae, and Freddie Mac. By the end of the 1990s, practically all GSE and private-label mortgage securities involved MERS. Despite the lack of public debate or legislative approval, this database commandeered the land recording system for a substantial majority of mortgages in the United States.

Instead of filing with county recording offices each time a mortgage transferred—and paying that fee—banks instead listed MERS as the "mortgagee of record" in the initial mortgage assignment. Then, for subsequent transfers, the parties would go to the MERS database and list trades on an electronic spreadsheet. Banks could make unlimited transactions inside MERS; the county recorder only knew about the original assignment.

Though frequently listed as legal title holder on borrowers' deeds, and though named on the assignment in the public records, MERS has no financial interest in the mortgage, does not receive payments from any borrower, and does not receive proceeds from any foreclosure sale. They make their money on the front end from mortgage originators, who pay to use the MERS database. MERSCORP, the parent company, owned a headquarters in Reston, Virginia, and a data center in Texas. They employed around sixty workers. MERS, Inc., the name on all the mortgage documents, was a shell company with no actual employees. Yet at the height of the housing bubble, most of the existing mortgages in the United States, more than sixty million, listed MERS Inc. as the "mortgagee of record."

Law professors such as Christopher Peterson of the University of Utah identified a couple of major problems with MERS. First of all, it operated like a tax evasion scheme, depriving local governments of recording fees by transferring mortgages internally. The far bigger problem was that the MERS database served as the repository of all knowledge about the various transfers from originator to trustee. Thousands of people could access the MERS database, which proved far more susceptible to human error than the recording office. Banks failed to record transfers within MERS in a timely fashion, if at all. Nobody took responsibility for flushing out errors or double-checking transfers. With millions of loans, that project could hardly be managed by a large team of operatives, let alone the few employees at the MERS data center. Law professor Alan White of Valparaiso University surveyed a sample of MERS loans and found that only 30 percent matched the ownership record in the public domain. MERS didn't so much track mortgage transfers as it *pretended* to track them.

If the borrower missed payments and the servicer decided to foreclose, MERS acted in one of two ways. In some cases they carried out the foreclosure process in their own name, as the mortgagee of record, despite the fact that they had no material interest in the loan itself. Alternatively, like in Lisa's case, they quickly made an after-the-fact assignment to the trustee, which under the pooling and servicing agreement is supposed to hold legal title on the loan. The difference depended on state laws surrounding foreclosures, whether the note was specifically endorsed to some other entity or not, and whether local courts had caught up to the fast-moving scheme.

Either way, MERS operated under questionable legal foundations. In depositions, MERS claimed to be merely acting as "nominee" for the lender while also claiming to hold legal title on the mortgage. They would argue their role as mortgage holder whenever possible but deny liability when pressed. In a March 2009 bankruptcy case in Nevada called *In re Hawkins*, MERS brought foreclosure action in its own name and as a nominee for others simultaneously. On page 9 of their brief in the Hawkins case, MERS asserted the "right to enforce the note as the note's holder"; on page 8 of the same brief, they asserted "authority to *act for* the current beneficial owner of the loan or its servicer." MERS didn't even seem to know what MERS did. (They lost that case, incidentally.) As Peterson wrote in a law review paper, "To grant MERS standing based on legal title held by someone else is to treat the notion of legal title as some magical nonsense where ownership means nothing other than a willingness on the part of courts to let financiers seize homes in whatever manner is most convenient for them."

In cases like Lisa's, where MERS assigned the loan to the trustee, the legal problems did not go away. First, the recorded assignments happened after the foreclosure commenced. Also, they were assigned after closure of the trust under the pooling and servicing agreement, after which time assets could not be conveyed. The PSA also barred trustees from putting delinquent or "nonperforming" loans into trusts, and by May 2009, the date on the assignment, Lisa's loan was delinquent.

MERS had, according to their corporate roster, just a handful of employees. How did Whitney Cook and Christina Trowbridge, named as MERS "corporate officers" on Lisa's mortgage assignment, work for them? MERS's corporate HQ was in Virginia and their data center was in Texas, and yet the mortgage assignment was signed and notarized in Ohio. Lisa did some more Facebook snooping and found a Whitney Cook, age twenty-three, living in Akron, Ohio, near the offices of Chase Home Finance. Furthermore, on the "Affidavit of Amounts Due and Owing" in the case, Cook's name appeared as a representative of Chase, not MERS.

Christopher Peterson, the Utah law professor, found that MERS sold their corporate seal on their own website for $25. Thousands of low-level workers across the country who worked at mortgage servicers or their law firms became "vice presidents" and "assistant secretaries" of MERS, despite never working for or receiving pay from them, so they could sign documents purporting to assign mortgages. Under the membership agreement, MERS empowered these "corporate officers" to execute whatever documents were necessary for loans in the MERS system.

Lisa couldn't believe it. Three centuries of American land title operations had been outsourced to a shell company created by big banks so they could save a buck—and they were using it to circumvent established procedures and kick people out of their homes. Every step of the process involved an alphabet soup of companies blithely ignoring the law to maximize profits. Originators neglected underwriting standards and served up predatory loans to anyone with a pulse. In securitization, banks chopped up the loans in faulty ways that clouded chain of title, and apparently didn't convey the notes properly. The same banks took bad loans and knowingly passed them on to investors to increase their profit margin. When this all crashed, servicers, foreclosure mill law firms, and trustees continued to neglect legal standards, using document fabrication and shady third parties to rush foreclosures through the system. In fact, foreclosure fraud was necessary to stay one step ahead of the origination and securitization fraud.

Chain of title is a long-standing concept in contract law based on the principle of privity, under which nobody can sue on a contract to which they are not a party. In any other legal context, from shoplifting to murder, breaking the chain of evidence would lead to a judge tossing the charges. If evidence in a judicial proceeding can be faked and nobody challenges the fakeries, the legitimacy of the system breaks down. Anyone can be swept up and condemned to eviction based on false documents or inaccurate testimony.

If actually reading your mortgage documents constituted a revolutionary act, then Lisa was among a handful of brave radicals, conscripted into a fight she never sought against the most powerful foe in America. But unknowingly, Lisa was actually building on twenty years of critical forensic work done mostly by one man, unsurprisingly based in Florida: a former sports agent named Nye Lavalle.

4

THE ORIGINATOR

It was 1989—before the housing bubble, before the widespread adoption of private-label securitization, even before the savings and loan industry blew up. Nye Lavalle was the great-grandson of an Argentinian president (Teatro Colon, one of the world's finest opera houses, sits on a Buenos Aires square named Plaza Lavalle, after his ancestor) who successfully managed professional tennis players in the 1970s. Nye's father, Ramon, was a diplomat, tight with the Kennedys and Ernest Hemingway. Ramon left Argentina to work in the Office of War Information during World War II, eventually becoming an executive vice president at the pharmaceutical firm Parke-Davis. Nye grew up in the tony suburb of Grosse Pointe, Michigan, and his dad liked to take him to inner-city slums in Detroit and New York City, telling him that people born into privilege had a duty to look out for those less fortunate.

In the 1980s Nye founded a consultancy and research firm called the Sports Marketing Group (SMG), which published groundbreaking studies into the popularity and viewing audiences of American sports. For many years he was a go-to analyst on sports trends and predictions, quoted in papers across the country. He called the rise of figure skating and NASCAR in the 1990s, and advertisers salivated over his detailed analysis. Nye's business successes accompanied a flamboyant style. He dressed sharply, laughed big, and was never at a loss for dates, as he would tell you. One friend quipped that, with his monogrammed blazers, he looked like the captain of a ship, minus the hat.

In 1989 Nye Lavalle was building his business, running part of it out of a home in Dallas purchased for his parents, Anthony and Matilde Pew (his

father, Ramon, died young, and his mother remarried). Savings of America
(SOA), predecessor to the crisis-era lender Washington Mutual and the nation's largest S&L, owned and serviced the loan. Though the Pews instructed
SOA to send monthly statements to their primary home in Michigan, the
company would either send them to Dallas or not at all. Nye paid the mortgage directly at an SOA branch. But SOA would mail the check to a servicing
center, and by the time it got delivered to the proper division, the payment
would be late. Nye protested that he held the check receipt, showing delivery well before the due date, but SOA would tack on a late fee anyway.

Nye started talking to banker clients—he represented Barclays and Visa
in his consulting firm—about these nickel-and-dime schemes. Loan servicers were mostly automated, with software programs tracking payments
and ringing up fees. They were paid through a small percentage of the
principal balance on the loans they serviced; they also earned "float," from
investments made in the time between receiving monthly payments and
sending them to investors. Most important, they kept all fees generated
through servicing. Fees represented the only real variable, creating a big
incentive to make customers delinquent. And the software could be dialed
to increase fees and maximize profits.

SOA's next attempted cash grab on the Pew home would become a
commonplace scam in the bubble years, known as force-placed insurance.
Homeowners are required to hold property insurance, so whenever that
lapsed, servicers automatically enrolled them in an overpriced replacement
policy, taking a kickback from the insurer in exchange. Homeowners suddenly got a giant charge for junk insurance automatically deducted from
their mortgage payment. Force-placed insurance served a dual function: it
racked up profits for the insurer while making homeowners late on their
full payment, leading to more fees. In this case, SOA's software program
force-placed the Pew house into homeowner's insurance whenever the policy came *within* thirty days of expiration. This happened three times on the
same loan, with SOA force-placing additional policies on top of the old
ones, charging for each by deducting from the monthly payment. All the
insurers who imposed new policies on the residence were actually owned
by the same parent company as SOA.

Nye and his family had enough. He told SOA he wanted out of the loan:
just give him the payoff amount and the loan histories, and he'd cut them a

check. When Nye finally got the data, he found that SOA overcharged by close to $18,000. Plus they failed to supply the promissory note. Nye refused to pay the charge-off amount, believing it fraudulent. The ensuing battle took over a decade and cost around $2.5 million in legal fees.

Throughout the dispute, Nye and his parents consistently made mortgage payments to stay current. But SOA kept demanding excess charges and court fees well above the loan balance, based on a delinquency they concocted. More frustratingly, Nye could never get a clear estimate of the amount owed. He received twenty different loan histories throughout the ordeal, none of which matched. Sometimes monthly payments were missing; other transactions were redacted or even manually whited out and typed over.

In 1991 SOA started charging the Pews monthly property inspection fees without telling them, taking the money from the mortgage payments. This generated additional late fees because the payment would come up short, though the deductions were unknown to the Pews until after the fact, and even then concealed as "miscellaneous advances." Nye's banker friends called the deliberate strategy "fee pyramiding," layering obscure overcharges to siphon as much extra cash as possible from every loan. Any attempts to fix these errors would only meet with stall tactics. SOA probably didn't think anyone read the payoff statements; surely none of their homeowners would have the resources or the will to fight them over it. And mostly they were right. But Nye had a sense of principle, a buildup of personal wealth, and a temper. "You can fuck with me," he said later. "But fuck with my family, my friends, or my dog and you have an enemy for life."

In September 1993 Savings of America claimed to have sold the Pew loan to EMC, a subsidiary of the investment bank Bear Stearns. (Interestingly, all of these entities—SOA, their purchaser Washington Mutual, EMC, and Bear Stearns—would after the financial crisis fall into the hands of JPMorgan Chase.) EMC rapidly filed for foreclosure, demanding nearly $1 million in excess fees, court costs, and late payments. Nye and his parents, who never missed a mortgage payment but were on the brink of losing their home, countersued in Dallas District Court to stop the foreclosure, which in Texas did not have to go through a judicial process.

It appeared that EMC operated as, to use Nye's phrase, a "mortgage toxic waste dump," taking over what the industry called "scratch-and-dent loans" in default and moving to foreclose, regardless of the homeowner's ability to cure past due amounts. Nye considered it a form of extortion. He demanded that EMC fix SOA's repeated misapplications of payments, fee pyramiding, and other fraudulent behavior, but EMC representatives openly threatened to ruin Nye's business credit and his family's credit if they weren't paid the full amount, arguing that they had no obligation to correct previous errors. EMC submitted loan histories to Dallas District Court that were pastiches of past SOA records, similarly flawed and incomplete, while swearing under penalty of perjury to their veracity.

And then there was the sale of the loan itself. EMC hyped the purchase from SOA, involving more than eight thousand loans with a total value of over $2 billion, one of the largest loan purchases in history to that point. But when Nye pressed EMC to fix the pattern of fraudulent charges on his account, EMC asserted that the master transaction records were destroyed. Nye asked EMC for a chain of title, including the promissory note and all the assignments and transfer documents on the loan, but EMC never provided them either, claiming several of them were also destroyed.

During his investigation, Nye learned that Bear Stearns, parent company of EMC, was an investment adviser to SOA. EMC created a shell corporation called California Loan Partners as a pass-through. SOA sold the eight thousand loans to California Loan Partners, and on the same day, California Loan Partners sold them to EMC. By structuring the deal this way, SOA could hide losses in the shell corporation, so they wouldn't have to take immediate write-downs. This would have led to technical insolvency and a takeover by the Resolution Trust Corporation, the entity President George H. W. Bush set up to unwind failing savings and loans. So the entire transaction was an elaborate game to get bad assets off SOA's books and ward off a government takeover.

EMC concealed the notes and mortgages to keep the scheme hidden, but that left them lacking proof of standing to foreclose. In addition, once EMC got hold of the loans, they included them in mortgage-backed security sales to investors. None of those transfers was ever recorded at the Collin County, Texas, land records office. Nye wondered if EMC even had custody of the mortgages, or if they were assigned willy-nilly to different investor pools without a proper chain of title. Nye also believed EMC officials gave false testimony under oath, particularly in sworn affidavits attesting to the loan histories. In a court filing, Nye questioned whether EMC was "the actual owners of the note or mortgage upon which they attempt to foreclose in their own name, rather than the name of the trustee or investor in the note or mortgage." This was the same complaint Lisa and her online friends would make years later.

In the 1990s the judicial system was not ready to hear about financial institutions creating false documents and lying to courts. After several years, the judge hearing the case unexpectedly recused himself, with a new judge brought in from retirement. The bank piled on frivolous challenges, even questioning Nye's adoption by his stepfather at one point. The family's own lawyers told them not to bother with the case, urging them to take an inadequate settlement; Nye suspected they were bought off. Ultimately the new judge ruled for EMC, and on January 4, 2000, they foreclosed on the Pew family property.

But the house in Dallas had ceased to be the point of the struggle.

Nye could tell he'd stumbled into something big; why else would a collection of financial institutions spend millions in legal fees to repossess a house worth, at best, $160,000? Only to conceal the fraud lurking underneath, inflicting enough emotional and financial distress to get away with it. If what Nye saw in his case occurred across the U.S. housing market, it would be the greatest consumer fraud scandal in history, affecting people far more financially vulnerable than his family.

Nye used the extensive discovery period to acquire and analyze tax records, prospectuses, SEC filings, internal audits, insurance documents, and more. He flew around, at his own expense, to courthouses in Florida, Georgia, California, and Texas, reading foreclosure case files line by line, making notes and even scanning documents into an early version of a Mac laptop. He found other foreclosed homeowners with similar horror stories. He deposed employees of Bear Stearns, EMC, and SOA and interviewed dozens of other mortgage bankers, industry experts, forensic specialists, and even local, state, and federal banking regulators. And once people on the inside learned of his investigation, they anonymously fed him bits and pieces of information, too. Nye Lavalle was a full-time sports agent and consultant but a part-time mortgage sleuth.

One day Nye met a woman in a bar, a certified cash manager with Bank of America. She told him that the board of directors set a profit number for the bank, and employees had to hit the target in any way possible. With the rise of computerization, they could do that simply by moving numbers on a spreadsheet. If a bank robber steals a million dollars, they go to jail. But if banks steal that sum from their customers every day in five- and ten-dollar increments, auditors and regulators pay no attention.

Nye connected this to mortgage servicers' financial incentives to drive borrowers into default and maximize fees. Servicers got paid first in a foreclosure sale, even before the owners of the loan. So there was no reason for them to help anyone in need or hire enough staff to handle requests for assistance. They devised ways to digitally extract profits through every stage of the mortgage process, from escrow accounts to homeowner's insurance to applications of monthly payments. When mortgages transferred to new servicers, the computer systems wouldn't reamortize the loan or reconcile the numbers, always benefiting the servicer over the borrower. At one point Nye counted forty-four different schemes to ring up additional fees, even if borrowers paid on time. These weren't back-office mistakes but deliberate financial engineering. Nye found a policy manual from EMC Mortgage that referred to its customers as "smucks," and if anything, that overstated the level of respect. Since smucks couldn't choose their servicers, they had to live with the consequences.

Furthermore, as Nye would later tell the *New York Times*, "nothing—and I mean nothing—that a bank, lender, loan servicer or their lawyer says or puts on paper can be trusted and accepted as true." No transfers of mortgages, which started to multiply with the rise of securitization in the late 1990s, were actually "true sales," as people like Lisa Epstein eventually figured out. The notes and mortgages in securitizations never made it to the trusts, and mocked-up documents submitted to county recording offices, bankruptcy trustees, and courts in foreclosure cases constituted an elaborate game to conceal that fact.

Nye also identified how banks would offer for sale interests in mortgages that they did not own. Banks would "double-pledge" mortgages into a loan pool and also as collateral with the Federal Reserve to obtain additional borrowing. It was as if a baker sold you a cupcake and then sold the same cupcake to the person in line behind you, letting you two fight it out over who gets to eat it.

Instead of documenting chain of title on each mortgage transfer and keeping assignments and notes in the individual loan file, investment banks made copies of the original documents, and when they needed to, they had foreclosure mills fill in the blanks with the necessary names and signatures. They couldn't really do it any other way: if the rules of evidence for all other trials also held in foreclosure cases, the cost of litigation would be enormous. You would need original promissory notes and assignments from every link in the securitization chain, along with certified testimony from each document custodian. But nobody preserved the records. Nobody tracked or verified evidence. One industry hand told Nye it was like taking a criminal suspect's lab specimen from the evidence room and letting someone else pee in the bottle. From a legal point of view, the chain of custody of hundreds of thousands if not millions of loans was fatally corrupted. And Nye's family trust had numerous investments in mortgage-backed securities through mutual fund holdings. He was helping *fund* this mess.

When you combine the spoliation of the data with servicers driving borrowers into default, anyone with a loan, current or not, could find themselves wrongly evicted with false documents. But the Great Foreclosure Machine was sloppy; you could uncover its traces. And Nye wasn't just willing to look. He wanted to expose it to the world.

As someone frequently quoted in the press, Nye knew how to get media attention. He presented his findings under the names of Pew Mortgage Investigations and Americans Against Mortgage Abuse, two nonprofit organizations that consisted mainly of Nye Lavalle, in long reports with provocative titles. "Predatory Grizzly 'Bear' Attacks Innocent, Elderly, Poor, Minorities, Disabled and Disadvantaged!" excruciatingly detailed the schemes of Savings of America, EMC, and Bear Stearns that led to foreclosure on the family home in Dallas. The next report, "21st Century Loan Sharks," took as its modest goal "to defend and protect Americans and the American dream of homeownership from unlawful, fraudulent, criminal, unethical and illegal acts." In that report, Nye described the modern financial industry as a white-collar mafia, using software and lawyers instead of guns and knives. "Well-known banks and mortgage companies in Florida," Nye wrote, "are providing perjured testimony, false affidavits and frivolous pleadings in cases involving mortgage foreclosure." Nye described a litany of false affidavits entered into courts by Florida foreclosure law firms, where they claimed control of documents the trusts never received, claimed ownership over notes when the entity merely serviced them, or claimed "to support knowledge of facts not known by the affiant."

This was a novel finding, that signatories on foreclosure documents had no understanding of the evidence they claimed to authenticate. Nye came to this realization while going through affidavits in the public records. The same names kept coming up over and over again, at a pace that suggested little or no examination of the loan files. Plus they signed multiple affidavits swearing to be vice presidents of different banks in different parts of the country. They were often the witness in one document and vice president in another. Finally, the signatures were inconsistent, with initials on one affidavit and full names on another. Signatures sometimes looked so different from one another, it seemed impossible for them to spring from the same hand.

Nye reckoned these were entry-level employees signing as bank officers—the lowest-paid vice presidents in history—with a corporate title rented by a foreclosure mill or document processor. He suspected that they lacked the personal knowledge of the facts of the case file, as required by law. Nye later published an entire report in 2008 about one of these document executors, Scott Anderson, who worked for Ocwen, a specialized non-bank servicer that dealt with distressed loans. Nye demonstrated that Anderson adopted the position of vice president for dozens of different banks and lenders, signing with initials or "squiggle marks" that looked different across multiple documents, possibly signed by other employees on his behalf. While Nye was more exercised by double-pledging notes and concealing rip-offs inside servicer computing platforms, he included these dodgy signing practices in his reports as a way to reach nonexperts with something they could easily understand. High-priced attorneys can explain away complicated securities maneuvers, but what about the physical documents that govern real estate transactions?

Nye intended to get these reports in front of anyone who could stop the abuse, from homeowners who could challenge their foreclosures to the highest levels of government. The effects of institutionalized fraud, Nye warned, would lead to drastic devaluations of securities derived from mortgages, widespread failures of major banks and a mass sell-off in the stock market, not to mention millions of foreclosures, job losses, vacant homes, and emotional distress. He predicted the financial crisis and Great Recession eight years in advance.

For years Nye was under a gag order imposed by the judge in his foreclosure case. When it was lifted in 2000 he sent his reports to top executives at practically every major financial institution: Banc One, Countrywide, Merrill Lynch, Washington Mutual. Nye not only contacted Bear Stearns but created several websites with names like EMCMortgageFrauds.com, BearStearnsCriminals.com, and BearStearnsShareholders.com. On these sites he listed numerous criticisms against Bear Stearns and EMC. Bear Stearns sued to get the sites taken down because they created customer confusion. A judge forced the closure of some, while allowing those whose addresses were "unmistakably critical" to remain up.

In 2000 Nye helped sponsor a conference of the National Consumer Law Center in Broomfield, Colorado. With his Italian suit standing out among the collared shirts and jeans of five hundred legal aid attorneys and housing counselors, Nye released his findings. "You're wrong if you call these errors," he told the assembly. "This is intentional and premeditated. Servicers want their customers in default, it's designed to increase revenues." Almost all of the lawyers thought he was nuts. Maybe they resented being lectured about their profession by a nonlawyer; maybe they just didn't like this guy with the fancy suit and brusque self-confidence. "Why is he wasting our time like this?" was the general reaction. "We're here to learn the law!"

The same year, Nye got to spend fifteen minutes with Arthur Levitt, chairman of the Securities and Exchange Commission at the end of the Clinton administration. He was in south Florida for a speech and Nye somehow secured a meeting. Levitt listened intently and agreed with Nye on virtually every point. But when Nye finished, Levitt leaned back and said, "I have as many lawyers at the entire SEC as one major law firm representing the banks." Levitt described a ten-year lag between identifying a financial fraud scheme and its ultimate exposure to the nation. "It won't come out for ten years, and the banks know it. By then they're already on to the next scam," Levitt sighed.

Undaunted and completely obsessed, Nye kept making his case. He published rants and critiques of the mortgage industry on consumer websites like RipoffReport and on a primitive blog documenting these issues, *Mortgage Servicing Fraud* (msfraud.org), run by another foreclosure-victim-turned-evangelist named Jack Wright. Nye infiltrated the corporate message board for MERS, the private database for mortgage transfers, accusing them of fraudulent activity. (The company's CEO, R.K. Arnold, personally responded in the comments, writing, "There's nothing sinister about who we are and what we do.")

But Nye's masterstroke was to purchase a piece of the companies he wanted to confront. He bought single shares of stock in several banks, mortgage servicing companies, and even the quasi-governmental entities Fannie Mae and Freddie Mac. Then he attended shareholder meetings and listed his grievances about pervasive mortgage misconduct and threats to the financial system. Nye studied every subsection of corporate shareholder rules, strategizing how to make himself heard.

In 2001 Nye and his parents flew to Seattle for Washington Mutual's annual meeting. Company bylaws stipulated that all shareholders had the right to inspect accounting books and shareholder lists fourteen days in advance. Washington Mutual didn't really make that information available. Nye found the woman who handled investor relations and asked to see the books. "I've been here sixteen years and nobody has ever made this request," she said.

"Well, guess what—today's your lucky day," Nye replied.

"But we just don't have this information!"

Nye smiled. "You'd better get it, because if not, that little party you're planning tomorrow won't go forward. I'll go to the Superior Court of King County and shut down your shareholder meeting!"

The woman turned white and left the room, returning a couple of hours later with William Lynch, Washington Mutual's corporate secretary, whom she pulled out of a board meeting. Nye handed Lynch one of his reports and reiterated his desire to see the shareholder lists and the books. Lynch pulled out his own file about the Pew family's long legal battle with Washington Mutual's predecessor, Savings of America. "You're just crying sour grapes because we foreclosed on you," Lynch said, smirking.

The smugness set Nye off. "You can wipe that fucking grin off your face before I knock it off," he said, banging the table in the conference room.

The startled head of investor relations rose. "How dare you speak to the corporate secretary that way! He took time out of his day to address your concerns!"

"The reason he's here," Nye replied, shooting her a look, "is because he knows I can shut down your meeting in a second. So you're going to listen to everything I have to say and take me seriously. This isn't a fucking joke."

Nye's parents thought security would haul their son out of the room. But William Lynch stayed there until eight o'clock at night going over Nye's reports. And the next day Nye met for hours with the company's head of mortgage servicing while the annual meeting went forward across the street. But while Nye forced Washington Mutual to be respectful, nothing really changed.

In fact, while major banks, accounting firms, and mortgage servicers accepted Nye's comments and vowed to address them, only one company, the mortgage giant Fannie Mae, took it a step further. Fannie did business with enough lenders, servicers, and law firms that changes to their practices would have ripple effects throughout the industry. Nye corresponded with several Fannie Mae executives, including CEO Franklin Raines. Eventually Fannie Mae hired an outside law firm, Baker Hostetler, to verify Nye's claims. Baker Hostetler conducted seventeen separate interviews with Nye over a six-month period. The deal for his participation was that Nye would get to review the final report and make comments, but when the time came, Baker Hostetler asserted attorney-client privilege and shielded it. Nye was blocked from reading a study based on his own work.

Years later, the *New York Times*'s Gretchen Morgenson published the 147-page report, which was authored in May 2006, at the housing bubble's peak. With the saccharine title "Report to Fannie Mae Regarding Shareholder Complaints by Mr. Nye Lavalle," Baker Hostetler corroborated most of Nye's allegations. The author, Mark Cymrot, distanced himself by noting, "Mr. Lavalle is partial to extreme analogies that undermine his credibility." But he agreed that Fannie Mae's foreclosure attorneys in Florida routinely filed "false statements" and affidavits, that MERS filed "sham pleadings" in cases across seven states, and that "Lavalle has identified an issue that Fannie Mae needs to address promptly."

But the report added one critical caveat. "Mr. Lavalle's assertion that Fannie Mae faces tens of billions of dollars of unenforceable mortgages and damages from class action lawsuits is overstated in our view," Cymrot explained, because borrowers were unlikely to robustly defend themselves from foreclosure. Most homeowners didn't have the resources. Plus Fannie Mae was insulated, one step removed from the attorneys who filed the false documents. Reaching Fannie would require multiple lawsuits, and borrowers would simply run out of money.

There was an eerie parallel to the infamous Ford Pinto memo. According to a 1977 exposé in *Mother Jones* magazine, Ford Motor Company discovered a design flaw in the fuel tank of its Pinto model that made it susceptible to explosion in a rear-end collision. But the company refused to fix it, because a cost-benefit analysis determined it would be cheaper to pay off individual lawsuits than to redesign assembly lines and repair the cars sold. They deliberately kept the public at risk rather than spend the money.

The Baker Hostetler report for Fannie Mae wasn't as explicit, but it made the same point: it would cost more to unwind the many problems with foreclosures than to keep everything in place and deal with borrower lawsuits on a case-by-case basis. As a result, Fannie Mae took no action on Nye Lavalle's claims. They certainly didn't make public the documented evidence of fraud.

Nye was hooked on exposing banking industry fraud, and years of setbacks wouldn't stop him. In his career, he always peered to the edge of the horizon and brought back the future. Now he saw tsunami waves on that other side, and he felt obligated to warn people. Nye started serving as a consultant and expert witness for some foreclosure defense lawyers who embraced his theories. Through those cases and additional reports, Nye believed, he could educate lawyers, judges, and the general public. It was hard to get people to listen; even Nye's friends would tease him, calling him Chicken Little, asking when the sky would fall. They stopped laughing when it did.

Nye left a trail a mile wide, so anyone could see what he called "the fraud of our lifetime." When the truth came out, as he knew it would, the corporate accountants, bank directors, judges, and federal regulators could not say they weren't informed. What would really bring down the whole charade, Nye thought, was the Internet. Without a way for people to talk to each other, banks could squash dissenters. But if victims could coordinate, and expose the fraud for themselves, everything would come crashing to the ground.

5

THE COMMUNITY

If Lisa Epstein was going to act as her own lawyer to fight her foreclosure, she figured she'd better observe the process. Once Jenna was well enough, Lisa returned to work, but shifted into a four-day-a-week schedule, reserving Fridays for the courthouse. On Craigslist Lisa found a babysitter named Mary Delaguila, who coincidentally lived on Gazetta Way, the same street as her foreclosed home. Every week she would pack a lunch, drop Jenna off with Mary, and drive to downtown West Palm Beach.

Bounded by the Intracoastal, downtown shimmered with fancy new buildings, as if a county commissioner happened upon a windfall of cash and decided its best use would be to make a giant movie backlot. The 1980s postmodernism of the eleven-story Palm Beach County Courthouse, all aqua and pink and granite and mirrored windows, fit the dominant aesthetic. The original courthouse, across the street on Dixie Highway, had traditional classical features; its replacement had the sobriety and seriousness of a shopping mall.

The last time Lisa stepped into the courthouse was to get her marriage license. Passing security, she reached the fourth floor, where one judge heard every foreclosure case in the county. A white folding table sat outside courtroom 4A, with well-dressed lawyers snaking down the hallway and back. Others loitered on their cell phones or hurried between floors. The bulletin board listing the day's cases in tiny type must have had a hundred docket actions scheduled. Lisa walked up to the entrance to courtroom 4A and put her hands on the door, whispering to herself, "Okay, God, let's see what we can do."

The small, wood-paneled courtroom had just a few benches, packed with lawyers awaiting trials. Lisa could not find anywhere to sit, and struggled over to the back wall. Plaintiff and defense counsels each had a small table and a podium, with a staging area in the back, almost like an on-deck circle for future cases. The judge sat in front of the official seal of Florida, with her assistants and the bailiff off to the side. The place was so thick with murmuring that Lisa couldn't always make out if any business was taking place. What she did manage to hear, she didn't fully understand.

Nobody in attendance looked like a homeowner, nor did their needs seem addressed by the obscure maneuvers on display. In the morning, the judge made motions and set future schedules; she also affirmed plenty of summary judgments, ruling for the plaintiff without a trial, based on glancing at the motions and supporting evidence for a few seconds. Veteran defense lawyers later told Lisa they almost never saw a summary judgment in any other area of the law; the judge would usually figure there had to be a fact worth proving in the case file. But in the foreclosure division, summary judgments were almost the norm, with homeowners evicted with all the effort of buying a soda.

In the afternoon were the trials, which were seldom, because virtually no homeowner mounted a challenge. If foreclosure defense attorneys showed up, most had little trial experience and would jump at any deal they could get, no matter how piddling. A trial with counsel often did not last more than a few minutes; as long as the judge heard the magic sentence "Your honor, the defendant is in default on their mortgage," material facts seemed not to matter. *Pro se* litigants put up more of a fight, but the judge appeared exhausted, if not outraged, by their mere presence. Even if the defendant managed to get the case withdrawn, the judge would almost never grant dismissal with prejudice, so plaintiffs could always refile. Servicers could try over and over again to foreclose, only needing approval once; homeowners lose any case and they lose their home. Some began to use a nickname to describe Florida foreclosure courts: the "rocket docket."

Lisa took notes in a composition book, then made her way to the file room on the third floor. This long, narrow room had a desk separating visitors from the clerks, with paperwork-lined shelves behind them. By this time Lisa had several files to check, not just her own. A couple of her new online friends were local, with cases in the Palm Beach County system. Her babysitter's in-laws had a problem with an underwater home. Even patients approached her for advice. Just by talking about foreclosures online or in public, Lisa became a valued source for desperate homeowners searching for information.

She had enough facility with her own documents to recognize what to look for in others. And many of the same discrepancies were evident: assignments dated after the foreclosure filing, the use of special document processing companies, the ubiquitous presence of MERS. She also pulled a couple of dockets she had just seen in the courtroom, tying together the motions and rulings. On many occasions the plaintiff's complaint purported to have the promissory note attached, but it was nowhere in the file.

Whitney Cook and Christina Trowbridge, the vice president and assistant secretary for MERS on her mortgage assignment, kept popping up on other homeowners' documents. Sometimes Cook and Trowbridge were representatives of MERS, sometimes JPMorgan Chase, sometimes Chase Bank, sometimes U.S. Bank, and sometimes Chase Home Finance.

It cost a dollar a page to photocopy files, and Lisa had no budget for this project. So she transcribed what she could and copied only what was absolutely necessary. The next week she brought in her Acer laptop and a portable scanner and started to scan the documents herself. The file clerk stopped her and said that was against court policy. "What is the policy?" Lisa asked. The clerk said she would discuss it with her supervisor, and Lisa heard nothing for months. All the while she scanned on the sly.

That summer of 2009, Lisa became a familiar presence at the courthouse. On Fridays she dressed professionally, always accessorized with a signature scarf. The rest of the week she would arrive in hospital scrubs. The cancer institute was a mile down Dixie Highway. Lisa estimated it took twelve minutes to walk from work to the courthouse, or seven minutes to run. Twelve minutes up and twelve minutes back gave her thirty-six minutes out of her lunch hour to scan files or observe hearings; if she ran, she'd get a bonus ten minutes. At first Lisa stopped by once a week; after a while she was there practically every lunch hour. There was always another theory to test, another case to watch, another file to check out. And she got really good at researching and identifying patterns of fraud.

Bailiffs started to recognize Lisa, along with attorneys from either side. She would meet homeowners in the hallways and tell them to observe court proceedings, talk to other borrowers in trouble, work together to solve the crisis that had befallen their communities. The only way to fight back, Lisa believed, was by relying on each other.

Amid the suffering of the 1930s, communities banded together to fight fore-closures, particularly in rural areas. T.H. Watkins's chronicle *The Great Depression* explains how farmers would disrupt their neighbors' foreclosure auctions. They would bid low, no more than a few dollars. Anyone who at-tempted a more robust offer would feel the cold hand of the biggest farmer in the yard on his shoulder; that bid would be summarily withdrawn. The winning bidder would sell the farm back to the original owner for the pittance. As Watkins writes, "So it was that in the fall of 1932, an $800 mortgage on Walter Crozier's farm outside Haskins, Iowa, was satisfied for $1.90, or that the horses, cows and chickens offered for sale at Theresa Von Baum's farm near Elgin, Nebraska, went back to her at a nickel apiece, for a total of $5.35." Sustained action led to several foreclosure moratoria throughout the Midwest. Farmers simply would not allow their neighbors to get swallowed up by the side effects of rampant speculation and greed.

When it began in late 2006, the foreclosure crisis didn't find the same level of public solidarity and organized resistance. Decades of neglect of the civic square weakened traditional activism, and the relentless depiction of delinquent homeowners as irresponsible deadbeats kept many silent, turn-ing their shame inward, asking what they did wrong to deserve foreclosure. That made it difficult to campaign for their rescue. And back in the 1930s the bank had a community face; now homeowners were not fighting the savings and loan in Bedford Falls but a thicket of servicers and deposi-tors and trustees, all attached to impersonal yet powerful Wall Street conglomerates.

A few scattered groups did protest repossessions, including remnants of the Association of Community Organizations for Reform Now (ACORN), which set up a Home Defenders campaign in early 2009, undertaking civil disobedience by standing in front of foreclosed properties and refusing to leave, while families barricaded themselves inside. They also mimicked Depression-era farmers by disrupting foreclosure auctions. In one case in Baltimore, ACORN members reclaimed Donna Hanks's abandoned fore-closure by breaking in and replacing the locks. Another group called the

Neighborhood Assistance Corporation of America (NACA) started demonstrating at the offices and even homes of top executives for major banks and lenders like Countrywide, demanding that they offer loan modifications. Encampments outside major cities, often referred to as "Bushvilles" in an evocation of 1930s Hoovervilles, raised awareness of the crisis.

But politicians didn't heed these cries for help and easily knuckled under to the persuasions of the financial services industry. The White House's HAMP incentives for foreclosure mitigation were voluntary and did not force servicers to offer principal reductions, the most sustainable type of loan relief. Treasury Secretary Tim Geithner reportedly saw HAMP not as a relief vehicle but as a way to "foam the runway" for the banks, allowing them to absorb inevitable foreclosures more slowly. The Obama economic team also resisted a policy called cramdown, which would have allowed bankruptcy judges to modify terms on primary residence mortgages, as they can other debt contracts. Liberal lawmakers believed this threat of bankruptcy modifications would give homeowners needed leverage to negotiate relief. But although then-Senator Obama endorsed cramdown on the 2008 campaign trail—banks even held meetings to prepare for its eventuality—his administration pressured congressional leaders against including it in must-pass bills like the economic stimulus. When it came up as a standalone bill, a dozen Senate Democrats sided with the industry and against cramdown, and Senator Dick Durbin, the bill's sponsor, remarked about Congress that the banks "frankly own the place." But they appeared to own the White House too. Liberal lobby groups complained that they would meet with senators on cramdown, and then Treasury Department bigwigs would come in afterward and lobby against it. Concern for fragile bank balance sheets outweighed concern for homeowners.

After losing the cramdown fight, housing activists focused primarily on the denial of modification requests. Mortgage servicers repeatedly lost paperwork, gave contradictory information, and showed little interest in granting mortgage relief. The banks blamed homeowners for sending incomplete financial documents, but the breakdowns were deliberate. Servicers turned HAMP into a predatory lending program, squeezing borrowers for every payment they could get and then foreclosing anyway. After keeping people in trial modifications for a year, servicers would suddenly reject permanent relief and demand the difference between the trial and original payment, under threat of eviction. Bank of America employees later testified they were given Target and Best Buy gift cards as bonuses for lying to homeowners, denying HAMP modifications, and pushing people into foreclosure.

While activists challenged the modification hustle, practically nobody went a level deeper to consider breakdowns in property transfers and mortgage documentation, or how lenders faked their way through foreclosures. It took victims connecting on the Internet, screaming about banks trying to seize their homes with trumped-up evidence, for foreclosure fraud to enter the conversation.

Writers for pre-crisis foreclosure fraud blogs typically had personal experience. Robert "Jack" Wright of msfraud.org lost his $200,000 home without ever missing a payment. Craig Kinney started FairbanksSucks.org after a dispute with Fairbanks Capital over incompetent loan servicing; Fairbanks would eventually settle with the Federal Trade Commission in 2003 for $40 million over unfair and deceptive servicing practices, changing its name to Select Portfolio Servicing in the aftermath. Mike Dillon, a freelance stage technician in New Hampshire, spent nine years fighting Fairbanks in the courts; his site was GetDShirtz.com. The bubble's collapse, throwing millions of families into foreclosure, pushed awareness of fraud beyond these personal blogs and allowed formerly concealed patterns to float to the surface.

Few visitors to *Living Lies*, by 2009 one of the larger anti-foreclosure sites on the Web, even knew each other's names. But they managed to build a knowledgeable community out of what is normally a mélange of craziness and unrestrained anger. There was Deontos and SF_Dan and baffledinga and usedkarguy and maineloanmodifications. Lisa used her name, Lisa E, as her handle; every so often Nye Lavalle would post a comment. A lot of commenters were first-timers asking for help: "My foreclosure was filed August 2008, never served. Should I file a motion to dismiss under the 120 day rule?" "Can a foreclosure, in Florida, still take place where there was no assignment recorded but the original note?"

Neil Garfield jumped into comments periodically to answer questions. And the site offered resources—sample motions, definitions of legal terms, and examples where homeowners beat the banks. But perhaps the most powerful resource was the other commenters. They would reply to newbies with information, suggest attorneys in different parts of the country, or detail what to look for in foreclosure documents. Most of all, they would fortify desperate homeowners who felt utterly alone in combating the most powerful institutions in America. The site became a salve to overcome that shame. This proved challenging, as foreclosure summoned up dark passions. One night an unidentified woman logged on and typed that she and her husband saw no other way out but a murder/suicide. Andrew "Ace" Delany replied, "It isn't your fault. I don't think it's my fault." He tried to prove to the woman that her life had meaning and support. Nobody at *Living Lies* was a licensed therapist. Their only weapons against depression were honesty and the comfort of another voice to kill the loneliness.

To shine hope through the darkness, *Living Lies* users passed around positive court rulings, which popped up with increasing regularity in 2009, illustrating that the walls protecting banks had begun to creak. In Miami, Ana Fernandez had her foreclosure sale vacated on February 11 (just days before Lisa got served) because Chevy Chase Bank could not prove it held the promissory note. Samuel Bufford, a federal bankruptcy judge in California, began to demand valid documentation in any case involving securitized loans. Judge Walt Logan in Pinellas County, Florida, stopped accepting any foreclosures precipitated by MERS. New York State Supreme Court justice Arthur Schack of Brooklyn halted numerous foreclosure cases with irregularities as varied as the same representative signing documents on behalf of two different banks in the same case, or a bank initiating foreclosure before they owned the loan—symptoms of securitization FAIL. Over a two-year period, Judge Schack rejected 46 of 102 foreclosure cases that came before him. "If you are going to take away someone's house," Schack told the *New York Times*, "everything should be legal and correct."

But *Living Lies* commenters were also tempered by pervasive horror stories about people who did everything right and played by the rules. In August, Anna Ramirez of Miami came home to find all her belongings out on the lawn and a stranger telling her to get off the property. Without warning, Washington Mutual sold her home at auction; she had never missed a payment. Miami-Dade County police officers tossed out the family, who had to collect their things and stay with friends for a few nights while Ramirez explained the situation to a judge. The bank eventually claimed the sale was a "mistake." Across town, physical therapist Tony Louzado was fighting two separate law firms, each one suing him on the same note, with both plaintiff banks asserting standing to foreclose.

These scenarios should be impossible. When borrowers close on a mortgage, they sign dozens of documents designed to verify chain of title, document exactly how much the borrower will pay every month, and detail what happens in event of late payment or default. The mortgage and the note get filed at the county recording office. The borrower receives title to the property and even purchases title insurance to guard against defects in establishing ownership. There should be no question about the owner of the loan, the purchaser of the mortgage, and the very detailed steps of the process, all put into fine print in a binding contract.

When multiple lenders filed foreclosures on the same note, or when a bank tried to auction a home when the borrower never missed a payment, it spoke to a deep rot in the property records system. If Lisa Epstein showed up at the courthouse claiming to own someone's home, the judge would sanction her. If a bank did the same, with no more reliable evidence, why should they get a free pass?

Cranks and naysayers liked to complain about foreclosure victims trying to get "free homes" on a technicality. Trolls would jump into the comments all the time, screaming about subsidizing deadbeat homeowners, demanding that they "pay up or move out." But the gang at *Living Lies* did not think they deserved free homes. They wanted to stop a chaotic, error-filled process, because without standards, anyone could get caught in the eviction trap, even those naysayers. And anyway, there was a little something called the rule of law. To argue that it didn't matter whether documents were accurate as long as the homeowner didn't pay the mortgage was like saying as long as the murder suspect was guilty, it didn't matter whether the cops planted the gun on him.

One day that summer, someone with the username "Fraud in FL" commented on a story about MERS, "I have been working with my servicer WAMU (Washington Mutual) to prevent foreclosure but now they have turned it over to Florida Default Law Group and had MERS assign my mortgage over to JPMorgan Chase to begin the foreclosure process. The problem I have is the 'Officers' of MERS that did the assignment are actually employees of JPMorgan Chase." The original lender, AmNet Mortgage, transferred the mortgage to Chase on April 20, 2009—a notable activity, since AmNet was out of business at the time. The commenter said he found the signing officers on his document, Chase employees, acting as MERS vice presidents on behalf of several other lenders in county databases. "In my opinion there is some major fraud going on here," Fraud in FL wrote.

Lisa replied within two minutes. "My story is so similar to yours," she said, noting the presence of MERS and Florida Default Law Group. "How did you look up the court records on the mortgage?"

Alina Virani, a paralegal and frequent commenter, stepped in to counsel Lisa. "You can search your county clerk's website," she wrote, pointing her to the recording office where public documents are kept. Lisa didn't know documents were available outside the courthouse. This meant she could continue her research anywhere with an Internet connection. Lisa immediately clicked onto the website for Palm Beach County's clerk of courts, discovering she could examine dockets and official records, including assignments of mortgage and deeds of trust. She couldn't search every document filed in a case, like the affidavits. But this would be a tremendous time- and money-saver.

"It looks like Alina answered your question," Fraud in FL wrote back the next day. "Let me know if you want to trade notes. Knowledge is power . . . Michael." Lisa replied with her email address, and she and Michael began to correspond.

Meanwhile, Florida media began to uncover foreclosure problems. Susan Martin of the *St. Petersburg Times* published an exposé of Nationwide Title Clearing, a document processing company inexplicably owned by the Church of Scientology. Martin unearthed documents from Brian Bly, an employee at Nationwide Title Clearing, alternately signing as vice president of Option One Mortgage, Deutsche Bank, and Citi Residential Lending. Martin tracked Bly down to a trailer park in Clearwater. Along with his coworker Crystal Moore, they signed dozens of mortgage assignments in the Tampa Bay area, as per corporate resolutions that authorized them to sign for various lenders and "fix" document issues. "They may sit there all day for a week and sign," admitted Jeremy Pomerantz, Nationwide Title Clearing spokesman.

Michael, the "Fraud in FL," commenter, left a message on Susan Martin's story explaining how widespread the practice was, in his experience, and not limited to Nationwide Title. Susan Martin wrote back and even tracked him down at *Living Lies*, asking for more information.

Throughout the summer, Lisa traded motions in her case with Florida Default Law Group, seeking discovery of documents. She also tried to strike Whitney Cook's affidavit of amounts due and owing, on the grounds that Cook represented JPMorgan Chase in the affidavit but MERS on the mortgage assignment. Florida Default Law Group withdrew that affidavit and then filed one with all the same information, this time signed by someone named Beth Cottrell. On LinkedIn Cottrell identified herself as an employee of JPMorgan Chase, but in the document she signed as a vice president of Chase Home Finance, a separate legal entity. So Lisa found another moonlighter working in a high-level capacity for multiple corporations. She added Beth Cottrell to her list of searches.

For Lisa, the day began at 6:00 a.m., three hours after going to bed. She would race to the computer to check the news, hoping to find a big headline, "Foreclosure Fraud Uncovered." Then she'd get Jenna up and ready for day care, intermittently checking headlines and blogs. A drive to the babysitter and back to the cancer center, maybe logging on to check foreclosure sites there, a bout of daydreaming about legal strategies in between caring for patients, seven minutes to the courthouse, forty-six minutes in the courthouse, seven minutes back, another check of the blogs, wrap up at work, run public records searches, pick up Jenna, a quick dinner, sit Jenna in front of the TV while researching securitization, cries of "Momma, come over here" and replies of "Just a minute, Jenna, just a minute, Jenna" until bedtime, after which more reading, more writing, more research, more learning, until three in the morning. Foreclosure news and information consumed Lisa's life the way a virus invaded the body.

Lisa regretted missing Jenna's childhood. And she couldn't focus on patients with the compassion and tact the job demanded. The nurturing side, the unspoken bond with her patients—that became harder, as something new always drew away focus. The computer beckoned her, the knowledge sustained her; a little voice told her to learn and fight and enlist others to stop the tragedy. And it never shut off.

Just after the Fourth of July, Lisa got a voicemail from a patient named Robyn Powell. Doctors discovered a tumor in Robyn's brain in 2006, while she was being treated for injuries suffered in a head-on auto collision. The subsequent illness, marital breakup, and long recovery wrecked her pool-cleaning business and left her well behind on mortgage payments. Robyn told Lisa she got a note from her servicer, Saxon Mortgage, informing her of an imminent hearing. "I'm calling to ask if you know any homeless shelters, because I could lose my house next week," Robyn said, her speech slightly slurred due to recovery from the tumor. Robyn had no income besides her disability benefit, and nowhere for her and her teenage son to go.

Lisa looked up the case file at the courthouse. The servicer's law firm, Shapiro & Fishman, filed a motion for summary judgment, which would eliminate all Robyn's options to save her home. But the case looked as muddled as every other. Saxon filed a lost note affidavit and didn't seem to have documented proof that it owned the mortgage. Lisa thought Robyn could at least get an extension, given the questions in the case as well as Robyn's handicaps. "It's going to be scary, but I think we could get the eviction delayed if we show up and challenge it," she told her. Lisa couldn't argue the case for Robyn, so instead she wrote a letter for Robyn to read in court. The two practiced for hours, working through Robyn's slurred speech. Robyn was nervous, but she agreed to go to the trial on one condition: Lisa had to come with her.

On July 15, 2009, Lisa, fresh from the hospital and decked out in scrubs, guided a limping Robyn into courtroom 4A. She stood by Robyn's side as Judge Meenu Sasser called the case. Robyn gingerly reached the podium and took out Lisa's letter, while Lisa tensed up with a mixture of pride and fear. But before the case began, Judge Sasser asked, "Where are the plaintiffs?" The local lawyers for Shapiro & Fishman, a statewide firm, never showed up. Judge Sasser asked if Robyn had her own lawyer, and Robyn glanced over at Lisa before saying no. But Robyn added that she wanted to make a statement. She recited Lisa's letter to the judge word for word.

Lisa had Robyn request an extension under the Americans with Disabilities Act, explaining her tragic story to the judge. If the extension could not be granted, Lisa's letter pivoted to a robust opposition to the motion for summary judgment, objecting to most of the material facts. "I dispute that I owe this plaintiff any money. . . . I dispute paragraph 7 of plaintiff's motion claiming this is a purchase money mortgage, when clearly it was a refinance. . . . I dispute that this plaintiff filed the original note with its complaint, as is required by Florida state statute," Robyn slowly read. Lisa contended that the obligation to pay was unenforceable and unsecured under standard contract law, that the servicer had no standing to foreclose, that the plaintiff did not hold the promissory note, and that the chain of title had been broken because the plaintiff never recorded assignments of mortgage or endorsed the note. She asked for an extension of "90–120 days from the day plaintiff provides the original note, proof that it is indeed holder in due course, evidence of the recording of the entire unbroken chain of assignments, and a full accounting of each and every payment I made." It was a neutron bomb of a statement, the kind only a nonlawyer acting in her own defense could get away with, and even then not so much. The chatter in the courtroom, typically constant, faded away, with the crowd actually hanging on every word.

Judge Sasser paused for longer than a beat and then explained calmly that, due to lack of plaintiff's counsel, she would deny summary judgment. She added that she would make arrangements to get Robyn a legal aid attorney to help with the case in the future. For now, Robyn would get to stay in her home. Lisa didn't recall her feet touching the ground on her trip back to the chemo center.

Lisa grew frustrated with the *Living Lies* website. It provided great information, but even experienced users found it hard to locate resources among the massive, haphazardly arranged topic list. Comments on posts would often not appear for days, and sometimes they would show up on a different page. It was hard to participate fully in a fast-moving discussion.

Lisa also had trouble keeping up with requests for help on foreclosure cases from friends, acquaintances, and random strangers. She would get a steady trickle of texts, emails, and letters. A homeowner with questions about his documents once addressed correspondence to Lisa at the county courthouse; the file room clerk handed her the mail. There wasn't enough time for Lisa to respond to everyone personally; even a law firm couldn't take every case, let alone a single mom with a nursing job. But Lisa did feel that millions of people in foreclosure needed guidance to help find what

they needed. She imagined a clearinghouse with easy-to-understand resources and knowledgeable people ready to answer questions. *Living Lies*
was not that place.

Alina Virani started an email group for attorneys, paralegals, experienced homeowner victims, and *pro se* litigants. Lisa was invited, along with
Michael, aka "Fraud in FL." A paralegal with a real estate background, Alina
encountered foreclosure complaints in her daily work and thought they were
completely subpar, with critical documents missing and written arguments
contradicting themselves in the space of a few paragraphs. On the email
group, participants could share press clippings, research, and case law in one
place, aiding attorneys who wanted to represent homeowners properly.

But Alina insisted on keeping that group private. First of all, she didn't
want to publicly reveal their litigation strategies to the world. Second,
most group members weren't attorneys, and Alina feared violating statutes outlawing the unlicensed practice of law by giving advice. Finally, there
were many scammers at foreclosure-related websites, "rescue" specialists
promising to fix everything for a thousand dollars up front. Alina didn't
want her resource center infiltrated by crooked lawyers with nefarious
ideas. So she closed the loop.

Lisa thought the email group solved only one of the problems. Yes, she
could communicate with other researchers and work on projects. But she
couldn't reach out to the newly foreclosed, the confused, the lonely. Without someone urging them on, they would only hear the dominant cries of
"Deadbeat, deadbeat," and become too cowed to fight back. Those people
needed a lifeline. The only hesitation Lisa had was a reluctance to enter the
spotlight. She hardly wanted to become the face of foreclosures in America; she never really wanted to be known to anyone but family, friends, and
patients. But the times demanded that she step up and do this work.

Lisa had limited computer skills and no aptitude for putting together a
website. So for $50 she hired a web developer she found on the Internet. The
main feature Lisa wanted was a chat room, where people could gather to
discuss their foreclosure cases. The web developer suggested a software platform called Ning. Dave Lehoullier, a fellow *Living Lies* commenter and
foreclosure victim with some Web experience, agreed to help out as a troubleshooter and tech guru. Lisa named the site *Foreclosure Hamlet*, with a

double meaning: *hamlet* as in a village or community, and *Hamlet* as in the Shakespearean tragedy. (She quoted the play in several early posts, including these lines from Act I, Scene I: "And then it started like a guilty thing / Upon a fearful summons.")

Foreclosure Hamlet launched in late September 2009, with the tag line "Supporting, Informing and Connecting People in Foreclosure." It was pretty spare: no images, no ads, just a white background and simple text. Lisa filled the site with disclaimers: "This Blog is NOT to be viewed as a source of competent legal advice. . . . We are NOT attorneys." Users had to pick a screen name and an avatar, giving them their own page on the site. They could post blog entries, submit questions to the forum, or comment on other people's posts. But the chat room was the centerpiece, a town hall where foreclosure victims could connect and find help, the avatars serving as people's faces. Lisa kept it on in the background all day long, and greeted everyone who entered. Some raised questions about their foreclosure cases, but others weren't that advanced; they had stumbled into the site off a Google search and just needed someone to talk to.

Lisa quickly discovered she would need moderators to get useful dialogue. Too many familiar types descended on blogs: the salesmen, offering services that Lisa had no way of verifying; the Internet trolls, who seemed to spring up everywhere, posting off-topic rants about everything from black helicopters to sex; the bullies, who took time out of their day to torment foreclosure victims. So Lisa found volunteers to scan the site and weed out the genuinely unhelpful. Dave Lehoullier filled in as a moderator, and Lisa also recruited Andrew Delany, who had talked the woman at *Living Lies* out of suicide.

Once Lisa organized *Foreclosure Hamlet*, she penned a few blog posts, as a lure for visitors to write their own. While legal motions in her case required a formal style, these were more freewheeling, allowing Lisa to draw on a previously untapped flair for writing. "I know this is starting from the middle, but that's the best I can do until I get the background posted," Lisa wrote in the site's first post, October 6, 2009.

When I get those large white envelopes in the mail, notifications of yet another filing from FDLG (Florida Default Law Group AKA Florida's Top Foreclosure Mill), an immediate sick feeling descends upon me like mercury; heavy, metallic, dangerous, toxic. I wonder, who am I, a simple working mother, to stand up against these attorneys in the lofty halls of the judicial system.

Then, 24 hours pass, and I regain my footing and my resolve to defend myself. I cope. I read. I Google. I search. I think. I research. I focus. I write a filing.

The post got twenty-one views. It was a start.

To those paying attention, September 2009 represented a turning point in the foreclosure fraud story. The Kansas Supreme Court decided the case of Boyd Kesler, who sold his house in bankruptcy to his original lender, Landmark National Bank. A second lien on the home was held by a separate lender, with MERS, the electronic database, named as the nominee, and no assignment recorded at the county office. The court ruled that since the MERS loan was never recorded, the lender was not due proceeds from the bankruptcy sale. In other words, MERS had no interest in the property. By implication, the electronic registry could not foreclose on Kesler's loan, either; it was as if the lien didn't exist in the eyes of Kansas. The Arkansas Supreme Court made a similar ruling. If replicated across the country, it would question the true ownership on millions of mortgages.

Tragedy accompanied the triumphs. On September 29, an angry homeowner in Phoenix refused to leave his foreclosed property and threatened the new owners with a gun. Police were dispatched, and after a standoff, the homeowner was shot and killed. The man, Kurt Aho, reportedly shared a beer with a neighbor earlier that day, saying he wanted to die after losing his home.

"May God watch over this man's family," Lisa wrote in the comments. But Michael, who had switched usernames from "Fraud in FL" to "Foreclosure Fraud," instead dug up the homeowner's documents. "I have been searching the Internet and public records for over a year now," Michael wrote, "and you wouldn't believe how many hats these people wear. I have seen hundreds of documents all using the same players assigning mortgages over to the lenders they work for using MERS as their shield."

Lisa, who was in touch with Michael through email, sent him a message asking him how he found the mortgage documents from Arizona. Michael sent her back an explanation of how he searched and what he looked for in the documents.

"Would you think about putting together a guide," Lisa wrote back. "Because this is great information. A lot of people are going to be asking you for this. It's going to be a lot easier if you just write it up." She offered to post the guide on her website.

Years later Michael would blame Lisa for getting him involved in all this.

6

MR. ANONYMOUS

Michael Redman doesn't want you to know who he is. He never did. Anytime he could separate himself from the outside world, he'd take the opportunity.

He came to Florida, like many before him, to sever links to the past, to mold a new life. Michael grew up along the Jersey Shore, in Toms River and Seaside Heights. Snooki and The Situation were *tourists*; living along that stretch of sand all year long, outside the frame of reality-show cameras, proved rougher. Michael's parents split up when he was young. He bounced from one home to another and mostly grew up on the streets. Lots of friends ended up either in jail or dead.

When Michael was a senior in high school, some buddies went to Florida for spring break; he was working and couldn't join them. The friends came back and told him they'd had a blast. That summer, 1993, Michael turned eighteen, and escaping New Jersey sounded pretty good. So did a place where nobody knew him. In a car stuffed with clothes and records and with $1,500 in his pocket, Michael, his girlfriend, and an acquaintance of hers drove down I-95 for two days straight. They kept going until they hit the exit for Boynton Beach Boulevard, as good a place to stop as anywhere else.

Michael's first impressions of Florida were in terms of color. The Jersey Shore was gray and drab; Florida was bright yellows and pinks, shades of rejuvenation. Outside of summer, you would hardly see cars driving through Seaside Heights; Florida felt alive.

Michael and his girlfriend bunked with a friend while they sought an apartment. They had no credit and no jobs. And though Florida welcomed fresh-faced young adults every year, landlords and employers didn't always take kindly to transients. Michael and his girlfriend spent all their cash just on the security deposit. He picked up shifts at a nearby restaurant and tried to acclimate to new surroundings. Before long the girlfriend split, and Michael found himself alone, waiting tables and spending many nights watching ballgames, just him and a six-pack. It took Michael a while to make his own luck.

Motorola, the phone and pager company, had their world headquarters in Boynton Beach, across the street from Michael's restaurant. One day he walked into the lobby and announced himself. "Are you guys hiring? Because I work across the street, and it sucks." The company actually had a job fair scheduled the next week. Michael landed a gig in the factory, making pagers on the graveyard shift. Despite lacking a college diploma, he picked things up quickly. Within seven years he moved into software development, heading up one element of the company's Y2K bug strategy and living the corporate life. The job even took him to Russia for a month, working out of frigid Vladivostok, the military gateway to the Chinese border. Michael loved it at Motorola. He had a parking pass, a bonus package, a health care plan, every accessory for the Organization Man. It was a mailroom-to-the-corner-office success story.

And then in 2001 the layoffs began. Michael got innovated out of a job; with the release of the BlackBerry and more advanced cell phones, nobody needed a pager anymore. First the manufacturing center closed, then engineering, then research and development. All 3,500 workers were eventually laid off, and the Boynton Beach campus shut down in 2004. It was later converted into a giant retail and residential development called Renaissance Commons, which after the crisis would slip into foreclosure.

Michael never expected a corporate job, but he was chastened by its loss. Young and unsure of his future, he took a break from working, spending his nights carousing and blowing through his severance package. On one of those nights out, he met Jennifer. She was a third-generation Floridian, and something about her signaled stability, roots, the comforts Michael hadn't known his entire life. They started dating.

When the severance ran out and the party ended, Michael had to figure out his next step. He excelled in a respectable industry; by his logic, he could really shoot up the ranks in a terrible one. Michael remembered how impossible a time he had buying a car a while back; that business could use some help. He hooked on at Carmax, industry leader in online auto sales. Michael ran the company's Internet department for a couple of years. Though he stayed behind the scenes, he also had a knack for promotions. In 2003 a team from Boynton Beach won the Little League World Series, and Michael pitched Carmax on a parade celebration, piling the team into thirty used cars and driving around town honking and shouting. The horn in Michael's car didn't work by the end of it.

Next Michael became Internet manager at Earl Stewart Toyota, a family-owned-and-operated outfit in North Palm Beach, one of the most successful local auto dealers in the country. Earl and his three sons owned the business and made themselves completely accessible to their employees. Red phones around the office were direct lines to Earl's cell phone; he would answer any question at any time of day. They charged no dealer fees, a rarity that kept prices well below competitors.

Michael built the Internet sales and marketing operation from scratch, leading a team of six. They ended up generating more volume from the Internet business than the storefront operation. Michael loved the power of the Web, how things could go viral and reach millions, how your credentials or personal history didn't matter. There's a saying that on the Internet no one knows you're a dog. This appealed to Michael tremendously.

While Michael was still at the Toyota dealership, he and Jennifer purchased a home together, a 1,200-square-foot wood-frame number in Lake Worth, twenty minutes from Michael's office. The unmarried couple kept the house in Jennifer's name. Michael would pay the mortgage but didn't want his fingerprints on the deed. And while he wore a wedding ring and considered Jennifer his wife, the couple never got an official marriage certificate; in the eyes of Florida, they were unmarried partners. Michael was always cautious.

The bubble was already inflating by 2004. Michael and Jennifer would get handwritten notes in the mail from real estate agents inquiring about buying the house. Michael's in-laws played the house-flipping game. They pooled all their savings and constructed a $4 million waterfront mansion on Manalapan Island, an oceanfront luxury getaway south of Palm Beach. They filmed part of the movie *Body Heat* on Manalapan, and it had a sultry feel and the smell of new money. Don King and Yanni lived there. Michael's in-laws planned to stay in the mansion for a while and then sell it, securing their retirement from the proceeds. The stratagem worked, but it took longer than expected. When the in-laws got out, it was late 2005.

Jennifer's parents moved from Manalapan to Vero Beach, an hour and a half north. At the same time Jennifer got pregnant, and she wanted more space for the family than the little Lake Worth cottage. She had her eyes on Port St. Lucie, about midway between Palm Beach and Vero Beach. Michael could still work at the Toyota dealership, and the baby could be near the grandparents.

Port St. Lucie and Vero Beach were on the Treasure Coast, so named after divers found precious trinkets among the wreckage of a Spanish fleet lost in a hurricane in the early eighteenth century. During the bubble years the treasure sat onshore: Port St. Lucie was perhaps the biggest real estate boomtown in America. Michael did like the control factor. He and Jennifer could purchase one of the city's plentiful vacant lots and build their dream house to exacting specifications. They could put the light switches where they wanted them. They could pick the moldings, the style of the windows, the roof shingles, and the built-in shelves. They could invest in their future.

A few years earlier, lots in Port St. Lucie went for around $5,000 a half acre. By 2005 that swelled to $50,000 and rising. Michael and Jennifer finally chose a lot for $75,000, but the financing didn't clear in time for the closing date. A week later they bought land two lots down and paid $15,000 more. The couple took out a construction loan for $280,000, to build a house that might have been worth half that in a normal market. It was steep, but Michael thought they could manage. Again Jennifer signed the papers. Michael had everything else in his name, from the auto loan to the credit cards. If things went south, he figured he could ditch other obligations to pay the mortgage.

As work began on the Port St. Lucie dream home, Michael and Jennifer put their Lake Worth house on the market. But in early 2006 the fish weren't biting in Florida real estate, compared to the prior feeding frenzy. Nobody bid on the house for three months, raising Michael's anxiety level. One day he and his wife sprawled on the couch after a sparsely attended open house. "This is not going well, we're going to get screwed," Michael ranted. Right at that moment, a hugely pregnant woman showed up at the front door and grabbed a flyer. She returned the next day with her husband and put in a bid.

Michael and Jennifer bought the house for $140,000; they sold it three years later to that couple for $260,000. Michael guesses it's worth $60,000 today. He thinks a lot about that young couple, so pleased to find their starter home. They probably went out that night and celebrated. Little did they know how rapidly they would be trapped inside a four-walled nightmare. Michael never kept up with the couple, but he could guess that they fell into foreclosure, and he couldn't help but feel a little responsible. Maybe they would have bought someone else's home, but they bought Michael's. Hearing their names makes him sad.

In June 2006, five days before their daughter, Nicole, was born, Michael and Jennifer moved into their new home in Port St. Lucie. A friend of Jennifer's converted the construction loan into a mortgage; before becoming a real estate broker, he fought fires. That was Florida in the bubble years; selling homes proved more lucrative than a public service job with a pension.

The conversion operated like a refinance. The ex-firefighter sold Michael and Jennifer an 80/20 loan, with a first lien for 80 percent of the mortgage price and a second lien for the remaining 20 percent. Michael and Jennifer paid with two separate checks. A wholesale lender named AmNet issued the mortgage, but they immediately flipped it to Washington Mutual, which then sold it to Freddie Mac. So Michael's loan was not securitized by a private Wall Street bank. Around this time, Freddie Mac jumped into the subprime and Alt-A markets, seeking to recapture a greater share of the housing market. They purchased the first lien; Washington Mutual remained the loan servicer.

Things floated along for a couple of years. The baby took her first steps. Jennifer scored a part-time job after maternity leave. Michael sold more cars than ever during Florida's boom years. Lawns were mowed and furniture dusted. The family led a normal, happy life. And then, in January 2008, they received a letter from Washington Mutual: "We are sorry to inform you that we miscalculated your escrow for the past two years."

In the mortgage contract, AmNet calculated property taxes based solely on the land value before construction. But two years later the servicer reassessed, taking into account the value of the home and making the amount due retroactive. This was the first Jennifer and Michael heard of a retroactive reassessment, and it added $600 a month to the $1,600 payment. If they had known the projected monthly payment at the time, they might have declined the mortgage.

Had house prices not exploded and then burst, Michael and Jennifer could have sold the house and paid off the loan. But instead they bought at the top of the bubble and were now desperately underwater. They had a newborn, with all the expenses that implied, and Michael's job relied on auto sales amid a tanking Florida economy. The family savings mostly went toward the new home, and they couldn't afford to pay 35 percent more than they budgeted on the mortgage.

Michael contacted Washington Mutual, requesting that they roll the payment back to the original amount quoted at signing. But WaMu had no interest in being charitable. Michael and Jennifer used their tax refunds to buy some time, but they knew they would only have about nine months before money would get tight. Jennifer believed strongly in paying her bills, but Michael saw no other choice. They couldn't continue to make this higher payment, and they weren't getting anywhere with pleading. Michael understood it was easy for him to say "stop paying," because his credit wasn't on the line. But eventually Jennifer had to forget her pride and give in to reality.

Michael devised a plan. He would put the $1,600 mortgage payment, the one they could afford, into a safe. He "paid" the mortgage there, in cash. When they straightened things out with Washington Mutual, they could draw on the nest egg to pay past due amounts.

The couple stopped paying the bank in September 2008, just as the U.S. economy teetered and credit seized up nationwide. The same month, Washington Mutual collapsed in the largest bank failure in American history. The federal government brokered a sweetheart deal for JPMorgan Chase to purchase WaMu and its $310 billion in assets for just $1.9 billion.

A few weeks later, Chase sent what is known as a breach/cure letter to Michael and Jennifer. This indicated that the missed payment violated the loan terms, and if the couple failed to cure this breach within thirty days, the loan would be accelerated, with the principal balance, all back payments, and late fees due under threat of foreclosure. Usually letters like this didn't come until three months of delinquency; Michael reckoned it had something to do with the liquidation of Washington Mutual.

According to the letter, JPMorgan Chase was now the creditor, having assumed the loan when they took over Washington Mutual. But Freddie

Mac owned it originally: WaMu was just the servicer. Unless Freddie sold it to Chase at some point in the past few weeks—a highly unlikely scenario amid the current upheaval—this was impossible.

Michael started poking around the Internet for answers, stumbling upon the reports of none other than Nye Lavalle. He learned about predatory servicing and securitization FAIL and the Great Foreclosure Machine. And he read Nye's report about Ocwen employee Scott Anderson, who would pass himself off as a vice president for multiple banks. Michael found Nye's phone number in one report and rang him up. Nye listened politely but ultimately blew him off; he got dozens of calls every week, a side effect of being outspoken about illegal foreclosures in a time of crisis.

But the bread crumbs Nye Lavalle laid down a decade earlier helped Michael navigate the foreclosure maze, which he felt compelled to keep traversing, like a video gamer spending days on end trying to reach the boss level. Michael's old habits—happy hours, nights watching the ballgame—faded to background. At work his mind drifted to foreclosures; at night he scoured the Web for information, fueled by Miller Lite and a desire to answer one simple question: who owned his loan?

Before the thirty-day deadline, Michael and Jennifer decided to dispute the debt, based on the erroneous claim of JPMorgan Chase as the creditor. The initial reaction from Chase was silence. Perhaps because of the Washington Mutual collapse and the subsequent turmoil, Michael didn't hear anything for nearly a year. With so many foreclosures streaming in, servicers and law firms lost many in the shuffle. Michael used the respite to become an expert in foreclosure fraud.

The turning point came when Michael discovered that all official public records in Florida were available online. He went to the St. Lucie County clerk's website and found the mortgage assignment for his home: MERS, as nominee for the loan originator, AmNet, transferred it to Washington Mutual, which was in the process of becoming JPMorgan Chase. The signers of the documents were Barbara Hindman, vice president of MERS as nominee for AmNet, and Shelley Thievin, also a vice president.

Michael Googled both of their names. LinkedIn profiles labeled Barbara Hindman and Shelley Thievin as employees of JPMorgan Chase. In the midst of the Washington Mutual crackup, Chase was apparently assigning mortgages to themselves, despite holding no interest in the loan and never putting up any money toward the transaction. It was easy to discern that Chase executed these assignments after the fact: AmNet Mortgage went out of business and was acquired by Wachovia in late 2005, shortly after Michael and Jennifer closed. This assignment was dated April 20, 2009, more than three years after that merger. Amid this wholesale theft of who knows how many mortgages, the surname "Thievin" struck Michael as darkly ironic.

The mortgage assignment listed the Washington Mutual address as Jacksonville, so Michael pulled up Duval County's public records, searching for Barbara and Shelley's mortgages to verify their signatures. It checked out. Michael even found Barbara Hindman's direct office line and called her up. He never got her on the phone, but on voicemail she called herself a "document executor."

Michael's mind was racing. Why should he give a couple thousand dollars a month to Chase? Because they said so? Who truly owned the loan? How many people were losing their homes from scams like this? And most of all, why would banks like JPMorgan Chase keep doing this despite a public-record paper trail for anyone with a laptop to locate? Did they think nobody would notice?

The next question became whether Chase assigned mortgages to themselves on a widespread basis. Over the next several months, Michael searched public records in every county in Florida. New York and Ohio also had excellent public records portals online, along with some counties in Illinois. And Michael kept finding Chase documents with Barbara Hindman and Shelley Thievin, usually with the same notaries and witnesses, all out of the same office in Jacksonville, which must have been some kind of document factory. Even when the lenders assigning the mortgage were out of state, the assignments had the Jacksonville address. The more clever assignments were backdated to make it look like they were executed at the proper time. But the names of the signers gave things away, along with the notary stamps: Michael found documents with impossible dates, because the notaries hadn't yet become notaries at that time.

Michael began to notice patterns among the documents. He saw the same combinations of names doing the signing, the same telltale mistakes in the documentation. And it didn't stop with JPMorgan Chase: Bank of America, Wells Fargo, Citigroup, all the big banks had the same evidence problems, including employees signing for different banks, suspicious-looking signatures, the works.

When Michael talked to his wife about his discoveries, she thought the pressure had cracked him up. But despite no prior experience, he was driven to dig through the public records almost every night, accumulating this dossier of a great wrong perpetrated on the public. The same banks that precipitated the crash and got paid off in the bailout were getting even richer off the leftovers. He saw it as the biggest transfer of wealth the world had ever seen.

After a couple of months Michael found *Living Lies* and started commenting under an alias. Michael built a separate life for his foreclosure fraud persona, walling it off from his everyday existence. He created a special email address for foreclosure fraud work. He established a phone number through Google Voice (the number ended in 5437, or LIES). And he set up boundaries, working on the issue during the week but keeping weekends free for the family. He thought he could compartmentalize, dividing the husband and father from the foreclosure fighter.

In June 2009 a process server finally delivered foreclosure papers to Michael and Jennifer. JPMorgan Chase was listed as the plaintiff, with Florida Default Law Group, the same foreclosure mill as in Lisa's case, representing them. Michael had met with foreclosure defense attorneys, but he felt he knew more about what was happening than they did. So even before they got served, Michael planned to have his wife act as a *pro se* litigant (only she could do it, because Michael wasn't on the mortgage). He assembled hundreds of documents from counties across Florida, with the same signers as in his case, to present to the court. He couldn't wait to see the faces of the bank lawyers. Jennifer filed a motion to dismiss, kicking off a protracted battle for their home.

Around this time, Michael set up Google Reader, a website aggregator, to track every news article related to housing, mortgages, and foreclosures. He would crawl through the headlines every day, looking for whatever stood out. He used Facebook, Digg, FriendFeed, and a Twitter feed, @4closurefraud, to spread what he found. Tweeting media stories and blog posts, Michael gained a thousand or so followers who thirsted for foreclosure news.

Michael would dive into comment sections of the stories Google Reader helped him find, pointing out document fraud and encouraging people to discover the truth. It was his few minutes a day to spread the message, a tentative foray into activism. But comment sections of mainstream media sites, notorious as the seedy back alleys of the Internet, weren't receptive to idealism of any kind. It was like holding an atheism rally inside a church. "Deadbeat" was the favored term of response. Or "pay your mortgage."

The commenting project connected Michael to Susan Martin, the *St. Petersburg Times* journalist who wrote about Nationwide Title document signers Brian Bly and Crystal Moore. Michael wrote in the comments: "I have researched this in my county records and this is being done to hundreds of documents per month. In most of the cases I have seen, the 'vice president' assignors of mortgage are actually employees of the lender it is being assigned to." Susan Martin asked Michael for evidence. He sent back a stack of assignments from Hillsborough County (in the Tampa/ St. Pete area, Martin's home base). "Hope this is enough to get you started," Michael said.

Susan appreciated the research but asked Michael, "How would this story be different from the one I already did on employees of Nationwide Title Insurance signing as vice presidents of various companies?" Michael responded that Nationwide Title was just a cleanup gang; JPMorgan Chase was doing it in-house with their own employees. "They are literally stealing homes that they have no right to for personal gain," he wrote. Susan saw his point but had other stories to handle. She told Michael to keep in touch.

Michael liked Lisa almost immediately. They had plenty in common, aside from both being sued by Florida Default Law Group. They were both ordinary people new to this crisis, with no doubts about who was to blame. And they were both so driven to expose the injustice that they could come off a little . . . obsessed. Maybe even crazy.

So when Lisa asked Michael to write a guide for searching public records, he considered it a good idea. He'd been creating formal presentations since his days at Motorola, and he'd been searching foreclosure documents for a year. It only took a weekend to compile. He gave it the spartan title "Looking Up Public Records," with a clip art cover that became his calling card: a magnifying glass focused on a house, with the dictionary definition of the word "fraud" swimming underneath. The guide begins:

Presented here is a guide to looking up public records online for possible forgeries, fabrications and fraud when facing foreclosure. . . .

During the housing boom, lenders passed around mortgages as if they
were whiskey bottles at a frat party. Notes were lost, destroyed, sold into multiple pools. Mortgages were not recorded and exorbitant fees were collected by
the big firms on Wall Street.

Now that the bubble has burst, "lenders" are trying to collect on loans they
do not own, in most cases never lent a dime on the transaction. . . . They are
steamrolling the courts because hardly anyone is contesting their foreclosures.

So I started digging around in the bowels of the Internets [sic] to see where
this rabbit hole led.

Using Florida as an example, the guide described precisely, complete
with screenshots, how to search official records online. Michael displayed a
mortgage assignment and annotated it with questions. Next to one signature,
Michael wrote, "MERS as nominee for First National Bank of Arizona, Barbara Hindman, assigning mortgage over to JPMorgan Chase while employed
by JPMorgan Chase?" He pasted in Hindman's and her partner Shelley
Thievin's work histories from LinkedIn to prove they actually worked for
Chase. To spot Hindman and Thievin in multiple documents, the guide
explained, you simply reverse-engineer the record searches, using the keyword of the foreclosing entity. It wasn't just Barbara Hindman and Shelley Thievin; the guide included assignments with Beth Cottrell, Whitney
Cook, and Christina Trowbridge, all of whom appeared on Lisa's mortgage documents.

One document, which Michael dubbed the "Triple Play," had Bill Koch,
signing for MERS as nominee for Pinnacle Financial Corporation, assigning the mortgage over to . . . *Bill Koch*, of Select Portfolio Servicing. Michael
imagined a conversation in court, where the homeowner's lawyer questioned this activity:

DEFENDANT: *But your honor, he works for the company he is assigning the mort-*
gage to. Isn't that a conflict of interest, fraud?

PLAINTIFF: *He may be employed by the company that the mortgage is being as-*
signed to, but at the time of the assignment he was acting as a representative of
MERS.

Other examples "appear to be blatant forgeries where they don't even take the time to match signatures," Michael wrote, illustrating this by comparing signatures of the same officials on multiple documents. Placing them side by side revealed wide varieties between signatures, allegedly from the same person. Michael explained how to check dates on the assignments, to see if they were filed after the notice of legal proceeding, a proof of fabrication. He instructed how to look up the notaries and check their business address against the address of the foreclosing agent. "I have found notaries that work in the next building over from the pretender lender foreclosing agent," suggesting an unsavory relationship of notaries signing masses of documents without scrutiny.

The guide included dozens of suspect signatures, misdated documents, and shady transfers. "There are thousands of them!" Michael exhorted, with "thousands" crossed out and "possibly millions" substituted. Summing up, Michael urged readers to perform their own searches and report back what they find. "Follow the Guide, research these matters deeper, and collaborate with others. . . . Let's use the Internet in what it was intended for, exchanging raw data between researchers. All the information is there. It just needs to be pieced together."

On October 11 Michael posted the guide on Scribd, where you can upload large documents. Lisa immediately posted it on the front page of *Foreclosure Hamlet*. Michael promoted the guide everywhere—on Twitter, Facebook, and in the comments at *Living Lies*. "Any feedback is welcomed, good and bad. . . . If anyone needs help finding information on your 'vice president' or 'assistant secretary' just let me know."

Two days after Michael posted it, Karl Denninger, a popular (and rather bombastic) libertarian finance blogger who ran Market-ticker.org, published the guide on his site under the heading "A Birdie on Possible Foreclosure Frauds." Denninger introduced it by saying, "This is so blatant and outrageous that if the federal government's law enforcement agencies (e.g. the FBI, et al) do not immediately bring federal charges they must be deemed intentionally complicit. Ditto for the state Attorneys General."

The page views started rising: two thousand, four thousand, six thousand, twelve thousand. Michael checked it every half hour at work, and while he didn't tell colleagues or his wife about it, he could hardly contain his excitement.

Michael started getting emails and phone calls (his Google Voice number was on the guide) from across the country, alternately thanking him and asking for help with their foreclosure cases. Many emails were addressed "Dear Sir or Madam": on the Internet, no one knows you're a dog. A Texas oil and gas landman emailed, claiming to have assembled 200,000 acres in leases along the Fayetteville shale. "Someone without this background who did this qualifies for some type of award," he wrote, suggesting Michael start a business helping people file fraud suits against lenders to recover damages. This led to a series of phone calls, with the oilman wanting to enlist Michael in running title on energy leases across Texas. Michael was fascinated but had no idea what to say. It wasn't long ago that he asked Nye Lavalle for help and was politely rushed off the phone. Now he was on the other end of the line.

A reporter from the NBC affiliate in West Palm Beach wanted to interview Michael about his findings. Being in front of a camera was the last thing on Michael's mind. He emailed Lisa and some others to see if they would do it, but nobody wanted to endanger their case or become the foreclosure poster child. This was the box foreclosure fraud activists often found themselves in: desperate to break the story, yet anxious about having their fingerprints on it.

Michael soon decided that instead of sending traffic over to *Living Lies* or Karl Denninger, he ought to hold on to it for himself. Using a blog template from WordPress, Michael started 4closurefraud.wordpress.com on October 18, 2009. The first post? The guide to searching public records for fraud.

While Lisa created a safe space to talk about foreclosures, Michael focused on collecting information about the scandal in one place. He posted links to foreclosure news, court opinions, commentary, and resources. One of his early posts was Nye Lavalle's report on Scott Anderson and Ocwen (Scott Anderson's varying signatures made it into Michael's public records guide, too). The motto for the site was, "Fighting Foreclosure Fraud by Sharing the Knowledge."

A week into his new blogging life, Michael heard from Neil Garfield, the man whose site had become a big part of his world over the past year. *Living Lies* was holding a seminar for homeowners and lawyers on November 1 and 2 at a Sheraton in Clearwater. Would Michael like to give a presentation about how to search public records?

Michael had never spoken at a conference before. Heck, he'd never given a *speech* before, at least not to more than five people. It just wasn't his thing. Michael looked at the calendar: November 1 fell on a Sunday. Going to the conference would break his unwritten family weekend rule. And Clearwater was across the state, he might have to go up the night before, miss Halloween, they were thinking about dressing up Nicole for the first time. There was no way he could agree to this . . .

"Sure, I'll do it."

7

WHEN MICHAEL MET LISA

November 1, 2009

At daybreak on Sunday, Michael Redman tried to quietly ease out of bed without waking his wife, putting on a shirt and tie and heading out for the Clearwater Sheraton. Jennifer's eyes peeked open just in time to see Michael walk out of the bedroom. She turned over in the bed.

The sun reflected off Michael's mirrored sunglasses as he sped through rural Florida, past herds of cattle and tall reeds of grass sticking out of swampland. He stayed home Saturday night to escort his daughter trick-or-treating; today he would trek three hours to give a presentation to lots of people who wanted to hear from him about highly technical real estate transactions and their paper trail.

The Sheraton Sand Key resort in Clearwater nestled against a white sand beach, on a strip of land in the Gulf of Mexico. From the top floors you could see deep-blue water on either side. Once Michael arrived, he found a quiet spot in the lobby and opened his laptop, reviewing the presentation one last time. The PowerPoint slides roughly tracked the guide he posted a couple of weeks earlier. A separate file included notes for what to say while each slide was on the screen. For a while Michael toyed with asking Neil Garfield to read the script, so he could stay out of the limelight. But he reconsidered.

Michael picked up the event schedule for the seminar and found out that he was actually the featured speaker, the final one on the bill. So he'd have the entire day to think about this. He stepped into the big conference room where the seminar would be held. The audience was bigger than he expected, and it looked like a bunch of attorneys, with only a smattering of more casually dressed homeowners. Michael found the only person in the crowd wearing a bright 1970s-style headscarf. He went over and introduced himself.

"So nice to meet you," Lisa Epstein said, smiling. With her heels she was a little taller than Michael, and his naturally ruddy complexion made it look like he spent too long in the sun. Lisa asked him where he drove in from. "Port St. Lucie," Michael answered.

"I'm in Palm Beach. Wow, we only live about an hour from each other."

"I work in North Palm, at the Toyota dealership," Michael said.

They walked around together, chatting with other attendees over morning coffee. Michael confessed to being terrified about the presentation, but Lisa told him not to worry: "Tell you what—after the speech, whatever happens, we'll go get some dinner." He agreed.

Living Lies ran seminars from coast to coast, and they all had the same format. The two-day conference split its focus, with one day concentrating on homeowners and one on attorneys, though given the expense, attorneys tended to dominate the room both days. Neil Garfield and his business partner, Brad Keiser, welcomed attendees, and Garfield gave a speech. He would tailor his remarks to wherever he found himself, be it a judicial or non-judicial foreclosure state, and depending on the attitudes and rulings of local judges. But it was usually the same patter. "We're not going to convert you into lawyers today," he'd say in his gravelly voice and rumpled, stakeout-cop demeanor. "We're not going to make you experts in securities and the securitization of loans. We're going to teach you the basic language and the basic concepts that are important, so that if you have to go to court, you'll know in a very short period of time whether the attorney, or the judge for that matter, understands a word that you're talking about."

Garfield also supplied an antidote to the truckloads of shame typically heaped on foreclosure victims. "You'll hear lawyers on the other side say, 'Well, you didn't make the payment due and so you're in default,'" Garfield said. "You will find that in many cases, if not most, they have been paid in whole or in part by federal bailouts or insurance. . . . Imagine if you could insure your house against fire for the full value, and then you could buy another thirty policies just like it. They insured those pools that they knew were going to fail, that they created to fail. They insured those pools thirty times over. So if you had a $300,000 mortgage, courtesy of the U.S. government and AIG, they were paid off $9 million."

In other words, banks were rewarded handsomely for their securitization schemes, unlike the poor stiffs living in the raw materials they bought and sold. Holding banks accountable for proper chain of title wasn't a trick or a technicality; it was the only way to put an end to the thievery. The banks had no place on the moral high ground, especially because their lack of attention to who actually owned the mortgage and note threatened every homeowner in America, regardless of whether they catered to the prevailing standard of being "responsible."

What made foreclosure defense such a slog was that each state—each circuit, even—had particular procedural rules. A defense might work on one judge but have no chance in the next courtroom over. Still, the banks' game plans were identical, whether they pursued foreclosure in California or Florida or Montana: conceal their fraud. "They're pushing you to the wall. They are doing everything they can to avoid an evidentiary hearing," Garfield explained. "They are doing everything they can to avoid appeal. . . . They will use every means to intimidate you. They will use every means to fool you."

While Garfield warned homeowners to avoid scam mortgage rescue specialists or substandard lawyers, he charged for access to the conference, asking that people come back more than once. Garfield also marketed "securitization audits," a forensic analysis that would track down the trust containing a particular mortgage. Garfield's rivals discounted the importance of these audits in court: the key evidence was not the trust location but the assignments and notes. Sometimes foreclosure relief specialists attacked each other more vociferously than the banks. Vulnerable homeowners had to negotiate a thicket of would-be saviors promising relief for a fee, and it was hard to know whom to trust. But Garfield's I'm-on-your-side pitch proved persuasive. "I'm on a mission here, I don't need to do this at all," he would say.

After Garfield wrapped up, a few other speakers covered securitization, Florida foreclosure procedures, and other topics. While Lisa awaited Michael's presentation, her cell phone rang. The number was unfamiliar. She walked out into the hall and answered.

"Hello, this is the Florida attorney general's Economic Crimes division. Am I speaking with Lisa Epstein?"

Holy shit, Lisa thought. *It worked.*

Once Michael explained to Lisa how to look up public records and directly identify instances of foreclosure fraud nationwide, she felt compelled to inform pretty much everyone. Whitney Cook could not be working for ten different banks simultaneously, and people had to know she was claiming this. So Lisa initiated a rule. She would send five letters every night to law enforcement, regulatory, political, and media figures across America, presenting her findings and urging them to investigate the Great Foreclosure Machine. It didn't matter how big or small their office or jurisdiction. She would start with Barack Obama and work her way down.

The campaign sprang from one of Lisa's old habits. She used to write thank-you notes to the clerk at the dry cleaner's or the waitress at the local diner, the invisible members of society who helped her inch through life. For years afterward, whenever Lisa walked into certain grocery stores or restaurants, she'd get treated like a visiting dignitary; the simple act of gratitude provoked an outpouring of kindness. Instead of thanking those anonymous Floridians, now Lisa wanted to fight for them.

The first letter went to the Florida Supreme Court and became a template for all the others. "By way of introduction, I am a working mother and also a *pro se* litigant fighting a residential foreclosure, in a state that ranks among the hardest hit," it began. "May I prevail upon you to read this lengthy letter, which I agree, may be too much to ask? I hope to shed light on what is befalling millions of us out here across the nation."

Lisa outlined the details of her case: the initial serving of papers by U.S. Bank, which she had no prior dealings with; her efforts at research, despite the lack of legal training; the fraudulent affidavits, unrecorded mortgage assignments, doctored notes, and sham pleadings submitted by Florida Default Law Group. She explained how the note was endorsed (using the legal term "indorsed") to a party other than the bank doing the foreclosing. She showed how a notary in Ohio purported to witness in person the signing of a document from a company with an address in Texas. She described other affidavits with signers attesting to personal knowledge of facts that hadn't happened until several months after the date on the document. She laid out the situation with Whitney Cook signing for MERS on one document and JPMorgan Chase on another. She ticked off all the financial institutions involved in her loan ("U.S. Bank NA, J.P. Morgan Mortgage Trust, Chase Home Finance, JPMorgan Chase Bank NA, MERS, DHI Mortgage . . . one could benefit from an organizational chart!") and the mounting absurdities of the documents they spat out. "I naively had assumed fabricating evidence wasn't a widely accepted practice, as surely it was punishable by appropriate jail time," she concluded.

Lisa attached the source documents from her case, along with other samples featuring the same signers representing themselves as officers of different banks. "May I assure you that my case is neither special nor unique, as I review hundreds of similar, local cases weekly," she wrote. Lisa tied this fraud to the ongoing suffering of the Great Recession, and expressed shock at judges rushing through foreclosure cases without respect for due process, against defendants challenged to obtain counsel with limited resources. "What most galls me is that these 'pretender lenders' are working the odds to unjustly enrich themselves, betting through their rapacious law mills that the low-lying fruit—those who easily cave and do not contest foreclosure no matter how illegal or unjust—will far outnumber those who put up a credible fight."

Every night Lisa postmarked the letter to another five people. If a newspaper article reported on foreclosures, the writer would go on the list of recipients. If a lawyer or a politician or a regulator gave a quote in the story, they would go on the list. She included federal banking regulators, the congressional oversight panel for the Troubled Asset Relief Program, state attorneys general, the Justice Department, the Federal Reserve, members of Congress on the relevant financial services committees, and anyone with a fancy title and a desk. Five a night, every night.

One morning in late September, while surfing the Web for scraps of information, Lisa found a short column in the Sarasota *Herald-Tribune* by Tom Lyons: "Filing Fake Documents to Establish the Right to Take Possession of Someone's Home? That's Not Something a Lawyer Should Do." Harley Herman, an attorney in Orlando and a member of the Florida Bar Association, told Lyons he had begun pressing the state bar for a "special review of ethics violations in foreclosure cases." Herman tried many foreclosure cases in central Florida, and the inattention to established principles of justice made him embarrassed for his profession. In his experience, judges and attorneys didn't even bother to check the authenticity of the documents. "If the courts can't depend on attorneys to a certain extent, the whole system breaks down," Herman told Lyons.

Lisa immediately sent Herman one of her letters, adding that she had also been badgering public officials to do something about the ghastly state of the Florida courts. Within a week or so Herman called Lisa back, thanking her for the letter, which he said showed a strong grasp of the situation. "We need citizens like you to provide a comment to the Florida Supreme Court; they're looking into this," he told her. The court had established a task force on foreclosure cases, and based on task force recommendations, were considering amendments to the state rules of civil procedure. According to Herman, nearly all of the previous public comments came from bank lawyers, who downplayed the problems and rejected any need to intervene. Herman wanted to push back, and he needed individuals, particularly people in foreclosure with firsthand experience, to contact the state supreme court and respond.

The next day Lisa called the Florida Supreme Court, asking how she might submit a comment about foreclosures. The clerk had her hold for a minute; then she returned and said, "Miss Epstein, it says here you already made a comment." It turned out that the Supreme Court used her letter, the first one she ever sent, as a formal comment, publishing it in the official record.

"Well, if I did one accidentally, maybe I can do one on purpose!" Lisa replied. The clerk said the court could accept a more formal "formal comment." Lisa redrafted her letter into a reasonable facsimile of a legal brief, urging the task force to force plaintiffs' lawyers to verify their client's document trail before filing cases, with real sanctions for failing to make the review. She even cited Florida law to show that the submission of false documents to courts constituted a felony. When she sent the formal comment to Harley Herman, he thought it read like the work of a competent second-year law student.

Despite Herman's admiration, Lisa's letters met mostly with silence, if not with irritation. The chief judge of Palm Beach County sent back an angry missive, saying he couldn't get involved in litigation and that if Lisa had a problem, she should report it to law enforcement; Lisa considered it odd for a chief judge to resist interfering with litigation. Robert Wexler, at the time Lisa's congressman, referred her letter to the Office of the Comptroller of the Currency, where it fell into a black hole. But here was the state attorney general's office, calling her back!

The woman from the Economic Crimes division explained that her office opened a probe into foreclosure mill law firms. Lisa already knew this; she had found a press release about the investigation and called them almost every day trying to submit evidence, to no avail. But now they wanted to talk. Lisa set up an appointment for the following week to speak with a staff attorney. "Thank you for your attention to this terrible set of crimes," Lisa said. After she hung up she allowed herself a little fist pump.

Lisa went back into the conference and found her seat right as Michael's presentation began. Michael approached the front of the room. During the hours of waiting, he brainstormed an idea. He dimmed the lights almost all the way down, ostensibly to get everyone to focus on the PowerPoint slides, but really to make sure nobody could see him as he spoke. Despite stepping into the spotlight, Michael made sure to keep the spotlight off himself.

This calmed Michael's nerves enough to get through the presentation. He'd been searching public records for nearly a year, so he could discuss the topic without notes. And the guide told the story: banks assigning mortgages to themselves, names repeatedly showing up as executives of multiple financial institutions, phony notarizations, blatant forgeries. The key point Michael wanted to get across was that this represented the beginning of the trail, not the end. There was enough intellectual firepower in the room to find enough irregularities to capture public attention and bring this whole scheme crashing to the ground. The Internet enabled them to collaborate, to use publicly available evidence to go where the traditional media and the judicial system refused to tread.

"Okay, that's about it," Michael said, motioning to the attendant in the back to bring up the lights. Michael wasn't prepared for what he saw next: an entire roomful of people standing and clapping. A crush of conference attendees swarmed Michael, thanking him for his work and asking a battery of questions. A lawyer from the Palm Beach area named Carol Asbury came up and gave Michael her card. "Maybe we can work together some-day," she said. The crowd made Michael slightly uncomfortable, but he managed.

After the attendees began to scatter, Michael ran into Lisa again. They broke away from the conference and got into Michael's car. There wasn't much around the Sheraton; they had to go up the street to find a nice din-ner spot.

The Bonefish Grill, with its jaunty logo of a cartoon sea creature carcass, has locations across Florida. Lisa and Michael grabbed a table in the back, and for the next couple of hours they might as well have been alone. The other patrons, restaurant staff, everyone disappeared into the background. It was just these two people, strangers really, who only knew each other from a few months of exchanges on the Internet.

Lisa and Michael got to know each other and their foreclosure cases. Michael explained his rituals: the $1,600 a month in his safe, the daily search for foreclosure news. Lisa had her own routines: the five letters a night, the lunch hours at the courthouse. She explained how bank plain-tiffs started producing more "found" notes, conjured up in time for a motion for summary judgment. Florida Default Law Group submitted two notes in Lisa's case, each of them different yet both claiming to be "true and correct copies" of the original documentation. Any effort to ask which note was authentic or where the mortgage traveled in the securitization process got this reply: "Defendant seeks confidential, proprietary, or trade secret in-formation."

They swapped horror stories about fraudulent foreclosures and loan res-cue scams. Because of their newfound notoriety, Lisa and Michael were hearing directly from borrowers in the trenches about lost paperwork, bait-and-switch schemes, and patterns of abuse. Mortgage servicers negotiated modifications with borrowers and simultaneously placed them into foreclo-sure, an activity known as "dual tracking." They used the HAMP program to create false promises and push homeowners deeper into debt. The two bloggers ticked off case studies: "Ever heard of this?" "Ever see this one?"

One case broke Lisa's heart. Isaac Dieudonné was two years old, a child of Haitian immigrants. When his family moved into a new home in Mira-mar, Florida, on October 11, 2009, he bounded out the front door in search of fun. The parents found young Isaac several minutes later, floating dead in the fetid pool of a foreclosed house. Foreclosures didn't just damage property values; they turned communities into deathtraps, attracting mosquitoes and rats, danger and tragedy. Incidentally, the Dieudonné family wanted to sue the owner of the foreclosed property for negligence, but they couldn't figure out from the public records who held title.

Michael told Lisa unusually personal details (for him, anyway) about the house he built from scratch, his wife's reluctance to default, his newborn child. Lisa and Michael's children were born a year apart, it turned out. Michael mentioned that he sold his property in Lake Worth right before the bubble collapsed. Lisa told Michael that the devastation there resembled the aftermath of Hurricane Andrew. The most depressed part of Lake Worth, not coincidentally the part with the largest population of people of color, was adjacent to Lisa's condo. Many lower- and middle-class African Americans there owned their houses outright before the bubble; cash-out refinances sapped their equity and made them vulnerable to collapse. In the crisis, families of color lost more of their homes, more of their wealth, more of their opportunity. Lisa made a habit of driving through Lake Worth, particularly the so-called alphabet streets, littered with boarded-up homes under sunken roofs, surrounded by overgrown weeds. The banks couldn't resell the properties, so they sat empty, becoming modern-day ghost towns, a visual depiction of the aftermath of fraud. Parts of Port St. Lucie, Michael's home base, looked just as bombed out.

Lisa's recent obsession was the imminent paralysis of the land transfer system once the cycle of false documents and inadequate standing to foreclose reached its conclusion. Buyers could purchase a home the seller had no right to sell. Titles would be permanently clouded. Properties would become monuments to the bubble, frozen in amber. Florida represented the greatest opportunity to force a reckoning, for one reason: banks still had to come before a judge and prove they could foreclose. The other hard-hit sand states—California, Arizona, Nevada—had non-judicial foreclosure processes. Only in Florida were the courts involved.

And then, over their seafood platters, Michael came to what he really wanted to say.

"Look, I don't know you from anybody, but we're obviously compelled to do this work. And we both know this is really, really big."

"I agree," Lisa replied.

"I want to dedicate my time and effort to this, and it seems like you do, too. I think we can work on it together. But we have to be very focused. We need to just commit ourselves to breaking the story. No bullshit, no drama. We can do this."

Michael had never been so blunt in his entire life. But he envisioned the makings of a great team. He had computer and research skills and could get information out fast. Lisa was personable and well-spoken and could present a public face for their actions. He couldn't pinpoint why, but he thought they could join together, educate the public and expose the truth.

"Great—that's what I'm looking for, too," Lisa said almost immediately.

Years later Lisa could not adequately describe the weirdness of that moment, any more than she could explain her transformation from bystander to activist. It fit with nothing in her character; she wasn't wired to be an extrovert, gadfly, or change agent. She didn't know this man across the table, and up until a few months ago, she hadn't shown the slightest interest in asset-backed securities or judicial rules of civil procedure or four-hundred-page pooling and servicing agreements. But with powerful certainty, Lisa realized this was her calling, her life's purpose, the only thing she should be doing.

8

HAPPY HOURS

The thing about making a pact to wage war on the banking industry is that at some point you have to figure out what to *do*. Lisa and Michael already had a full plate: websites, outreach to government and media, contact with other victims and activists, research, courtroom visits, and so on. What more could they juggle on top of their overstuffed schedules?

Besides, even the activism Michael already shouldered was taking a toll on his relationship. Jennifer was unhappy about Michael leaving her alone for two days. He tried to explain how exposing fraudulent foreclosures could get them their financial stability back. But Jennifer insisted that Michael not abandon her and the baby again. Michael decided to make another pledge, this one to Jennifer: the informal rule about keeping the weekends for the family would be made official. He wouldn't schedule any extracurricular activities for Saturdays and Sundays.

As for Lisa, she was focused on her call with the state attorney general's office, her first opportunity in front of anyone with real clout. But a chance bit of research threw that into disarray. Among the many documents in Lisa's case was a seemingly perfunctory affidavit establishing that attorney's fees in conjunction with the case were reasonable. A witness named Lisa Cullaro signed the affidavit, and Erin Cullaro notarized it. The handwriting looked like it came from the same person, but Lisa figured if they were related, maybe that made sense. In fact, she didn't think much about the affidavit at all, just because it seemed so tangential. How could the law firm foul up an affidavit about reasonable attorney fees? Wouldn't that be the one document they'd get right, the one that guaranteed payment?

But one night after wrapping up her tour through the Web, Lisa didn't feel like sleeping, so she Googled Erin Cullaro. Up came a link to the Florida attorney general's office. Someone with the name Erin Cullaro was working as an assistant attorney general in the Economic Crimes division, the very division Lisa was scheduled to speak with. In fact, Lisa was planning to tell them about fraudulent foreclosure processes at Florida Default Law Group, where Cullaro apparently moonlighted as a notary. It had to be the same person; how many Erin Cullaros could there be in the legal community in Florida?

Reasonable attorney fee affidavits were not online, available only at the courthouse. So she frantically Googled the Cullaros to find out everything she could about them. One link seemed to confirm her suspicions. It was from the almost comically titled U.S. Foreclosure Network, a coalition providing resources for the mortgage servicing industry. A short piece about the "right of redemption" (whether a defendant could redeem property by paying off the arrears after a foreclosure sale) was written by Erin Collins Cullaro, listed as a "USFN-FL" member with the foreclosure mill law firm of Echevarria, Codills, and Stawiarski. That was the former name of Florida Default Law Group. And the link was dated 2006. So Cullaro had been with FDLG for at least a few years, while working for the Florida attorney general's office simultaneously.

The day of the call, Michael gave Lisa some advice over email: "It might be a good idea to ask outright if Erin Cullaro is in the room." A little after three o'clock, after her patients had gone home for the day, Lisa's phone rang. The woman on the line introduced herself as June Clarkson, a new attorney with the division who had come from the private sector. June joined law enforcement because she wanted to catch companies who tried to steal from their customers. Lisa had plenty of information on that. They talked for ninety minutes about document fraud, the corruption of public records, and the situation in Florida courts. June asked good follow-up questions, and Lisa got the feeling she really wanted to help. She put the Erin Cullaro thing out of her mind. When June suggested that Lisa come into the offices for a video deposition, Lisa eagerly accepted.

But when Lisa called back later to make the appointment, the office had no recollection of a June Clarkson. She left messages and never heard back. The brief hope had been extinguished. "They acted like I was some kind of crazy person," she told Michael. "I mean, all right, so I'm a little different, but I'm not crazy!" Michael turned to the possibility that Cullaro quashed the investigation and that Lisa was now being targeted. "We have to be careful," he said.

Meanwhile, Michael tested his newly won fame by contacting Susan Martin of the *St. Petersburg Times* again. He forwarded her links to the guide he had created, the pickup from Karl Denninger and other websites, and his presentation at the *Living Lies* conference. "Perhaps this information, growing in acceptance and renown, would be of more interest to you now as a true investigative journalist who has published articles denouncing foreclosure fraud," Michael wrote.

Susan Martin wrote back, thanking Michael for the links. But her tone had changed since the summer. "My problem with all this, however, is that too many distressed homeowners are jumping on these 'foreclosure defense' tactics thinking that they will be able to save their homes when in reality they are just prolonging the inevitable," she wrote. She criticized lawyers who asked for too much money from homeowners, as well as *pro se* litigants with their incoherent, "frankly ridiculous" motions. These were practical points—homeowners were paying lawyers when they could pay down their debts—but to Michael, it ignored the widespread fraud Martin herself had documented.

What really got to Michael, though, was this statement by Martin: "Frankly, too, it is extremely complicated to write about for a daily newspaper of general circulation." She was implying her own readers were too stupid to understand foreclosure fraud, and it wasn't worth the effort to get them to understand.

"It's too complicated to write about in a newspaper?" Lisa raged in an email. "The news is 'TOO COMPLICATED'? WAS 9/11 'TOO COMPLICATED'? WAS THE EARLY STAGE OF THE HIV EPIDEMIC 'TOO COMPLICATED'? WAS WATERGATE 'TOO COMPLICATED'?"

Michael shrugged it off. "On to the next arena."

Lisa saw the problem not as stupidity but as ignorance, and thought that ignorance could be reversed. After attending court hearings for months, she was convinced that judges weren't paying attention to the fraud. Lisa had no access to judges, but attorneys had the respect of the court, what with their diplomas and fancy initials after their names. If Lisa could teach them about the fraud and have *them* teach the judges, they would get more of a hearing. And everything would get resolved.

If it sounded deceptively simple, that's probably because it was. Lisa and Michael's lack of experience with political and social movements allowed a certain naïveté to creep in. They were appropriately cynical about Wall Street's land grab depriving millions of a basic human need and profiting massively off economic dislocation, but they had no problem thinking they were just a few allies away from fixing it. Moreover, they believed that if someone in power prevented banks from using fraudulent documents, their sharp executives would surely devise a reasonable solution that gave people a fair shot at saving their home. And then Michael and Lisa could go back to their lives.

Lisa had met a number of attorneys at the Palm Beach County courthouse. Most of them came out of real estate law and weren't trained trial lawyers, with no grasp of the epidemic of fraud or how to present it to the court. Whenever she showed attorneys false assignments and notarizations, they reacted with total shock. Instead of instructing them one by one, Lisa wanted to bring them together in one space. She envisioned an informal gathering where foreclosure victims and lawyers could have a few beers, discuss the issues, and maybe spark something more, without the intimidation factor of a lecture. The shame and humiliation attached to foreclosure demanded safe spaces, where people desperate to hide their financial catastrophe from the neighbors would feel comfortable unburdening themselves and sharing their stories. She wanted an offline version of her *Foreclosure Hamlet* chat room: a foreclosure fraud happy hour.

At the courthouse, Lisa started to approach lawyers she knew, asking them, "If we had a get-together, would you come?" The lawyers, almost all men, would always respond the same way: "Are there going to be any women there?"

Lisa would answer, "Hey, I'm a nurse, I've got women!"

So the first step in the movement to expose the largest consumer fraud in U.S. history resembled a matchmaking event for young professionals. Lisa chatted up her single nursing friends, who were happy for the chance to meet successful potential mates. That was the origin of the Nurses' Co-

alition Against Homelessness, official sponsor of the foreclosure fraud
happy hour.

Lisa called Michael and said, "I have a crazy idea." The only problem was
that she knew nothing about the local drinking scene. "I don't think I have
ever gone to a bar by myself in my life." Fortunately, Michael's instinct about
the two of them having complementary skills was accurate—he spent plenty
of time at happy hours.

He immediately thought of the perfect location: E.R. Bradley's Saloon.
The huge, beachfront-style bungalow with the bright green canopy in downtown West Palm Beach faced the Intracoastal Waterway and the marina
yachts. The outdoor tables were protected from the sun by umbrellas made
of old palm fronds, the kind of thing Jimmy Buffett would write a song
about. Almost everyone in the area knew Bradley's, especially the legal
community, since it wasn't far from the county courthouse. Lisa and Michael talked to the manager, and he offered half-price appetizers for the
event. The drink prices were a little high, but Michael considered Bradley's
welcoming vibe enough of a draw to attract people.

Lisa and Michael promoted the happy hour in true grassroots fashion:
with flyers at Starbucks. Jim Chambers, a *Foreclosure Hamlet* regular, made
the flyers. In fact, visitors to Lisa and Michael's websites became unpaid
volunteers for the cause, using fax machines to spread the information to
area law firms. The first happy hour was scheduled for November 18, 2009.

A few days before the happy hour, a homeowner emailed Lisa with a
question. The bank hadn't moved on her case in nearly a year, and she
wanted to know how she could get it out of the court system. This was a
common query—lots of people experienced long delays, with the banks
making no effort to foreclose. It caused tremendous stress, because homeowners never knew when they would have to find somewhere to live or
scrounge up a security deposit. For all the claims by banks about "improper" defense motions clogging up the courts, their inaction had much
more to do with it.

Lisa thought the homeowner raised an interesting question, so she set
out to find the answer at the county courthouse. While riding the escalator
to the fourth floor, she approached the man in front of her, whose suit gave
him away as an attorney. "Are you a lawyer?" she asked. The man's eyes

nearly bulged out of his head at the prospect of having to listen to some civilian's horror story.

"Don't worry, I don't want legal advice," Lisa said, "I just have a question." The man relaxed, and Lisa continued. "If a bank files a foreclosure case and doesn't do anything to it, is there a way to take it out of the court system?"

The attorney looked at Lisa. "Come with me."

They ran down two floors into the law library, which was filled with recitations of Florida statutes and case law. The lawyer pulled out a book and flipped through the pages. He came to a stop and said, "This refers to exactly what you were talking about."

According to rule 1.420(e) of the Florida court rules of civil procedure, if there's been no docket activity on a case for at least ten months, any "interested person," whether party to the case or not, can file a notice of lack of prosecution. "You have to send a certified copy of that notice to all the parties in the case," the attorney said. "And if they still don't file anything in sixty days, you can set a hearing for dismissal. And the judge has to dismiss it. Says it right here—the action shall be dismissed."

Lisa discovered her newest project.

She did some research, finding *Chemrock v. Tampa Electric*, an opinion out of the Florida First District Court of Appeals. Tampa Electric filed a motion to dismiss for lack of prosecution, under rule 1.420(e). Within sixty days, Chemrock filed a motion in opposition to the motion to dismiss for lack of prosecution, but the district court sided with Tampa Electric and tossed the case. The appeals court ruled that any filing in the sixty-day grace period would have to be "an attempt to move the case toward conclusion on the merits," not just a dummy motion to restart the clock. Everything checked out: not only the rule but case law supporting it.

Lisa called up Michael and said she wanted to run reports throughout the state for all cases with no docket activity for ten months, and then file motions en masse. Maybe they could get local law school students to help, telling them that if they wanted to acquire experience, this was a way to appear before a judge and get a case dismissed. "This is it," Lisa enthused. "All we need is a practice case to see how this goes."

A couple of days later, Michael told Lisa that he found the practice case. His receptionist at the Toyota dealership had a daughter, Tami Savoia, who was in foreclosure on a home in Greenacres, southwest of Palm Beach. Tami and her husband actually abandoned the home in 2007 and moved to North Carolina, but the case, brought by U.S. Bank (as trustee for First Franklin Mortgage Loan Asset-Backed Certificates, Series 2005-FF7), was still in the courts, lying cold. Michael asked the receptionist if they could give this motion a try, and she handed over the keys. Lisa filed the notice that month:

> PLEASE TAKE NOTICE that it appears on the face of the record that no activity by filing of pleadings, order of court, or otherwise has occurred for a period of 10 months immediately preceding service of this notice, and no stay has been issued or approved by the court. Pursuant to rule 1.420(e), if no such record activity occurs within 60 days following the service of this notice ... this action may be dismissed by the court on its own motion or on the motion of any interested person. ...
>
> Lisa Epstein, Interested Person

Lisa added a "Suite 508" to her apartment address to make it look official. She mailed the notices and marked off sixty days on her calendar, waiting for a response.

After a classic Florida sunset, a nearly full moon shone over E. R. Bradley's on November 18, 2009. Lisa and Michael arrived first to set up and corral guests. And it went pretty well. The lawyers showed up because of the nurses, the nurses showed up because of the lawyers, and several foreclosure victims stopped by. These were people who knew one another only by aliases they used on the Internet. Intellectually, they knew others were out there, but meeting them in person confirmed they had allies in the fight.

James Elder called himself "Jazzy" on *Foreclosure Hamlet*; he met Lisa at the courthouse. His auto repair business was literally blown away by Hurricane Wilma in 2005, and his wife later fell ill, stressing the family finances. PNC Bank put James into foreclosure while negotiating a loan modification. Foreclosure mill law firm David J. Stern backdated the assignment of mortgage; it wasn't filed until 2009, but the date of assignment was listed as 2005, a bungling attempt to cover up the post-foreclosure production of the document. Grace Rucci's son got the same message from Chase Home Finance that Lisa did: *stop paying for three months and we'll give you a modification.* He did, and Chase put him into foreclosure. Grace, a home health care worker, got activated by Lisa's website. Dave Lehoullier, Lisa's tech troubleshooter at *Foreclosure Hamlet*, came down, too. In all, about thirty people made it, which Lisa and Michael judged a success for a couple of weeks' notice and a whirlwind campaign of posting flyers on every utility pole and faxing every foreclosure defense and bankruptcy attorney in south Florida.

The big topic that week concerned the lending industry's comments to the Florida Supreme Court's task force on foreclosures. The Florida Bankers Association bluntly stated, "Virtually all paper documents of the note and mortgage are converted to electronic files almost immediately after the loan is closed. . . . The reason 'many firms file lost note counts as a standard alternative pleading in the complaint' is because the physical document was deliberately eliminated to avoid confusion immediately upon its conversion to an electronic file."

This was an amazing admission. First, the pooling and servicing agreements for the securitization trusts explicitly stipulated that only notes and mortgages with "wet-ink signatures"—that is, original documents—would make a transaction valid. The Florida Bankers Association unwittingly admitted that, as a matter of course, these original documents were never delivered. Second, for months Lisa watched lost notes become miraculously found whenever plaintiffs were challenged to produce them. This happened in Lisa's own foreclosure case, with the "original note" conjured up months after the foreclosure action. How could they be found if they were destroyed? Either the Florida Bankers Association was lying or the notes were fraudulent.

Robert Bostrom, executive vice president at the mortgage giant Freddie Mac, made an even blunter statement in a comment that Michael found: "Typically, the plaintiff in a foreclosure action does not own the underlying note or loan that is secured by the property subject to the foreclosure proceeding." This is precisely what Michael had spent the better part of a year trying to prove! Information of this nature would acquit a shoplifter. If the chain of custody of evidence cannot be established and the prosecuting attorney cannot produce the stolen items, the case falls apart. And this was not a bottle of nail polish but someone's home, the store of most of their wealth.

Michael and Lisa encouraged defense attorneys to introduce these comments in their cases. And they wanted to prove that victory was possible against the banks, despite their power and prestige. So they ticked off a series of recent wins. Homeowner Antonio Ibanez just reversed his foreclosure in Massachusetts, after U.S. Bank failed to execute the assignment of mortgage until after the foreclosure sale. Federal bankruptcy judge Robert Drain canceled a $460,000 mortgage debt for a borrower in White Plains, New York, because PHH Mortgage couldn't prove their claim. Even a bankruptcy judge in Idaho objected to an incomplete chain of title routed through MERS. Defense attorneys hadn't entered law school to facilitate the Great Foreclosure Machine, so they were eager to pick up new strategies to fight back.

People broke off into their own groups, but Lisa and Michael made sure to talk to everyone. The happy hour lasted all night. For a brief moment lawyers and homeowners were actually working together to solve the problem. Though Lisa and Michael planned to skip December because of the holidays, they hoped the happy hours would build momentum when they resumed in January.

A couple of days later, Michael got an unexpected call from Nye Lavalle. The same guy who blew Michael off several months before was now asking to collaborate. They met for drinks one night in Delray Beach and compared notes. Michael thanked him for leading the way, and Nye praised Michael's guide to looking up fraud. "We didn't have records online when I started out doing this," Nye told him. "I had to go to the courthouses one by one." Michael told him about the happy hours, and Nye said he would try to make them whenever he was in town. Michael drove back to Port St. Lucie that night thinking he had been let behind the velvet rope into an exclusive club.

Meanwhile, Dave Lehoullier, Lisa's tech guy at *Foreclosure Hamlet*, decided to throw a get-together for activists at his home, which he called "The Ranch." Michael and Lisa attended, along with a few others. They talked a bit about foreclosures and documents, but more about themselves and what brought them to this point. "I don't know what I'm doing half the time," Lisa confessed. But she was compelled forward, she said, by the same impulse that led her to become a nurse. Then she told a story that nobody, not even Michael, knew. Lisa happened to be visiting New York City as a tourist on September 11, 2001. When news of the planes flying into the Twin Towers broke, she ran to help. Within a matter of hours, Lisa found herself in a triage center in lower Manhattan, tending to victims of the attacks for a couple of days. That's what she was doing now, she said—providing triage to those suffering from foreclosure.

Everyone left The Ranch that night a little closer to their compatriots. But they were wrong about one thing. They kept framing the goal as educating attorneys about the sorry state of the public records, as if no lawyer had it figured out. At some level they understood that was wrong; there wouldn't be any positive developments to tout if there weren't some attorneys out there trying cases. But Michael and Lisa didn't know about a robust coalition of lawyers—a giant virtual law firm—challenging lenders. Some had been doing it for decades. The activists, not the lawyers, needed to be educated.

9

THE NETWORK

April Charney did it first in 1992. A Miami native with long jet-black hair who shuttled between Florida and Arkansas in her legal career, she had just started working at the nonprofit Gulfcoast Legal Services in Sarasota. April's humility was evident in who she chose to defend. Back in Arkansas, clients would pay with money carried in their boots, which they withdrew from the "bank"—their backyards. In Sarasota, April represented many renters improperly evicted from apartments. But this was a home mortgage case.

All mortgages have language entitling homeowners to special delinquent servicing prior to foreclosure. Once a borrower misses a payment, the loan servicer must contact them with a delinquency letter, advising the borrower of the amount due and how to cure the problem and bring the loan current. That letter must arrive within forty-five days of the missed payment. Servicers must take partial payments and cannot begin foreclosure until the window for the borrower to fix the default closes. Borrowers fund this servicing entitlement themselves through part of their mortgage payments. On Veterans Administration or Federal Housing Administration loans, special servicing directives are even more stringent.

April Charney started getting cases where none of these requirements had been satisfied. She tracked down the federal statute mandating the delinquency notice, 12 USC 1701x(c)(5). It was part of the National Housing Act of 1934. Early intervention made sense: if struggling borrowers got special assistance when they missed a payment, they might have a chance to prevent foreclosure. Yet many servicers did not even seem to be aware of the obligation.

You could count on one finger how many lawyers realized this in 1992. Fortunately, the lawyer who figured it out was April Charney. She began to fight foreclosures on grounds of inadequate servicing, first on VA and FHA loans, where requirements were very rigid. Her main contention to the judges was that the consumer paid for this service and wasn't getting it, just like if you went to a repair shop and bought a spare tire and they forgot to bring it out to you.

April began to train lawyers on foreclosure defense for the Sarasota Bar Association, explaining how servicers routinely broke a fundamental consumer right. She had a knack for breaking down complex legal issues into accessible bits, like a high school math teacher. For years April and her colleagues fought bad servicing practices. Servicers ran a low-margin business, and they couldn't afford to follow federal law and hire enough staff to counsel delinquent borrowers. So they took their lumps from a handful of rabble-rousers in 0.005 percent of their cases, rather than change their practices.

The rise of securitization made improper delinquent servicing look quaint. In 2004, April moved to Jacksonville Area Legal Aid as a consumer attorney, and before long the foreclosure cases rushed in. Almost all the plaintiffs filed "lost note affidavits," claiming that they owned the loan but just didn't hold the required paperwork. And the plaintiff was usually MERS, the electronic database that had no financial interest in loans but nevertheless claimed standing to foreclose. Nobody goes to law school to learn about foreclosures, April was fond of saying, and that was especially true in the securitization era. April taught herself about the various actors in the chain of ownership, spending nights reading intricate pooling and servicing agreements and obscure tax laws. The paperwork in her Jacksonville office piled up so high, she had to meet clients in the lobby.

But while the topics were obscure and the cases complicated, at the heart of the matter were insights available to any novice law student. First of all, April reckoned, Americans simply didn't make enough money to keep up with the demand for mortgage bonds. As a result, underwriting guidelines had to be scrapped. But REMICs, the tax-exempt trusts set up for mortgage-backed securities, were supposed to invest only in safe assets, not subprime loans. Wall Street banks that sold the securities didn't want the Internal Revenue Service to notice they were consistently violating the REMIC rules. So they purposely didn't create a paper trail, despite clear language requiring such documentation in the pooling and servicing agreements. April would explain it with one of her colloquialisms. It was like closing on your house and not signing the closing papers. Then ten years later you sign the papers and try to get everyone to believe that you owned that house the whole time.

Worse, there was no set schedule of mortgage loans pooled in a securitized trust, or if there was, the trustees were extremely loath to provide it. Sometimes the principal payments went to one trust and interest payments went to another. April saw cases with the same loan pledged into multiple trust pools, so when the loans went into default, different entities would try to foreclose on the same note. April called the mortgage-backed securities from the bubble years "nothing-backed securities."

April was preparing to put her arguments about securitization FAIL to the test in court when she attended a consumer attorneys' conference in Minneapolis and met the one person who independently came to similar conclusions about the mortgage industry and already won cases on these points. His name was O. Max Gardner III.

Max, whose grandfather was once governor of North Carolina, carried himself with the courtly mien of a political scion. One friend said that listening to Max was like listening to the prophet Elijah—if Elijah had a syrupy Carolina accent. After law school and clerking for the state supreme court, Max set up shop as a small-town lawyer in his southern Appalachian birthplace, Shelby, eventually specializing in consumer bankruptcy. Many of his clients struggled with mortgage payments, forcing him to deal with servicers. Starting in the mid-1980s, he began to see improper fees, misapplication of payments, and other unlawful activities. His Chapter 13 bankruptcy clients would get charged for monthly property inspections that were never carried out. Servicers also ignored the bankruptcy stay, a designated stoppage of debt collection during the bankruptcy process. And they would try to recapture fees in asset sales. Max hooked up with a forensic accountant named Kevin Byers, who discovered that servicer software was actually programmed to violate the bankruptcy stay, so that servicers could try to collect windfall revenue. Servicers could also change nonrecoverable fees to recoverable ones with a couple of keystrokes, and add them into pay-off statements.

Unlike other bankruptcy attorneys, Max had trial experience, and he believed he could fight these improper charges in court. The bankruptcy judges were initially indignant. "Max, are you on a crusade against the banks?" they would ask. In his calm manner, Max explained that his client wasn't behind on the court-ordered payments; the servicers were just tacking on charges using their software codes. The presumptions of industry innocence lingered, but Max did start to have modest success, because the servicers would rather pay him off than correct their systems.

In 2000 Max attended the same National Consumer Law Center conference in Colorado where Nye Lavalle made his presentation. Max sized up Nye as the kind of guy who would play golf in a suit and tie. But unlike the rest of the room, Max didn't laugh at Nye's hyperbolic contentions, because he had seen hints of them in his cases: affidavits, assignments, and endorsements of questionable legality. No other lawyer had put it all together, but this civilian did. Max pulled Nye aside at the conference, and the two spent a few hours together in the hotel bar. They talked about the newfangled securitization model and how it was working on the ground. They bonded over being outcasts, lone voices in the wilderness.

Over the next several years Max came to discover the lost note affidavits, faulty mortgage assignments, missing transfers, and dubious signatures that infected courts nationwide. He theorized that passing authenticated, notarized documents along every link in the securitization chain and into the trusts was too costly for the fly-by-night originators that sold the loans, let alone everyone else involved. So they didn't do it.

When the borrower defaulted and trustees needed standing to foreclose, they would call special fix-it companies. Max wrangled a copy of a quarterly newsletter put out by Fidelity National Title Group called *The Summit*. Fidelity actually created the main servicer software platform used to dial up profits. It had a subsidiary called Fidelity National Foreclosure Solutions. And *The Summit* described how the Document Execution team at Fidelity National Foreclosure Solutions generated whatever assignments or promissory notes were needed for its clients, after the fact. Team manager Dory Goebel explained how "FNFS has signing authority for a number of our clients" and how plaintiff attorneys could simply request any mortgage document and receive it within twenty-four hours. "The Document Execution team is set up like a production line," Dory explained. "On average, the team will execute 1,000 documents per day." There was even a flow chart showing the trail, from document request to fabrication to return to the foreclosure mill law firm. In 2008, Fidelity spun off its mortgage division into a public company called Lender Processing Services, or LPS. When foreclosures exploded, LPS controlled most of the market in servicer software and third-party document fabrication.

Max began to speak at national seminars about these issues. He also questioned whether the parties trying to claim payment from his bankruptcy clients actually established a proof of claim. He would use these challenges as legal leverage to secure better terms: reduced principal, forgiven past due balances, whatever. And he started to win. "Max has a better record than Roberto Duran, 103–0," said one observer. Bankruptcy judges, who were accustomed to proofs of claim, began to understand Max's arguments. When the big cases started to move, bankruptcy judges were well ahead of state and federal courts.

In 2004, Max's wife, Victoria, who bred Cavalier King Charles spaniels, needed more land for a kennel. So the family packed up their menagerie (they have seven Great Pyrenees, along with three other dogs, two donkeys, and five horses) and moved into the mountains, to a remote log cabin and farm twenty-five miles northwest of Shelby, reachable only along a gravel road. Victoria made a suggestion: instead of flying around the country giving seminars on fighting improper mortgage claims, why not have people come to the farm? That was the beginning of Max Gardner's bankruptcy boot camp, one of the more unusual legal training sessions in America. Lawyers paid $7,775 for the four-day retreat, room and board included; Victoria did all the cooking. Holed up in the woods, attendees had nowhere to go and could only focus on the good food, the homemade Carolina rye whiskey, and how to beat the banks in court. April Charney attended one of the initial events, on a scholarship.

In day-long strategy sessions Max counseled a cool, almost laconic strategy in the courtroom. Since the plaintiffs had nothing but false documents to use, he recommended having them present their evidence before jumping on it—letting them "dig their own grave," in his words. An entire wall of the classroom displayed settlement checks from Max's cases, a testament to his success. Eventually Max brought in expert guests, including Dick Shepherd, former general counsel of Saxon Mortgage; Margery Golant, a foreclosure defense attorney who previously worked at mortgage servicer Ocwen and two different title insurance companies; and Kevin Byers, his forensic accountant friend. With insight from those who spent their careers on the other side of the table, defense lawyers learned how to anticipate opposing counsel's arguments.

Max also handed out materials on a thumb drive for each attendee, including a file called "Max Gardner's Top Road Signs of Bogus Mortgage Documents." By 2010 this would include sixty-six independent features of false documents, including a list of 295 names, a roster of fraudulent document signers from around the country. Once participants graduated from bankruptcy boot camp, they would get access to Max Gardner's private email listserv, which included case files from a growing number of lawsuits, all stored and indexed. Competing attorneys in the same field rarely collaborated like this, but boot camp graduates operated like a networked foreclosure defense practice, using the listserv for strategy and information sharing. Between 2005 and 2010, six hundred lawyers from forty-seven states attended boot camp and discovered this new support system. They all returned home ready to take on the mortgage industry. One of these lawyers was April Charney.

April set out to prevent every foreclosure in her case file, because the plaintiffs possessed no legitimate evidence that they owned the loan with a right to enforce it. In the bubble years, virtually every mortgage she saw was placed into a securitized trust or sold on the secondary market. If the originators tried to take over and claim the right to foreclose, they would be admitting that they never transferred the mortgages to the trusts—a major violation of securities law. So trustee plaintiffs were stuck asserting ownership without proof. April's pleadings got a reputation—they were known as the "show me the note" defense.

Hanging over every case was this notion that judges might grant someone a "free house." But April directly challenged that point. Societies constantly make legal rules that cannot be violated, even if they lead to a guilty person going free. Police cannot coerce a confession and have that be admissible in court. They cannot falsify evidence. Even failing to read criminal suspects their rights should result in dismissal. Nevertheless, judges who would have no problem throwing out a criminal case if they found planted evidence wrestled with the moral and psychological implications of giving homeowners a windfall. Everyone had to follow the law, except for banks, which could wave a piece of paper and get a foreclosure affirmed. To April, stopping these foreclosures represented a critical step to preserving the whole concept of justice.

April believed the mortgage market was ripe for collapse, with tragic consequences, and lawyers needed to be trained to protect clients. She went to Ohio, California, Minnesota, Missouri, South Carolina, wherever she was asked. She never took money for her seminars, charging only enough to recoup the cost of the facility. And she required that everyone taking the class perform twenty hours of pro bono work.

Between 2004 and 2008, as foreclosures became a growth industry, fifteen hundred lawyers took April's seminars. Like Max Gardner, she also maintained an enduring relationship with those she trained, inviting attorneys throughout Florida and the nation onto two listservs where they could collaborate, share pleadings, and develop strategies. Between April's and Max's listservs, young attorneys could access the accumulated knowledge in foreclosure defense with the click of a mouse.

April produced results, albeit mixed ones. She froze dozens of cases in place because plaintiffs possessed no legitimate proof of ownership. In others, servicers agreed to loan modifications so her clients could afford the payments. In 2005 she got Judge Walt Logan to throw out twenty-four Florida cases in which MERS attempted to foreclose without possession of the note. But an appeals court reversed the decision two years later; the banks had the means to keep trying until they found someone to wave cases through. The stops and starts angered April, who believed that any judges allowing foreclosures to advance by plaintiffs without standing failed to uphold their constitutional duty. But she was gaining a following; the *New York Post* dubbed her "the Loan Ranger."

Among the many young Florida lawyers seeking guidance at the dawn of their careers was a lanky guy out of St. Petersburg named Matthew Weidner. His family had a tradition of civic engagement. His father joined the air force, one uncle became the executive director of the state Republican

Party, and the other liked to walk around in Benjamin Franklin costumes. After graduating from Florida State University, Matt did political campaign work, but found it laced with corruption, so he moved on to practicing law. He filed his first case while still in law school, over the denial of a public records request. It went nowhere because he didn't turn in enough copies for the process servers. The combination of earnest principles and reckless abandon never faded.

Matt thought of foreclosure defense as the subsistence farming of the legal profession: the $500 retainer he charged would barely cover expenses, and clients couldn't pay much more. When he realized he could get attorney fees from the banks instead, it changed his life. A couple of key moments stuck out. Once Matt sat in a judge's chambers before a hearing, reviewing a mortgage document. The judge pointed to one of the amount-due figures that looked improbable, and the plaintiff's attorney interrupted, "We can change that right away and give it back to you." Matt wondered how much of the document could be legitimate if the attorney could alter it by snapping her fingers.

Later he hired a law school clerk, who ran down a provision in the rule book requiring plaintiff's attorneys in foreclosure cases to attach internal records for the borrower. Matt didn't believe him, but after looking it up himself, he agreed. Matt took it to a local judge, who immediately responded, "Weidner, what the fuck are you doing?"

"Look at the rule book!"

After the judge found the rule in question, he said, "Holy shit, you're right!" Not even judges with extensive experience in foreclosure cases knew the required steps to take away someone's home. And they didn't really have to know; until the crisis, most cases went untried. In fact, when Matt took April Charney's seminar, with her insistence that securitized mortgages constituted the largest criminal scheme in the history of mankind, most of the lawyers in the audience feared that judges would find such defenses frivolous. Lawyers often try to build relationships with judges; they don't want to be seen as wasting the court's time. If they believed they would lose and that judges would consider them ridiculous for even bringing the case, they would stay away from filing.

Matt didn't see it that way. April inspired him that the rule of law was at stake. He watched April's 2005 trial, in which Judge Logan threw out all those cases where MERS tried to foreclose in its name, as the smoke heralding the fire of the collapse. If the judges paid attention, the foreclosure crisis might have been avoided. And he'd be damned if he would keep quiet out of concern for career advancement.

April Charney's insistence that lawyers collaborate rubbed off on Matt. He met Greg Clark, a title attorney in Clearwater, who worried that broken chains of title would make existing homes unmarketable, creating ghost properties without resale potential. "The judges can do whatever they want," Greg told Matt. "But I'm a title attorney. This is unfixable."

Greg assembled a group of local attorneys in St. Petersburg, and Matt joined up. They called themselves Jurists Engaged in Defending Title Integrity, or JEDTI. The whole thing was vaguely related to the concept of Jedi knights; maybe the membership had seen *Star Wars* too many times. They bought a broadsword, engraved it with the initials "JEDTI," and held roundtable meetings where only the attorney in possession of the broadsword could speak. They found a meeting room on the twenty-sixth floor of the county administration building in downtown Tampa, which took two elevator rides to reach. They even had a JEDTI motto: "The light of truth, the strength of defense, the heart of passion, and the leadership that follows from integrity."

Matt built a website to market his law practice, and colleagues convinced him to include a blog. In fact, before Lisa and Michael published their blogs, Matt Weidner started his own, in July 2009. Matt filled the blog with the kinds of rants he couldn't say out loud in court: contempt for the Great Foreclosure Machine and the judges' nonchalant acceptance of bank attorney lies.

Judges initially viewed Matt and his JEDTI friends as clowns fighting the equivalent of traffic tickets. But inside the system, clerks who worked with mortgage documents on a daily basis knew something was tragically wrong. They were disquieted by the behavior of the foreclosure mill law firms, filing hundreds of cases a week in the sloppiest way imaginable. They thought the courts desperately needed the leadership that follows from integrity. As the crisis raged and the lost notes and fabricated documents mounted, judges in the Tampa/St. Petersburg area began to listen.

When people around the state discovered what was happening in St. Petersburg, new faces would show up at JEDTI meetings. Once an attorney stood up and said he had to come to Florida's west coast to see JEDTI for himself. He'd driven four hours from Palm Beach, known locally as "Corruption County," where he couldn't get anything done because the judge who handled all the cases wouldn't listen to foreclosure defenses. In fact, she would sanction attorneys for stepping out of line.

As the attorney from Palm Beach discussed his litigation strategies, Matt immediately recognized him as a much higher-caliber advocate than the JEDTI lunatics, someone with deep experience. The attorney's name was Thomas Ice.

Tom Ice started as a corporate lawyer, spending twenty years defending companies in accident cases, eventually becoming a partner with the international firm Holland & Knight. But he got burnt out and decided that early 2008 was the perfect moment to put out his own shingle, recession notwithstanding. He opened Ice Legal in Royal Palm Beach, in a strip mall on Okeechobee Road, one of those six-lane Florida boulevards with a continuous loop of car dealerships and chain stores. His wife, Ariane, formerly an executive director at nonprofits, joined the firm as part paralegal, part researcher, and part counselor. Tom would joke that Ariane knew more about the law than any attorney.

Tom originally planned to try consumer bankruptcy cases, as his brother did. But the first client who walked into Ice Legal was a trucker who couldn't declare bankruptcy because he'd lose his truck, and therefore his entire livelihood. He wanted to mount a foreclosure defense to save his home. As far as Tom Ice knew, there wasn't any such thing as a foreclosure defense; if you didn't pay, that was it. He sent the trucker on his way, apologizing that there was simply no way to help. He thinks about that guy a lot.

The next person also wanted to fight a foreclosure, as did the next, and the next. Since primary mortgages couldn't be modified in bankruptcy and practically every homeowner in Florida was deeply underwater, most clients would have no chance to make payments in a Chapter 13 workout. Tom realized that he'd better research foreclosures. He read English case law, like the 1677 Statute of Frauds, and dove into the various requirements for bank repossessions. Early on, Ariane kept alerting Tom to outlandish add-on charges from mortgage servicers for things like property inspection. Tom would ask for documentation to prove the charges, and the creditors would immediately drop the claims, saving his clients $5,000 to $10,000 by making a phone call. That made the Ices recognize they couldn't trust bank figures. Ice Legal rapidly changed focus from bankruptcy to foreclosure defense. The main judge in the Palm Beach County foreclosure division at that time, Jeffrey Colbath, personally asked Tom to take cases, saying that homeowners needed lawyers. The evidence Tom encountered looked suspicious: bad signatures, vice presidents signing for multiple banks, the whole bit. He and Ariane got sucked down the same rabbit hole as so many other lawyers, victims, and activists, scouring the public records, amazed by the systemic misconduct of the nation's largest financial institutions. So when Tom first went into court on a foreclosure case, despite no experience in this area, he felt enormously confident that the judge would nail the other side. But it was the exact opposite. The judges were where Tom had been a few months earlier: if the homeowner didn't pay, there was no defense.

Tom observed cases across the state and decided that the best way to fight was to litigate. He started with the process service defense. When a defendant is served with a summons, the process server must include four separate items on the document: their initials, their ID number, date, and time. Ariane was doing document intake, and the information was consistently missing. Tom at first balked at the idea, saying, "I don't see a court getting excited about this."

Ariane said, "Come on! Tell me why you can't raise that!"

Upon further research, Tom learned that defendants weren't getting served the papers. The point of the notations was to prove whether process servers did their job. Foreclosure mill law firms often owned the process servers, and therefore had an interest in failing to inform defendants about their court cases—it meant uncontested foreclosures and pure profit. Investors in mortgage-backed securities paid for process service, and they had no way of knowing whether the charges were legitimate.

Ariane talked Tom into filing one case, *Vidal v. SunTrust Bank*. Palm Beach County judge Diana Lewis, who initially heard it, indignantly grabbed the copy of the process server's papers and wrote the notations in herself, saying, "There, does that satisfy you? Now stop all this quibbling!" But where Judge Lewis saw quibbling, Tom and Ariane saw a legal process that should never be defied for convenience's sake. *Vidal v. SunTrust Bank* ended up going all the way to appellate court, and Ice Legal won.

Tom discovered that some process servers "cleaned up" the documents by testifying they couldn't locate the defendants. Dozens of affidavits outlined the same scenario, where the server would talk to a neighbor who hadn't seen the defendant in months. It was always fictitious. Others would have managers forge signatures for the process servers, whether they went out and served papers or not. Ice Legal obtained an affidavit from Liz Mills, a process server whose name appeared on hundreds of papers in Lee County. She swore that she had never visited Lee County in her life. Ice Legal prosecuted many of these cases, finally prompting the companies to bother to serve papers correctly.

There were other defenses. The standard mortgage contract included paragraph 22, which required that the borrower get written notice of default and guidance on how to cure it before filing for foreclosure. This was the delinquency letter defense April Charney had been using since 1992, but even in 2008, servicers failed to provide all the required elements on the letter. The Ices, along with lawyers across the state, made numerous paragraph 22 defenses.

Plaintiff's attorneys attacked Tom for his motions, which they said clogged the courts and delayed the inevitable. But simply by doing some real lawyering, Tom succeeded in breaking the stranglehold that bank attorneys had over the foreclosure process. Ice Legal spent most of 2008 and 2009 in discovery, filing motions to compel depositions. They wanted to talk to the employees who signed assignments of mortgage and other documents, to see if they could live up to their claims. Tom and his colleagues traveled across the state to locate judges who would order depositions. Ice Legal lawyers were prepared to go wherever necessary to depose employees, even after the judges would ask, "You really want to fly to Michigan for this case?" Tom and Ariane hired a couple of paralegals whose entire job consisted of answering emails about the four hundred or so deposition requests the firm had open. Everyone spent long nights at the office. And gradually it paid off.

The first deposition was with Erica Johnson-Seck, a "vice president of foreclosure and bankruptcy" with OneWest Bank, formerly the subprime lender IndyMac. Tom had a client named Israel Machado; IndyMac, his servicer, sued him for foreclosure, and Johnson-Seck's signature appeared on the assignment of mortgage (as a vice president for MERS), the affidavit of amounts due and owing, and a response to a defense motion. Johnson-Seck turned up in a case thrown out by Brooklyn judge Arthur Schack because she had both assigned a mortgage to Deutsche Bank and executed an affidavit on behalf of Deutsche Bank. This was a similar instance, with Johnson-Seck appearing as multiple officers in the same case. But nobody, to Tom's knowledge, had deposed her.

Johnson-Seck lived in Texas but traveled to Palm Beach for the meeting, on July 9, 2009. She stated that she had authority to sign for MERS, despite not being employed by them. In fact, Johnson-Seck could sign for MERS, OneWest, IndyMac, the FDIC as conservator for IndyMac, Deutsche Bank, Bank of New York, and U.S. Bank. "And that's all I can think of off the top of my head," she added. Tom Ice asked Johnson-Seck how many foreclosure-related documents she signed every week. She estimated 750.

"How long do you spend executing each document?" Tom asked.

"I have changed my signature considerably," Johnson-Seck said proudly. "It's just an *E* now. So not more than thirty seconds."

These were sworn affidavits, where Johnson-Seck attested to reviewing business processes at the servicer and all relevant information on the document, material facts that would lead to someone losing their home. She gave each case thirty seconds.

"Is it true that you don't read each document before you sign it?" Tom Ice continued.

"That's true," Johnson-Seck replied. She didn't know who inputted the figures on the documents, or how the records were generated. She relied on an on-site specialist from Lender Processing Services to run a quality control check on a 10 percent sample. And she admitted to not signing in the presence of a notary, undermining the purpose of notarization.

Johnson-Seck's casual admissions shocked Tom. But Johnson-Seck was just a foot soldier, assured by her superior that blindly signing documents was part of her job. Tom didn't blame her, just thanked her for giving up the scheme. More important, Johnson-Seck revealed the underlying crime in the Israel Machado case: the plaintiff, IndyMac, never held the promissory note or the mortgage and was trying to foreclose without standing on behalf of a trustee. IndyMac fraudulently tried to assign the mortgage to themselves after the foreclosure case was filed, to cover up the standing

problem. Tom immediately filed a motion to dismiss the case. Florida Default Law Group, IndyMac's lawyer, countered by striking Johnson-Seck's
affidavits, attempting to bury the evidence of fraud. But the judge sided with
Ice Legal in the case, throwing out the foreclosure and ordering that FDLG
pay Ice's $30,000 legal bill. Despite this success, in many cases judges pushed
the paper through, willfully blinding themselves to the misconduct. Those
foreclosures trudged along, and Tom and Ariane prepared appeals while
working their other cases.

One day in early November 2009, Tom ran across a letter to the Florida
Supreme Court from Lisa Epstein. Like many lawyers, he had been following
the task force on foreclosure processes—one of the task force members, in
fact, was April Charney. Lisa's letter knocked Tom's socks off. She presented
herself as a nurse and a working mom, but Tom figured she had to have some
legal training; she could really write. He and Ariane thought Lisa might
be able to help them with filing appeals. They contacted Lisa and asked if
she could come in. Lisa was shopping at a produce stand when she got the
call, and she quickly agreed to meet. She brought Michael along.

Tom and Ariane were not only shocked that Lisa and Michael weren't
lawyers but also that they held full-time jobs despite all the work they were
doing and all the knowledge they had acquired. "When do you get your
work done?" Ariane asked them, and Lisa and Michael just shrugged. Sleep
being optional helped.

Tom showed them a couple of early depositions, including the one featuring Erica Johnson-Seck. Michael and Lisa knew this behavior was going
on but never saw an employee cop to it in testimony. It made the fraud
too real. "You should let me put this on my site; people have to see this,"
Michael said. Tom had toyed with publishing the depositions, but Ice
Legal's site didn't have any readers. They already revealed the contents of
the deposition in a public motion, so Tom didn't see how it would violate
any privileges.

Tom talked about some other cases, too, including one involving Florida Default Law Group over some suspicious-looking affidavits for reasonable attorney's fees. The signer's name was Lisa Cullaro, and the notary was
Erin Cullaro. At least that was the case on this particular affidavit; sometimes Lisa Cullaro would be the notary. Erin's notarizations had a variety

of different signatures, from her full name to just an *E* and everything in between. Ariane put all the signatures on one long piece of paper to make the comparisons easier; even the short versions didn't seem to come from the same person, and Lisa Cullaro's signatures looked off as well. Ice Legal recently requested a deposition with the Cullaros.

"They're on my documents, too! Do you know Erin works for the attorney general's office?" Lisa said.

"What?" Ariane replied.

Lisa showed them the links. Even Erin's previous employment with Florida Default Law Group was suspect: these were supposed to be independent assessments of attorney's fees, not assessments from ex-employees. But working for the attorney general's office took it to a whole other level, completely changing the Ices' thinking on the deposition. Tom wanted to know if Erin was working on anything at the Economic Crimes division involving foreclosures. Ariane wondered if Cullaro revealed to her employers that she was moonlighting as a notary. A public records request could uncover those documents if they existed. Also, they wanted her official travel records. If she went out of state on any of the occasions when she purportedly notarized documents for Florida Default Law Group, that would be serious evidence of forgery.

Michael focused more on how much the Cullaros were paid per affidavit. "Two, three bucks a signature, thousands a week? Plus an assistant AG gig? That's a lot of cash flow."

A few days after the meeting Tom Ice sent the transcript of Johnson-Seck's deposition over to Michael, and on November 15 Michael posted it at *4closureFraud* with the headline "Full Deposition of the Infamous Erica Johnson-Seck." He added Ice Legal's pleading for sanctions in the case, for filing documents "in complete disregard of the truth."

Across the state, Matt Weidner read the deposition and had the same incredulous reaction. Prior to that point, Matt's blog mostly contained short commentaries and outbursts with titles like "Mortgage Modification, Santa Claus and Other Fairy Tales" and "The Stock Market Is a Ponzi Scheme." He'd posted a couple of court decisions before, but never a deposition. Matt had access to transcripts like this, through contacts around the state and April Charney's listserv. Instead of just ranting, he could use the blog to make them available. Matt believed in full transparency, that anything occurring in a courtroom should be public. And if the disclosure put pressure on the outlaw banks, all the better. Matt republished the Erica Johnson-Seck deposition on his site. And in January he wrote one of his patented tirades, based on a conversation with Tom Ice about the deposition. "Jesus, they're like robots," Matt told Tom, referring to the signers. In the blog post, Matt put it all together:

> In the vast majority of cases where these documents are produced, the person signing the documents does not have the legal basis to swear to the facts placed on the paper they are signing. We know from depositions taken of these "robo signers" that they don't even read the documents placed in front of them and the notaries and witnesses that are supposed to watch them sign are not present.

Some lawyers didn't like the term "robo-signing"—it softened the crime, made it sound like an automated labor-saving device instead of an improper process—but it caught on.

Meanwhile, Florida Default Law Group played the same games with the Cullaro case that they did with the Erica Johnson-Seck matter. First FDLG denied requests for communications between the Cullaros and the law firm, terming them "privileged and confidential." Then they filed an objection to making the Cullaros available for questioning, which they called a "fishing expedition." Ariane sent an email to her counterpart at FDLG, asking if they were operating as the Cullaros' lawyer; they replied that they were. But the Cullaros were supposed to be independent experts. When Tom pointed out how inappropriate that was, FDLG replied that "upon further investigation, our firm does not represent the Cullaros," and then they withdrew all Cullaro affidavits, arguing that depositions would now be unnecessary.

The Ices subpoenaed Lisa and Erin Cullaro as fact witnesses to misconduct involving FDLG. The Cullaros hired their own attorney—John Cullaro of the Cullaro Law Firm, their brother. Ice Legal scheduled hearings to force Erin and Lisa to testify, while issuing public records requests for any communications with the attorney general's office around Erin's FDLG employment. The fish was trying to wriggle off the hook, but Tom and Ariane were patiently reeling it in. And of course, they kept Michael and Lisa, their newest colleagues, apprised of the developments.

Over in North Carolina, Max Gardner stood outside a courtroom, in heated conversation with the vice president for a big mortgage company. "Do you understand what's going to happen?" the vice president thundered. "You're going to destroy the country. And if you don't stop, we'll just go to Congress and get the laws changed!"

Max thought about it. "You know, we have some changes we'd like to make, too!"

10

THE SPECIALIST

December 2009

As the economy sputtered back to life, winter brought a few more snowbirds back to Palm Beach than the previous year, but nothing like before the recession. Still, on her trips around the city, Lisa Epstein had to dodge the sudden lane changes of elderly drivers desperate for a good lunch table at the nearest deli. Away from the busiest avenues, Lisa would usually find herself back on the alphabet streets in Lake Worth, among the abandoned homes. A couple of years earlier, families trimmed the Christmas tree in those living rooms. Kids opened presents and hugged their loved ones. Now they were who knows where, the memories left out in the yard with the rotting furniture.

Throughout that winter, the Great Foreclosure Machine careened forward, flailing away like a boxer in the dark. In December, a Las Vegas woman named Nilly Mauck returned home to find every room in her condo emptied and her belongings thrown away. Her condo was 1156, and 1157 was in foreclosure: subcontractors hired to "trash out" the repossessed property got the numbers mixed up. A few days later, the television station that reported the incident heard from another man who claimed the same thing. Nilly contacted the trash-out team, and they only offered $5,000 as compensation for everything she owned.

The Horoskis of East Patchogue, New York, won a case against Indy-Mac, with the judge canceling their mortgage entirely. Two weeks later, IndyMac sent the couple a letter demanding $474,936.78 anyway. In Sarasota, Wells Fargo filed suit on a condo owner; they named the junior lien holders in the lawsuit, which led to the spectacle of Wells Fargo (the holder of the first mortgage) suing Wells Fargo (the holder of the second). The defendant Wells Fargo hired a law firm to represent itself in a lawsuit against itself.

Before Christmas, Citigroup made a big announcement that it was "suspending" foreclosure activity nationwide for thirty days. Everyone got excited until Matt Weidner explained on his blog that this affected only four thousand loans that Citi owned in their portfolio and didn't securitize. It was no wonder a company in England created a hit version of the Whack-a-Mole game, with bank executives dodging the mallets instead of moles.

Lisa spent the holidays trying to secure funding to fight foreclosures full-time. Added to her letters to public officials were letters to charitable foundations, describing plans for a nonprofit organization. "I am working until the wee hours long past midnight, after my child goes to sleep each night," Lisa wrote. "I then awaken early to start my workday, exhausted but determined to make a positive impact and help whomever I can. There are other hard working, tireless activists whose full-time, salaried efforts would make a similar impact in the great mountain of work facing us."

Ariane Ice became one of those sleepless activists; her job required scouring the public records. She would call Lisa late at night to talk about a filing she just discovered, or ask for help with a particular document. They would cackle on the phone at two in the morning, overtired and slap-happy, picking through the remnants of a criminal enterprise.

On the last day of 2009, Lisa wrote in her online diary, with her daughter, Jenna, at her side, "More and more each day I stare blankly into space, eyes brimming with tears, unable to comprehend how and why this is allowed to continue." Michael posted a different sentiment: "Happy New Year Banksters!" He included a link to a macabre song by Gene Burnett about financial executives in their C-suites on the fiftieth floor, called "Jump You Fuckers." Whether emotional or defiant, both Lisa and Michael held a cockeyed hope that 2010 would finally expose Wall Street's massive secret.

A couple weeks after New Year's, Michael was checking his feeds when he found an interesting essay called "An Officer of Too Many Banks." It cited case law where judges threw out foreclosures because the signing officer represented multiple banks in the same complaint. "In thousands of foreclosure cases, key documents may have been fabricated by employees of mortgage servicing companies who have falsely held themselves out as bank officers. . . . [I]n 2010, the issue of the validity of Assignment is likely to finally come under examination by regulators, courts, lawyers and distressed homeowners." It was familiar stuff to Michael, but he put the story up at his site.

The author of the piece was Lynn E. Szymoniak, Esq.

She was born in Buffalo, New York, but only stayed there thirty days. The family lived on military bases in Hawaii and California before settling in Antioch, Illinois. Lynn Szymoniak's father, a Marine Corps sharpshooter who served in World War II (at Guadalcanal) and Korea, left the family in the States after being assigned to duty in Japan, and when he returned home, he would come and go. Lynn's mom raised the family, working as a secretary at the State Bank of Antioch during the day; Lynn would help run the drive-through teller on weekends.

Antioch, a farm community on the Illinois-Wisconsin border, was barely visible on the map; they would turn on the stoplight on weekends. Lynn had a cloistered, small-town childhood, excelling at a strict Catholic girls' high school. She went to mass and took communion every morning and wore a uniform every day to class. Lynn earned a full scholarship to Bryn Mawr, one of the Seven Sisters liberal arts women's schools, located in the Philadelphia suburbs. The year was 1967, late in the 1960s but near the dawn of The Sixties. And a Catholic schoolgirl got her first taste of freedom.

It didn't take long for Lynn to become radicalized amid the freewheeling spirit on campus. She attended lectures by feminist author Kate Millett and took classes from Communist Party USA National Committee member Herbert Aptheker. One day Aptheker had his students sign a birthday card for Angela Davis while she languished in prison; he was Davis's godfather. Lynn protested to end the war, organized marches and school building takeovers, railed against racial and wealth disparities, and occasionally went to class. During what she would later call a "racial identity crisis," Lynn spent a summer working for the Black Panther Party in Kansas City on a free community breakfast program. Her best friend at Bryn Mawr, Dianne, would eventually return to Kansas City and marry Congressman Emanuel Cleaver, Eldridge Cleaver's cousin.

On March 8, 1971, antiwar activists known as the Citizen's Commission to Investigate the FBI broke into a field office in Media, Pennsylvania, liberating files showing that agents had infiltrated and investigated student organizers and dissenters. One of the files was Lynn Szymoniak's. William Davidon, a friend and professor at nearby Haverford College who organized the burglary, asked Lynn at an antiwar rally a few days later if she wanted to see her file. Lynn said she just wanted it destroyed.

All that spring, a black sedan often parked outside Lynn's house on the Main Line, with the two men in suits inside making no effort to be inconspicuous. The men followed Lynn to campus and to her part-time waitressing job. Katherine McBride, the dean of Bryn Mawr, pulled Lynn out of class to tell her that the FBI considered her a suspect in the break-in. Lynn couldn't take it. One night she cut her blond hair short and dyed it black, climbed out of her back window, and drove off with a friend. They bought a bus ticket and fled to a commune in upstate New York.

A few months later, Lynn made it back to Antioch, working as a teller at the community bank with her mom. Within three days, the same FBI agents confronted her at the office. They told Lynn they had solid evidence she played a role in the break-in, and also accused her of burning down a draft board in Indiana. They interrogated her for hours in a bank conference room. Lynn initially refused to answer, and one of the agents retorted, "How do you think it would affect your father's recovery if we had to tell him about all this?" At the time, Lynn's father was holed up in a mental hospital, trying to shake off the latest in a series of nervous breakdowns that followed his military career. Lynn finally complied, detailing her activist and sexual exploits, to the delight of the prurient agents. But she never gave up Professor Davidon's secret. In January 2014 the perpetrators finally revealed their role in the burglary, which led to the first-ever reforms of FBI domestic surveillance.

Lynn thought that was the end of her activist days.

Switching gears, Lynn left Antioch and wound up in a management training program for Bryn Mawr Trust Company back in Philadelphia. After a couple years, she noticed that she was the only female trainee, and the only one who never got promoted. She informed the bank of this, and they paid her to keep quiet and leave the program.

Using the bank's hush money, Lynn entered Villanova Law School, in one of the first classes that enrolled women. Mark Cullen, who would become the father of Lynn's children, met her at Villanova. After graduating in 1976, Lynn and Mark took jobs at various legal aid societies, doing poverty and civil rights law. There was a stint at a battered women's shelter in Merion, Pennsylvania, and a period representing Choctaw Indians in eastern Oklahoma. Anything that allowed them to agitate for social change, they liked. Mark loved to watch Lynn stare down injustice, wheels turning, formulating a plan to fight.

The search for a cause brought Lynn and Mark to Florida Rural Legal Services in Palm Beach County in 1980. Migrant workers picking sugar cane in Belle Glade, on the western outskirts of the county, toiled under dreadful conditions. Farmers would prepare the fields by spraying them with defoliant and setting them ablaze. Lynn would drive along two-lane highways with lit-up fields on either side forming a tunnel of fire, running the windshield wipers to push away ash. She filed hazardous workplace cases for workers stricken with tuberculosis and lung disease; at one point Lynn and Mark tried to get Belle Glade declared a farm labor camp so it could be brought up to *those* minimal standards.

Florida Rural Legal Services got defunded within a year, and after opening a poverty law practice with Mark, Lynn left the firm and had three kids—Zach, Mark Elliot, and Molly—becoming less a flower child and more a mom. She shuttled through several jobs in academia and the corporate sector, always on the move, changing employers every three years. Eventually Lynn became senior litigation counsel for the National Council on Compensation Insurance, working to bust large corporations defrauding insurance companies and worker's compensation funds for millions of dollars. Rooting out corporate fraud had a link to the social justice impulse, even while assisting big insurers. And while training at the National Association of Certified Fraud Examiners, in a course taught by retired FBI agents, Lynn became a real white-collar crime buff. She liked working backward from the claims forms, analyzing documents, partnering with private investigators. She learned how to find fraud, and became quite adept at it.

The white-collar cases put Lynn in close contact with numerous FBI and U.S. attorney's offices, in particular several officials in the Middle District of Florida, in Jacksonville. She even taught a class in insurance fraud at the FBI Academy in Quantico. She and the fraud investigators would drink together and trade stories. The FBI agents would always refer to "Lynn's people" when talking about liberals—she couldn't shake her bleeding heart—but they all got along. After working for a few other firms, Lynn opened her own law practice in Boca Raton, building an office with Mark that grew to twenty-five employees.

By 1998 Lynn achieved enough success to purchase a four-bedroom house for her and the kids in a gated community in Palm Beach Gardens, northwest of downtown. The house on Man O' War Road had an open plan and high ceilings, with a covered patio and a pool, on a handsome one-acre lot with palm trees. It was impossible to spend time there and not feel relaxed. But after purchasing the house, Lynn suffered a series of setbacks.

In 1999, Lynn was diagnosed with breast cancer. She waged a successful two-year battle, undergoing multiple surgeries and nine months of chemotherapy. The bills used up most of her fallback savings. Around the same time, she and Mark split up. They remained good friends—they even kept open the law firm after the breakup—but she got custody of the children. Meanwhile, Lynn's mother moved down from Antioch to stay with the family, and rapidly fell ill. She was diagnosed in 2006 with late-onset Parkinson's disease and Alzheimer's at the age of eighty-eight, and Lynn became her caregiver. She had to pull back on litigation work and needed another source of income.

So many Floridians managed during this period by trading on home equity. Lynn used her house as an ATM, twice writing off her old loans and refinancing into bigger ones, while taking money out. She used some of the cash to engage in the state pastime of house flipping, trading multiple properties and winding up with an eighth-floor condo in a swanky downtown West Palm Beach building with a rooftop Jacuzzi and pool, which she used as an office when the law firm downsized. Lynn found another business venture through one of her insurance fraud buddies in Jacksonville. The U.S. attorney needed an expert witness to explain workers' compensation to a jury. Lynn testified in the case in early 2008. Word gets around in the small world of expert witnesses, and before long Lynn was flying to New York, South Carolina, and elsewhere to give testimony.

None of this alleviated the financial stress. And as the 2008 crash hit, insurance companies cut back on legal work. Meanwhile, Lynn's mother was deteriorating. She would forget to use her walker and fall down. Lynn or her son Zach, who went to college nearby and lived at home, would have to sleep on the couch near the bedroom in case her mother would wake up at night. Sometimes the men tending to the yard would find her wandering the grounds, with no idea how to get back to the house.

Lynn thought about selling the big house and converting the office back into a condo. Throughout her childhood and professional career, she frequently moved on and started over. But Lynn promised her mom she would never stick her in a "hell-hole nursing home," by God, and with the condo there wouldn't be any other choice. Getting her mom to use an elevator, managing cramped quarters: it just didn't seem like it could work. At the house, Mom had a perfect little life, with her own bedroom, her own bathroom. Her doctors were nearby. It was awful enough to watch the woman who raised Lynn, someone who solved the newspaper crossword puzzle every day of her life, fall apart mentally. But Lynn thought that if she couldn't keep the promise to stay by her mother's side as she lived out her days, nothing else made sense. So she dug in her heels, cutting her budget to the bone to keep making mortgage payments.

The last refinance Lynn made, with a company called Option One, was a "2-28" loan, where the interest rate would reset upward after two years. Per the mortgage contract, Option One had to make the adjustment by March 1, 2008, or else wait until September. They missed the March 1 deadline but then adjusted the loan at the end of the month, increasing the monthly payment by nearly $1,000. This would have cost Lynn around $6,000 in extra interest; more important to a stickler lawyer, it represented a breach of contract. If Lynn allowed this, she thought, Option One could change her payment whenever and however they wished. Lynn protested the adjustment, but the lender wouldn't listen. So in an attempt to gain leverage, she stopped paying the mortgage at the new rate.

Lynn got sued for foreclosure in July 2008, by "Deutsche Bank National Trust Company as Trustee for Soundview Home Loan Trust 2006 OPT-2," an indecipherable mystery to her. Deutsche Bank filed a lost note affidavit but nonetheless asserted standing to foreclose. Lynn hired her ex, Mark Cullen, as her lawyer, and they attempted to have the case dismissed because Deutsche Bank did not attach the mortgage or the note to the complaint. As per usual in any case defendants actually challenged, the bank took no action for a long time. A natural investigator, Lynn began to dig into the situation. She found a lot of cases like hers: mortgages adjusting at the wrong time, unknown entities named as plaintiffs. Lynn trekked the same online route as Lisa and Michael and other victims, learning about mortgage-backed trusts and securitization FAIL and Wall Street's Great Foreclosure Machine.

After her mother died in mid-2009—she did live out her life in that Palm Beach Gardens home, dying on her birthday—Lynn put the home on the market. But by that point the housing crisis was in full swing, and her chance to sell vanished. Lynn began to see the devastation in her own gated neighborhood: U-Hauls in the driveways, washing machines on the front lawn, abandoned homes, shattered lives. She figured she'd be another one of those suckers soon enough. She was just hoping to walk away without any debt.

Finally, on the day after Christmas, 2009, with her kids all home for the holidays, Lynn got her knock at the door. Miraculously, Deutsche Bank found the note. They also found the mortgage assignment, certifying the legal transfer from American Home Mortgage Servicing—another new name—to Deutsche Bank. Lynn had never filled out a check to either one of these companies, but they were passing her mortgage back and forth. American Home Mortgage Servicing was listed in the notice of filing as "successor-in-interest" to her lender, Option One. But something else on the assignment caught Lynn's attention: the effective date, October 17, 2008. That was three months *after* Deutsche Bank filed for foreclosure. Just as in Lisa Epstein's case, at the time of the foreclosure filing Deutsche Bank didn't yet own the loan over which they sued her. *I don't think so,* Lynn thought. She dialed Mark Cullen, who was representing her in the case. "Merry Christmas," he answered with a smile in his voice.

"They served me the notice of filing," Lynn said breathlessly. "But something's wrong here. The date on the assignment says Deutsche Bank acquired the loan three months after they sued me."

"Oh, really?" The words just hung there. Mark had tried only a couple of foreclosure cases, but while he knew all about the dodgy paperwork, judges evinced very little sympathy for delinquent borrowers they perceived as deadbeats. Anyway, Mark's usual response to his clients' overexcitement was to try to calm them down. He told Lynn he would take a look at the papers when he went back to the office. "I know you think I'm nuts, but I'll call you back," Lynn said, clicking off the cell phone. Mark heard that familiar intensity in her voice.

Lynn went into the kitchen to pour herself some coffee. She was going
to be here a while.

She pulled out her laptop and set it on the dining room table. Through a
little Googling, Lynn ascertained that American Home Mortgage Servicing acquired Option One in mid-2008, after Lynn stopped paying; that
explained why she never sent them a check. But she didn't know anything
else about the company. Through her work, Lynn had access to a database
called Accurint, basically a more sophisticated form of LexisNexis. The
mortgage assignment featured a notary stamp from Fulton County,
Georgia, so Lynn ran a business search in Georgia for American Home
Mortgage Servicing. Nothing turned up, in Fulton County or anywhere else.
American Home Mortgage Servicing executed the assignment, but they had
no offices in the state where the paperwork was notarized.

Linda Green signed the assignment as vice president of American Home
Mortgage Servicing. That name was too common for Lynn to work with.
But one of the witnesses on the document, Korell Harp, would fit the bill.
Was it too invasive to run a background search on the poor office worker
who signed her mortgage document? Maybe. But Lynn the homeowner re-
ceded into the background. Lynn the investigator had control now. Twenty
years of training taught her to dig deeper, to follow the chain back and de-
construct the facts. She wasn't going to stop.

Lynn typed "Korell Harp" into Accurint. Up popped someone who at
one point lived in Barnesville, Georgia. She read his address and work history, none of which mentioned American Home Mortgage Servicing. But
there was this: Korell Harp had an arrest record for a federal crime. Lynn
switched over to PACER, the database that contains federal legal pleadings.
As a lawyer, Lynn would often run names through PACER to search for
outstanding litigation or criminal records. She found that Korell Harp was
charged with identity theft in Oklahoma in January 2009. That was three
months after he signed her document.

Lynn poked around some other databases for more information about
Korell. If the charges were filed in December, he may have been arrested
earlier. Finally Lynn landed on the website mugshots.com. She typed in Korell Harp, locating his mug shot and booking number. On the date in Oc-

tober 2008 when he allegedly witnessed the mortgage assignment, Korell Harp was in state prison in Oklahoma.

Korell Harp may have committed identity theft, but somebody had stolen *his* identity, using it to sign mortgage documents that were submitted to courts as evidence to take people's homes. To take *Lynn's* home. Plus the documents were notarized in a state where none of the companies involved had any branch offices. And the dates were all wrong.

The copy of Lynn's promissory note included an allonge—a strip of paper, separate from the note, that included the most recent endorsements. Allonges weren't supposed to be used unless room ran out on both sides of the original note, but they were commonplace during the crisis, as they were easier to fabricate. Allonges were also supposed to be permanently affixed to the note, but the corner had no staple holes or other signs of attachment. In fact, nothing on the allonge looked official, except a line at the top with a Palm Beach County "book and page number." That meant a corresponding allonge must be on file at the county courthouse. Book 19933, Page 1827.

Mark Elliot Cullen, twenty-three, one of Lynn's two sons, walked lazily into the living room, stretching his neck to work out the kinks after a night's sleep.

"Come on, we're going to the courthouse," Lynn said to her son.

"It's the day after Christmas."

"Good, that means there won't be a crowd."

In the courthouse file room, Lynn asked the desk clerk for Book 19933. The clerk went into the back and returned with a large binder.

Lynn flipped to page 1827. What she found there wasn't the allonge but the first page of her original mortgage with Option One. She took out what Deutsche Bank sent her and compared it to the document on page 1827. *Why didn't I notice that before?* she thought. There was a strip across the top and bottom of the allonge, with some words cut off along the bottom. Lynn had seen this in phony tax returns. Somebody at Deutsche Bank, or whoever they outsourced this work to, copied the first page of the mortgage in an attempt to make the allonge look legitimate, and then did a cut-and-paste job. Not a digital cut-and-paste with Photoshop, but a literal one: someone cut off the top part of the page, taped it to another piece of paper, and photocopied that, adding the endorsement signature. But the line across the top and bottom, residue from the bad tape job, gave away the game. When Lynn lined up Page 1827 with the allonge, it was an exact match.

Deutsche Bank or American Home Mortgage Servicing never attached a new allonge to the note; this was a fabricated endorsement mocked up after the fact. Adding the book and page number simply made it look official. Lynn figured they probably just had one allonge they copied over and over whenever they came across a note that needed an endorsement. Who but Lynn would bother to check the documents?

Lynn returned the book and page binder to the desk clerk. "I need an affidavit from you that says this is what's really at this book and page number," she said.

"Sure, but you know you don't have to come down here to look all this up, right?"

"What do you mean?" Lynn said.

"You can search public documents online."

Lynn brightened. She turned to her son. "Mark, come on—we're going home!"

When they arrived home, Lynn informed Mark Elliot that the dining room would remain off-limits for the rest of the day. She had work to do.

To a fraud investigator, finding a searchable public records database for mortgage documents was like finding a pot of gold. Lynn started at the Palm Beach County site by looking up every mortgage assignment from American Home Mortgage Servicing around the same date as hers, October 2008. Dozens popped up. A few of them had Linda Green signing as vice president of American Home Mortgage Servicing. But in one document Linda Green was listed as vice president of MERS. Lynn didn't yet know what MERS was, but she wondered how Linda Green could be vice president of two different companies at the same time.

So she looked for mortgages containing the name Linda Green. This resembled how Lynn would handle insurance fraud investigations, searching for patterns in files prepared simultaneously by the same people. It turned out that Lynn got it wrong—Linda Green was not vice president of two different financial institutions. She was vice president of at least a dozen, according to signatures all over the official Palm Beach County records. Korell Harp's name kept appearing in different job titles as well, sometimes as witness, sometimes as vice president, despite being in the slammer in Oklahoma the entire time. And other familiar names repeated themselves, all with different job titles depending on which company assigned the mortgage.

The Linda Green documents shared one thing in common: at the top of the page, they said that DocX, a company from Alpharetta, Georgia, prepared them. The notary stamps came from Georgia as well. What if Linda Green didn't work for any of these banks, but worked for DocX? What relationship did DocX have to these banks and mortgage companies? And what was MERS?

Lynn decided the only way her lawyer or anyone else would ever believe her would be to physically stick these documents in front of their noses.

She called to her family, "I'm headed to OfficeMax!"

Lynn returned home from OfficeMax with reams of paper and several ink cartridges. She planned to print out every DocX document she could find, and compare them for patterns. Lynn moved her operation into the dining room, and for the next thirty-six hours, the hum of the laser printing process rang throughout the house, all day and all night, much to the chagrin of the three kids trying to sleep upstairs. Lynn herself didn't sleep during Christmas week.

Mark Cullen read the notice of filing at the office, finding the same fishiness with the fabricated allonge. He tried to re-create the allonge on the office copier and couldn't manage it. Mark also had Deutsche Bank's motion for summary judgment, and the allonge in there was different from the allonge in the notice of filing, lacking the strip across the top and the bottom. Though their forgery skills improved, Deutsche Bank's skills in presenting evidence hadn't: it filed two separate allonges in the same court case. Mark hadn't seen such a blatant example of evidence tampering in his legal career.

Since 2004 Lynn maintained a blog called *Fraud Digest*, mainly so she could stockpile details about past cases. At first she only let friends access it, but later she made it public, as a promotional vehicle for her litigation and expert witness careers. The site usually contained information about insurance companies, letters of credit, or workers' compensation fraud. In the last week of 2009 *Fraud Digest* featured articles like "DocX Mortgage Assignments Filed in Palm Beach County, FL (A-H)." Site visitors could peruse an alphabetic listing of every individual with a DocX mortgage assignment in the county, cross-referenced by date. There were hundreds and hundreds of names. And Lynn was churning out hard copies on three-hole-punch paper, fitting them into binders.

By the end of this thirty-six-hour period, Lynn found that Linda Green acted as the vice president of more than twenty mortgage servicing companies in just one month in 2009. She listed the names of those companies in a separate *Fraud Digest* article. And she highlighted other frequent signers, like Tywanna Thomas and Christina Huang. These names, which meant nothing to Lynn a couple of days ago, now became the most important people in her life.

Then Lynn started to focus on the signatures. On one assignment, Linda Green's signature was very smushed, with a large loop for the *L*, a sharp line for the *d*, and a hastily scribbled last name. The next one had a perfectly legible *Linda* and a proper cursive *G*. A third was mostly illegible except for the *G* in *Green* (see below).

The other names on the documents also had wide discrepancies among their signatures. These documents didn't just look fabricated; they looked forged. DocX, a vendor for mortgage servicers and law firms that needed assignments and affidavits to prove standing to foreclose, was supplying felonious evidence.

Mortgage Electronic Registration Systems, Inc., acting solely
as a nominee for HLB Mortgage

Linda Green
Vice President

Amtrust Funsing Servicies, Inc., by American Home
Mortgage Servicing, Inc as Attorney-in-fact.

Linda Green
Vice President

Seattle Mortgage Company

Linda Green
Vice President

First Franklin, A Division of
National City Bank Indiana

Linda Green
Vice President

American Home Mortgage Acceptance, Inc.

Linda Green
Vice President

Arbor Mortgage

Linda Green
Vice President

Mark Cullen would get a call from Lynn approximately every three hours, with updates on the investigation. "This is nuts, this is absolutely nuts," Lynn would say. Mark continued to humor her, but even he couldn't deny how it looked. There seemed to be more fraudulent paper out there than legitimate paper.

Lynn progressed from American Home Mortgage Servicing and Palm Beach County to more companies and more localities. She discovered searchable online databases in North Carolina and Massachusetts. She found fictitious assignments prepared not just by DocX but by its parent company, Lender Processing Services—the company Max Gardner tracked down in that newsletter about the Document Execution team. LPS produced the documents out of offices in Jacksonville, Florida, and Dakota County, Minnesota. Lynn found assignments prepared by employees at the servicers and foreclosure mill law firms, too, claiming to be corporate officers of the banks. The Great Foreclosure Machine had many elements, but almost every assignment Lynn looked at, no matter who generated it, exhibited telltale signs of fraud. Ninety percent of the documents had errors, by her estimates. How many innocent people were going into foreclosure based on lies?

She went back to OfficeMax for more paper and ink three times. She wore out the family with the constant printer hum. The binders piled up along the floor of the dining room, grouped by company; Lynn could stack them up and build a small wall separating her from the outside world, leaving her alone with the documents.

Lynn didn't yet understand why these companies fabricated the assignments and notes. But she believed she had enough raw evidence of criminality to write an official fraud report to the U.S. attorney's office in Jacksonville, Florida. DocX's parent company, Lender Processing Services, was headquartered in Jacksonville, giving that office jurisdiction over at least one facet of the case. Lynn had several buddies there, prosecutors she partnered with on white-collar criminal cases. She sent the fraud report to a friend, assistant U.S. attorney Mark Devereaux, who managed all the mortgage fraud cases in the office. Devereaux replied that he needed to clear it through the FBI agent in charge, Doug Matthews, who was on assignment at the time. So Lynn would have to wait. In the meantime, she had thousands of mortgage assignments to examine. The banks had foreclosed on exactly the wrong person.

Throughout January, while urging her contacts in Jacksonville to open a criminal case—she called Devereaux probably three times a day—Lynn tried to get local lawyers interested in her discovery. She drove to law firms and hand-delivered *Fraud Digest* articles in manila envelopes to mildly confused secretaries. She even took one to Ice Legal. Lynn also sent letters, much like Lisa, to state and federal officials, attaching her findings. Sheila Bair, the head of the Federal Deposit Insurance Corporation, wrote back that she didn't have jurisdiction over mortgage servicers or trustees. At least she answered.

Attracted by her writing at *Fraud Digest*, foreclosure victims around the country sent Lynn copies of their documents, which featured the same discrepancies. Michael Redman found Lynn's pieces too, and reproduced them at *4closureFraud*. The community was still small enough that a few weeks of research and a handful of well-informed articles made Lynn one of the nation's leading foreclosure fraud writers.

Late in January, Lynn found a notice for a February 2010 "foreclosure fraud happy hour" down the road in West Palm Beach at E. R. Bradley's Saloon, an old Marine hangout where she had knocked back a few beers. She didn't really like the sound of it; if you were in foreclosure, she figured, at least be contrite. But there would probably be other homeowners there, and maybe some lawyers. She could give a little presentation, bring along her findings.

There was a phone number on the happy hour flyer. So Lynn called, and for the first time she talked to Lisa Epstein.

11

BLACK DEEDS

Sixty days had passed since Lisa filed the notice of lack of prosecution in the Tami Savoia case, and U.S. Bank and their law firm, David J. Stern, never responded. So Lisa filed a motion to dismiss with the Palm Beach County Court. A week later, she got notice of a scheduled hearing on Monday, February 8, 2010, before Judge Meenu Sasser. "Interested Person, Lisa Epstein, will appear," the notice read. Because the hearing fell on a Monday, she had to take the day off work. She also had to hire a court reporter for $100, because Palm Beach County did not provide transcripts for civil cases. But Lisa happily made all the plans. It would be a busy week; the monthly happy hour was the following day, February 9. Lisa hoped to have something to celebrate.

In the meantime, Lynn Szymoniak called, asking who came to the happy hours and whether she could have seven minutes to show off some of her research. "We'd love to have you," Lisa replied. Michael didn't recognize Lynn's name, though by this time he had cross-posted a number of her *Fraud Digest* articles. They mostly contained raw data, evidence that could be used to build a criminal case. Lynn compared signatures from DocX employees like Linda Green, Korell Harp, Christina Huang, and Jessica Ohde, none of which looked the same. Another of Lynn's stories listed the dozens of job titles held by Linda Green and her DocX co-workers.

Lynn bombarded assistant U.S. attorney Mark Devereaux with phone calls and emails, sending along every document she had proving her claims. Finally FBI agent Doug Matthews, the Jacksonville office's point person for white-collar fraud, returned to town, which Lynn figured was a great relief to Devereaux. Matthews called Lynn up. "I know you want me for this thing, but we already gave it to another agent."

"Get it back!" Lynn said.

Matthews found the report sitting on the agent's desk, untouched. He picked it up and flipped through it, and within days the FBI opened a case. Lynn learned that investigators visited DocX offices in Alpharetta, Georgia, asking why their employees signed documents with different signatures as vice presidents for several different banks. The FBI couldn't officially comment to Lynn about an open investigation—she was lucky to find out they went to Alpharetta—but she wanted to know what was happening. So she called up Henry Clark, a specialist with the Florida Department of Insurance Fraud, who often worked with Doug on these cases. Henry was a good old boy, a whip-smart southerner who usually pretended to play dumb. Everyone, including Lynn, called him "Tommy."

"Tommy, am I on the right track?" Lynn queried.

"Oh, no," Tommy replied. "It's ten times worse than you think it is, no matter how bad."

Lynn knew how long FBI investigations took, and wanted to exert additional pressure. She thought about organizing a class action by homeowners with fabricated DocX documents, to challenge their mortgages. She had been involved in a lot of class actions before, from life insurance discrimination to farmworker conditions. Lynn's lawyer and ex-partner, Mark Cullen, wanted no part of it. He tried many class action cases but had others in the queue, didn't know much about mortgages, and, as a solo practitioner, couldn't front the $250,000 or so needed for expenses on a suit of this type. So Lynn had to shop around for representation, which proved difficult. She met with a lot of lawyers who started looking at their watches five minutes in. There was a built-in resistance to the idea that banks mocked up practically every mortgage document used in foreclosures.

One lawyer did perk up when Lynn gave her presentation. He told her that his brother was a senior officer at JPMorgan Chase. "He's been telling me that the bankers have been waiting for years for this to come out." Even with that admission, his law firm declined to represent Lynn.

After a couple of weeks, Lynn remembered Dick Harpootlian in South Carolina. Harpootlian ran the state Democratic Party for many years; when he went to Washington he ate lunch in the West Wing. He used Lynn as an expert witness on a case involving AIG, the insurance giant the U.S. government bailed out during the financial crisis. AIG falsified insurance claims to shortchange a workers' compensation fund, and the class action translated into a $4 million rate rollback for policyholders. Lynn's friends in South Carolina all told her that Dick, a former district attorney, wasn't afraid of suing anybody.

Lynn requested a half-hour to pitch the case, and Dick agreed. She drove eight hours to Columbia, South Carolina, to meet with Dick and his old high school buddy Ken Suggs, the former president of the American Association of Trial Lawyers, whose firm also tried class action cases. Dick and Ken combined could handle the up-front costs. Dick listened to the pitch, reviewed the documents, and liked the idea. He had prosecuted people for bank fraud, and if they misstated their income to get a loan, they were guilty, regardless of whether they made all their payments. This seemed like the same thing, only on the bank side. If the mortgage company fabricated documents to enforce the foreclosure, it didn't matter whether the homeowner paid the mortgage. But Dick wanted someone other than Lynn as the lead plaintiff, someone who wasn't a lawyer. "I don't have any plaintiffs," Lynn said.

"You can find them," Dick replied.

Ken Suggs immediately raised several issues. Under the Fair Debt Collection Practices Act (FDCPA), damages were limited to $1,000 per plaintiff. You would need a massive amount of plaintiffs to justify the up-front cost, which he put at $500,000. Attorney's fees were also limited under the FDCPA. And a case filed under the federal Racketeer Influenced and Corrupt Organizations (RICO) Act, which could implicate Deutsche Bank in DocX's activities the way a mob boss is implicated in the work of their hitmen, didn't apply where they lived, in the Eleventh Circuit, because case law made it impossible to get a RICO class certified.

Somehow Lynn convinced Harpootlian and Suggs to fund the case anyway, with the hope of opening the class nationally down the road. She wanted to be first to file so they wouldn't get edged out if other cases were consolidated. Harpootlian placed newspaper ads in hard-hit states, seeking people injured by foreclosure. They got a stream of replies, which Lynn answered personally. The stories were miserable, tales of people facing evictions with nowhere to go, people convinced of their failures as human beings. Lynn would tell them they were worth more than their credit scores. Not every homeowner had DocX documents, but Lynn knew that didn't matter; she typically found the same fabrications, the same forgeries. She sent two sets of reports on her findings: one to her class action lawyers on the civil side, and one to the U.S. attorney in Jacksonville on the criminal side.

One discovery stayed in Lynn's head, like an earworm of a song you can't drum out. She was trying to search public records in Nassau County, New York, where a state judge had just issued a ruling favorable to homeowners. But she ended up instead at the site for Nassau County, Florida, and it led her serendipitously to a remarkable mortgage assignment. The opening sentence contained the standard boilerplate, except for one piece near the end:

> American Home Mortgage Acceptance, whose address is 538 Broadhollow Road, Melville, New York, does by these presents hereby grant, bargain, assign, transfer, convey, set over and deliver unto BOGUS ASSIGNEE FOR INTER-VENING AS[SIGN]M[EN]TS, whose address is XXXXXXXXXXXXX, the following described mortgage . . .

The property address, for a home in Fernandina Beach, Florida, was on the document. So was the name of the original borrower (Ann Patton), the loan amount ($150,430), and the assignment date (October 31, 2008). But instead of the company receiving the mortgage in the transfer, DocX recorded "BOGUS ASSIGNEE FOR INTERVENING ASMTS." Linda Green signed this notarized document as the vice president of American Home Mortgage Acceptance, but transferred it to a bogus company. Literally.

Since DocX only created mortgage assignments so companies could prove standing in foreclosure cases, eventually this document, BOGUS AS-SIGNEE and all, would get filed with the clerk of courts in Nassau County, Florida, and go into a courtroom as evidence. It was obviously a placeholder document DocX never changed by filling in the name of the actual company involved in the transfer. Whoever created the template for mortgage assignments at DocX apparently designed a subtle commentary about the company's production of bogus documents for a living. That person probably never expected anyone on the outside to see this little joke.

On February 8, the day before the happy hour, Lisa Epstein found her court reporter in the hallway outside courtroom 4A. Lisa was a bundle of nervous energy for her first-ever appearance in front of a judge; her personal fore-closure case had gone a year without a trial date. Unfortunately, she didn't get a chance that day, either. Judge Sasser never called the hearing, as the other cases went long. The judge rescheduled Lisa for Friday. Lisa had to give the court reporter $100—they get paid whether they work or not—and make plans to come back in a few days. That meant more money for the court reporter, more money for Jenna's babysitter, and three more days of waiting.

The next evening, on a clear, cool Tuesday, Lynn Szymoniak parked a block away from E. R. Bradley's Saloon. She wanted to get there early and scope out homeowners as they arrived; she needed more class members for the law-suit, and this would be a target-rich environment. After briefly greeting Lisa and Michael, Lynn began to place poster boards against windows and stools all around Bradley's, like a litigator prepping the courtroom for a big case. Michael excused himself from Lisa. He wanted to size up the evidence.

The poster boards contained blown-up mortgage assignments and other documents. Michael scanned them one by one. The different renderings of Linda Green's signature made him chuckle. But he stared at the BOGUS ASSIGNEE document for a long time.

Nye Lavalle walked in, wearing a blue blazer with a large crest on the front pocket. Some other lawyers and homeowners congregated, and an-other guest speaker named Lane Houk, a former employee of several large mortgage banks and an expert in securitization, began his presentation.

Michael approached Lisa and Lynn, who were chatting, and pulled Lisa aside. "You've been talking to this lady, right? How does she sound?"

Lisa said, "Fine, I guess. Why?"

"I think she's a fucking kook."

Michael was always cautious of scam artists, tinfoil hat types, the kind of people who sometimes flitter on the edges of social movements. And he didn't put it past the banks to use a mole to discredit them. He brought Lisa over to the BOGUS ASSIGNEE document. "This lady's crazy. There's no way this is a real document." While Michael had a low opinion of the mortgage industry, the idea that they would be this stupid was quite a stretch. "Bogus assignee? Come on, man!"

While Lane Houk wrapped up his talk, Lynn struck up a conversation with Nye. "What do you think happened to the original notes and the assignments?" Nye asked. Lynn said she didn't know, and Nye pitched a theory about a secret warehouse in Tijuana with trucks loading up documents. Lynn just smiled.

When Michael interrupted the conversation, Lynn figured her turn was up. "Where do you want me to stand?" she asked.

"That assignment over there," Michael said, pointing to the BOGUS ASSIGNEE document. "Where did you get it?"

Lynn recognized Michael's tone; she'd heard it before, from her lawyer, her children, and virtually everyone else inclined to dismiss her claims. "Oh, the bogus one. Nassau County. You can look it up yourself."

"Is there a book and page number?"

"I think so."

They walked over, and the top of the document read "Book 1592, Page 444." Michael had his laptop with him; it was that kind of happy hour. So he logged on, went to the Nassau County clerk's website, and plugged in the book and page number. Sure enough, the same assignment came up on the site. "Holy shit, this is real!"

Not only did DocX file the mortgage assignment to BOGUS ASSIGNEE, but the clerk of courts even entered the grantee as "BOGUS ASMTS." In other words, someone in the office read that document, saw it was made out to BOGUS ASSIGNEE, and, instead of raising questions, typed it into the system that way. Not only that, but the docket showed that Ann Patton, the homeowner, lost her home to repossession. Given Florida law, that meant there had to have been a trial, or at least a hearing, where a judge, sworn to uphold the law, issued a final judgment for foreclosure, even though the assignment dictated that the beneficiary of the home would be a company called BOGUS ASSIGNEE.

Michael went to the front of the room and quieted everyone down. "Thanks for coming," he said. "I want to introduce you to someone. When she walked in the room I thought she was nuts, but now I think we actually have a lot to learn from her. Here's Lynn Szymoniak."

Lynn delivered her presentation, giving the short version of her document discovery—she had repeated it so much, she could tailor it like a political stump speech. Lynn stressed that she needed plaintiffs who could show injury from phony documents for her proposed class action suit. Lynn referred to the poster boards arrayed around the room, including the BOGUS ASSIGNEE document. The crowd buzzed at that one. The whole speech didn't last much longer than five minutes, but Lynn received a warm ovation.

The happy hour congregants broke into small groups. Lisa wound up at a table with Lynn and a young man wearing a black baseball cap low on his head. His name was Damian Figueroa, and he drove up from Fort Lauderdale for the meeting. The David J. Stern foreclosure mill filed an imminent action on his home, where he held a permit to house his dogs and his pet monkey, Misha. He told Lisa and Lynn he had to avoid eviction, because no landlord would let him keep Misha.

Damian's métier at the time was online video, and he'd produced a five-part series over the past week about his own mortgage, an IndyMac loan with assignments from Erica Johnson-Seck, she of the infamous deposition at *4closureFraud*. The same officers were signing for both IndyMac and MERS in his case. Matt Weidner, the lawyer and blogger from St. Petersburg, picked up the videos for his site. Lynn had seen them, too, emailing Damian to praise his "excellent work." Lynn left shortly after her presentation, but she exchanged business cards with Damian and some others, promising to follow up later about class action opportunities. The happy hour didn't break up until late that night.

Michael fired up his laptop the second he got home. He grabbed a copy of the BOGUS ASSIGNEE document from the Nassau County public records. By seven o'clock the next morning, he published it at *4closureFraud*. "Looks like DocX's 'art department' forgot to change the wording on their assignment of mortgage template before they filed this one."

At four o'clock that afternoon, Michael saw a comment on the post from a familiar name, DinSFLA. "Wait . . . there is more. INCREDIBLE," DinSFLA wrote, with a link to a YouTube video. DinSFLA was the online nom de plume of Damian Figueroa. Like Michael, he couldn't stop thinking about the BOGUS ASSIGNEE document from the previous night's happy hour. So he ran a search in his home county, Broward, and found another one.

"I am going to show you something that is going to make you extremely mad," Damian's video began. He stuck the original BOGUS

ASSIGNEE document next to a new mortgage assignment, also created by DocX, for a home in Pembroke Pines, Florida. It used the same language as the original document: "hereby grant, bargain, assign, transfer, convey, set over and deliver unto BOGUS ASSIGNEE FOR INTERVENING ASMTS." Damian also showed the book and page number, so anybody watching could call up the document themselves. Korell Harp, the jailed identity fraudster, was the vice president of the mortgage servicer, Qualified Financial, on this assignment. Damian finished the video by channeling the expected thoughts of the average viewer: "Seriously, this has got to be a joke."

In Michael's experience searching public records, as soon as you find two of anything, with a little persistence you can find thousands. So he started digging, and by the end of the day he tracked down seven more BOGUS ASSIGNEE documents. A couple of them added a new wrinkle: the company doing the transferring was also absent, replaced on the template with A BAD BENE, short for "a bad beneficiary." The signers of the document were from the company transferring the mortgage (at least that was the theory), so right on the assignment, Korell Harp was listed as the vice president of A BAD BENE. The person who made the DocX templates had a wicked sense of humor.

Michael posted a new story with the headline "Bogus Assignee for Intervening Asmts All Over the Public Records!" He stressed that judges were allowing foreclosures to proceed based on obviously phony documents. Karl Denninger picked up the story.

Lisa and Michael talked all day about these assignments, which seemed so blatantly fraudulent that they couldn't be ignored by the media. The more they could track down, the bigger they could build the story. So they brought in Damian and Lynn and decided to split up the country. For the next seventy-two hours the four researchers would divvy up every searchable public records database in America and look for BOGUS documents. Because they didn't have the funds to pay search fees, this limited them to Arizona, California, Florida, Georgia, Kentucky, Illinois, Michigan, and Nevada. But that included all four of the "sand states," those hit hardest by the housing bubble's collapse. There would be hundreds of thousands, perhaps millions, of records to search. Lisa called the operation "Project BOGUS."

Damian emailed Lisa that day: "Wowzers! That Linda Green has like 20 different signatures!" Lisa replied: "Only 20? Keep looking!"

That week felt like a dam bursting. Lynn brought the BOGUS assignment to the happy hour on Tuesday. More BOGUS documents were found on Wednesday. On Thursday, while Lisa, Michael, Lynn, and Damian searched for more, the Florida Supreme Court amended its rules of civil procedure. They accepted the recommendation of the foreclosure task force, endorsed in Lisa's comment letter, to require plaintiffs to review and verify ownership of the note and the accuracy of all documents in their complaints prior to foreclosure. The court specifically established the amendment to "prevent the wasting of judicial resources" on lost note counts and lawsuits brought without standing to foreclose, and "to give trial courts greater authority to sanction plaintiffs who make false allegations." The court also specifically acknowledged to Lisa that she made "well-reasoned arguments."

That next day, Friday, was the rescheduled hearing for Lisa's motion to dismiss for lack of prosecution. This time Judge Sasser called the hearing to order promptly at 11:05 a.m. Lisa approached the podium with butterflies in her stomach. But the adversary in the case, the David J. Stern law firm, did not even send a representative. Judge Sasser told Lisa she put a call in to Stern's office, and after a short recess the judge decided to proceed without them.

Judge Sasser asked Lisa to state her name for the record. For months Lisa had watched this judge stand mute, while homeowners lost their homes to foreclosure, without ever casting a critical eye at the evidence. But her broad smile didn't betray any frustration. "My name is Lisa Epstein, I am here as an interested person, not a party to the case." The judge asked Lisa if she served the sixty-day notice for lack of prosecution, and Lisa replied that she sent the plaintiffs notice by fax and mail. After verifying that, Judge Sasser looked straight at Lisa and said, "I've read the entire court file, I've read your motion, and I'm going to grant your motion."

Lisa went silent for a second. "Motion to dismiss granted?"

"Motion to dismiss granted."

A tear started to form in Lisa's eye. She could hear her heart beating. "Are you okay?" Judge Sasser asked. "Do you need some tissues, Ms. Epstein?"

"No, ma'am."

The motion to dismiss was without prejudice, so U.S. Bank could always refile. But for the moment it actually worked. An "interested person" without legal training, Lisa got a foreclosure case kicked out of the Palm Beach County court system. Judge Sasser told Lisa she could have the lockbox taken off the door of the home. Tami and Vincent Savoia could move back in if they wanted.

Before going home, Lisa stopped off at a bar and had the most satisfying glass of wine of her life. When she finally got home, she scanned the one-page order granting the motion and posted it at *Foreclosure Hamlet*. The caption read, "Happy Valentines Day America! This is for you!"

By Sunday night, the volunteer research team—Lisa, Michael, Lynn, and Damian—downloaded thirty-six BOGUS ASSIGNEE documents, at least one in all eight states tested. None of them believed these were the only BOGUS documents out there; they came from just a few days of limited searches. "The Whole Country Is Bogus," read the headline at *4closureFraud* Monday morning. "At first I thought it was some kind of joke," Michael wrote. "Well it is, and the joke is on all of us. Doesn't anyone look at these papers before filing them? Do the courts even care they are allowing people's homes to be taken away by some BOGUS document?"

Lisa punctuated her update on Project BOGUS at *Foreclosure Hamlet* by quoting the English dramatist John Webster:

Let guilty men remember, their black deeds
Do lean on crutches made of slender reeds.

A week later, Tom Lyons of the Sarasota *Herald-Tribune* wrote about the BOGUS documents. And in April, acting on a tip from Lynn, the *Wall Street Journal* ran a story about DocX and its parent company, Lender Processing Services. The paper published several examples of mortgage assignments "that incorrectly claimed an entity called 'Bogus Assignee' was the owner of the loan." A spokeswoman for LPS reassured the reporters that the word "BOGUS" was merely used as a placeholder.

12

THE REVOLUTION WILL BE BLOGGED

February 2010

Matt Weidner, the young JEDTI warrior, sat in his office on the second floor of a historic building on Mirror Lake Drive in St. Petersburg, the light dancing on the lake in the warm sunshine. When not in court, Matt was usually in this office, blogging. His secretary buzzed that he had a call.

"Hey, I've been following your blog and I wanted to let you know what was going on," the voice on the other end said.

"Who is this?"

"My name's Michael Redman. Do you know the FBI, CIA, and Department of Justice have been coming to your site?"

Matt, who knew Michael's name from *4closureFraud*, was as used to receiving strange phone calls as any lawyer. But this seemed a little outrageous. Nevertheless, when he installed Michael's tracking software and checked his site's visitors, he saw the same IP addresses: FBI, DoJ, even state agencies and district courts, from which people logged onto the site at crazy hours—3:00 a.m., 4:00 a.m.

Michael tracked visitors with a program called Stat Counter, and it may have been his favorite part of running his own site. It monitored activity in real time, so he could see individuals come in and out, click on different links, and so on. This was Michael in his element: in the shadows, watching those who watched him. In one week in February 2010, *4closureFraud* logged visits from Georgetown University, MERS, Lender Processing Services (the parent company of DocX), the county of Los Angeles, and, oddly, a

Dairy Queen. On February 22, someone from DocX popped around the site for four hours, visiting dozens of different pages. Practically every mortgage servicer, foreclosure mill law firm, major bank, regulator, and law enforcement office spent some time on Michael's site. And he watched them all.

Michael devised a simple yet labor-intensive system for *4closureFraud*, through his optimized Google Reader feed. He took in headlines from all major news sites and scraped the Web for stories tagged with several keywords (like "foreclosures" and "evictions"). This allowed Michael to find obscure reports that other people might miss. On February 13, WINK News in Fort Myers profiled an anonymous homeowner, "Mark," who made a modified mortgage payment to Bank of America that they erroneously posted 40 cents short. As a result of BofA's mistake, Mark was headed into foreclosure. A week later, an NBC affiliate in Moscow, Ohio, reported on a man facing foreclosure who decided to bulldoze his own home rather than give it to the bank. Only Michael was digging up all these random bits from local news affiliates or small-town papers, revealing the crisis at its most personal level.

But it took tremendous effort. All told, his Google Reader would reel in around thirty thousand new headlines every single day. And between waking up and going to bed, Michael had to scan every headline and mark them as read, getting thirty thousand down to zero. If he didn't, the unread headline count would rise to fifty thousand the next day. Bloggers checked off their Google Reader headlines daily the way farmers cleared invasive plants. You had to cut back the kudzu constantly, or more would return. So it became an all-consuming demand, bigger than Michael's job at Toyota, bigger than his family, bigger than everything. It weighed on his brain while he slept, and hung over his every move while awake. And out of those thirty thousand headlines a day, Michael would pull maybe three stories.

As the site grew, Michael annotated posts with images, though his graphic design skills were fairly crude. Someone named Howard Davidson contacted Michael and offered to build graphics, from parodies of bank logos to clever-looking Photoshops (one altered a For Sale sign to say "No Sale by Owner—Clouded Title"). Later Michael met Howard in New York and discovered that Howard was a woman. She was in foreclosure and didn't want to reveal her identity, even to Michael, but the graphics allowed her to make a contribution to the cause.

Michael didn't just aggregate local foreclosure horror stories. He published dodgy documents, recent court opinions, and his own research. He briefly featured a "Foreclosure Fraud of the Week," taking ten Palm Beach County foreclosures at random and picking the one with the most fraudulent documents. (The winner the first week had an allonge with an obviously Photoshopped endorsement. The signature had a looping *y* that dipped below the line, at which point the line disappeared.) He would track down authors of interesting rants or opinion columns and ask permission to cross-post. One of the first was Sam Antar, the former CFO of Crazy Eddie, who served jail time for fraud and penned inside stories about how he ripped off the public. Another was Matt Weidner.

Matt and Michael maintained a healthy rivalry, competing to be the first to post key depositions or rulings. They shared many sources, so the race to publish would often involve being in the right place at the right time. Matt had an employee in his office handle the blog when he was away from a computer. Once when Matt was on vacation, a juicy filing came out, and he frantically struggled to call his office while driving, imploring the blog minder to throw it on the site. Lisa would sometimes forward documents she found, copying Michael and Matt. Michael would call Lisa and say, "Can't you just send things like that to me first?"

At its height, *4closureFraud* received half a million unique visitors a month, modest compared to the *New York Times* but substantial for a niche website. And there weren't just one or two sites but a network, a foreclosure fraud blogosphere. Michael had *4closureFraud*; Lisa had *Foreclosure Hamlet*; Lynn had *Fraud Digest*. There were blogs by lawyers like Matt Weidner and Mark Stopa (stayinmyhome.com). There was Martin Andelman at *Mandelman Matters* and Jack Wright at *MSFraud* and Mike Dillon at the *Home Preservation Network* and Denise Richardson at GiveMeBackMyCredit .com, all of whom had been around for years. There were newcomers like Damian Figueroa, who started *Stop Foreclosure Fraud* after Project BOGUS, and Virginia Parsons at *Deadly Clear*. On really big stories, finance blogs like Karl Denninger's *Market Ticker* or *Zero Hedge* or *Naked Capitalism* would jump in. The bloggers amplified each other's posts, so one site's reach wasn't limited to its own readers but could spread throughout the entire network. Everybody read and gained insights from each other. They weren't officially working together, but they operated like a team.

Once Lisa welcomed more visitors to *Foreclosure Hamlet*, she knew she had built exactly what homeowners fighting foreclosure needed. Americans have what counterparts in other countries might call a curiously personal attachment to their homes. They don't see it as just a domicile, or as collateral against a promise to pay. The home is a repository of memories, an investment in financial security, and a reflection of self-worth, all wrapped into one. The home is where their kids learned to walk and talk, where they signified their commitment to marriage and family, where they exemplified their arrival to friends and neighbors. One *Foreclosure Hamlet* reader wrote Lisa of his deep affection for the tree in his backyard, which held a swing he used as a child. He couldn't lose his home any more than he could lose his heart. For him and so many others, *Foreclosure Hamlet* represented the most important resource in the world.

The site's best asset was its community. Paralegal Alina Virani was a constant presence, highlighting new cases and legal strategies. Ronald Gillis, a notary from Port Charlotte and a *pro se* litigant for three years, hung out at the site and would drive 150 miles to attend the happy hours. Andrew "Ace" Delany, one of the moderators, always left positive comments. Like Ace, Paul Muckle also hailed from Massachusetts. As a *pro se* plaintiff, he filed a lawsuit against every sitting governor and Presidents George W. Bush and Obama, arguing that mortgage abuse violated the Fourteenth Amendment to the Constitution. He sought no monetary damages, just a cease-and-desist order on every foreclosure in America. Muckle uploaded several videos about property rights, much of the information pulled from an eighteenth-century manuscript he found in his house. He also posted alien videos.

Kim Thorpe, a stay-at-home mom from Harrison, Maine, went by "KT." She posted a comment on *Living Lies* late one night, explaining how the local sheriff handed her foreclosure papers even though she never missed a mortgage payment. The first response came from Ace, recruiting her to *Foreclosure Hamlet*. She joined up in March 2010 and never left.

After the victory on the motion to dismiss for lack of prosecution, Lisa wanted to follow up by sending sixty-day notices on dead dockets all over the state. Lisa even checked with the Florida bar, making sure she could continue to file as an "interested person" and not get sanctioned for unlicensed practice of law. In the meantime, she paid to have Palm Beach County run a report on all cases with no docket activity for over ten months. Andrew Delany called other counties, but they wanted cash up front to produce the report. When Palm Beach County's data came back, they found thirteen thousand cold cases. So just sending a notice to each party would cost tens of thousands of dollars. Lisa needed a grant to get the project off the ground, but it never came together. In fact, Lisa was about to lose a source of income, not gain one.

She could not concentrate anymore. Previously a hard worker, she performed her nursing duties less capably, preoccupied with foreclosures and unendorsed notes and fabricated assignments. Projects filled her head: letters to public officials, requests for grant assistance, lists of documents to examine. Many days Lisa would stop in the small chapel before work and look up at the ceiling, whispering, "I need some guidance here." She felt impossibly entangled in a strange world. Returning to a normal routine would be like climbing back up the sheer sides of a deep hole. Oncology nursing was a good job at a time when there weren't many good jobs available. But though Lisa didn't know where her foreclosure obsession came from, she finally decided she had to see it through.

She went to management and told them she wanted to take a leave of absence. An administrator asked her if she was experiencing menopause, and she said no. "This is a huge story and I have to work on it," she told them. The practice had always accommodated her requests: they gave her maternity leave in 2007 and sick leave for Jenna in 2009, and they let her restructure her schedule to a four-day work week. And it initially looked like they would accommodate her again. Lisa trained her own replacement before the leave of absence. But in March 2010, before she officially left, she was fired. The cancer center never gave a reason; Lisa believed they wanted to save a buck instead of paying two nurses for one job. Under Florida law, fired workers were ineligible for unemployment. Lisa checked her savings and made some calculations. Stopping payment on the Gazetta Way mortgage in 2008 allowed her to rebuild savings; if she cut way back, she could use the money to keep herself and Jenna fed for a while.

Lisa had gone from married and employed to no husband and no job in just over a year. And yet she was doing exactly what she wanted.

Lynn Szymoniak, along with co-counsels Dick Harpootlian and Ken Suggs, filed a class action lawsuit in U.S. District Court in Florida on February 17, 2010, on behalf of four plaintiffs picked up through newspaper ads. Michael posted the complaint on *4closureFraud*, of course. Lynn sued two trustee banks, Deutsche Bank and U.S. Bank, and their third-party document fabrication providers, Lender Processing Services and DocX, for violations of the Fair Debt Collection Practices Act. The complaint distilled Lynn's six-week whirlwind of research to twenty-nine pages. She summed it up succinctly: "The entity seeking to foreclose can never prove the chain of ownership." That was the original sin, the failed securitizations that broke chain of title by neglecting to transfer notes and mortgages to the trusts. The document fraud merely covered this up.

Though filed on behalf of only four plaintiffs, the lawsuit asserted that the class action could include thousands of similarly situated homeowners. The complaint sought damages incurred in the foreclosures plus the maximum allowable $1,000 per class member in statutory penalties, along with attorney's fees. More important, Lynn hoped, a successful class action would bar trustees from foreclosing with false documents.

The case was assigned to William Zloch, the most conservative judge in the Eleventh Circuit. Dick and Ken were wary of trying the case in front of an ideologue, but Lynn said, "Maybe that's who we want! He sentences harshly in white-collar cases!" However, presumed allies at the National Association of Consumer Attorneys went ballistic, screaming at Lynn on the phone for days, calling her unsophisticated in consumer law and bound to lose. Lynn figured these consumer lawyers wanted to protect their turf from well-heeled attorneys like Dick and Ken. Finally Lynn got a message from a legal services office in Chicago: "I hated to do it, but you didn't return my last two calls, so I just filed a bar complaint against you." Lynn hadn't received a bar complaint in thirty years of practicing law. She called the man back to yell at him. He replied, "You don't know what you're doing!" The attorney explained that an unreported Eleventh Circuit case held that the Fair Debt Collection Practices Act didn't apply to banks. He said Judge

Zloch would take the opportunity to extend that to servicers and trustees. "You're going to screw us all!"

Lynn found the unreported case and broke the news to Dick and Ken. Luckily, they were able to withdraw the case before the judge entered orders or served anyone. The worst part was calling the plaintiffs, homeowners in the middle of foreclosure, and telling them that the case had to be dropped.

The timing was excellent in one respect. As a public company, Lender Processing Services needed to submit a financial statement to the Securities and Exchange Commission, disclosing any legal actions against them. The company must have turned its statement in after the class action was filed but before it was dismissed. "The complaint essentially alleges that the 'industry practice' of creating assignments of mortgages after the actual date on which a loan was transferred from one beneficial owner to another is unlawful," read the disclosure. "The complaint also challenges the authority of individuals employed by our document solutions subsidiary to execute such assignments as officers of various banks and mortgage companies." LPS added that they identified an unspecified "defect" in the notarization of certain documents from DocX, and claimed to be working on rectifying it. But this was the real bombshell: "Most recently, we have learned that the U.S. Attorney's Office for the Middle District of Florida is reviewing the business processes of this subsidiary," referring to DocX.

That was Lynn's case out of Jacksonville. In fact, she learned that a grand jury had been empaneled, because whenever she gave her contacts the name of someone who might have new information, they would immediately respond, "Would they be willing to speak to a grand jury?" Lynn's friend Tommy, the insurance fraud investigator who partnered with the FBI on these cases, also knew how to slip Lynn hints of progress. He would say things like, "I can't talk this weekend—some stupid woman is making me go to Alpharetta, Georgia," the home of DocX. All the prosecutors in the U.S. attorney's office boasted about how everyone associated with this scheme would go to jail. Lynn even learned that DocX moved its operations out of Alpharetta and into the main LPS headquarters in Jacksonville, fleeing the scene like burglars after a heist.

One person willing to speak to the grand jury was Nye Lavalle. After the happy hour, he called up Lynn and asked to take her to lunch. "You and I seem like we're working on the same things," he said. They went to Lynn's favorite restaurant in City Place, a multistory outdoor mall in downtown West Palm Beach. Within ten minutes Nye took photos out of his wallet. "I want to show you my new girlfriends," he said to Lynn, pointing to a picture of him with two women young enough to be his daughters. Lynn smirked. They talked about the various investigations they had embarked on. "What I'm really involved in is filing claims," Nye said. "But I can't talk to you about it here."

"At City Place?" Lynn said.

"I mean I don't want to talk to you about it within the boundaries of the United States." Nye proceeded to ask Lynn to accompany him on a boat into international waters, saying it would protect them from charges of conspiracy.

Lynn took about half a second to politely decline. Foreclosure fraud made her crazy, but not *that* crazy.

Lynn also kept up with Damian Figueroa, the homeowner from the happy hour. When Lynn was searching for plaintiffs on the class action that later fell apart, she sent Damian a retainer agreement to act as his lawyer, which he happily signed. Stuck with a dead case, Lynn thought she could still represent Damian in a class action against his plaintiffs, the David J. Stern law firm and MERS; neither of them was a bank, so the Fair Debt Collection Practices Act stumbling block might not apply. But she'd have to sell the lawyers with the cash on it.

Damian asked Lynn about filing something he heard about, called a *qui tam* action. "Here is the problem with the *qui tam*," Lynn emailed back. "The VICTIM must be the government—as a plaintiff, you stand in the shoes of the government that has been defrauded. The government is a victim as it is financially investing in these over-valued securities—but we both know that the homeowners are the real victims." The other problem with a *qui tam*, which could be pursued under a federal statute called the False Claims Act, is that the relator—the plaintiff who acts on behalf of the government—must have knowledge unknown to the general public. Lynn's information came from publicly recorded documents, and deciding whether they were "known to the general public" would be up to a judge. Dick Harpootlian and Ken Suggs did suggest a *qui tam* case, with Lynn as the relator. She mentioned this to Damian, and threw out the possibility that they could file together. Damian was willing to co-file. The two continued to exchange information; by this time, Lynn had a coterie of pen pals and collaborators from all over the country, helping her build a body of evidence.

Lynn had her own foreclosure case to worry about. She filed for sanctions against Marshall C. Watson, the foreclosure mill, for fabricating evidence. She also wanted to depose Linda Green and her DocX bosses. Mark Cullen, her lawyer, encouraged her to go to the courthouse and watch foreclosure cases, mainly so she could understand her chances of success. "You'll see—they will give you thirty seconds, and you'll lose."

In the courtroom, Judge Meenu Sasser dispatched cases at almost precisely that rate. Lynn focused on the handful of homeowners in the room. They all looked tired, as though they had been in this fight for so long it would almost be a relief to see it end. Being in foreclosure took a physical toll on homeowners, a daily puncturing of their already reduced self-esteem. Activists heard constantly about stress-induced illnesses, heart problems, depression. You could read it on people's faces.

Lisa ran into Lynn in the courtroom. Every time a plaintiff's lawyer would move to drop the lost note count and claim that they found the note, Lynn would say "liar" under her breath. Lisa just laughed. It kept happening, case after case. Found note, found note, found note. If Judge Sasser considered this unusual, she didn't let it show.

After the session gaveled to a close, Lisa told her new friend about how she would drive around the alphabet streets in Lake Worth, looking at boarded-up homes. "There are streets like that in Palm Beach," Lynn replied. They got in Lynn's car and drove to Pinewood Avenue, just a couple of miles away, literally across the train tracks from downtown. The homes were one-story ranch-style models built in the 1920s and 1930s, and their current state revealed the passage of time. Many still had the antiquated wiring and plumbing from the original installation; none had central air conditioning. Yet Lynn found sales in this area as high as $250,000 at the height of the bubble. Nearly all of the mortgages from these homes were securitized and put into trusts, and now few of the properties were inhabited.

Lisa was amazed by how Lynn could tick off the names of the trustees for every home on Pinewood. "That's a Deutsche Bank, that's Bank of America, that's Fannie," Lynn said as she passed each property. The neglect stood out: damaged roofs, black mold. Once the mold set in there wasn't much to do but bulldoze; the property couldn't be sold anymore. Passing by one house, Lisa spotted an extension cord that ran into the neighbor's home, from which the first house's residents were siphoning power. "They call this the historic district," Lynn said.

After touring Pinewood, Lynn and Lisa decided to get some lunch. Lynn got through about half her salad when Lisa asked if she was going to finish it. She admitted that she wasn't working at the chemo center anymore, and every little bit helped. Lynn wasn't in the best financial condition, either: once foreclosure fraud invaded her life, she mostly gave up legal work. She and her son, Zach, started selling old stuff on eBay to pay the electric bills and keep the grass cut. But Lynn marked the expression in Lisa's eyes, and gave her the leftover salad in a to-go box.

Michael got a call in late February from someone he hadn't heard from in months: Carol Asbury, the defense attorney from the Neil Garfield seminar. Carol had a business proposition: she wanted to sponsor *4closureFraud*. Michael met Carol at her office to go over the particulars. They would take *4closureFraud* off WordPress and onto its own server, and Carol would cover all webhosting expenses. Michael would still be the lead writer, free to post whatever he wanted without interference. Carol might write posts every now and then, but that wasn't central to the deal. She really wanted an ad for her law firm in a prominent spot. And Michael would do all intake of new clients brought in from that ad. For this, Carol offered $40,000 for the first year.

Michael liked Carol; she seemed like someone who wanted to fight for people. And it was hard to overcome the flattery of having something he did in his spare time turn into a valuable commodity. Michael wasn't sure about the intake, but he was hearing from foreclosure victims anyway; at least now he'd get paid for it. So he agreed to let Carol underwrite the site. It shifted from 4closurefraud.wordpress.com to 4closurefraud.org. Unbeknownst to Michael, Carol listed it as her law firm's website in official registries.

Carol set Michael up with a meeting location for prospective clients, in a rickety two-story building in Lake Worth. The first floor was a telemarketing office, and the employees always seemed to be loitering at the entrance on a cigarette break, no matter what time of day. Prospective clients had to stagger through a haze of smoke to reach Michael's desk. But they came, one by one, as the crisis metastasized in south Florida.

Michael had to lead a double life to make it work. He drove every day from Port St. Lucie to the Toyota dealership in North Palm Beach. At some point he'd announce that he had to go to the port to check on some cars they were exporting overseas. But instead he'd head to the new office, meet with homeowners, write a couple of posts, and check feeds. Then he'd race back to Toyota in the afternoon, and then home to Port St. Lucie. Life had already been a grind dealing with just the blog; this took Michael completely over the edge.

Like Lisa, he had foreclosure fraud on the brain twenty-four hours a day. Mentally, he checked out of his day job. And he felt guilty about it. So he told his managers that he wanted to quit. "This isn't fair to you guys; I'm spending 90 percent of my time here on something other than what I'm supposed to be doing," he told them. The lead manager replied that Michael's 10 percent beat most of the staff's 100 percent. They wouldn't let him resign. So Michael kept making the trips back and forth, from Port St. Lucie to North Palm Beach to Lake Worth and back, up I-95 and down.

The same week he made the deal with Carol Asbury, Michael heard from Tom and Ariane Ice. Two months had passed since they sent him a deposition, but this was a good one. Cheryl Samons worked for the David J. Stern law firm, a foreclosure mill that ballooned to nine hundred employees during the crisis, filing more than seventy thousand cases in 2009 alone, diligently forcing people out of their homes all week long and sometimes on weekends. The company also owned several ancillary services, making money at every stage of the foreclosure process. Stern lived like a captain of industry, with a $15 million mansion on the Intracoastal and a 130-foot yacht named *Misunderstood*. According to rumor, he initially considered calling it *Su Casa Es Mi Casa*. He recently bought his neighbor's $8 million property to tear it down and build a tennis court.

Samons had been Stern's operations manager for fourteen years. The first half of the deposition, taken back in May 2009, spun a familiar story: Samons signed an untold number of documents per month ("it's definitely not more than a million," she said when asked), without any personal knowledge about the contents, without even reading them. She signed as a vice president or assistant secretary of MERS without being paid by them or having any other official duties.

But near the end, Tom Ice brought up something new. He showed Samons a document she signed that was notarized by Valerie Nemes, a notary in the Stern office. The date of execution on the document was June 19, 2007, three days before the foreclosure case was filed. But Tom had another piece of evidence. "Here's a printout from MyFlorida.com Notary Public Commission for Valerie Nemes," he said. "And it shows that the issue date for her commission was August 20, 2008. So how is it possible that this was notarized on June 19, 2007, over a year before she was issued that commission?"

"I can't testify to that," Samons said brusquely.

Tom showed Samons another assignment where the notary wasn't a notary at the date of execution. Samons breezily dismissed it as a mistake: "There would be no purpose in backdating an assignment." But the backdating was necessary because the mortgages weren't assigned at the time of the transfer, which violated the pooling and servicing agreement. Stern's assembly-line operation, which got a flat fee for every foreclosure rather than billing hourly, foreclosed first and mocked up the documents later. But if the foreclosure predated the assignment, Stern's client could not possibly have standing; they wouldn't own the loan on which they were trying to enforce the terms. Backdating the assignments was the only way to win cases.

Tom kept pulling out backdated assignments with impossible notarizations. He had twenty-one in all. Eventually Samons grew angry. "Do I have to say the same thing on every single assignment? Because I can tell you I don't remember. You're going to ask me if I think it was backdated. I'm going to tell you no. I'm going to tell you I don't know what the mistake is. I don't know if I want to answer the same question every single time."

After she finished her rant, Tom calmly went forward. "You are a notary?" he asked Samons.

"I am a notary."

"How often does it get renewed?" asked Tom, referring to the notary stamp.

"I don't remember off the top of my head."

"I'll represent to you it's every four years."

"Okay."

"When it gets renewed every fourth year, you get a new stamp, right?"

"Correct."

Tom pointed down at the mortgage assignment. "If you just look at the document itself, you will see that the expiration date is more than four years after the execution date."

"Okay."

"Which means that unless they are capable of time travel," Tom said, his voice rising slightly, "they couldn't have used that stamp that wasn't going to be issued until after this document was executed."

At that point Samons's personal lawyer, David Bakalar, requested that the deposition be taken off the record. When they came back, Bakalar stipulated that every one of the twenty-one notarized assignments in Tom's pile had fraudulent dates, based on the notary stamps.

Michael posted the Samons deposition, and so did Matt Weidner, at virtually the same time. Shortly afterward, Matt got a call from an unidentified Stern employee, saying there was plenty more to come. A national reporter, Andy Kroll from *Mother Jones* magazine, had been poking around the operation for months, interviewing former employees. The anonymous insider worked in the process service department, and started feeding Matt information about dual sets of books and massive overbilling. Matt told them this was just what he needed to take Stern down. The insider replied that it would never happen, because Stern was too tied into the power structure in Florida.

"But if I put everything in public, it can't be ignored," Matt insisted.

"That's what you think," was the reply.

13

THE NINTH FLOOR

Like Lisa, Lynn delivered a stack of letters to state and federal officials, urging them to investigate foreclosure fraud. The Federal Deposit Insurance Corporation, the Securities and Exchange Commission, the House Financial Services Committee, the Financial Crisis Inquiry Commission, the state attorney for Palm Beach County, and every one of Florida's sixty-seven county clerks of courts got detailed information, with binders an inch and a half thick. "It is very possible that one letter to any of these authorities will be ignored," Lynn wrote in a February 9 *Fraud Digest* post. "If they receive 10, they may open a file. If they receive 100, they may be compelled to act. If they receive 1,000, they may actually conduct an investigation, discover the truth and demand an end to these shameful and illegal practices."

Only Lynn's friends in the U.S. attorney's office in Jacksonville had opened any sort of investigation. Lynn spent hours on the phone with prosecutors, teaching them about mortgage-backed securities. It was a slow process. But even without deep knowledge of securitization, they had the physical evidence of fraudulent documents polluting state courts. Somebody was creating those documents, and somebody else was authorizing them to do it. To Lynn, it seemed like a relatively easy white-collar criminal case, where you work your way up the ladder to prosecute those responsible. But because so many people in the Jacksonville office knew Lynn, she wondered if they were overcompensating by casting undue skepticism on her claims. She would write to her friends in Jacksonville stressing her restlessness: "I just drove by an underpass under I-95, I think that's where I'll be living next."

Prosecutors strongly hinted that DocX executives were on the short list for indictment. But when Lynn tried to depose them in her own foreclosure case, suddenly New York–based "TBLs" (tall-building lawyers) for Lender Processing Services marched into court. They claimed the depositions constituted harassment of LPS employees. In court, with Lisa and Michael in the gallery—they all attended each other's hearings for moral support—Judge Diana Lewis granted LPS's motion for a protective order. "You can revisit it later if you give me a better reason," the judge told Lynn.

Lynn filed an IRS whistleblower claim over REMIC tax law, which stipulates that mortgage assignments and note endorsements illegally made after the trust closing date trigger major penalties equaling 100 percent of the late "contribution" (i.e., the full value of the mortgage). Lynn wrote up a long, detailed complaint explaining that these trusts were acquiring defaulted loans two or three years after the closing date, with a mountain of physical evidence confirming it. The IRS brought Lynn to New York for an interview. Agents displayed little understanding of trusts and securitization, and mostly focused on questioning Lynn's credibility as a witness. Then one of them asked, "Ms. Szymoniak, exactly how much money is at stake here?"

If every securitized mortgage in the United States were taken into account, the total could equal trillions of dollars. Lynn said she couldn't know without further analysis.

"But that's your job as a whistleblower," the agent said.

The meeting broke up.

After the class action lawsuit withered, the notion of a *qui tam* case, which Lynn initially found impractical, reentered the conversation. Dick Harpootlian didn't know much about a *qui tam*, but Ken Suggs, the other lawyer, suggested a New York firm named Grant and Eisenhofer, which specialized in False Claims Act cases. Lynn got a loan from her ex, Mark Cullen, to return to New York and meet with Grant and Eisenhofer attorney Reuben Guttman. He had won some of the largest awards in the history of the False Claims Act; there was really nobody better for this case.

Lynn took her class action draft and restructured it as a False Claims Act complaint, supplemented by evidence uncovered by her, Damian

Figueroa, and other homeowners across the country. The critical challenge was proving how the government was harmed by these schemes. First Lynn alleged plain old securities fraud. Through bailout programs like Maiden Lane, intended to help Bear Stearns and AIG, the government purchased tens of billions of dollars' worth of mortgage-backed securities. And the Federal Reserve bought trillions in mortgage-backed securities after the crisis in an attempt to lower long-term mortgage rates. When trustees spent money to mock up documents, they charged investors in the securities. So because the trusts failed to receive mortgages and notes, investors— including the government—had to pay for the cover-up. Lynn asked Damian for help, and the two of them found the trusts for federal government mortgage bond purchases and identified forged mortgage assignments associated with them.

In addition, Fannie Mae and Freddie Mac, the government-sponsored mortgage giants, used servicers for the loans they acquired, meaning that they paid for fraudulent mortgage assignment preparation. The REMIC tax issue, which the IRS seemed disinclined to pursue, provided another count. There was a final possibility with the Federal Housing Administration, which provided insurance to mortgage companies on qualifying loans; they paid out insurance on foreclosed homes based on fraudulent mortgage documents, literally false claims.

While Lynn wasn't enthused about winning money for the government after they ignored subprime lending, bailed out banks, and did little to help struggling homeowners, she did think her *qui tam* could serve as a template for investors in mortgage-backed securities to force payback. She saw any possibility to increase pressure on the banks as positive.

Before the meeting, Lynn sent her three-hundred-page draft complaint to Reuben Guttman at Grant and Eisenhofer. Upon her arrival, Reuben greeted Lynn and said, "I started to read this but I couldn't understand any of it. Why don't you just explain to me what this is about?" Lynn gave him the remedial version, and at the end of it, Reuben said, "I maybe understood 25 percent of what you just said, and I get the feeling you dumbed it down a lot for me, but you said it very convincingly." Lynn thought, *This is what it must be like to have Jon Stewart as your lawyer.*

Another lawyer in the room, who specialized in securities law, said maybe Reuben should get some lunch while he met with Lynn privately.

They reviewed several technical issues, from statutes of limitations to provisions of the pooling and servicing agreements governing the securitizations. When they finished, Reuben said they'd give Lynn an answer within the week.

When Lynn returned home, she pulled out a map of the United States and a box of red round-headed pins. Leafing through her wall of mortgage assignments, which dominated the front room, Lynn located the cities where they were made and stuck a corresponding pin on the map, the way a cop would analyze where bad drugs originated. Lynn only wanted to meet with prosecutors in places with a pin: venue and jurisdiction meant a lot. Select Portfolio Servicing documents came out of Utah. Citi's came from Missouri. Litton Loans, Saxon Mortgage, BAC Home Loans, and American Home Mortgage Servicing all had various sites in Texas. JPMorgan fabricated documents in Louisiana. Then she put a pin in Fort Mill, South Carolina, the home of America's Servicing Company, a division of Wells Fargo. Almost all the Wells documents originated there, really sloppy stuff, including assignments that were notarized but *unsigned*. South Carolina could provide an inroad; Dick Harpootlian knew everybody there. Maybe she could get a prosecution going against America's Servicing Company, the way she got one in Jacksonville against LPS and DocX.

Before she could get a chance to pitch Dick, he called her. "I just want you to know we're all in. We're all going to do it." The *qui tam* case was on.

Dick flew Lynn up to Columbia to meet Bill Nettles, who had just been installed U.S. attorney for South Carolina. Nettles worked on voting rights issues in the 2008 Obama campaign. He brought his criminal staff to meet with Lynn, and she recognized a couple of them from the insurance fraud days. Lynn presented the scheme and named all the various law firms and document shops in the state. One of the biggest robo-signers in the Fort Mill office was named John Kennerty; Lynn found him signing as a MERS officer on behalf of at least twenty different banks. When Lynn mentioned Kennerty, one of the criminal staff exclaimed, "You mean they're forging the name of John Kennedy?" She had to talk them down on that one.

Nettles's staffers promised to assign an FBI agent right away, but that never really happened. The FBI claimed a lack of resources, though Lynn suspected it involved friction between Nettles, a former criminal defense attorney, and local agents resisting orders from someone who used to be on the other side. Later Nettles's office asked Lynn if she wanted to meet with the U.S. attorney for the Western District of North Carolina, Anne Tompkins. Lynn consulted her map, finding that Fort Mill, South Carolina, was actually closer to Charlotte than to Columbia.

So Lynn flew out to Charlotte, the trip again paid for by her lawyers. While at home Lynn was broke, on the road she'd have an expense account. She'd pay for hotel rooms with old Marriott points; if she confined herself to the restaurant downstairs, she could eat for free as well. It was a strange life, jet-setting across the country but penniless in Palm Beach.

Tompkins, another recent Obama appointee, came with the FBI agent in charge of the region; they were on the same page. About twenty civil and criminal staffers attended the meeting. Tompkins agreed to investigate. A relieved Lynn got on her return flight, wanting only to go home and relax. Just before the plane took off, she reached forward for the in-flight magazine. The stranger sitting next to her, a thin, unassuming-looking man wearing a dark shirt, dark sport jacket, and glasses, leaned forward at the same time. He turned to face Lynn.

"You know what happens to people who sue banks?"

"What?"

"They end up *dead*."

If it were a movie, the music would swell, the camera would dolly in to capture Lynn's terror, and the screen would cut to black. But because it was really happening, Lynn had to sit there for two hours next to the man who'd just threatened her life, while he casually flipped through magazines and ordered a drink. Cloak-and-dagger films don't teach you how to react for those two hours. *Should I call the flight attendant?* Lynn thought. *What would I say? That this man threatened to kill me if I sued a bank?* That was the other strange thing. Nobody at this point really *knew* Lynn had sued a bank. The class action was only live for a few days before being withdrawn.

Lynn opted to just gaze straight ahead catatonically, playing the words over and over in her head. She didn't move an inch the whole way to Palm Beach.

At the March happy hour, Michael told Lisa they needed to go to Miami that weekend. The Florida attorney general's office and something called the Interagency Mortgage Task Force scheduled an event called "The Housing Crisis: Who to Trust and Where to Turn." A dozen state and local agencies and the federal Department of Housing and Urban Development planned to take part, soliciting information from the public about "mortgage fraud."

Mortgage fraud meant something very particular to law enforcement: individual borrowers lying on their applications to acquire home loans, or scam artists ripping off homeowners with false promises about mortgage modifications. Nobody at this forum would expect allegations about phony documents and broken chains of title. But Lisa agreed they had to attend. She remembered the missed opportunity after she spoke to the lawyer from the Florida attorney general's office for ninety minutes but never heard back. This event offered a chance for a reboot.

There was one problem: the seminar fell on a Saturday. Attending would break Michael's vow to reserve weekends for his wife, Jennifer, and daughter, Nicole. Jennifer agreed that JPMorgan Chase tried to steal their house, but she didn't see why Michael had to investigate anyone else's foreclosure, especially if it took him away from his family.

For months Michael held to the separation between weekday and weekend, a wall between the online and offline worlds. Michael would log off 4closureFraud on Fridays and not return until Monday. Lisa wouldn't be able to contact him. But Michael told his wife he was making an exception, just this once. The whole point of his preoccupation with foreclosure fraud was to hand it off to law enforcement, and this presented an opportunity. Jennifer didn't like it. When Michael walked out the door that Saturday morning in Port St. Lucie, he said in parting, "I'm doing this for us." She slammed the door behind him.

At Lisa's co-op, Michael had to watch her put together dozens of printouts to hand to officials at the forum. "Let's go already," Michael said. "We're like an hour late!" Lisa hurried up and finally made it into the car. They got a mile down I-95 before Lisa realized that she brought none of the printouts with her and they had to go back. Michael could only shake his head.

They drove seventy-five miles from West Palm Beach to Florida International University, a pleasant, palm-tree-lined campus that looked more like a corporate office park than a college. One massive building abutted a man-made lake, the white façade reflected in the water. Inside, in a large hall, various agencies set up booths where individuals could present complaints or ask questions. The seminar was open to the public, but there was also a closed session with the Florida Department of Law Enforcement, the state Office of Financial Regulation, and the Miami-Dade Police Department. Lisa and Michael walked into the closed session, acting like they belonged there, and nobody stopped them. But as they suspected, the agencies were prepared to hear about mortgage fraud, these small-time scams. Banks trying to prove ownership of a loan by forging a document was a foreign concept. As Michael put it, mortgage fraud happens when you defraud a bank; foreclosure fraud is when the bank defrauds you.

Finally they found the attorney general's table, manned by a short blond woman with glasses. Lisa approached angrily. "I called in a complaint a couple months ago. I had a ninety-minute conversation with someone in your office, and I was supposed to give a video deposition, but nobody followed up. I really need to speak to June Clarkson."

The woman looked at Lisa and said, "I'm June Clarkson. I'm happy to hear from you."

When June spoke with Lisa in October, she'd just started working at the Economic Crimes division. She didn't even have a phone extension. None of the secretaries knew who June was when Lisa called in, and so they couldn't figure out where to transfer the call. It was just a mix-up.

The Economic Crimes division had been early in identifying trouble at Countrywide, the subprime giant, and played a role in the multistate enforcement order against the lender. It investigated a wide range of consumer fraud issues, from puppy mills to pill mills and even foreclosure mill law firms. Complaints from individuals got reviewed at the main attorney general's office in Tallahassee, then referred back to the regional offices. Republican Bill McCollum, a twenty-year congressman and a House manager in the Bill Clinton impeachment trial, became Florida's attorney general in 2006, with clear designs on the governor's mansion. It didn't hurt someone running for governor to build a record of protecting consumers. So there was an opening for prosecutors to get aggressive.

June told Lisa and Michael to drop by the Fort Lauderdale office the following week and to bring in all the evidence they had gathered. Lisa said,

"You don't get it. There are hundreds of thousands of documents across the state."

"Just bring in everything," June replied.

Before Lisa and Michael went to Fort Lauderdale, they checked with Tom Ice about the status of the investigation into Erin Cullaro, the Economic Crimes division lawyer who moonlighted notarizing Florida Default Law Group affidavits. Ice Legal discovered that Erin Cullaro used to be the expert witness on these affidavits, with her sister-in-law Lisa Cullaro serving as the notary. When Erin left for the attorney general's office, they switched places. Tom Ice obtained Erin's "Request for Approval of Dual Employment Outside State Government," filled out months after she entered public service. Erin wrote that she planned to "notarize documents," without naming the employer, Florida Default Law Group. She also stipulated that the dual employment would "not create a conflict of interest nor the appearance of impropriety," and that it would not take up too much time. According to the request, she would only notarize documents from 7:00 to 7:15 p.m. on Mondays, Wednesdays, and Fridays.

Despite such a cramped work schedule, Erin Cullaro managed to notarize 150,000 FDLG documents in just over three years. She received a $2 fee per notarized document, putting her annual compensation from FDLG close to six figures for what she alleged was forty-five minutes of work a week.

Tom and Ariane cross-checked the affidavit dates with a calendar, finding that Erin notarized documents on days other than Monday, Wednesday, or Friday. She also signed on days when travel records indicated that she was outside the state, meaning she couldn't have possibly witnessed the document preparation. Ice Legal also found Erin's signature in several different handwriting styles, suggesting that she didn't sign those documents herself but just lent her name to the process, allowing her and her sister-in-law to split the proceeds. This was exactly the conduct the Economic Crimes division should be investigating, and one of its own staff was engaged in it.

Tom hadn't yet deposed Erin and Lisa, as FDLG filed a motion for a protective order to stop any testimony. Foreclosure defense attorney Matt

Weidner also had a case going with the Cullaros, and when he tried to take their depositions, their attorneys released an old document that they claimed included Matt's forged signature. A contractor installing a driveway for Matt signed a permit himself when Matt wasn't around. The difference was that the contractor never filed the document with a court, it had nothing to do with the foreclosure case Matt was defending, and they found one signature of Matt's versus 150,000 from the Cullaros. With typical understatement, Matt raged about secret-police-style blackmail. Whatever the analogy, it showed that the Cullaros were willing to do anything to cover up their actions.

The week of Lisa and Michael's meeting, a judge ruled that Ice Legal's deposition of the Cullaros could go forward; FDLG doggedly filed a motion to reconsider. They also withdrew Cullaro affidavits statewide, including in Lisa's case. FDLG wanted to pretend 150,000 Cullaro affidavits never existed; like the familiar effort by weekend hackers on Florida golf courses, they sought a mulligan.

After hearing all this, Lisa decided she would have to tell June Clarkson about her colleague's extracurricular activities. This made Michael highly uncomfortable. "We're going to go into their offices and tell them that they're a bunch of frauds?" But Lisa was adamant. June told her to bring everything, after all.

The reddish brown 110 Tower in downtown Fort Lauderdale, near the Broward County courthouse and the local jail, took up a city block. The Economic Crimes division of the Office of the Attorney General was located on the ninth floor. A security detail led Michael and Lisa to the offices. They had to go up in one elevator, change cars, and then go back down to reach the ninth floor. Security brought them into a conference room obscured by tinted glass. They had to turn off their cell phones, and they couldn't leave the room without an escort, not even for the bathroom. Lisa asked for a glass of water; security said no. Michael wondered whether this was a meeting or an interrogation.

After a few minutes June walked in with a colleague, Theresa Edwards, a taller woman with red hair and piercing blue eyes. June said hello curtly and sat down. Their demeanor made it clear this was a business meeting, not a social call.

"Before I start," Lisa blurted out, "I'm just a little concerned about your colleague Erin Cullaro."

"We do have a colleague named Erin Cullaro. She works in the Orlando division," Theresa said. "What's your concern?"

Lisa slid a set of documents across the conference table. "Here are my papers, with my name on them," Lisa said, "and here's her signature on my papers. Now, I heard you're investigating this foreclosure mill, Florida Default Law Group, and Erin Cullaro is signing documents and foreclosure papers for the same firm."

June scowled. "This can't be the same person," she said. She and Theresa told Lisa and Michael to wait there, grabbing the documents and storming out.

Lisa turned white. They could not contact anyone outside the building. They could not leave the conference room. These state prosecutors had her foreclosure documents. And they looked angry. Michael, who earlier said he was attending this meeting under protest, gave Lisa an I-told-you-so look.

"What?" Lisa said in response. Did Michael really think these prosecutors would arrest them for telling the truth? Then again, it was her word against a colleague's. Anything was possible.

With the situation heightening his existing paranoia, Michael conjured visions of secret jail cells in the basement. The day before, Michael texted friends, telling them where they were headed. "If you don't hear from me, you know what to do," he told them. He even set up his friend Deirdre with bail money. Michael pulled out his phone and turned it on, desperate to reach the outside world, but he couldn't get any service. Lisa's phone also had no bars. Michael pointed to a computer in one corner of the room, but neither of them wanted to appropriate government equipment for their own purposes.

"How are we going to get out of here?" Michael asked. Lisa began to tremble.

They could do nothing but sit. And wait. And wait. It seemed like hours went by. Nobody checked on them; nobody came to the door.

Finally, after what was in fact only thirty minutes, June and Theresa returned, their expressions changed from fury to something more like embarrassment. June spoke first. "We want to apologize. This is the Erin that we work with. We'll be looking into this."

That set the tone for the meeting. Lisa and Michael showed them the BOGUS documents, the impossible notarizations, the faulty endorsed notes. They pulled out a new assignment Lynn had written about, where DocX forgot to change the effective date, so it read 9/9/9999 (meaning the homeowner didn't have to worry about foreclosure for around eight thousand years). They traced these bad documents back to specific third-party processors and foreclosure mills, and provided examples of fellow Floridians who were kicked out of their homes using this questionable evidence. After months of practice, Lisa and Michael crafted a persuasive case that banks had botched the ownership records on an untold number of properties and, instead of fixing their mistakes, decided to fudge it.

June Clarkson and Theresa Edwards had to acknowledge how plausible it sounded. These were official documents submitted to state courts and recording offices. And the Erin Cullaro situation enabled Lisa and Michael to earn their trust. They all exchanged information and agreed to stay in touch.

Immediately after the meeting, June and Theresa told their supervisor, Bob Julian, about Erin Cullaro's extracurricular activities with Florida Default Law Group. They discovered what Michael and Lisa already knew: Erin had special dispensation to act as a notary on certain days and certain hours of the week. But Lisa and Michael told them how Ice Legal determined that Erin couldn't have signed all the notarizations on those dates.

On March 26 Matt Weidner couldn't wait any longer. Fuming about the Cullaros' sleazy effort to muzzle him, he posted one of Ice Legal's court memos, showing Erin Cullaro's position with the attorney general's office and her array of signatures. Michael had been holding back on this for months, but after Weidner's release he ran with it, too. Michael added a screenshot showing that Erin Cullaro, who was supposed to be an independent "expert" for Florida Default Law Group, was actually their lead attorney before changing jobs. "The best way to stop a criminal investigation is to become one of the investigators," Michael wrote.

In their bid to avoid depositions, Erin and Lisa Cullaro promised to never again sign affidavits for Florida Default Law Group. But a week after everything went public, Michael found an FDLG affidavit for reasonable attorney's fees signed by *John* Cullaro. Apparently he replaced his wife as FDLG's expert witness. Could the employment pool in that part of Florida really be so thin that it narrowed down to one family? Meanwhile, Lisa sub-poenaed the Cullaros for testimony in her foreclosure case, prompting tele-phoned threats from John, who was also his wife's lawyer. "Let the judge decide," Lisa yelled back, and hung up the phone.

June and Theresa got another lead when the FDIC's Sheila Bair for-warded Lynn Szymoniak's letter about foreclosure fraud to them. Lynn came to Fort Lauderdale for a meeting with a binder of examples from DocX and Lender Processing Services, gift-wrapping the entire scheme for the prosecutors. June and Theresa were initially skeptical of an industry-wide conspiracy, but it was hard to retain such doubt amid the evidence. They asked Lynn a familiar prosecutor's question: what's the worst thing someone will say about you? Lynn replied that she had children out of wed-lock. Theresa cracked up. "So did I," she said.

On April 29, attention-hungry attorney general Bill McCollum an-nounced that his office was investigating FDLG and Lender Processing Services/DocX, which was unusual because he hadn't yet filed charges. The release noted that the civil investigation concerned "fabricating and/or pre-senting false and misleading documents in foreclosure cases." The Eco-nomic Crimes division in Fort Lauderdale, aka June and Theresa, would handle the case. The attorney general also opened an inspector general in-vestigation into Cullaro's activities with FDLG.

It would take more than a year before Cullaro was fired. But after hav-ing their pleas for support met with indifference, skepticism, or outright laughter, Lisa and Michael finally had some positive reinforcement. This was a crack in the foundation. And they wanted to ensure that crack would grow.

14

THE RALLY IN TALLY

February 24, 2010

At a local costume shop on Okeechobee Road, Lisa Epstein helped Michael Redman zipper himself into a plush pig outfit, complete with anime-style large eyes and a cartoonish smile. Michael looked like the mascot for a local sports franchise (*"Ladies and gentlemen, here are your West Palm Beach Swine!"*). Lisa rummaged through the aisles, finding a tuxedo with glittery lapels, dollar-sign earrings, white gloves, a top hat and cane, and a bushy moustache. She was a monocle away from being the Monopoly man.

The costume shop clerk, who rarely saw customers outside of Halloween, asked, "What are you guys doing this for?"

"You wouldn't believe it if we told you," Lisa answered.

The clerk hesitated for a moment. "Oh, wife swapping?"

"What? No!"

A few days later Michael and Lisa were heading to the massive Palm Beach County Convention Center, which they had been scoping out for two days. For a few years the Neighborhood Assistance Corporation of America (NACA) had been holding multiday Save the Dream events all over the country, for tens of thousands of homeowners. NACA rented out large arenas and brought in mortgage servicers, encouraging them to negotiate one-on-one workouts on the spot, into NACA-approved loan modifications. They operated through a combination of radical activism and pragmatic partnerships with the banks.

Now NACA brought Save the Dream to West Palm Beach. Michael thought NACA would be an excellent location to call attention to legislation pending before the Florida legislature to strip away homeowners' rights and allow the Great Foreclosure Machine to hurl forward unmolested. The fight had to reach beyond the foreclosure blogs to generate maximum pressure, he insisted.

Lisa and Michael planned to crash NACA on Saturday—by now Michael's weekend prohibition had gone out the window. That gave them two days to strategize. They walked among desperate homeowners, mostly low-income Latino and African American couples waiting hours for assistance. They identified security guards and where they patrolled. They mapped out a route for breaking in and for escaping. Michael wedged golf tees in the emergency exits to keep them open in case they needed a quick getaway.

Near sunset on Saturday, Michael, Lisa, and Deirdre, their videographer, pulled into the loading dock at the downtown convention center. The costumes were in the trunk; they also brought flyers to pass out. A security guard stopped them and asked them where they were going. "We're with the radio station," Michael said. He'd noticed disc jockeys broadcasting from the lobby the day before.

The security guard nodded and waved them through. Michael parked, and the pig and the banker donned their costumes right there in the loading dock. They entered through a back door, with Deirdre behind them, and walked onto the wide-open convention center floor. At the JPMorgan Chase and Wells Fargo tables, they passed out flyers and shook their fists. Michael held a big sign reading "PigsAss.org." People cheered, thinking it was part of the program. But after a few minutes NACA organizers spotted the pig and the banker, confirmed they were uninvited, and alerted security.

Earlier that month, the Florida Bankers Association presented state lawmakers with legislation to make Florida a non-judicial foreclosure state. If the bill passed, judges would no longer have to rule on the validity of foreclosures. Instead, as in twenty-seven other states, banks would merely file notice, give homeowners a nominal time frame to cure the debt, and then kick them out. Under the bill, that period could be as little as ninety days. If homeowners wanted to challenge the foreclosure, they would have to pay a $1,900 filing fee and carry the burden of proving their case. Mandatory mediation between homeowners and lenders, which Florida judges could order, would go away. The bankers pitched the bill as a way to unclog the cash-strapped court system and somehow prevent neighborhood blight caused by abandoned homes. They gave it an Orwellian title: the Florida Consumer Protection and Homeowner Credit Rehabilitation Act.

Fraudulent documents were so visible in Florida because of its judicial process. Servicers and foreclosure mills manufactured evidence in other hard-hit states—Arizona, California, Nevada—but without judicial foreclosures, they were buried at county recording offices and harder to find. Eviction rates soared in non-judicial states, too. If bank lobbyists could convert Florida, families facing foreclosure would have fewer protections, and hopes of exposing the scandal would dissipate.

The week before Lisa and Michael's NACA infiltration, state senator Michael Bennett, a Republican from Bradenton, filed a version of the bill called the Non-Judicial Foreclosure Act for Non-Homestead Properties. Florida had broad homestead protections for most homeowners, restricting forced sales upon death or in response to creditor demands. But if homesteaders abandon the property, they lose their protections. "Abandonment" under the proposed statute could mean a homeowner who never responded to the foreclosure notice, left for vacation for three months, failed to pay property taxes, or "act[ed] in a manner that manifests the intent to surrender the property owner's interest." It looked to Michael like banks wanted to create enough loopholes to let them foreclose on anyone. The day before Senator Bennett's language came out, Wells Fargo tried to evict William Berta of Sarasota because they claimed he "could not be found and might even be dead," when he was actually living in the residence with his son and two dogs at the time. A process server gave Berta eviction papers at his house after Wells Fargo took the deed in an uncontested foreclosure. Wells's arbitrary designation of abandonment could end up becoming legal under Bennett's bill.

Michael created a mini-site about the legislation, uncharitably called PigsAss.org, referring to Senator Bennett. Jim Chambers, the graphic designer who helped with the happy hour flyers, created a form letter people could fax to their legislators, urging them to vote against the bill. The graphic displayed a homely looking pig with the Monopoly man logo stamped over its posterior. PigsAss.org included contact information for Bennett's Tallahassee and district offices along with the names of all his legislative assistants and their phone and fax numbers. "The Bankers have thrown down the gauntlet," Michael wrote at *4closureFraud*. "Let's accept their declaration of war and fight back."

At the convention center two security guards approached Michael, and he zigzagged away from them, waving his arms to whoops and shouts from the crowd. Bruce Marks, CEO of NACA and a former organizer for the Hotel Workers Union in Boston, tried to take the PigsAss.org sign away. Eventually Michael and Lisa got cornered. They were both certain they were headed to jail for trespassing. But security just led them out to the loading dock and left. They headed to the car before anyone changed their mind.

A minute later a security guard came back out and said, "Bruce wants to talk to you." The guard brought Michael and Lisa, still in costume, to see Marks, who had one of their flyers in hand. "I'm the one who crashes events, not you," Marks said, and he was right: NACA was known for picketing bankers at their homes and disrupting congressional hearings. "What's all this about?"

Michael and Lisa explained their efforts against fraudulent foreclosures in Florida and the non-judicial foreclosure bill. Marks smiled. "Well, why didn't you just call ahead and say so? We would have let you in!" Michael, still dressed as a pig, shrugged. He never thought of *that*.

NACA Save the Dream events all had a small stage in the middle of the convention center so that homeowners could express their gratitude or organizers could announce the latest statistics on successful modifications. Marks pointed to the stage and said, "Why don't you go up and make a speech?" Michael, naturally, nominated Lisa.

She hadn't given a speech since junior high school, never as an activist, certainly never to thousands of homeowners, and really never while wearing a moustache.

"What are you going to talk about?" Michael asked her.

"I don't know!" she replied.

Lisa stepped onstage, Michael behind her. And they rapidly came face-to-face with America's digital divide. Lisa started talking about the proposed legislation and how they could stop it. "This is a bill written by the Florida Bankers Association for their own benefit!" she shouted. "It would take away our right to a day in court and allow the banks to cover up their massive fraud!" But the audience consisted of low-income victims of predatory lending, who didn't spend their days reading blogs and who were not attuned to foreclosure fraud. They had no idea what Lisa was talking about. It was certainly entertaining to see a banker and a pig giving a speech, but it didn't penetrate any further. Everyone smiled politely, if they listened at all.

Special interests depend on a disorganized public. They don't want people understanding what lawmakers decide in ornate committee hearing rooms. Keeping the masses preoccupied with their own struggles is critical for unmolested profit-taking. For all their successes, Michael and Lisa's reach was relatively limited.

Bruce Marks took a picture with the pig and the banker, Michael proudly holding up his sign, Lisa's face mostly covered by the moustache. And then everybody went home. Michael took a break and spent all of Sunday with his wife and daughter. By Monday, he was back trying to figure out how to stop the damn bill.

In March, Florida House member Tom Grady introduced a broader version of the non-judicial foreclosure bill, subtitled the Homeowner Relief and Housing Recovery Act. That moved through the state Civil Justice Committee and then the Insurance, Business, and Financial Affairs Committee with little resistance. The Senate version, meanwhile, reached the Banking and Insurance Committee. Two Democrats, state representative Darren Soto and state senator Dave Aronberg, crafted response legislation to preserve homeowners' access to the courts and add additional protections—they called it the Foreclosure Bill of Rights—but Republicans controlled the legislature, so it didn't have much of a chance.

On one of her research jags, Lisa noticed that the Florida Bankers Association held a Capitol Day every year, blanketing Tallahassee with lobbyists to argue its priorities. The 2010 version featured a golf outing and a Taste of Florida dinner at the association's headquarters. Lisa figured that if the bankers could spend a day lobbying the legislature, why couldn't homeowners? Rather than calls or emails or petitions, it was time to get right in the face of the decision makers. When she explained the idea to Michael, Lisa called it the Rally in Tally. He loved it.

Lisa wanted the entire state to participate; after all, this would affect every homeowner in Florida. She asked Matt Weidner if he would be willing to get people on the west coast to the capital for a rally. In public, Matt joined the chorus of opposition to the non-judicial foreclosure bill, but he knew, because of his family's history in politics, how things worked in Tallahassee. The first year a politician introduces legislation, they view it not as a potential law but as a moneymaking opportunity. The politician can extract campaign donations from people on both sides of the issue, to ensure that "their voices are heard" when the bill gets closer to passage. When the legislation returns for a second year, stakeholders get nervous that it has staying power and might someday happen. That triggers more campaign donations. Only by the third year would the legislature actually do something about it. But in a less cynical moment, Matt recognized the power ordinary citizens wielded in the foreclosure fraud battle, and thought a show of force could help.

They set a date, April 21; buses would drive overnight to the capital for a day of events. The first goal was to raise enough money to get everyone there. Foreclosure defense firms were an obvious target, given their interest in stopping legislation that would make their business irrelevant. Ice Legal sponsored two buses to transport supporters on the east coast. Matt and a colleague, Chip Parker, put together an ad hoc group, Lawyers for Homeowner Rights. Some of his buddies at JEDTI lent financial support, and Matt also got attorney Mark Stopa to pony up for the west coast bus. A group of homeowner activists from Sarasota, in bill author Michael Bennett's district, called themselves the Mortgage Justice Group—they had capes and everything—and made plans to attend.

Lisa was the worst person to handle logistics for a statewide bus trip— she had seemingly no concept of time or cardinal directions, and barely knew how to get to Tallahassee, let alone how to coordinate pickups along the way. But this was her life now, so she gave it her best shot. Lisa ultimately scheduled stops in Miami, Fort Lauderdale, Orlando, Gainesville, and Live Oak, as well as west coast buses for Sarasota and Tampa. She wrote talking points for participants to use when speaking with their legislators, and urged them to incorporate their own foreclosure stories. For those who couldn't make it, Lisa solicited and received letters from homeowners that she would hand-deliver. Lisa contacted the grounds department at the capitol and applied for a permit for a staging area, across the street from the state supreme court. She rented a public address system and speakers from a soundstage company. She promoted the rally fanatically to the press, connecting it to civil rights–era Freedom Rides. Through Matt, Lisa got April Charney, the founding lawyer of the foreclosure defense movement, to make a speech. Within a couple of weeks it was all set.

While they were planning all this, the bills actually stalled in committee. It was too late to stop the rally, and anyway, as Matt Weidner counseled, the bankers planned to come back next year. So they pushed forward as scheduled.

Late at night on April 20, several dozen homeowners boarded buses across Florida to make the hours-long ride to Tallahassee. Lynn decided not to go; where her partners in foreclosure fighting had grassroots energy, she believed in working the legal process from the inside. Michael drove up separately with his family. He took a vacation from his job at the Toyota dealership and never came back. The rally served as an introduction for Jennifer and his daughter to what he'd been fighting for all these months.

Lisa left Jenna with the babysitter and boarded the bus herself. A light rain fell as they motored up I-95, and Lisa watched raindrops collect on the bus windows. She met several people whom she knew only as case studies of foreclosure madness. They talked about their struggles, and their hopes that the trip would lead to something positive. Before long the night got the better of everyone, and they settled back for the long ride. The darkness and the rain imbued Lisa with an eerie calm as she prepared to intrude on the heart of Florida's political power and demand to be heard.

As day broke, the group stopped at a roadside Cracker Barrel to freshen up. Grace Rucci, whose son was in foreclosure in Palm Beach, walked into the bathroom and saw two children brushing their teeth; they were homeless and living in their family's car. Foreclosures hit the middle class in Florida; Rucci hadn't been exposed to real poverty like that. But it symbolized why she traveled eleven hours through the night: to help stop millions of others from experiencing the same fate.

The capitol in Tallahassee sits high on a hill, the rotunda and legislative office tower behind it visible for miles. Buses from east and west converged as the sun rose, stopping near the staging area in Waller Park, at the west front of the capitol. The podium sat just above "Stormsong," a local artist's statue of large metal dolphins frolicking over a working waterfall.

During the layover, Lisa changed into a blue suit jacket and shirt; a trademark bright green scarf held her hair in place. She disembarked and ascended the capitol steps, past a replica of the Liberty Bell. Michael found her and introduced his family to Lisa for the first time. As they waited for the rally to begin, they greeted other homeowners, as well as attorneys like Matt Weidner, Chip Parker, and April Charney. Cory Luttrell, a film student who jumped on the bus at the last minute, set up equipment to record the rally. The clouds cleared overnight, and the view from the steps, out toward the state supreme court, was all blue sky.

Matt Weidner emceed the rally, while Lisa and Michael held up signs with their website addresses on them; Ice Legal had a sign as well. Jennifer, Michael's wife, retreated into the crowd; this was her husband's moment, and she wanted a good view. "We gotta give credit to the consumer activists that joined this fight," Matt said, motioning to the homeowners behind the podium. He warned of bankers conspiring to remove fundamental due process rights, and how this battle would reverberate across the country.

State representative Darren Soto and state senator Dave Aronberg, who co-authored the Foreclosure Bill of Rights legislation, thanked attendees for their energy. "Your being here today is sending the message that we need to stand for people," said Aronberg, who was in the midst of a campaign for state attorney general. Matt also introduced foreclosure defense attorney Chip Parker, who thundered at the mortgage industry's daily injustices: "We're living in the steroid era of foreclosures. The banks are juiced in order to win." April Charney, in her understated drawl, argued that "foreclosure is a failed business model, and we need to stop it at the courthouse door." If Florida went the way of California and Nevada, Charney said, homeowners' rights would be bulldozed and foreclosures would skyrocket. "Without our homeowners, we have nothing."

The sign got too heavy for Lisa to hold, so she passed it off, but by that time her moment had arrived. Naturally, Michael nominated her to speak for homeowners. Since the NACA speech, Lisa started attending Toastmasters for public speaking tips. The leaders there instructed her that she had to expand her repertoire beyond foreclosures; Lisa responded, "But I'm only here to speak about one issue." Matt Weidner introduced Lisa as a "*pro se* patriot, for all the work she's doing to spread the message that you have a right to defend your home." And she stepped up to the microphone.

The most important part of the speech was the first line. "Hi, my name is Lisa Epstein and I am in foreclosure." Power loomed behind the affirmation. She did not hide reality, safeguarding her credibility out of fear that everyone would stop listening to a deadbeat seeking a free home. She owned her struggle because only through that could she highlight the rot at the heart of the biggest market in the world. She owned it because shame was the tactic the mortgage industry used to sell mortgages to people who couldn't afford them and forge documents to take back the homes when it all unraveled. Only a raised voice could overcome that shame and help others reject humiliation.

Her voice cracked by the second line, but Lisa held it together. "I cannot believe that I am a citizen of a country that feels it is okay to evict millions upon millions upon millions of its citizens from the only homes that they have," she said. Lisa said the titles were so dirty that property transfers would be maligned for the next fifty years, if not a century. "And I am here to say, defend your homes, America!"

Lisa used words she found etched in a display outside the Palm Beach County courthouse, among a series of quotations about the American justice system. Daniel Webster, the Massachusetts senator and orator, once said, "The protection of life and property, trial by jury, the right of an open trial: these are principles of public liberty existing in the best form in the republican institutions in this country."

"Now I don't know what happened, but that's etched in stone," Lisa continued, "and when you go inside the building, we have banks producing fraudulent paperwork and showing them to judges that could never conceive that an officer of the court would show up with something so criminal and so fraudulent." Lisa told of her days observing at the county courthouse and her efforts to educate judges about the fraud, including her comment to the state supreme court, whose building she could see from the podium. ("Isn't that just beautiful?" she remarked of the courthouse.) She explained how she never paid a bill late in her life, how she faxed her modification applications to Chase Home Finance for eight months, how she tried her best to stop this horror from being visited upon her and her family, to no avail. She even told the story of September 11, her voice trembling again as she described the scene. "I could smell the jet fuel emanating from their bodies, and I saw the soot and glass particles in their eyes and in their skin. . . . And I thought this is the worst that I am ever going to see in my country. But I was wrong. Because that evil came from outside. And this evil was born within."

She closed by inviting homeowners to join them in fighting pretender lenders, criminal entities coming to evict them with false documents. "We don't want free homes," Lisa insisted. "We want to pay for our homes. We don't want to be victims, we don't want to be deadbeats, and we don't want to be taken advantage of anymore."

Amid cheers, Lisa walked back toward Michael, smiling and raising her eyebrows. Michael nodded back. And then everyone went off to lobby.

The capitol was a hive of activity, with lawmakers, staffers, and lobbyists scurrying across the marble floors. Rally participants broke off to find their legislators. Lisa told everyone to deliver written copies of their stories if nobody was available to hear them. Some ended up briefing staff, while others got to speak directly with state representatives or senators. Lisa stressed to her legislators how the stereotype of the foreclosure deadbeat needed an update. Hard-working Floridians exposed to unemployment or medical debt fell victim to the crisis and naively trusted mortgage servicers or lending companies. "If I pulled any of the things they pulled, I'd be hit with felony criminal charges," she told them. Michael stayed back with his family, handing in a written statement and coordinating other citizen lobbyists.

The Mortgage Justice Group was determined to confront Senator Bennett. First they were told they needed an appointment. But Bennett came out of his office and chatted amiably—until they mentioned the non-judicial foreclosure bill. As a homeowner named Tammy would later tell Michael, Bennett flipped out. "This is a wonderful bill! Why would you even want to fight for your home?" He stomped out of his office and down the hallway. The homeowners were stunned.

That day Bennett told a local news station that he put the non-judicial foreclosure bill on hold because the banking industry claimed he made it "too easy to protect the consumer." When Michael got back home, he posted a story on PigsAss.org listing all of Bennett's campaign contributions from bankers, but it wasn't necessary. The bill died in the Banking and Insurance

Committee on the final day of the legislative session, nine days after the Rally in Tally.

Whether it was the Freedom Ride imagery, the novelty of citizen-organized protest in a state known more for political apathy, or the sight of digital warriors leaving their houses and hitting the streets, the Rally in Tally got the media's attention. Television stations from Pensacola and Tampa Bay, local radio stations, and print outlets like the *Sunshine State News*, *Tampa Tribune*, and *Tampa Bay Times* all covered it, pushing something previously confined to niche blogs into the living rooms and onto the front porches of many Floridians. Michael described the rally at *4closure-Fraud* as the culmination of "one of the most influential months we have seen in the fight for justice since we started our crusade." And, he added, "May will be more interesting than April."

15

BY ANY MEANS NECESSARY

You don't live through a south Florida summer: you *endure* it. Clothing clings to sticky bodies, and the air is so thick it could be weighed on a scale. Everybody just slows down. The foreclosure fighters powered through the heat to keep the momentum going. They had no choice, as the horrors piled up. Rick and Sherry Rought of Gowen, Michigan, filed federal suit after Deutsche Bank broke into the home they purchased in a foreclosure auction, took their possessions, and changed the locks. Deutsche Bank said it thought the house was still abandoned. In another trash-out mix-up, Bank of America stole a woman's pet parrot. Glazy and Jose Ruscalleda had two lenders seeking to repossess their Miami condo, both claiming to hold the note. Keith and Julie Hanover never missed a payment, and Bank of America wasn't their lender, but the bank served them with a foreclosure notice anyway. The Great Foreclosure Machine also produced tragedy: police in Houston found a married couple shot to death in a murder/suicide. The note blamed the deaths on an imminent foreclosure.

At *Fraud Digest*, Lynn posted highlights of a case granted summary judgment in Pinellas County, where the judge learned that a different plaintiff was also pursuing summary judgment on the same home. Both plaintiffs filed an affidavit in support of summary judgment signed by the *same* robo-signer, as an officer of two separate corporations. Judge Anthony Rondolino, upon hearing the news, informed the plaintiff's attorney, "I don't have any confidence that any of the documents the Court's receiving on these mass foreclosures are valid."

The most terrifying story that summer concerned Keith Sadler of Stony Ridge, Ohio. Sadler faced foreclosure on a home he owned for twenty years, and he decided not to leave. With six members of an ad hoc group called the Toledo Foreclosure Defense League, Sadler barricaded the doors with PVC piping. Sadler webcast live from inside the house for six days, saying he wanted to wake up the nation, and *Foreclosure Hamlet* members linked to it. On May 7 a Wood County sheriff's SWAT team stormed the house, guns drawn, pushing everyone to the ground. The group was charged with obstruction of justice and criminal trespassing. Activists seethed that government resources were put into pulling people out of their homes while the real criminals went free.

Michael and Lisa highlighted these stories, as they had for months. But something changed after the Rally in Tally. National media still didn't care, but Florida reporters dug through Lisa and Michael's archives, finding leads for stories. One was Paola Iuspa-Abbott of the Miami trade publication *Daily Business Review*. A native of Argentina, Iuspa-Abbott recalled how breakdowns in the Argentinian legal system in the 1970s led to dictatorship and chaos. She believed the system was being similarly corrupted in the United States.

Iuspa-Abbott read a *4closureFraud* report about John Watson, a foreclosure defense attorney in Fort Lauderdale, who also represented mortgage servicer Aurora. He had foreclosure clients who were fighting Aurora, giving him an interest in both sides of the lawsuit. Watson's brother, Marshall C. Watson, ran one of the largest foreclosure mills in the state (they were the firm in Lynn Szymoniak's case). John Watson's clients confronted him over these ties, and he claimed no relationship with his brother's foreclosure mill, even though his address, office phone, and email were routed through Marshall C. Watson's firm. Iuspa-Abbott re-reported the *4closureFraud* account, adding that the homeowners filed a complaint to recoup the attorney fees they paid to Watson. *Daily Business Review* was not a likely candidate to break foreclosure fraud news, because much of its revenue derived from publishing notices of foreclosure from the law firms. But there was a wall between editorial and advertising, and Iuspa-Abbott had documented proof, so *Daily Business Review* ran the story.

A *Palm Beach Post* writer, Kim Miller, was watching, too. Miller had just transferred from the higher education desk and expected little from the real estate beat, just boring stories on home sales reports. But she found Lisa and Michael's sites, and they became primary sources. Lisa would send Miller email tips and find them in the newspaper a few days later. Miller wished she learned all this earlier: she and her husband bought a house at the top of the bubble, in 2005.

It wasn't just reporters. Insiders at a couple of foreclosure mills contacted Lisa, who started having clandestine meetings with them in restaurants. They felt guilty about what was happening but could only give hints, which Lisa ultimately couldn't prove. One insider told Lisa their mill lost an entire filing cabinet full of original notes.

Someone from MERS's communications department left a comment at *4closureFraud* insisting that MERS did not support filing lost note affidavits, even though they were found in MERS cases. Michael annotated the comment with a GIF of a cartoon character lighting himself on fire. Michael then found a private Facebook group for ex-DocX employees, and he published the Facebook pages of Brittany Snow, Tywanna Thomas, Korell Harp, and even the company's CEO, Lorraine O'Reilly Brown. A commenter named "Concerned" criticized Michael for making insinuations about the group. Michael pulled up his IP address; "Concerned" was writing from a DocX facility. A few DocX employees privately contacted Michael, asking him to take down the post because they didn't want future employers to see their names associated with fraud. Michael had no sympathy. To him, their job resulted in innocent people losing their homes, and he did not feel compelled to be nice about it.

Commenters sympathetic to banks—or perhaps industry-paid shills— claimed that Michael and Lisa were using technicalities to luck their way into free houses. If you didn't pay, they said, you should go. Lisa wasn't even living in her house at the time, so she always found that amusing. But the misaligned moral responsibility, where homeowners had to sacrifice everything to make payments in a depressed economy but companies without proof of ownership could use bogus documents to kick them out with impunity, angered her.

There used to be a social contract attached to the mortgage contract: borrowers agreed to pay no matter their hardships, and lenders agreed to foreclose only as a last resort. Borrowers still bore the first compulsion. Most of the homeowners Lisa interacted with demonstrated a deep desire to save their homes, saying they would forgo food or electricity or medical attention to make the mortgage payment. It made no rational or financial sense to plow through savings when the loan was designed to fail. But homeowners, their emotions poured into their homes, didn't care.

The same moral compulsion did not influence lenders, who drove homeowners into foreclosure with underhanded tactics designed to fatten their profits, and used phony documents to finish the job. Industry leaders warned of "strategic defaults," where homeowners deliberately missed payments to secure a government-supported loan modification. But it almost never happened, because homeowners could not be certain of receiving a modification and the consequences of default were so drastic. In fact, the highest-profile strategic default that summer came from the Mortgage Bankers Association, a trade group for the lending industry, which walked away from its ten-story headquarters in Washington. Its spokesman argued just a few months earlier that borrowers had to keep paying. The spokesman asked, "What about the message they will send to their family and their kids and their friends" if they defaulted? Indeed.

Some veterans of the foreclosure fraud blogosphere grumbled about the new wave's lack of credentials and its flair for grabbing attention. Steve Dibert, a loan auditor and former mortgage broker, considered rhetorical flourishes about tearing down the banking system simplistic, if not dangerous. He particularly had a problem with Neil Garfield overpromising that *pro se* litigants could win based on demanding notes or other strategies. In blog posts, he characterized Garfield as an Elmer Gantry–like figure, selling false hopes the courts would extinguish. Of course, Dibert also took on clients to help avoid foreclosure, but he claimed to give them more realistic expectations.

Foreclosure Hamlet regulars defended Garfield, noting that Dibert used to post at *Living Lies*, trolling for customers for his loan audits. Others claimed Dibert ripped people off when he was a broker, implicating him in the same system he was now fighting. Dibert shot back, calling the Garfield supporters uninformed amateurs, though he did say, "I won't hold it against Lisa Epstein who operates *Foreclosure Hamlet* because she is pretty cool." *Huffington Post* blogger Richard Zombeck sided with Dibert after Lisa asked him if he could request a Palm Beach County courthouse press pass for her, so she could film rocket docket cases. Zombeck thought the foreclosure fighters were asking him to lie to his editors, and he decided they were dilettantes. Battle lines were being drawn within the blogosphere.

Michael's willingness to attack led to collateral damage. Lisa was observing in court one day when Judge Meenu Sasser, out of nowhere, said, "Ms. Epstein, approach the bench!" Lisa uneasily wedged through the packed room of attorneys to the podium; she had nothing scheduled in her case that day. "I just want to let you know that civility and respect are very important to me," Judge Sasser said sternly. "And disrespect like you've shown is intolerable." After the dressing-down, a couple of attorneys asked Lisa what that was all about. "I have no idea," she replied.

Lisa called Dustin Zacks at Ice Legal, who in May became her defense attorney. Ice had its own run-ins with Judge Sasser—the firm's lawyers claimed she treated them with hostility—but they didn't understand why she would attack Lisa in open court. The next call she made was to Michael, who said, "Oh, yeah, that's probably my fault." That day Michael posted Judge Sasser's financial records, which any candidate for judicial election had to submit. The statements showed several mutual fund investments associated with banks, including equity stock in Bank of America. Though Ice Legal used the equity stock holding to try to get Judge Sasser disqualified from a Bank of America case, most mutual funds have some banking investments in them. To some, particularly Steve Dibert, the charges were gratuitous. But, lacking resources or power, Michael felt he had to call people out to get noticed.

Judge Sasser thought Lisa ran Michael's website, so she blasted her. A few weeks earlier, Sasser had denied Lisa's motion to dismiss her case. Impugning a judge's integrity was a sure way to lose cases. Michael put Lisa in a difficult spot, and future trips to Judge Sasser's courtroom became significantly more uncomfortable. But Lisa didn't recoil from the courthouse.

She started Moratorium Monday, a weekly call for a pause to foreclosures, so document fraud could be thoroughly assessed and a workable solution found to keep people in their homes. The protests weren't that large—five to ten people at most—but for months Lisa never missed a Monday, passing out leaflets and holding up signs.

Moratorium Monday often had a three-year-old participant: Jenna. Lisa couldn't afford to constantly leave her daughter with a babysitter. More important, too many nights were spent in front of screens, Lisa at the computer buried in research, Jenna left to television. Lisa had a profound desire to raise a child, even enduring a miscarriage to get there. Now she was losing her connection to motherhood because of an unrelated passion. So Jenna would come to Moratorium Monday with a sign and her own set of chants: "Banks got bailed out, we got sold out!" "Stop the looting, start the prosecuting!" They were just a pile of words to her, but fun to yell in public. One day Jenna showed off these chants at her babysitter and "second mom" Mary Delaguila's house, and Mary's son said, "Mom, how come you don't teach me any cool songs like that?"

Lisa brought Jenna inside the courtroom as well, finding her a spot on the benches to lie flat; the scar from the spina bifida surgery was still sensitive. Jenna would happily lie next to her mother, oblivious to the legal proceedings; Lisa would buy her an ice cream sandwich at the commissary. Others joined Lisa at court periodically, from Lynn to Grace Rucci to James Elder ("Jazzy" on *Foreclosure Hamlet*). But Jenna was her favorite companion.

To Lisa, the attorneys and bailiffs and file clerks were co-workers. But her reputation at the courthouse evolved after she filed an amicus brief in an HSBC case that contained one of the BOGUS documents. "A BOGUS ASSIGNMENT OF MORTGAGE filed in the public records is a key piece of information," Lisa wrote in the brief, "leading to conditions that make it difficult to identify the true owner of the property, to transfer title to another, for subsequent owners to obtain title insurance, and for an unbroken chain of possession to be determined."

Trial courts in Florida were not set up to receive an amicus brief; that was an appellate court technique. So the only strategy available was to file a motion to have the brief accepted. Lisa filed two motions, one in Port St. Lucie and one in Palm Beach.

At a hearing for the motion in Palm Beach, the bank's attorney kneeled down beside Lisa and asked, "Are you the homeowner?"

"No."

"Are you an attorney?"

"No, I have an amicus brief."

Lisa handed the attorney a hundred-page report, which included LPS's financial disclosure tying it to DocX, an old study on missing mortgage documents, the BOGUS assignment, and her amicus brief.

The attorney flipped through a few pages and said, "I'm going to step outside and call my office."

Bank attorneys always looked at her sideways after that. But anytime Lisa showed up in court, attorneys and judges paid a bit more attention to the law, or at least gave it more lip service. Maybe it didn't alter rulings, but it did make the Great Foreclosure Machine creak a little.

Plaintiffs had a new innovation in their cases: the "ta-da" endorsement. "Original notes" would magically appear on the day of the hearing, without time for the defense attorney to examine them. Previous notes were frequently unendorsed, in violation of the pooling and servicing agreements governing the securitization. But these new "original" notes would sprout endorsements on them. Evidence was manufactured to custom-fit whatever the banks needed. Lots of these suddenly appearing endorsements came from Countrywide, which like most of its mortgage originator counterparts was no longer technically in business. Lynn compiled dozens of examples.

As for the Florida Supreme Court's new verification standard, most law firms simply ignored the requirement. Shapiro & Fishman, a large foreclosure mill, tried to get a rehearing from the supreme court, stating outright, "Holders of the notes are often unfamiliar with the status of the notes." Lisa summarized the claim this way: "Your Honors, all we know is that someone, at some point, owed something to someone else." She teamed up with Nye Lavalle, writing a sixty-six-page response to Shapiro & Fishman. The verifications that law firms did produce looked odd. Michael found one from PNC Bank signed by an "authorized officer" (of what, it didn't say). It looked like the industry just switched from robo-signers to robo-verifiers.

Lisa wanted copies of these ta-da endorsements and weird verifications. But in June the file room supervisor handed Lisa an official-looking cease-and-desist order, forcing her to stop all personal scanning of documents. The supervisor gave Lisa two choices: go back to paying $1 per page, or cover the $22.75 hourly wage and benefits of one file clerk, who would pull files and monitor the scanning. Lisa considered it ridiculous to have a foreclosure document babysitter, especially because of the supervisor's reason: fees were necessary to keep the court running. The court could have tossed out every case without a proper verification, forcing mortgage companies to refile and pay a new $1,900 filing fee each time. And they were worried about $1 a page? Nevertheless, she doled out the $22.75 an hour for the document babysitter.

Lisa obsessed over what to do about blatant violations of the verification standard, something she helped get through the state supreme court. She emailed the chief judge in Palm Beach County and other court officials. One day she learned that the Palm Beach County Bar Association Professionalism Committee held monthly lunch meetings. Lisa contacted Kara Rockenbach, the committee co-chair, asking them to address this issue. "How is anyone to have faith in our judicial system," Lisa wrote, "if the opposing counsels' officers of the court can unilaterally elect to opt out of the Rules of the Court?"

Rockenbach wrote back, "I will add your issue to our agenda and can provide 5 minutes for presentation and 5 minutes for discussion."

The day of the meeting, Lisa and Michael (as usual, they went as a team) arrived at a West Palm Beach office building. Kara Rockenbach invited them into the cafeteria for lunch; Lisa helped herself to a Diet Sprite. "We're very excited for your presentation," Rockenbach said. "I hope you don't mind, we invited someone who's very interested in professionalism, Judge Sasser—"

Lisa spat her Diet Sprite all over the floor. Michael didn't move a muscle. When Rockenbach walked away, Lisa said, "How come you didn't react!"

"You can't react," Michael replied. But he knew exactly how bad this was: Lisa delivering a presentation to the presiding judge in her foreclosure case asserting that unprofessional, clueless magistrates stood mute in the face of widespread fraud.

The co-chairs of the committee told Judge Sasser that Lisa Epstein would be speaking, so that was probably why Sasser never showed. A relieved Lisa gave the presentation, focusing on the lack of verifications as well as fraudulent foreclosure documents. The attendees, including other local judges and an assistant U.S. attorney, made knowledgeable comments. One participant said to Michael, "It is all about awareness, and then sanctions can and should be applied."

On June 3 the state supreme court denied Shapiro & Fishman's rehearing on the verification procedure. A couple of days later Lisa was walking into the courthouse as Judge Sasser was walking out. Lisa described it to Michael later as one of the weirder moments she ever experienced, as the two locked eyes and exchanged looks like they were football quarterbacks from rival high schools.

Lynn Szymoniak helped draft subpoenas for the Jacksonville U.S. attorney's office to trustees like Deutsche Bank. They asked for the mortgage, note, endorsement, assignment, and title policy on the roughly five thousand loans in each trust. Nobody ever wanted to see these files, but it was a critical step in unraveling the scheme. Fabricated foreclosure documents were the cover-up; failing to transfer mortgages to the trusts was the original sin. And Lynn was hearing that the trusts had almost none of the paperwork in their files. Where trustees should have delivered 25,000 documents, they were delivering twelve. Lynn learned through a Bloomberg report that prosecutors in the Jacksonville office interviewed April Charney in connection with the case. The U.S. attorney told Charney they were working on formal grand jury depositions for employees of Lender Processing Services and DocX.

On June 4 Lynn filed her *qui tam* lawsuit in U.S. district court in South Carolina. Another would get filed in North Carolina, and the two were eventually consolidated. Lynn's lawyers rewrote much of the complaint but used her evidence to allege that the government was defrauded. "The defendants concealed that the notes and the assignments were never delivered to the MBS trusts and disseminated false and misleading statements to the investors, including the U.S. government," read the complaint. Government investors paid for the document cover-up so banks could prove standing to foreclose. Other parts of the government paid off mortgage guarantees based on invalid notes and assignments. The heart of Lynn's case was that the industry broke the housing market by screwing up securitization, with the government among those paying the price.

The Justice Department got involved right away, setting up big meetings with fifteen different agencies, including the FBI, the Department of Housing and Urban Development (HUD), the special inspector general for the Troubled Asset Relief Program, and the Federal Housing Finance Administration. Some around the table simply identified themselves as "consultants," without specifying whom they consulted for. All the prosecutors boasted about their prowess in sending bad guys to jail; Lynn didn't know these people, or whom to believe. But her lawyers were happy, because

Justice Department involvement meant that DoJ would supply the resources for pretrial proceedings.

Lynn's new contacts at Justice asked for her help in drafting confidential information disclosures, or CIDs, which functioned as requests to produce evidence. Justice needed one CID for each of the eighteen defendants in the case. They took hours and hours to draft, and after Lynn submitted them, the team in D.C. would give notes: "Can you pare this down to the thirty most pressing issues?"

Despite these glimmers of progress, at home Lynn was having trouble paying her electric bill. A light fixture in the kitchen let water through when it rained. The air-conditioning was busted. Lynn couldn't afford payments on the condo, and it fell into foreclosure. The complaint, from foreclosure mill David J. Stern, didn't include a verification affidavit, required by the Florida Supreme Court's rules. Lynn contested the nonverified complaint. She now had two foreclosure suits, separate from the criminal and civil cases. And in April, disaster struck. Lynn's daughter, Molly, a freshman at Hofstra University, had a massive aneurysm. The chances of surviving such an event were minimal, but somehow Molly hung on. Lynn would succumb to tears at random moments. The family was fortunate Molly survived, but medical bills ate into their finances further.

Eventually Lynn stumbled into opportunity. A homeowner from New York with DocX documents faced summary judgment, the final step before eviction and sale. He contacted Lynn and asked, "Would you give us an affidavit and be our expert?"

Lynn asked for $300. She built a standard affidavit template, with her name, her legal background and training, her expert witness experience, and links to articles about mortgage securitization and foreclosures. She examined the mortgage assignments and other supporting documents, looking for falsehoods. That wasn't a terribly taxing job; the myriad problems were by now familiar. Lynn would list the errors—robo-signing, assignments executed after the foreclosure filing, whatever—and write, "For all of the reasons set forth above, I conclude that the Assignments herein are fraudulent." This wouldn't automatically save someone's home, as Lynn made clear to homeowners. But it was successful enough in raising questions to hold off summary judgment in cases that might otherwise race through the system. After the first affidavit, word got around among foreclosure defense attorneys, and more requests came in, first from New York and then from Florida. They brought in enough money for Lynn to pay utilities and keep things stable.

The research led Lynn deeper into the bowels of the Great Foreclosure Machine. For an affidavit on a loan from BAC Home Loans, she uncovered several new document shops in Texas. She found a series of trusts from Ace Securities, with documents produced by Ocwen, right in West Palm Beach. So she researched everything Ocwen put out. Each trustee, servicer, "default services" company, and originator led Lynn to a new bounty of documents, and she surfed from one to the next.

Lynn's front room filled with more documents. She took out all the furniture except for the dining table, and piled up the binders. There were collections for each trust and each robo-signer, to easily identify the signature variations. The printer kept running out of ink, prompting more trips to Office Max. Before it finally keeled over, it churned out enough evidence to implicate virtually every low-level signer, supervisor, and executive at every mortgage-related business in America.

Lynn had to keep some research to herself. The bad news about *qui tam* cases, aside from recovering money for the federal government instead of homeowners, was that they were filed under seal. So when she communicated with Damian Figueroa, whom she still technically served as a lawyer, she could not divulge anything about the case. Damian sent Lynn news about a *qui tam* suit filed in Nevada against MERS, the electronic mortgage registry. She played it coy. "Have you been approached by anyone about filing a *qui tam* against Stern and IndyMac? I cannot get anyone interested— but I think they should be interested."

Damian replied, "You told me to keep it between us. You would be the only person who would take me serious [*sic*] and not think I am nuts!"

"Just so you know that I have *not* filed a qui tam," Lynn volunteered. It was unclear whether she was referring to a case against Stern or a *qui tam* in general. "So if you are approached, you should consider this. Despite all the hype, no one is beating down doors to help us."

A week later someone did beat down Damian's door. An attorney in Fort Lauderdale was organizing a class action against Stern. Damian asked Lynn, "He might ask me to be the class rep for it. Does it conflict on anything we plan to do in the future?"

Lynn released Damian from her retainer by replying, "I cannot get my group to act—please take any opportunity you can to get justice."

Damian hired Kenneth Eric Trent, an attorney in Fort Lauderdale, and they filed a class action against Stern's law firm. Kim Miller at the *Palm Beach Post* wrote a big story on it, noting all the backdated and fabricated assignments in Stern cases. Miller asked Judge Meenu Sasser about it, and the judge claimed, "I haven't seen any widespread problem." The bloggers were certain that would come back to haunt Sasser.

The suit was the latest in a host of setbacks for Stern, who endured bad press over his waterfront mansion and stable of sports cars, while an old Florida bar complaint over fee-gouging hit the blogs. Damian's new lawyer, Trent, released a deposition of Shannon Smith, a Stern notary, whose signature, two big looping initials, looked exactly like the signature of her colleague Cheryl Samons. A separate class action alleged that Stern refused to stop foreclosure on a couple who never missed a payment, instead demanding $17,000 in legal fees. DJSP Enterprises, the firm's publicly traded parent company, was hit with a suit from investors alleging lies about future profits, which exposed ugly secrets like an SEC disclosure in which David Stern insisted that, no matter how hard the government tried to mitigate foreclosures, he would find a "way to create a profit center." The controversies hurt the company's referral business, and the stock tanked.

Most damaging to Stern, the Florida attorney general's office was investigating. June Clarkson and Theresa Edwards asked Lynn and Lisa for documents: "Find me fifty backdated Stern assignments," or "Find me documents where the same person signs for different banks." Lisa and Lynn busily honored the requests, sometimes seeking help to run searches from local fraud researcher Michael Olenick, Damian, or any visitor to *Foreclosure Hamlet* willing to pitch in. Between that and the paperwork flowing in from homeowners who heard about the investigation, June and Theresa's offices started to look like Lynn Szymoniak's front room, with foreclosure files scattered everywhere.

Tony Webster was one of Lisa and Lynn's unofficial research assistants, a *Foreclosure Hamlet* member from Brevard County, near Orlando. Tony would drop a letter in the mailbox of every new foreclosure victim in his area, urging them to join *Foreclosure Hamlet* and fight their cases. He also sent daily blog links to his county's clerk of courts, Scott Ellis, highlighting bad assignments and fraudulent notes: "Our public land records are being turned into a public sewer system!" Ellis was not amused, replying, "I'm not an investigative agency. You claim fraud, no law enforcement agency seems interested." So Tony Webster got law enforcement interested.

Thanks to Tony, Lisa drove up to Orlando and sat for ninety minutes with special agent Michael Giddens of the Florida Department of Law Enforcement, detailing the criminal frauds. Representative Darren Soto, who spoke at the Rally in Tally, showed up, too. Giddens asked for case files in his central Florida jurisdiction. Lisa put it on the list; she'd have to go up to Orlando again to dig through the courthouse file rooms.

Finally, in early August, after an eight-month investigation, Andy Kroll at *Mother Jones* released his story on David Stern. It was among the first pieces of reporting from national media about foreclosure mills. The story pulled together a lot of threads: the Ice Legal deposition with Cheryl Samons on impossible notary stamps, Judge Rondolino's statement that he had "no confidence" in foreclosure mill documents, Damian Figueroa's class action, the investor lawsuit, the old bar complaint, and Stern's incalculable wealth from foreclosures. Kroll explained how the mills—and the servicers they worked for—had financial incentives to foreclose rather than help homeowners. And he uncovered wild details about life inside Stern's offices, with contests among lawyers to see who could foreclose fastest, "routinely doctored" case files, and job security based mostly on kicking people out of their homes. Stern was depicted as repugnant, subject to a sexual harassment lawsuit for grabbing female employees, making lewd jokes, and miming sex with them. He settled that suit out of court.

Though some of the information in the *Mother Jones* story had been on the blogs for months, it collected everything on Stern in one place and painted a damning portrait of homes being illegally seized. Florida attorney general Bill McCollum, days away from a close gubernatorial primary against health care executive Rick Scott, took the opportunity to announce new investigations of Stern and two other mills (Marshall C. Watson and Shapiro & Fishman) over "improper documentation . . . filed with Florida courts to speed up foreclosure processes." June and Theresa would handle that inquiry, too.

A couple of weeks later McCollum lost the primary. A new attorney general was on the way. But none of the activists paid any attention, because the walls were shaking.

Florida judges started to get it. Summary judgments were reversed. Motions to dismiss were granted. Foreclosures were stopped. Judge Tepper dismissed a Pasco County case with prejudice, meaning it couldn't be refiled. Judge Traynor did the same in St. Johns County: "The plaintiff is not a proper party to the suit." Judge Bailey in Miami-Dade imposed sanctions on Florida Default Law Group, thundering in her order, "I want responsible attorneys who meet the basic standards of knowing what the Sam Hill is going on in their files." Lisa started keeping a list.

With the judges more receptive, Lisa had another idea: attend the Florida Bar Association's annual convention at the lavish Boca Raton Resort and Club, and educate more attorneys. Lisa asked the bar association if it could accommodate a seminar about foreclosure fraud, but a representative said all the rooms were taken. So Lisa called the hotel and asked, "What's the closest conference room to the bar association convention as possible?" The hotel told her she could take the Mizner Room, right next door.

Lisa dragged Michael along to reserve the room. The resort's giant pink tower would have stood out anywhere but in Boca. Lisa and Michael walked into the ornate lobby; the marble floors and vaulted ceilings might as well have been wallpapered with $100 bills. Convention staff showed Lisa and Michael the conference room and told them it was free to rent for the day; all they had to do was spend $2,000 or more for catering. *How are we going to spend $2,000 on food?* Lisa thought. Then she saw the menu. A quart of orange juice was $36. Twelve cookies were $48.

They bought the bare minimum to reach the $2,000 threshold, and it wasn't enough for a decent spread. Lisa supplemented it with items from Dunkin' Donuts and McDonald's, probably a first for the Boca Resort. Carol Asbury, *4closureFraud*'s underwriter, paid the bill. The team also offset costs with a "fraudulent document graveyard." For $20, you could have the foreclosure document of your choosing pasted to a headstone and displayed before bar association attorneys.

On the day of the convention, Lisa distributed information cards surreptitiously in the other conference rooms, hinting that their seminar was an official bar event. Dozens of people came, maybe for the high-priced cookies and juice. Most stayed for the presentations, from the likes of Lynn, Carol Asbury, and Matt Weidner. Lisa and Michael handed out awards to the heroes of the crisis—people like April Charney, Tom Ice, and judges Jennifer Bailey and Michael Traynor. The sign-in list included judges, attorneys, and elected officials. Even Alex Sink, the Democratic candidate for governor, stopped by. Two men dressed entirely in black and wearing wireless earpieces stood in the back. Were they Secret Service? It wasn't clear. But Michael recorded the event for a *4closureFraud* live stream, and when he pulled the report of who watched, he found visitors from the Department of Homeland Security, the CIA, and eop.gov, the Web server for the executive office of the president of the United States.

Michael wrote a gushing reminiscence of the convention seminar:

> I never thought that being in Foreclosure could be so invigorating and rewarding. . . .
>
> Since I started this process over TWO years ago, I have done things I would of [*sic*] never thought possible. I have met people who are so real/true to themselves/passionate on what is right and what is wrong . . . and have come to a realization of it is not about me anymore. It is about making a difference in this crazy corrupt world we are living in.
>
> Now, this is never who I was. For the most part, I never really gave a hoot about anyone else. Now I find myself addicted to helping/educating/networking/sharing with anyone and everyone who will listen, hell, I try to do all that even if they don't!

A few days after the convention, Lisa was with Jenna in the Palm Beach County courthouse as the foreclosure division took a midday break. She was packing up when Judge Sasser approached her. "Is that your daughter?" Sasser asked, motioning to Jenna, who was lying flat on one of the benches.

"Yeah, that's my little love bug."

Judge Sasser asked if Jenna had a medical condition, and Lisa explained her spina bifida surgery and the rehabilitation process. The judge nodded. "I know what it's like to have a child with medical problems." In fact, the judge told Lisa, she had lost a child.

16

DOWNFALL

As the Florida judiciary and attorney general's office grew skeptical of the Great Foreclosure Machine, the state legislature had other ideas. Instead of the aborted plan to push foreclosures out of the courts, lawmakers authorized $9.6 million to bring back retired judges, with the stated goal of reducing the backlog of roughly half a million foreclosure cases by 62 percent within a year. If foreclosure divisions were pursuing a "rocket docket" before, the legislature supercharged it to break the speed of sound.

The only way to unload cases in the manner the legislature decreed was to finalize summary judgments as fast as possible. Accuracy of the evidence became a secondary consideration. In July alone, Orange and Osceola Counties completed 1,319 cases, the chief judge for the area boasted to the *Florida Bar News*. Palm Beach County's chief judge maintained that courts had to "clear the foreclosure cases so that vacant and dilapidated homes can go back on the market." Of course, there were no buyers for distressed homes in moribund Florida, and lenders didn't like to pay for maintenance; the likely outcome of flushing foreclosures through the courts was more properties in ruin.

Lisa and Michael got reports from the trenches. Two-minute trials were reduced to twenty seconds. Judges routinely declined to read the case file. One retired judge in Miami-Dade denied dozens of requests to stop foreclosure sales, actually saying out loud, "What is this HAMP that these people keep claiming they are approved for," unaware of the federal government's signature loan modification program. Another judge in Palm Beach lectured from the bench, "I know all about sickness, I know all about divorce,

I know all about anything else," commanding that homeowners stop making excuses for nonpayment (excuses by banks for noncompliance with the laws of evidence were still allowed). Attorney Mark Stopa saw a judge in one of his cases file final judgment *before* the hearing. Other summary judgments were entered without informing the homeowner.

With no courtroom space, hearings were held wherever a free spot could be found: judge's chambers, a conference room. In Broward County they did it in the hallway. A judge there told a homeowner her job was to "dispose of cases," refusing to stop a foreclosure even after the borrower and lender agreed to postponement. Because the retired judges were paid specifically to reduce caseloads, they had a financial incentive to dispossess people.

This was wonderful news for the Great Foreclosure Machine. Document processors got additional business manufacturing mortgage assignments and note endorsements. The foreclosure mill law firms who hired them pumped out cases and earned fees faster. Servicers who hired *them* recouped their fees upon foreclosure sale. Trustees finally got troublesome loans off their books, pinning losses on investors. And evidence of the whole scheme—securitization FAIL, violations of tax and securities laws, broken chains of title, and invalid standing to foreclose—could be buried, shoveled over by retired judges cashing a check to bang their gavels and say no a lot.

Worst of all, Lisa heard that the courts didn't want anyone watching this embarrassing violation of hundreds of years of civil jurisprudence. Signs on the doors of the makeshift courtrooms said that only parties to the cases and their attorneys could attend; critics claimed that violated the First Amendment. April Charney snuck *Rolling Stone* journalist Matt Taibbi into a conference room/courtroom in Jacksonville. The presiding judge, A.C. Soud, bragged to a local paper that his job was to finish twenty-five cases an hour (even though in the very first motion Taibbi saw, the plaintiff both claimed ownership of the note and admitted that it was lost, all in the space of a few paragraphs). Taibbi tried to talk to a homeowner after the session ended, and Judge Soud called everyone back into the room, lecturing that nobody should talk to the journalist. April got an email an hour later from Judge Soud, threatening her with contempt for bringing in a reporter to observe.

Lisa couldn't fathom that the situation in the courts could ever get *worse*, but it did. Judges with actual experience hearing foreclosure cases were incensed about their courtrooms being turned into crime scenes, but homeowners had to hit the lottery and draw the right magistrate to receive anything resembling justice. Saddest of all, retired judges appealed to a twisted sense of fairness, denouncing homeowners who got to stay in houses "for free." That perceived benefit, a side effect of lenders failing to follow established legal practices, trumped the rule of law.

Lisa contacted Laurence Tribe, the well-known Harvard law professor (he taught President Obama), who was serving as "senior counselor for access to justice" at the Justice Department. Tribe's portfolio at DoJ focused on the challenges of providing legal services to the poor, but Lisa stressed how the rocket docket denied due process. To her amazement, an associate named Daniel Olmos emailed her back, and in September they had the first of several conference calls. Olmos followed up with requests for information on the rocket docket and foreclosure mill misconduct. Tribe had clout, Lisa thought, so she jumped on the information requests.

In darker moments, Lisa wondered whether she would ever make a dent in stopping a broken justice system. But the rocket docket would soon seize up, not because Florida suddenly recognized the damage it was inflicting but because foreclosure fraud would finally burst into the public consciousness.

4closureFraud routinely posted depositions from mortgage industry employees across the country, whether document processors like Nationwide Title or foreclosure mills like David J. Stern. But the two that cracked the case involved robo-signers who worked directly for mortgage servicers: Jeffrey Stephan and Beth Cottrell.

The Stephan revelation originated years earlier. Jim Kowalski was a straight-arrow assistant state attorney prosecuting homicides and sex crimes until 1996, when he moved to the defense side, joining a small firm in Jacksonville specializing in consumer fraud. In 2005 Kowalski's client Robert Jackson paid his mortgage with a certified cashier's check. GMAC Mortgage, initially the financing arm of General Motors but subsequently America's fifth-largest mortgage servicer, returned the cashier's check for insufficient funds. That's impossible: you pay for a cashier's check up front.

Jackson received a foreclosure notice, along with an affidavit in support of mortgage indebtedness. As a trial lawyer accustomed to seeking discovery, Kowalski wanted to depose the person who signed the affidavit. Her name was Margie Kwiatanowski, from Hatboro, Pennsylvania. Kowalski went up to take her testimony, and it became obvious within a couple of minutes that she knew absolutely nothing about the case. Despite signing a sworn statement certifying the veracity of all elements of the loan file, in reality Kwiatanowski simply double-checked a summary of the payment history against computer records she didn't generate. "Did you sign the document in front of a notary?" Kowalski asked.

"No," Kwiatanowski replied, explaining how she would leave documents in a folder that the notary picked up later. She signed hundreds of affidavits a day as a "limited signing officer"—what Matt Weidner would years later term a robo-signer.

Kowalski immediately flew back to Jacksonville and moved for sanctions for fraud upon the court. And in early 2006 the judge agreed that GMAC submitted false testimony, awarding $8,134.55 in legal fees to the defense and demanding that the servicer fix affidavit processes within thirty days, so they represented actual reviews of the material facts. GMAC promised it would.

Kowalski didn't realize that Kwiatanowski admitted to a standard practice replicated throughout the industry, as cover for securitization FAIL. But he did learn that wherever you find process problems in foreclosures, inevitably you find substantive problems. Nothing the banks claimed could be believed. And despite the sanctions, GMAC never changed procedures. In fact, Margie Kwiatanowski got a promotion, and a new employee slid into the limited signing officer role: Jeffrey Stephan.

Nearly four years later, GMAC would be caught again, this time by Thomas Ice. His wife, Ariane, kept finding Stephan's name on GMAC affidavits. So in December 2009 Ice Legal brought Stephan to West Palm Beach for a deposition, conducted by one of their young attorneys, Chris Immel. Stephan and his thirteen-member "document execution team" signed documents for GMAC and also for MERS, on behalf of dozens of mortgage originators; said Stephan, "It's too many entities for me to actually quote."

"How many documents would you say you sign on an average week?" Immel asked.

"I'd say a round number of 10,000. That's just an estimate, of course."

There are 21.7 workdays in a month, on average. So that meant Stephan was signing his name 460 times in an eight-hour day, or 57.5 times an hour, assuming no breaks of any kind. Consequently, he could spend a little over a minute on every document he signed. Maybe the documents were accurate, maybe not; the evidence strongly suggested the latter, as did the swift process of manufacture. But certainly Jeffrey Stephan would have no idea in one minute of review.

"So these documents wouldn't be actually executed on your own personal knowledge?" Immel pressed.

"Right."

The standard affidavit in support of mortgage indebtedness begins with this sentence: "The statements appearing herein are based on the Affiant's personal knowledge."

Stephan explained that foreclosure mills created all the documents he signed; the document execution team just put their names to paper, without consulting specific business records or anything in the complaint. And notaries still weren't present when team members signed; they didn't even notarize on the same *day* as the signatures. Stephan answered everything matter-of-factly, placidly describing the quotidian toil of office drones like him: *I take this, I sign that.* He did not display any recognition of the criminal aspect of his job duties.

Ice Legal forwarded the Stephan deposition to Michael Redman, just one among many. Michael posted it at *4closureFraud* on March 22, 2010. "These depositions would be comical if it weren't for the fact that people are losing their homes," he wrote. The Stephan deposition lingered in public for months, and substantiation of GMAC's illegal practices lingered for years, with nobody taking notice. And then an attorney named Thomas Cox stumbled upon them.

Cox practiced law for over thirty years, at one point working for Maine National Bank in commercial loan transactions. In those days, small-business loan guarantees were often backed by a mortgage on the owner's house. During the savings and loan crisis, many loans went bad, and Tom Cox had to prosecute the foreclosures and shut down the businesses. Maine's a small state, and Cox personally knew a lot of the people he had to evict.

He battled depression for years, bruised from acting as the undertaker for someone else's dream. He even gave up the law for a while.

In spring 2008 Cox returned to part-time pro bono work. He signed up with Maine Attorneys Saving Homes (MASH), a project run out of the small nonprofit Pine Tree Legal Assistance. MASH made Cox the volunteer program coordinator; he would review foreclosure cases and refer them out to pro bono lawyers. That forced him to peruse every file. And he couldn't believe what he was seeing. His foreclosure work ended by 2000, so the practices in these cases were brand-new to him and, in his mind, offensive.

Cox spent a year in referrals, reading the files and noting patterns. Then, in summer 2009, Nicolle Bradbury's case came over the transom. She lived in a tiny wood-framed house across from a construction site in Denmark, a western Maine town near the New Hampshire border. The purchase price in 2003 was just $75,000, and from the looks of the squalor, she overpaid. Bradbury lost her job and could no longer pay the mortgage. Fannie Mae, the loan owner, moved for summary judgment; GMAC was the servicer. The man who signed the affidavit in support of summary judgment was Jeffrey Stephan. Cox fixated on that name; he had seen it dozens of times.

MASH didn't have any lawyers in that rural area, which was about as far as you could get from the continental United States while still being in it. So Cox decided to take it, his first foreclosure case in a decade. The year of examining shoddy files made him progressively angrier, and he craved an opportunity to fight. Stephan's title, "limited signing officer," implicitly admitted that he knew nothing about the underlying facts of the case, Cox alleged. Plus the amount due Stephan verified was wrong; it didn't fit the amortization schedule.

Judge Keith Powers, an old colleague (Cox was involved in hiring Powers at his first law firm), didn't want to hear it. In January 2010 Judge Powers approved summary judgment on everything except the amount due, keeping the case alive by a thread. Cox thought the order stank. He walked into a colleague's office at Pine Tree Legal Assistance and vowed, "I'm not going to let this stand."

He served a notice of deposition for Jeffrey Stephan. At first GMAC and Fannie Mae's lawyers wouldn't allow it; maybe someone remembered Stephan's deposition with Ice Legal a month before. But Cox issued a letter rogatory in Maine court to compel Stephan's testimony in Pennsylvania, a rare tactic typically used between countries to subpoena witnesses out of jurisdiction. The plaintiffs were caught flat-footed. The judge signed the letter, and a Pennsylvania court issued the subpoena for Stephan.

A couple of months before the deposition, Chet Randle, who ran MASH, stopped by Cox's office. "Somebody beat you to it," Randle said. "They deposed Stephan down in Florida." Cox got a copy of the Ice Legal deposition. He contacted Chris Immel and had several lengthy discussions, which helped him prepare questions. Through a lawyer listserv, Jim Kowalski contacted Cox about his deposition four years earlier with Margie Kwiatanowski. Cox recognized the name; Ice Legal got Stephan to admit that Kwiatanowski was his boss. Incredibly, Cox was able to quickly locate four years of significant evidence of GMAC's illegal schemes, but nobody in law enforcement ever did. Cox alerted the Maine attorney general's office that they should have someone sit in on the deposition. Nobody ever responded.

On June 7, 2010, Cox arrived at the law offices of Lundy Flitter Beldecos & Berger in Narberth, Pennsylvania, for the deposition. GMAC didn't even have a lawyer attend; she was conferenced in on the phone, with a local attorney standing in her place. Despite the Ice deposition, Cox thought GMAC seemed remarkably unprepared for his questioning. During the ninety-minute interview, Cox steered the same path as Chris Immel, getting Stephan to admit he signed up to ten thousand documents a month without personal knowledge of anyone's case; nor did he or his document execution team check the physical data for accuracy. "I compare the principal balance. I review the interests. I take a look at the late charges," Stephan said. "That's about it."

"So is it correct that you do not know whether any other part of the affidavit you sign is true?"

"That could be correct."

Cox raised his voice a little. "Is it correct?"

"That is correct."

After GMAC's representative left the room, Cox asked the court reporter if he could get a rush copy of the transcript within two days. "It'll cost you $300," the transcriber said.

Cox passed that transcript to several lawyers, including Jim Kowalski and the Maine attorney general. The transcript wound up on April Charney's listserv, where Matt Weidner found it. He posted the Stephan deposition on his site on June 15, eight days after it was taken. Michael Redman saw it and cross-posted it at *4closureFraud*.

Shortly thereafter, Cox got a call from a tall-building lawyer newly attached to the Nicolle Bradbury case. The TBL angrily questioned how the Stephan deposition got leaked to websites. "I don't have to tell you anything," Cox said. GMAC never called Matt Weidner and demanded he take it down; if they did, he would have told them to fuck off. But GMAC did attempt to block public release of the transcript and to sanction Cox for "malicious dissemination." Cox counterfiled to dismiss the case based on fraud. "When Stephan says in an affidavit that he has personal knowledge of the facts stated in his affidavits, he doesn't," Cox wrote in his motion. "When he says that he has custody and control of the loan documents, he doesn't. When he says that he is attaching 'a true and accurate' copy of a note or a mortgage, he has no idea if that is so, because he does not look at the exhibits."

GMAC "replaced" the Stephan affidavit with a new one. And the TBLs had one response: Nicolle Bradbury didn't pay her damn mortgage. But Judge Powers ruled against the TBLs. Even the new affidavit was flawed; it didn't include the street address of the home, among other inaccuracies. And GMAC's practices irked the judge. "The Court is particularly troubled by the fact that Stephan's deposition is not the first time that GMAC's high-volume and careless approach to affidavit signing has been exposed," Judge Powers wrote, referring to both Jim Kowalski's case and Ice Legal's Stephan deposition. "It is well past the time for such practices to end."

Judge Powers vacated the summary judgment with prejudice. He told GMAC to pay $27,000 in attorney fees. He wouldn't force a takedown of the transcript, because the Ice Legal deposition was on the Internet anyway. And GMAC must have gotten plenty nervous. Several other GMAC cases in Cox's office settled quickly. Michael started seeing multiple users from GMAC spending hours on *4closureFraud*, reading everything GMAC-related on the site. Then Lisa discovered Florida Default Law Group withdrawing a series of affidavits of indebtedness, all of them signed by Jeffrey Stephan. The notice of withdrawal spelled it out: FDLG "has recently been notified that the information in the affidavit may not have been properly verified by the affiant." Lisa posted this at *Foreclosure Hamlet* and reported it to June and Theresa at the state attorney general's office. They asked for all of Lisa's Stephan-related documents. Lisa put out an APB to her network and collected sixty-nine documents in a few days. As Lynn was searching, she found a mortgage assignment Stephan had signed on *her own condo*, a document she'd never seen before.

On September 20, 2010, Michael and Lisa were trying to find shelter for Ramsey Harris, a sixty-two-year-old disabled vet evicted from his rental home in Rocky Point, Florida. Harris was initially told he could stay in the foreclosed home while he set up financing to buy it from the bank. But suddenly the bank informed him on Tuesday he would be evicted on Thursday, and subsequently threw all of Harris's belongings on the side of the road in the rain.

Michael was furious. He looked into every aspect of the case. The foreclosure was fraudulent; Harris lived in the property but never received a summons, a violation of state law. The assignment of mortgage was dated six months after the suit was filed from Bear Stearns, which had already collapsed. Liquenda Allotey, a known robo-signer, affirmed the assignment, but the signature differed from other Allotey signatures. Michael and colleagues exchanged dozens of emails, trying to get Harris a place to stay and legal representation. But while Michael was working so diligently on Ramsey Harris, the thing he'd been trying to provoke for over a year dropped: GMAC announced a suspension of all its foreclosures in twenty-three judicial foreclosure states while they investigated the faulty Stephan affidavits.

Lisa was having her car serviced when she gazed up at the TV screen in the lobby. "GMAC Moratorium on Foreclosure Sales," read the headline on CNN. At that instant, Michael called her cell phone. "This is it!"

Robo-signing was just one cover-up for the banks' lack of standing to foreclose. But Lisa and Michael believed this was finally the crowbar in the window. So many media outlets declined to publish their claims because the banks never admitted to problems. Now GMAC admitted it. Lisa tested her newly serviced car engine by speeding home. She and Michael planned to bombard the media with links to their evidence. But before they could, the media started contacting them. The *Financial Times* asked Michael questions for a story. So did a reporter for the *Washington Post*, who visited Stephan's house to ask him about the charges (Stephan "said only 'No, thanks' before retreating inside"). Local media already valued them as a source: Paola Iuspa-Abbott of the *Daily Business Review* ran a profile two weeks before, with a picture of Michael and Lisa, arms folded, on the rooftop of the courthouse. Now the national media were following suit.

Eight days after GMAC's announcement, *4closureFraud* posted video of Jeffrey Stephan's Ice Legal deposition. Viewers were shocked to see Stephan dressed for legal testimony in a black heavy metal T-shirt and jeans, with spiky blond hair and a chin-strap beard completing the look. Matt Taibbi wrote that Stephan looked like "an advanced-age Beavis or Butt-head." Toward the end of the video, Stephan burst out laughing; he later made a paper airplane and sailed it toward the camera. Commenters at various sites that cross-posted the video were horrified. "That can't be real," one exclaimed.

It wasn't real. Lisa Epstein played Jeffrey Stephan; Michael Redman played the lawyer asking questions off-camera. They shot it at Carol Asbury's office, the one with the telemarketers on the first floor. Lisa was getting into costume in the bathroom when one of the telemarketers came in, took one look, and helped her put on the chin-strap beard. Lisa couldn't hold character by the end, her loud cackle reverberating off the walls. But despite how farcical it looked, the deposition initially fooled everyone.

Lisa and Michael weren't just beating the banks; they were having more fun.

"How do we keep this momentum going?" Lynn wrote to Damian, Nye, Lisa, and Michael the day after GMAC's announcement.

Michael replied: "Keep republishing the most relevant articles that we already have. It is all there. We just need to lead them to it. We have been preparing for this moment for a year."

The first thing Michael reposted was a deposition from a Chase Home Finance employee named Beth Cottrell, adding the line, "This deposition is even better than Jeffrey Stephan's depo."

Chase's downfall tracks back to Nye Lavalle. In 2009 he shuttled between south Florida and Savannah, Georgia, working with a woman battling foreclosure on several vacation properties. He would write briefs by day, and hang out at night with his friend Paul DeAgnes in Atlanta on his big yacht. DeAgnes had a friend in Hilton Head, South Carolina, not far from Savannah, who was having trouble with his loan. Nye told Paul to send the guy over.

The man visited Nye and brought along a friend, Dan Junk, an expert in electronic legal discovery with a similar mortgage problem. Dan tried to rescind his loan after learning that the originator, American Home Mortgage Servicing, went out of business. Though he followed all specifications for a rescission, the servicer, Citi Mortgage, wouldn't let him out. Nye and Dan struck up a friendship and started collaborating. They would build out the facts of foreclosure cases and work with lawyers to introduce them into courts.

In May 2010 Dan and Nye received an Ice Legal deposition with Beth Cottrell, an operations supervisor at Chase Home Finance. Cottrell's name appeared on a replacement affidavit of amounts due and owing in Lisa's case. The eight-person Chase team in Columbus, Ohio (which included Whitney Cook and Christina Trowbridge, Lisa's robo-signers), signed eighteen thousand documents a month, from assignments to affidavits to allonges. And like every other robo-signer, Cottrell had no knowledge of what she was signing, leaving that to whatever attorney had created the document. "I have personal knowledge that my staff has personal knowledge," she said.

In the case in question, there were two "original" notes filed on the same property. "So when you signed the affidavit and said 'Plaintiff is entitled to enforce the note and mortgage,'" Ice Legal attorney Dustin Zacks asked Cottrell, "you didn't know which of these two notes you were referring to?"

"No," Cottrell answered.

Of particular interest to Nye and Dan Junk was how the documents would get notarized. Cottrell would sign a stack of documents, put them in a folder, and hand them over to the notaries, who stamped and signed everything later. Nye read over that part and said to Dan, "This is notary fraud in the state of Ohio." That was important because Dan Junk's sister was Jennifer Brunner, the Ohio secretary of state. And secretaries of state had jurisdiction over notaries.

Brunner served as a common pleas judge in Franklin County, Ohio, for several years, and during the housing bubble she saw plenty of odd foreclosure cases. Either the defendant was never served papers, or the plaintiff would get suddenly substituted, or the bank claimed they lost the note. Brunner always wondered how a bank could lose a note. But most homeowners never mounted a defense, so there wasn't much she could do. As secretary of state, Brunner built a reputation for integrity. She entered the Democratic primary for Senate in 2010 but lost in May, making her a lame duck.

After the primary, Dan sent his sister the Beth Cottrell deposition, highlighting the section on notarizations. When she read the deposition, she and her legal staff agreed that Cottrell admitted to notary fraud. But after some research, she learned there weren't many options for secretaries of state to sanction notaries. The best she could do was forward violations to the Justice Department as a criminal referral.

Brunner had been working on a separate matter with Steve Dettelbach, the U.S. attorney from Cleveland. In August, Brunner hand-carried the deposition to Dettelbach with a criminal referral, and awaited a response. Unbeknownst to her, a fellow statewide officer, Ohio attorney general Richard Cordray, was also investigating robo-signing, particularly the Jeffrey Stephan affidavits. Cordray planned to file a lawsuit against GMAC for fraud against Ohio courts. When Brunner got wind of this, she asked Dettelbach if she could announce her criminal referral in the Chase Home Finance case. Dettelbach said sure.

Two days before Brunner went public, on September 29, Chase Home Finance announced it would suspend foreclosure operations in all judicial states. It would have been customary for Dettelbach to inform Chase they were being targeted for investigation. It certainly looked like Chase was preempting disclosures about the criminal case.

The Great Foreclosure Machine could maybe explain away one mortgage servicer's corrupt practices. But now a second admitted to the same misconduct. There's an old Monty Python sketch about the Amazing Mystico, a conjurer who imagined a block of flats with his mind. The tenants had to believe in the building for it to stay upright; if they stopped believing, it would tumble. By September 29, everybody stopped believing in the Great Foreclosure Machine.

Nye chuckled at the timing. In 2000, former SEC chair Arthur Levitt told him about the ten-year lag between the identification of financial fraud and its exposure. September 29, 2010, was almost exactly ten years from the day Levitt made that comment.

Lisa Epstein and Michael Redman, after toiling in obscurity for a year, were suddenly among a small collection of experts able to talk about this scandal. Journalists they hadn't heard from in years solicited comments or interviews or document requests. CNBC wanted to film Lisa asking questions for a town hall meeting with President Obama. Ariana Cha, a *Washington Post* reporter, asked Michael if there were documents signed by Jeffrey Stephan in non-judicial foreclosure states, where GMAC hadn't yet halted foreclosures. The next day Cha wrote an article, "Ally's Mortgage Documentation Problems Could Extend Beyond 23 States," based on Michael's research. Kim Miller at the *Palm Beach Post* published a tip from Lisa that GMAC withdrew affidavits from another one of their robo-signers, Kristine Wilson. Lisa found other withdrawals, including documents signed by Linda Green, the infamous DocX robo-signer from Lynn's papers. Michael Olenick found Beth Cottrell's name attached to dozens of foreclosure cases for banks other than Chase. "The GMAC announcement was the mushroom cloud," Matt Weidner soberly told the *New York Times*. "The fallout will burn through the entire mortgage servicing industry."

An anonymous tipster passed Michael a remarkable document. DocX printed a catalog for foreclosure mills and mortgage servicers, with an online order form called GetNet for missing documents. Curing a defective mortgage would cost you $12.95. Lost note affidavits and allonges were also $12.95. Creating a "missing intervening assignment?" $35.00. Re-creating "the entire collateral file"—that means the note, mortgage, securitization agreement, everything? It's yours for the low, low price of $95.00.

So a company under state and federal investigation for fabricating documents had a document fabrication menu: choose one from column A and one from column B. As finance blogger Yves Smith of *Naked Capitalism* explained, this proved that trustees did not hold the evidence necessary to foreclose. Smith later relayed a heated conversation between a colleague and an anonymous subprime lender CEO, who acknowledged, "If you're right, we're fucked. We never transferred the paper. No one in the industry transferred the paper."

Now roused to investigate, the media proved adept at finding examples that the destruction of the land records system was something everybody should be concerned about, not just so-called deadbeats. The Fort Lauderdale *Sun-Sentinel* reported that Jason Grodensky received a foreclosure notice on his door. But he paid cash for his home. He bought it in a short sale in 2009, but Bank of America never stopped foreclosure on the previous owner, and Fannie Mae bought the home at auction. So both Jason Grodensky and Fannie Mae owned the home. North Carolina attorney general Roy Cooper found Bank of America foreclosing on another house with no mortgage, according to the *Triangle Business Journal*.

Martin and Kirsten Davis of Cleveland lost their home to foreclosure after accidentally paying 14 cents too little on a monthly payment, wrote the *Cleveland Plain Dealer*. Their servicer charged late fees, pyramiding them on top of one another until 14 cents became thousands of dollars.

Matt Weidner got a call from a woman named Nancy Jacobini. She was on her couch one evening when she heard someone kicking in her door. Terrified, she retreated upstairs and called 911: "Help, I'm locked in my bathroom, somebody broke into my house!" It turned out to be a "property preservation" specialist hired by her bank, JPMorgan Chase, to change the locks on an abandoned property. But Jacobini was still living there, and while she was behind on mortgage payments, foreclosure proceedings had not even begun. Weidner used to holler about these breaking-and-entering cases, never getting a response. But because nobody believed in the Great Foreclosure Machine anymore, Nancy Jacobini appeared on ABC News, MSNBC, and *Democracy Now.*

The stories incensed Barry Ritholtz, Wall Street analyst and author of a popular finance blog called *The Big Picture*. In a post, "Why Foreclosure Fraud Is So Dangerous to Property Rights," he listed every document homeowners sign during closing to ensure clear title. A system created and refined over three hundred years, with multiple checks, safeguards these rights. "There is no room for errors," Ritholtz thundered, explaining how capitalism breaks down if a buyer cannot be certain that someone else does not have a legal interest in the property they purchased.

Hence, we end up with the wrong house being foreclosed upon, the wrong person being sued for a mortgage note, a bank without an interest in a mortgage note suing for foreclosure, and cases where more than one note holders are suing on the same property that is being foreclosed . . . The only way these errors could have occurred is if several people involved in the process committed criminal fraud. This is not a case of "Well, something slipped through the cracks." . . . There is simply no reason we should tolerate unlawful property seizure merely when it is done by banks. They are not the State, not the King, and not above the law.

CNBC's Larry Kudlow brought Ritholtz on to discuss this with network correspondent Diana Olick. In characteristic embedded-reporter style, Olick downplayed the corporate malfeasance, asserting that most of these homeowners were not paying for their homes and "they shouldn't be in them."

"When you have people in Texas and Florida being foreclosed on, and they don't have mortgages," Ritholtz replied in his thick New York accent, "something's wrong with that process."

Olick interrupted him. "You're always going to see those stories—"

"No, you never see those stories!" Ritholtz shot back. "That has never happened before! That is a legal impossibility!"

"That's a very small minority of cases—"

"It should be zero! For most of American history it's been zero!"

Although business reporters covered for the scandal, banks knew they'd been caught. That last straw was when Old Republic National Title Insurance announced it would not insure title on properties foreclosed upon by companies that used robo-signers. The company simply couldn't guarantee who owned the homes. And without title insurance, nobody would risk a purchase.

The Amazing Mystico's buildings all fell down. Bank of America suspended foreclosures in judicial states October 1, 2010. The same day, Connecticut called a moratorium on all foreclosures in the state, and Texas, Massachusetts, Maryland, North Carolina, and California followed suit. Congress got involved, too; Senators Al Franken and Jeff Merkley and Representatives Gabby Giffords and Alan Grayson demanded investigations and moratoria. Grayson made an easy-to-understand video about foreclosure fraud that went viral ("We are reaching a point where the easiest way to make a buck is to steal it"). Ohio attorney general Richard Cordray announced his GMAC lawsuit, seeking $25,000 per fraudulent Jeffrey Stephan affidavit, a penalty that could reach into the billions of dollars. Federal banking regulators opened formal reviews of all foreclosure processes at major mortgage servicers. On October 8 Bank of America extended its moratorium to all fifty states. Chase, GMAC, Litton Loans, and Citi followed suit. Wells Fargo held out for a while, claiming they were the "good" bank, but their robo-signer Xee Moua, who signed five hundred documents a day without verification, eventually got deposed, and they started slowing down their cases. On October 13 the attorneys general of all fifty states announced an investigation into foreclosure fraud, and the leading foreclosure operations in America were mostly at a standstill.

The game plan, hatched almost a year earlier at the Bonefish Grill, worked to perfection. Michael and Lisa assumed law enforcement would now move in, expose the scandal, stop it cold, and hold those responsible to account. They had dinner to celebrate. "We had so much hope," Lisa later reminisced. "We thought we did it."

17

THE BIG TIME

Foreclosure fraud bloggers had to contend with something new: notoriety. Their obsession became front-page news: *Good Morning America*, *The Daily Show*, and nightly newscasts led with the story. And Lisa and Michael became front-page news as well, with profiles in the *Washington Post*, McClatchy Newspapers, and the *Palm Beach Post* ("The Deadbeat Took On Wall Street"). Ordinary people exposing a complex financial scandal provided a compelling media angle. Not that Michael was satisfied with the newfound interest; he wrote on *4closureFraud*, "Funny how we have been screaming this for about a year and no one would listen until GMAC made their announcement."

CNN asked Michael to come on. Michael, of course, forwarded the request to Lisa. They rushed to a local affiliate, where Lisa sat in a tiny studio while anchor Mary Snow asked her questions for thirty minutes. At the end, the cameraman told her, "I know three people in foreclosure; thanks for what you're doing." Lisa and Michael decamped to a nearby bar to watch her first national interview. Right before it was supposed to air, CNN broke away for important breaking news: a tractor-trailer filled with pigs flipped over on a Canadian highway. Authorities tried to corral the swine as they strolled across the road. Lisa headlined the *Foreclosure Hamlet* recap "Preempted by a Passel of Pigs Being Put in the Pen (Hopefully Foreshadowing Reality)."

MSNBC's Dylan Ratigan didn't preempt Lisa, bringing her on live. "MBS? There are no mortgages backing these securities, they didn't put

them in. I think we should call these 'malicious bankers with syphilis,'"
Lisa said, reciting a line she'd practiced that whole day. Ratigan remarked
on the air that Lisa could take over for him if she was available some after-
noons. A thousand miles away in Massachusetts, Andrew "Ace" Delany
watched the show with his dad. After the syphilis line, his dad said he
wanted to adopt her.

Every second of every day was filled. Michael and Lisa set up "emergency happy hours" statewide, including Tampa and St. Petersburg. The
documentary filmmakers behind *Inside Job* contacted Lisa. Michael got to
blog at the cranky yet high-traffic finance site Zero Hedge. While in Sarasota for a seminar, Lisa bumped into Florida governor Charlie Crist, who
was running for U.S. Senate. Halfway into a black SUV, Crist turned around,
pointed at Lisa, and said, "I want to talk to you." Lisa couldn't believe *she*
was the one being recognized.

After hearing about the accelerated rocket docket, two attorneys with
the American Civil Liberties Union's (ACLU) Racial Justice Program, Larry
Schwartztol and Rachel Goodman, called Lisa and Michael for information
about potential constitutional violations of due process. They filed public
records requests, finding that the Office of State Courts Administrator distributed court funds based on the percentage of cases completed. Schwartztol
and Goodman flew to Palm Beach to meet with Lisa and Michael, who set
them up with statewide contacts.

Lisa and Michael enjoyed their unusual moment in the spotlight because
they finally saw an ending: people in charge would take over, and they could
fade away. But they had to stay prominent for now, because there was a lot
of nonsense to knock down. Lisa found a flood of "replacement" mortgage
assignments and affidavits being filed across Florida. Michael wondered
how they managed to find people with deep personal knowledge of hundreds of thousands of foreclosure cases so quickly. Particularly amusing
were the "found allonges," when the rules stated that allonges had to be attached to original notes and therefore couldn't simply be found.

The industry next dismissed the scandal as a matter of "bad paperwork,"
as if someone in the back office just forgot an initial somewhere. They didn't
want the public to understand that they had no proof of ownership on the
homes they were seizing in foreclosure cases. The American Securitization

Forum, a leading trade group for Wall Street banks, invented a clever refrain: "The mortgage follows the note." That way, faulty mortgage assignments were irrelevant. Of course, the notes were faulty, too. The theory also contradicted the securitization agreements, which clearly stated that assignments had to be conveyed into trusts for the asset to be valid.

The Service Employees International Union started a campaign called Where Is the Note? Under the 1974 Real Estate Settlement Procedures Act, homeowners, whether in foreclosure or not, could ask servicers for original mortgage documentation and be guaranteed a response within sixty days. SEIU uploaded a "qualified written request" form for homeowners, and servicers got six thousand letters in the first few weeks. SEIU organizers sifted the replies into three categories: "we don't know," "we won't tell you," and "no comment." If this was the reaction to notes, what the industry considered the good paper, what did the really bad stuff look like?

A remarkable "news" piece in the *Wall Street Journal* entitled "Niche Lawyers Spawned Housing Fracas" carried a distinct attitude of *And we would have gotten away with it, if it weren't for you meddling kids.* "Lawyers in the field now commonly use a technique more identified with corporate litigation: probing depositions, designed to uncover any lapses in judgment, flaws in a process or wrongdoing," author Robbie Whelan wrote, intimating that forcing plaintiffs to prove their cases was unfair. Industry mouthpieces warned that clogging foreclosures would trigger economic disaster, reducing cash flows to mortgage companies and delaying market "clearing." Of course, foreclosures hurt the economy, lowering property values and tearing up communities. *The Daily Show*'s Jon Stewart asked, "So we can improve the economy by throwing millions of families out of their houses just in time for the holidays? . . . Because apparently now we have a foreclosure-based economy."

The most common argument was that borrowers deserved to lose their homes for missing payments, which ignored not only the foreclosures on people who were current on their mortgage but also several hundred years of judicial procedure. "Fraud doesn't erase the fact that the borrower agreed to make payments or face the penalty of losing her home," sniffed CNBC's John Carney. But it actually *does* erase that: that's how the criminal justice system works. If the prosecution violates procedures, it loses, regardless of the status of the defendant.

Behind the rhetorical effort was a quieter strategy that reached the desk of Ohio secretary of state Jennifer Brunner. On September 30, the same day she announced the criminal referral in the Beth Cottrell notary fraud case, she received an email from Leslie Reynolds, executive director of the National Association of Secretaries of State: "We just learned that HR 3808, Interstate Recognition of Notarizations Act, which passed the House under a suspension of the rules in April 2010, was passed by the Senate on September 27." In a near-empty chamber, Senator Bob Casey's motion to approve HR 3808 by unanimous consent passed without debate. Reynolds's group, which opposed the bill, was never informed; in fact, they were told in August it wouldn't get a vote.

HR 3808 came from an obscure Alabama Republican named Robert Aderholt, who claimed he introduced it upon a constituent's request. It would require state and federal courts to "recognize any lawful notarization . . . commissioned under the laws of a State other than the State where the court is located." Brunner discovered that three states allowed electronic notarizations: Nevada, Minnesota, and Arizona. E-notarizations meant that signers of official documents would not need to personally appear before a notary. Brunner envisioned mortgage companies moving their document assembly lines into those three states, forcing courts to accept electronic notarizations, and the underlying paperwork, as presumptively valid. States could challenge the statute, but that could take years of appeals, with untold numbers of foreclosures processed in the meantime.

Congress was out of session, with campaigning intensifying for the midterm elections. HR 3808 was just sitting on President Obama's desk. Brunner sent the bill text to Dan Junk, and he and his colleagues agreed HR 3808 could make it more difficult for attorneys to challenge documents. Brunner did two things. First she blasted her old Senate campaign email list, asking a half million subscribers to contact the White House and tell the president to veto HR 3808. Then she called Campbell Spencer, political liaison to the White House during her Senate race. Spencer, who was still working in the West Wing, promised to pass word to her colleagues.

News of HR 3808 reached Michael and Lisa. Michael reposted Brunner's email at *4closureFraud*. Thousands of people contacted the White House; at one point the switchboard lines jammed. Once the veto movement went viral, legal experts split over whether HR 3808 would truly grease foreclosures through the system. Some argued that even with valid e-notarizations, bad assignments and affidavits could be challenged. But activists weren't interested in a debate: they just wanted the bill stopped.

On October 7 the White House announced that the president would give HR 3808 a pocket veto, refusing to sign the legislation because of the "unintended impact of this bill on consumer protections, including those for mortgages." Like 99 percent of America, Michael didn't know what a pocket veto was. A president could withhold his signature from a bill and prevent it from becoming law when Congress was out of session. But Congress was still holding pro forma meetings while away from Washington, to block recess appointments. Some observers were anxious that a pocket veto would not take, and the bill would become law without the president's signature on October 12, ten business days after passage, unless he sent it back to Congress. Michael published his findings, including emails from readers featuring arcane discussions of veto procedures and constitutional law.

That night Michael got an anonymous email that read, "You're right and you need to follow through on this." He ignored it—by this point he was getting wacky emails all the time—but the same emailer sent another one the next day: "Keep at this, keep going." The tone made Michael believe this was not a random oddball, but someone with inside knowledge.

White House reporters peppered spokesman Robert Gibbs with questions about whether a pocket veto would hold during pro forma sessions. Michael's alert about whether the pocket veto was valid became the most-read page in the history of *4closureFraud*. And on October 9 the White House issued a *second* press release: "To leave no doubt that the bill is being vetoed, in addition to withholding my signature, I am returning HR 3808 to the Clerk of the House of Representatives." Lisa told Michael, "They're talking to you about that."

In President Obama's first six years in office he vetoed only two bills, and one was a stopgap defense bill made redundant by passage of a separate appropriation days later. So HR 3808 represented the only time in six years anyone stopped Barack Obama from signing a bill that passed Congress, all thanks to people power.

Well, plus one other individual. A couple of months after the veto, Jennifer Brunner heard from Elizabeth Warren, the Harvard professor who had been installed in September 2010 as a special assistant to the president, overseeing the implementation of her brainchild, the Consumer Financial Protection Bureau. Warren thanked Brunner for warning about HR 3808; her staff found out via Campbell Spencer, Brunner's White House contact. There were rumors on the blogs that Warren personally intervened to convince the president to veto; when Brunner asked about that, Warren would only say, "One person really can make a difference."

Lynn Szymoniak also delighted in the Great Foreclosure Machine's collapse, though not as publicly as Lisa and Michael. Instead she went back to every contact she made over the past year, with links to every deposition, every exposed bank, every false document. There would have to be prosecutions now, Lynn thought, not because of any commitment to right and wrong but because the negative publicity raised the pressure in Washington. A package of 150 robo-signer depositions from Deerfield Beach defense attorney Peter Ticktin only turned up the heat. Deponents couldn't define the terms "affidavit," "promissory note," or even "mortgage," which might have been fine if that wasn't what they worked on for a living. Before becoming vice presidents on paper, robo-signers held jobs like hair stylist, Walmart greeter, and assembly line worker. "I don't know the ins and outs of the loan, I just sign documents," said one robo-signer.

So when attorney general Eric Holder said on October 6 that the Justice Department was "looking into" the allegations, Lynn was nonplussed. A federal grand jury had been empaneled in Jacksonville for nine months. And DoJ was intensely involved in her *qui tam* case, holding meetings and deputizing Lynn to write confidential information disclosures. Even if Holder knew nothing, someone in Washington could pull up the pending cases, from Jacksonville to Lynn's inquiries in North and South Carolina. There was a ready-made latticework of legal actions waiting for DoJ to grasp. So far Justice was playing dumb.

Meanwhile, the Jacksonville case moved at the speed of a man walking through quicksand. Lender Processing Services, parent company of DocX, hired a Bush-era assistant attorney general, Paul McNulty, among their flotilla of lawyers in the case. Agents told Lynn that LPS denied the Linda Green inaccuracies by calling their practice "surrogate signing," as if it were routine for multiple employees to forge a colleague's name on legal documents.

At the Florida attorney general's office, June Clarkson and Theresa Edwards subpoenaed information on six former DocX employees and LPS's internal records, and LPS responded in typical firehose fashion, sending enough notebooks and files to overwhelm the office. June and Theresa began to wade through the records, but David J. Stern's embattled law firm also drew their focus.

Right around the time of the GMAC moratorium announcement, June and Theresa took a deposition from Tammie Lou Kapusta, a former senior paralegal with Stern. She testified that all foreclosure documents were created and signed in-house, without input from servicers or default services providers. How would a law firm have the manpower to create thousands of documents, June and Theresa wondered. "Well, there was work being done offshore," Tammie Lou said, identifying facilities in Guam and the Philippines. Offshore doc shops generated the "casesums," specific file information like unpaid principal balance and fee calculations. It resembled Firm Solutions, the Panamanian facility where Lisa Epstein's documents were prepared. All the paralegals at Stern did was sign their name.

Tammie Lou kept talking. Homeowners frequently didn't get served legal papers, even though Stern goosed fees by charging for serving nonexistent tenants or unknown spouses. Mortgage assignments were always produced after the foreclosure case was entered. Affidavits of indebtedness went out with incorrect figures. Notes got lost all the time, as entry-level employees threw things out or placed documents in the wrong files. And the business with the signatures was completely illegal. "I don't think any notary actually used their own notary stamp. The team used them," Tammie Lou said.

"There were just stamps around?" June asked.

"Correct. We would stamp them and they would get signed."

"Who would sign them?"

"Other people on the team that could sign the signature of the person or just a check on there or whatever."

Cheryl Samons, whom Ice Legal deposed earlier, instituted this system. Though she had exclusive signing authority for many lenders, three different people regularly penned Samons's name, Tammie Lou explained. Paralegals sat around a big table and signed as witnesses and notaries in assembly-line fashion, placing the documents in a folder for Samons. Nobody read anything, just signed. This happened on six floors of the office, every single day. The fourth-floor mass signing sessions took place right outside David Stern's office; it was impossible for him to plead ignorance. Tammie Lou got fired because she refused to falsify military documents used in process service; two weeks later, she was told to pack up. Nobody challenged the situation because everybody knew the consequences. Question the system and you're out.

June and Theresa leaked the deposition, hoping to heighten interest in the Stern case and bring more people forward to testify. Michael posted it at 4closureFraud. The state prosecutors sent another deposition later, with Kelly Scott, one of Cheryl Samons's former assistants. Within a week Fannie Mae and Freddie Mac, amid pressure from Congress, terminated referrals to Stern for cases in Florida. Citigroup and GMAC followed suit. That wiped out a large chunk of the company's business. But seeing Stern crumble financially wasn't enough for the activists. They wanted indictments.

June and Theresa had data coming in from Lynn and Lisa. But they also received information from just about everyone involved in a case with foreclosure mills, LPS, or DocX. They were early movers in a rapidly growing scandal. Assistant attorneys general in Nevada, California, and Ohio traded information with them. Regulators started visiting the office. The banks called them, lobbying for leniency. June and Theresa's superiors supported their efforts; they even formally reprimanded Erin Cullaro for her foreclosure mill moonlighting (though, amazingly, she kept her job for another year). But just as June and Theresa verged on announcing indictments, their boss changed.

Foreclosure fraud's blast into the public consciousness coincided with the 2010 midterm elections. Democrats, from congressional leaders Harry Reid and Nancy Pelosi on down, pounced on the issue, demonstrating concern for struggling homeowners. Thirty-one California House Democrats co-signed a letter calling for a federal criminal investigation and attaching twenty pages of horrific case studies from constituents—tales of dishonesty and misrepresentation. Alan Grayson wanted foreclosure fraud monitored by the Financial Stability Oversight Council, a new super regulator created by the Dodd-Frank reform law, as a systemic risk. But Republicans had little interest in the story, save for a few in hard-hit foreclosure areas. Their electoral strategy instead focused on Obamacare and allegations of presidential lawlessness.

When the scandal broke, Sheila Bair, chairwoman of the Federal Deposit Insurance Corporation, thought the government should capitalize on its leverage with legally exposed servicers. She drafted a proposal called the "super-mod," which would take every loan over sixty days delinquent and write it down to face value. Borrowers would have a shot at making reduced payments, and lenders would get a share of the upside as home values appreciated, giving them a stake in neighborhood stability. Bair formally sent the proposal to Treasury Secretary Timothy Geithner. It never went anywhere.

The White House took foreclosure fraud seriously enough to convene a high-level economic meeting in the Roosevelt Room. President Obama asked National Economic Council director Larry Summers about robo-signing, and he assured the president that there was no systemic threat to the economy. Around the room they went, everyone agreeing with Summers: a mild problem, nothing existential. Finally Obama pointed to newly minted assistant Elizabeth Warren, whom one of his staffers invited. She expressed much stronger concern, laying out how foreclosure fraud covered up a larger crime, deeply damaging homeowners and investors and putting the housing market at risk. But the rest of the group moved on to the next topic. It was one of the few times Warren would get into a presidential-level meeting; Summers tried to keep her away after that.

Throughout the crisis, the Obama administration would not endorse a national foreclosure moratorium, which Michael, Lisa, Lynn, and virtually all the other activists demanded. While the president couldn't automatically stop state court activity, advocates thought a show of high-level support could create political pressure for a moratorium. Instead, Obama adviser David Axelrod told *Face the Nation* that foreclosures with proper paperwork should go forward. Michael didn't know of any cases with "proper" paperwork; in his eyes, every land record in America had been corrupted.

On a hunch, Michael checked Illinois public records for the president's mortgage documents. Sure enough, he found the Obamas' satisfaction of mortgage on their first condo in Hyde Park, signed in 2005 by Marshe Craine, a Chase robo-signer. Michael found Craine's name on three other satisfactions of mortgage with different handwriting styles, sometimes for Chase, sometimes for MERS. Even people who paid off their mortgage—even the Obamas—couldn't be certain the payoff documents were legal.

Michael posted the Obama robo-signer story at *4closureFraud* and Zero Hedge. The hit count soared by the minute after an irreverent Dutch blog called *GeenStijl* linked to it and thousands of websurfers from Holland streamed in. The next day Michael found a second robo-signed Obama mortgage document. "Feel free to call or email me to discuss this further, Mr. President," Michael wrote. But the phone call didn't come, nor did the White House change its position on a moratorium.

Within three weeks Bank of America pronounced themselves free of errors, returning to the courts with 102,000 "replacement" affidavits. The rocket docket hearings resumed. After an internal audit, BofA found "10 or 25" problems in the first "several hundred" files studied, a vague figure made more embarrassing by a report in the New York *Daily News* detailing 4,450 errors just in the five boroughs of New York City, including banks foreclosing on homes they didn't own. Michael bet he could find "10 or 25" problems in his own loan file.

Some courts fought back. In Cuyahoga County, Ohio, a judge ruled that any plaintiff substituting documents must explain within thirty days why that case should not be dismissed. Supreme courts in New York and New Jersey forced attorneys for the foreclosing entity to personally attest, under penalty of perjury, that they reviewed the loan file and verified all its elements. It was even stronger than Florida's verification standard because of the personal consequences, and as a result, foreclosure filings in these states initially vanished. Nobody would put themselves on the line for these documents.

Bank stocks sank throughout October; investors were as skeptical as the courts. Owners of mortgage-backed securities, who had to pay for all the document manufacturing and legal shenanigans, began to organize themselves. Under securitization agreements, if banks failed to convey mortgages to the trusts, investors could sue to force the banks to repurchase bonds. Major institutional bondholders BlackRock, Pimco, and the New York Federal Reserve, which bought oodles of mortgage-backed securities during the bailouts, asked that Bank of America take back $47 billion. Before filing a repurchase lawsuit, at least 25 percent of all bondholders had to agree to it. Mortgage-backed securities investors were scattered around the world, and banks were, let's say, protective about releasing who owned what. But Talcott Franklin, a lawyer in Dallas, was amassing bondholder lists. Analysts put the ultimate cost to the banks at $120 billion.

Behind the scenes, banks were freaking out. Michael got passed notes from a conference call between Citigroup and Adam Levitin, a law professor from Georgetown University and expert on securitization. Citi gave the document the subtitle "Foreclosures Gone Wild." Levitin forthrightly told Citi executives that the affidavit issue was secondary to the big question of whether loans "were never properly transferred at each step of the securitization process." This transfer failed to take place "in many instances," Levitin said, raising questions about loan ownership as well as "the validity and tax exempt status of the trusts." Citi even acknowledged that "it is unclear in many cases where the actual paperwork rests today." Michael uploaded the conference call notes, and Citigroup immediately threatened legal action. Eventually Citi did get the notes scrubbed. But Michael gave readers a brief window into the anxiety in the C-suites.

In the end, foreclosures couldn't stem the Tea Party tide on Election Day 2010. Some communities were so dislocated that politicians couldn't find their voters. Alan Grayson's campaign staff would walk precincts around Orlando and find only a couple of occupied houses per block. He ended up losing by eighteen points. Democrats relinquished the House to Republicans. In lower-profile races, the roster of attorneys general changed over, just after every office agreed to a fifty-state investigation of foreclosure fraud. Republicans picked up six seats. Richard Cordray, who had sued GMAC, lost in Ohio to former GOP senator Mike DeWine. Former AGs Andrew Cuomo and Jerry Brown became governors of New York and California, respectively, and Eric Schneiderman and Kamala Harris, both seen as more liberal, replaced them. And in Florida, Bill McCollum's tenure ended, supplanted by an assistant state attorney known for appearances on Fox News named Pam Bondi.

When Congress returned in November for a lame duck session, Democrats announced hearings on foreclosure fraud. While hearings were normally exercises in grandstanding, because Congress knew so little about the issue there was an opportunity for education. Jim Kowalski and Tom Cox testified before the House Judiciary Committee, flying up to Washington on their own dime. Tom Ice and Lisa talked to Senate staff about appearing, but staffers were primarily interested in people who lost their homes even though they never missed a payment. While such cases certainly happened, Tom and Lisa tried to explain that the issue was bigger than that, it was about judicial integrity and the rule of law. They weren't invited.

The hearings were often lively. Politicians came armed with constituents' horror stories of victimization by mortgage servicers. Executives from Bank of America, JPMorgan Chase, and other Wall Street giants had to run for cover. Diane Thompson of the National Consumer Law Center made clear that many of these illegal foreclosures were also unnecessary, driven by servicers who engaged in fee pyramiding, force-placed insurance, and other schemes to push homeowners into default. Servicers would tell borrowers to miss payments to become eligible for loan modifications, and then foreclose on them, just like in Lisa's case. Thompson, an attorney, claimed that half her clients fell victim to servicer-driven defaults. Foreclosure fraud was the last stop on a well-traveled road of abuse.

Damon Silvers, of the congressional oversight panel for the Troubled Asset Relief Program, cited the $47 billion Bank of America repurchase request. "Five such requests will amount to more than the market capitalization of Bank of America," he howled at a Treasury official. "We can either have a rational resolution to the foreclosure crisis or we can preserve the capital structure of the banks. We can't do both."

Law professor Katherine Porter cut to the heart of the matter: if the banks never transferred mortgages to the trusts, which lawyers on the ground confirmed to her was true in virtually all cases, confusion would reign for years. "Just because a homeowner hasn't paid his mortgage doesn't mean anybody in the world can kick him out," she observed. At the House Financial Services Committee, Adam Levitin summed up why nobody had undertaken a real investigation: "The federal regulators don't want to get information from the servicers, because then they'd have to do something about it." It was more convenient to remain in the dark about whether mortgage-backed securities were backed by anything than to uncover a problem that could end up too big to fix.

In early November the Roosevelt Institute, a progressive think tank, invited Lisa, Michael, and Lynn to Washington for a private meeting on foreclosure fraud with lawyers, writers, academics, analysts, and activists. The group would discuss where things stood and brainstorm the path to solutions. Without funds to get to Washington, Lisa and Michael put out the tip jar at *4closureFraud*. Readers gratefully pitched in. "I donated my last $10, good luck you guys," wrote one commenter.

Lisa and Michael flew up and held a D.C. happy hour the night before. The next morning they entered an office building on Massachusetts Avenue, just steps from the White House. Lisa was back where she grew up, the slate-gray sky a reminder of her perennial sadness at the loss of the sun. But today she was happy. People she and Michael heretofore only wrote about or linked to were in attendance. Damon Silvers, Katherine Porter, Tom Cox, and Adam Levitin, all involved in those hearings, gave presentations. Writers from *The Nation*, the *Huffington Post*, and *The American Prospect*, congressional staff, and researchers for the Financial Crisis Inquiry Commission made it. There were activists from unions and faith groups, community organizers with more foot soldiers than Lisa or Michael could ever scrape together. It was loftier company than the nurse, the car salesman, and the forensic expert ever expected.

The Florida activists got to tell their stories, describing the situation to people with no personal exposure to it. Lisa talked about how she could find fifty foreclosed homes in a two-mile walk around her neighborhood, and how the land records had been defiled, perhaps permanently. "The response from people I see is no different than to anyone attacked by a predator: shame, confusion, fear, terror and embarrassment," Lisa told the group. "But my role is that I will overcome my embarrassment to better this country."

At one point meeting organizer Matt Stoller, a longtime blogger who worked with Rep. Alan Grayson and MSNBC's Dylan Ratigan, pulled Lynn aside. During the meeting she had hyped the federal criminal investigation in Jacksonville. Stoller said to Lynn, "You know, this is not going to work out well for you with the Justice Department." Stoller went on to explain his skepticism about Attorney General Eric Holder and the head of the Criminal Division, Lanny Breuer. Both had worked as corporate lawyers for Covington & Burling, which not only represented every major bank but provided the legal opinions that created MERS. So far the Justice Department hadn't pursued prosecutions against anyone associated with the financial crisis. Former DoJ officials complained that Holder and Breuer weren't interested in bringing cases unless they were sure they could win. That guaranteed timidity.

Lynn still believed in the justice system, that it was possible to bring enough evidence to nail the worst actors. And she had the evidence, undeniable incidents of fraud a million times over. But Stoller's words, along with the White House's tepid moves on the scandal, stuck in her head.

18

WE WILL PUT PEOPLE IN JAIL

When Michael, Lisa, and Lynn returned to south Florida, several rapid-fire events dropped like dominoes. Damian Figueroa found an intriguing New Jersey bankruptcy court ruling, *Kemp v. Countrywide*. Linda DeMartini, a supervisor for Countrywide's successor, Bank of America Home Loans, acknowledged in a deposition that "to her knowledge, the original note never left the possession of Countrywide . . . the original note appears to have been transferred [directly] to Countrywide's foreclosure unit, as evidenced by internal FedEx tracking numbers." DeMartini also testified that "it was customary for Countrywide to maintain possession of the original note and related loan documents." Hilariously, most of this came out on redirect from Countrywide's own attorney. Judge Judith Wizmur ruled for the debtor that the trustee, Bank of New York, could not prove its claim on the mortgage.

The suspicions of securitization FAIL, that mortgage lenders neglected to transfer notes to the trusts, finally had some hard evidence behind it. Countrywide packaged hundreds of billions of dollars' worth of mortgage-backed securities, or rather non-mortgage-backed securities. At the finance blog *Naked Capitalism*, Tom Adams tracked down the pooling and servicing agreement for the Kemp loan—CWABS 2006-8—and saw no exemption from conveying the mortgage and note, with complete chain of title, within ninety days of closing. Bank of America hired a tall-building lawyer from K&L Gates to argue, "We believe the loan was sold to the trust even if there wasn't an actual delivery of the note." But that violated the language of the pooling and servicing agreement. There was a very simple way to find out who was right: subpoena the trust documents. The U.S. attorney's office in Jacksonville had been doing that for months. But so far they were alone, and as Adam Levitin told Congress, the bank regulators didn't want to look, in case they found something.

The same week as the Countrywide bombshell, Florida Supreme Court chief justice Charles Canady, amid pressure from the ACLU's Racial Justice Project, issued a directive to courts across the state, ordering them to grant access to observers of foreclosure proceedings, a rebuke to the judge who reprimanded April Charney for bringing Matt Taibbi into a courtroom in Jacksonville. Observing the rocket docket was the first step toward exposing and stopping it.

Lisa started hearing from contacts inside the foreclosure mills that David Stern was laying off dozens of employees and filing motions to withdraw from cases in bulk. The Sarasota *Herald-Tribune* published an investigation on Stern, finding hundreds of improper mortgage assignments and faulty notarizations in the public records—following the same path of discovery in Michael's guide. The reporter went to Stern's offices in Plantation, and security threatened to have him arrested. The top foreclosure mill in Pennsylvania, Goldbeck McCafferty & McKeever, had problems, too: they were caught prosecuting thousands of foreclosures with complaints prepared and filed by nonlawyers, which risked having all those cases thrown out of court. The biggest cogs in the Great Foreclosure Machine were belching exhaust and sputtering.

Sarasota defense lawyer Chris Forrest posted video depositions, real ones this time, of Brian Bly, Crystal Moore, and Dhurata Dako, three employees at Nationwide Title Clearing who manufactured documents for several servicers. Michael thought Bly resembled cubicle drone Milton from the movie *Office Space*, and he posted the comparison at *4closureFraud*. Bly signed mortgage assignments in batches of two hundred for over twenty different banks but couldn't explain what one was. Dako, a native of Albania, went a step further: "We don't do mortgages in my country."

Michael, Lynn, and Matt Weidner embedded the video deposition at their sites, and Nationwide Title Clearing's parent company, the Church of Scientology, fired off cease-and-desist letters. They even got a court injunction to remove the videos, arguing that their employees suffered death threats and "highly offensive" criticisms about their looks. Forrest took the videos down, but they were reposted so many times, he couldn't locate them all. Nationwide Title Clearing later sued Weidner for slander and libel; he ended up removing several posts. You don't mess with the Scientologists.

In early January the Massachusetts Supreme Court delivered a lightning bolt, confirming a lower court ruling for homeowner Antonio Ibanez against Wells Fargo and U.S. Bank. State law was quite clear: the plaintiff must hold the mortgage through a properly conveyed assignment in order to enforce foreclosure. In this case, the assignments of mortgage were executed after the foreclosure sale. Wells Fargo and U.S. Bank argued they had the intent to transfer (the "I meant to do that" defense), but to no avail; the foreclosures were canceled and Antonio Ibanez got his house back. Ibanez's was the first major securitization FAIL case decided by a state's highest court. It only applied to Massachusetts, but bank stocks plummeted anyway.

Alongside court victories came a new willingness to challenge the system. In Simi Valley, California, a couple broke into their foreclosed house, on the recommendation of their lawyer. In Los Angeles, the Alliance of Californians for Community Empowerment (ACCE), built from the rubble of the defunct community group ACORN, installed bedroom furniture in a JPMorgan Chase lobby; if Chase moved out homeowners, the homeowners would move into the bank. PICO, a national faith coalition, rallied on the Treasury Department steps for months before getting a sit-down meeting with Timothy Geithner. Community groups—ACCE, PICO, National People's Action, Alliance for a Just Society, Right to the City, and more—formed anti-foreclosure coalitions, like The New Bottom Line and the Home Defenders League.

Lisa had been doing her Moratorium Monday protests for months without much traction, but now, capitalizing on the breakthrough, she and Michael announced a big demonstration at the courthouse. Scheduled just before Christmas, they called it Homeless for the Holidays. Local media picked it up; even a French TV crew arranged to cover the protest. Courthouse officials got so panicked that they sent an internal email, leaked to Lisa, announcing that they would hire extra security and cordon off parts of the building.

The night before Homeless for the Holidays, the temperature in Palm Beach dropped forty degrees. The morning brought heavy winds, as palm trees swayed and rain came down sideways. Every day that week was beautiful *except* for the protest day. Grassroots organizing in south Florida proved difficult even in perfect weather, let alone a hurricane. Nobody showed up except the French camera crew, a couple of stragglers, and Evan Rosen, a defense attorney from Fort Lauderdale. Rosen's presence impressed Michael, but overall it was a disappointing day.

That week Michael's wife, Jennifer, told him that after the holidays she wanted him out of the house. Tensions had grown over the past year, with Michael trying to draw a line between his activism and his family life but never being able to hold himself to it. In the end he didn't even argue, just packed a bag.

Officially the fifty-state attorney general investigation started in October 2010, but within a month anonymous reports hyped an imminent settlement, focused on improvements to the mortgage servicing industry and a compensation fund for homeowners. Michael immediately posted contact numbers for all fifty state attorneys general, demanding, "Don't sit down with the banks, stand up against fraud." He believed a compensation fund would make nice headlines, but the flood of phony documents and chain of title problems would remain. And it would allow banks to buy themselves out of trouble without individual accountability, without even an attempt to determine the extent of the damage. As the congressional oversight panel for the Troubled Asset Relief Program pointed out in a tough report, "If the public gains the impression that the government is providing concessions to large banks in order to ensure the smooth processing of foreclosures, the people's fundamental faith in due process could suffer."

Iowa attorney general Tom Miller, who orchestrated a major settlement in 2006 with now-defunct subprime lender Ameriquest, led the investigation. The *Washington Post* asked Miller whether he was interested in a cash settlement or acquiring a set of facts for civil and criminal prosecutions. "It's both," he answered. Miller received $261,000 from banking interests for his 2010 reelection campaign—eighty-eight times the total from the previous decade. In a subsequent report in *Time*, Miller acknowledged asking bank lawyers for contributions. Miller told the Senate Banking Committee in November 2010 that he held two settlement negotiation sessions with Bank of America in the first month of the investigation.

Deacon Tom McCarthy of the faith and justice group Iowa Citizens for Community Improvement (CCI) buttonholed Miller at a meeting in Des Moines and asked what he wanted out of the investigation. In addition to cash assistance for people in foreclosure, Miller said, "we will put people in jail." Michael didn't believe it. The French TV crew that covered Homeless for the Holidays had just interviewed Miller in Washington, and they said he was far more passive, saying that the fraud wasn't so bad and that everything would get tidily worked out.

Within days Miller's office claimed he wasn't referring to the fifty-state investigation when he mentioned jail, but to a mortgage fraud probe in conjunction with a U.S. attorney's office in Iowa. Michael knew what "mortgage fraud" usually meant—people who duped banks, not banks that dupe people. Miller also described the fifty-state investigation as "inherently civil." Iowa CCI held follow-up meetings with Miller and said it seemed like "the big banks had knocked the wind out of our state's top law enforcer." Miller kept a low profile after that.

Parallel to the state-level attorney general probe, every bank regulator and law enforcement agency even tangentially attached to housing, eleven in all, opened their own civil and even criminal cases. The opening salvo was an intensive eight-week review of servicer practices, with what Treasury Department official Michael Barr called "hundreds of investigators crawling all over the banks." But eight weeks seemed to experts like no time at all, and some of that time stretched over Thanksgiving and Christmas. Barr claimed that individual file reviews took between five and eight hours, which both highlighted the inadequacy of the time frame and made him sound absurd, because anyone spending eight hours looking at a loan file didn't know what to look for.

White House officials kept talking up a "global solution," presumably where every investigation or pseudo-investigation would merge into one big settlement, so the banks would only have to write one check for their failures. As a result, promising leads funneled up to Washington, where they would disappear. Thomas Cox, who helped break open foreclosure fraud, heard that the Justice Department didn't want U.S. attorneys pursuing cases in the states. His own U.S. attorney in Maine, whom he presented with information, was quite interested in the matter initially, but that faded.

Perhaps the biggest tell that the mishmash of investigations wasn't very serious was the lack of outreach to anyone with deep knowledge of the issues. Tom Ice, armed with the most comprehensive set of depositions on foreclosure fraud in the country, never got a call from investigators. Tom Cox sent his Jeffrey Stephan deposition everywhere, but had no takers. Jim Kowalski also sent information to Congress, to the Treasury Department, and to the FDIC, and heard nothing back. Securitization experts weren't consulted. Nye Lavalle wasn't consulted. Matt Weidner wasn't consulted. Max Gardner was, but he found that investigators were beginning from a blank slate, with no understanding of the modern mortgage system.

Lisa Epstein didn't feel like waiting. To her, the fifty-state investigation offered the best possibility for justice; the federal government was just playacting. So she built customized document bundles, state by state. For Illinois, she found fifty Linda Green forgeries on Illinois homeowners' documents. Then she assembled fifty California-specific Linda Greens, and so on. Lynn custom-built evidence files for attorney generals' offices, too. After Ohio's Richard Cordray sued GMAC, Lynn sent him hundreds of robo-signing examples. When Texas's Greg Abbott made a statement, Lynn had a bundle for him.

A foreclosure fraud blogger named Virginia Parsons had contacts in Hawaii state government. Lisa created a file of dodgy Hawaii documents, and even appeared via Skype at state legislative hearings in Honolulu. Some of the legislators maintained that, with federal banks servicing the mortgages, there was nothing they could do. "But this is Hawaiian land, these are Hawaiian people getting evicted," Lisa insisted. "You have jurisdiction over your own land." In May 2011, Governor Neil Abercrombie signed the toughest foreclosure law in the nation, based partially on Lisa's work. It mandated mediation between homeowners and banks, and required servicers to submit to the mediation board the full chain of title on the note and the mortgage prior to any foreclosure. Banks not negotiating in good faith or filing fraudulent documents could be heavily sanctioned. Hawaii transformed from a state with fairly lenient hurdles for taking a house to one where banks had to follow the law.

Through the Roosevelt Institute conference in Washington, Lisa met a staffer for New York attorney general Eric Schneiderman. A former state senator who took office in 2011, Schneiderman's initial pronouncements about foreclosure fraud stressed the need to bring people to justice. New York law governed nearly all securitization trusts, and state prosecutors wielded the Martin Act, a financial fraud statute with a relatively low burden of proof. Lisa sent some targeted New York materials to the staffer, and they wrote back asking for more. So Lisa sent more. Lynn held a conference call at her lawyer's offices in New York City with representatives from Massachusetts, California, Nevada, Illinois, and New York. Schneiderman's associates sent follow-up requests. Lisa and Lynn supplied different sets of evidence to separate contacts at the same office.

Before long, attorney general's offices in dozens of states—Iowa, Michigan, North Carolina, Kentucky, New Jersey, Washington, Tennessee—received Lisa's reports. Sometimes she sent them to activists who said they could get them to state officials; sometimes she sent them directly. Lisa was an unofficial, unpaid, unknown research volunteer for the fifty-state investigation. And unrequited, too; most offices didn't even acknowledge receipt.

Lynn couldn't get answers, either. When she asked the Justice Department about the results of the confidential information disclosures she spent hundreds of hours drafting, they'd reply, "We can't share that information with you."

Banks restarted the Great Foreclosure Machine by December 2010. Servicers used euphemisms like "irregularities" to describe systemic fraud, insisted that said irregularities had been repaired, and maintained that they had to resume operations to limit the number of abandoned properties, employing the image of a crime-ridden vacant lot to justify evictions. "We have not discovered a single instance where the foreclosure sale was unjustified," said GMAC Mortgage CEO Thomas Marano.

In Florida, clerks of courts wanted more information about whether their offices, full of property records, had become crime scenes. They asked lame duck attorney general Bill McCollum to send someone to speak about foreclosure documents at their annual meeting on December 8. McCollum sent June Clarkson and Theresa Edwards.

The state prosecutors didn't have a ready-made presentation. But they did have Lynn Szymoniak's old PowerPoint slides. Almost a year earlier, Lynn's friends from the U.S. attorney's office in Jacksonville visited her house to look at all the documents. She prepared slides with help from her son Mark Elliot, an MFA candidate at the New School in New York. They had fun with it, using images like an animated safe with legs, the game board from Candy Land (to show the movement of mortgages through the chain of title), and stock photos of worried-looking businessmen surrounded by paperwork. Behind the humor was a strong introduction to the topic, sort of Foreclosure Fraud 101.

When Lynn first met June and Theresa, she gave them a copy. In December, June asked Lynn if they could use her PowerPoint slides, and Lynn said that was fine. "Do we need to credit you?" June asked. Lynn said no: "Use me like a rented mule, take my stuff."

June and Theresa modified the presentation—the Candy Land board still appeared—and showed it to the clerks of courts. They titled it "Unfair, Deceptive and Unconscionable Acts in Foreclosure Cases." In ninety-eight slides, it reviewed the history of mortgages, securitization, the failure to follow the pooling and servicing agreements, and the document fabrication to cover it up. It identified fake signers, fake witnesses, and fake notaries. It included a dozen different Linda Green signatures and fourteen of her job titles. It showed Lynn's cut-and-pasted allonge, with the lines at the top and bottom giving it away. It had BOGUS documents. It had the 9/9/9999 document. It had documents that were notarized but unsigned. It had assignments with servicers transferring mortgages to themselves. It had assignments executed three years after the closing of the trust, and months after the initiation of foreclosure. It had assignments from defunct companies with no address. It had assignments with impossible notary stamps. It had documents with stamped instead of wet-ink signatures. It had deposition excerpts with David Stern employees talking of forgery.

If you knew nothing about foreclosure fraud, even if you knew nothing about mortgages, after this one-hour presentation you would recognize that county recording offices were polluted with garbage. More important, you would know why. June and Theresa were the first law enforcement officials in the country to produce a detailed, airtight depiction of what was happening.

June and Theresa's immediate supervisor, Bob Julian, attended the meeting. Trish Conners, also from the Economic Crimes division, used the presentation in remarks before the Florida Senate. That got the presentation leaked to Kim Miller at the *Palm Beach Post*, days before the end of McCollum's term. The PowerPoint slides included a limited power of attorney agreement from Chase to Lender Processing Services, showing all the LPS employees who could sign for Chase. LPS immediately complained. "We object to the Florida Attorney General's characterization of the mortgage industry and the securitization process as a game of Candy Land," LPS attorney Joan Meyer wrote to June and Theresa. The letter argued that LPS's operations were too complex for mere state prosecutors to understand. June and Theresa laughed it off.

But the complaints filtered up to Tallahassee. Pam Bondi, the incoming attorney general, received thousands of dollars in campaign contributions from LPS and its affiliates. A few weeks after Bondi's inauguration, Richard Lawson, a former lawyer for bank executives and the new director of the Economic Crimes unit, visited Fort Lauderdale for a meet-and-greet with June and Theresa. It turned into a meet-and-scream. Lawson said that attorneys for the target companies told him the two women acted aggressively and unprofessionally. "You're all I ever hear about. You're acting like hyenas!" Lawson yelled. He made June and Theresa justify every slide of the presentation. At the end, Lawson said he could probably take the heat for them. "Just don't let me hear anything else about you for the next six months."

Life under Pam Bondi proved different. June and Theresa were deliberately not assigned to the fifty-state investigation, despite knowing more about foreclosure fraud than any other state prosecutors in America. They were ordered not to speak with other AG offices or share documents. Only Tallahassee could file discovery requests, take depositions, or speak with target attorneys; June and Theresa could merely prepare memos guiding their work. And when their secretary quit, they didn't receive funding to replace her. As documents streamed in from across the country, June and Theresa had to share one secretary with two other colleagues. They had to personally respond to public records requests from LPS and other investigation targets, turning them into glorified clerical workers. Bob Julian, their supervisor, expressed frustration about what was happening, but he couldn't do anything about it.

Like Tom Cox, Lynn seethed at how the same federal prosecutors and FBI agents who had previously expressed great interest in her case now said they couldn't get authorization to pursue it further. When she talked to contacts about LPS or DocX or fraudulent assignments, they would change the subject. Lynn read a ruling that referenced a foreclosure fraud investigation by bankruptcy trustees in Pennsylvania and Delaware, and asked the U.S. attorney's office in Jacksonville about it. They said Main Justice brought that under their umbrella. This was a common occurrence; local investigators could interfere with cases above them, so they deferred. It seemed like every criminal inquiry was getting swallowed into that umbrella in Washington.

Michael Olenick, one of Lynn's researcher colleagues, contacted her. He was working with an associate producer at CBS, who was poking around the foreclosure fraud story. "Meet with us and have dinner," Olenick asked. Lynn knew she'd have to be careful, with her *qui tam* case still under seal. But she dreamed of raising a ruckus about fraudulent documents and forcing the government into action. So she went to dinner.

The associate producer was Dan Ruetenik; he worked for *60 Minutes*. In Lynn's pitch, Ruetenik saw the makings of a story. The two spent a couple of days in Lynn's front room, poring over mortgage assignments and poster boards. A week later Ruetenik returned to Palm Beach Gardens with senior producer Robert Anderson. After several email exchanges, Ruetenik told Lynn that *60 Minutes* was ready to run a story, if she'd agree to be interviewed. Lynn checked with her lawyers, and they gave their blessing. They knew they couldn't stop her anyway.

One sunny morning in February 2011, a team of cameramen and sound engineers arrived at Lynn Szymoniak's house. They emptied the living room, moving all the furniture onto the driveway. The neighbors must have thought that, at long last, Lynn lost her case and was being evicted. The crew spent four hours positioning lights and cameras. Scott Pelley, the correspondent, didn't arrive until that afternoon. "Let's take a walk," he said to Lynn, and the two strolled around the subdivision, framed by the man-made lake and aimless fountain in the distance. Pelley said he worked on a story about credit cards where low-level employees spent every day signing court affidavits, using names of people who had been dead for years. So he didn't need much convincing.

They went back inside and began the shoot. Lynn sat in front of her poster boards, the same ones she'd lugged around since that happy hour at E.R. Bradley's. Lynn handled interrogations from the FBI, so she could handle a TV interview. But every now and then Pelley would stop Lynn and give her tips: "When you lean forward it doesn't work as well; you look like you're trying to sell me something."

Pelley keyed in on the information about Linda Green and DocX. When they wrapped, he turned to his producers and asked, "So when are we going to Georgia?" The producers hadn't set up a trip to DocX; LPS had shut down the office the previous spring, and many of its workers had scattered. But Pelley was insistent that without interviewing DocX employees, there was no story.

Dan Ruetenik pulled Lynn aside and asked for some DocX contacts. There was one man, Chris Pendley, who had written to Lynn telling her that he signed so many documents he couldn't remember his own name anymore. *60 Minutes* did go to Georgia, but the ex-employees they found were worried about how the FBI in Jacksonville would react if they went public. Ruetenik asked Lynn to call her FBI contact, Doug Matthews, to see if he would allow the ex-employees to come forward. Doug just laughed at her.

Lynn didn't know if or when the story would air. She kept asking Dan Ruetenik over email. Ruetenik had to go to Japan to cover the Fukushima nuclear disaster and responded only intermittently.

Meanwhile, Michael and Lisa continued branching out beyond the Internet. Moratorium Monday continued and expanded across the state. Dozens of protesters marched on the Fort Lauderdale courthouse in January 2011. During a popular beach bonfire event in Lake Worth, Lisa and Michael held Torch the Fraud, setting fraudulent documents ablaze in the night sky. Lake Worth routinely attracts a few thousand people for the bonfires, and homeowner activist Nicole West edited the video to look like they were all there for Torch the Fraud. "How'd you organize that big crowd?" people asked in the comments. Lisa didn't give up the secret.

Lisa brought Jenna to every protest, even the bonfire. Once she gave her coins to throw into the fountain in front of the Palm Beach County courthouse. "What did you wish for?" Lisa asked. Two things, Jenna replied: a bunny, and "that the judges will understand."

Michael filmed a county sheriff serving Virtual Bank in Palm Beach Gardens with a writ of possession when the bank failed to pay court-ordered attorney's fees after losing a foreclosure case for inability to prove standing. The sheriff ordered deputies to remove money from ATMs and other assets to satisfy the lien. "Deadbeat bank" actions became more widespread, with a Philadelphia homeowner "foreclosing" on Wells Fargo and another in Naples, Florida, "foreclosing" on Bank of America. That one made it onto *The Daily Show*.

When the Florida legislature returned, bills to convert the state to non-judicial foreclosures reappeared, just as Matt Weidner expected. So Lisa and Michael collaborated with the Mortgage Justice Group of Sarasota and organized the second annual Rally in Tally, another day of speeches and citizen engagement. This Rally in Tally was held the same day as the Florida Bankers' Association Capitol Day. Hundreds of bank lobbyists and homeowners passed each other in the hallways, each with their own agenda. This time Lisa worked with a lobbyist in Tallahassee, Candice Ericks, to schedule lawmaker meetings. She and Michael even got forty-five minutes in Pam Bondi's office, where staffers praised their efforts. Jenna attended the rally, but just as the little girl stepped off the bus, Grace Rucci lost control of a plastic protest sign in a strong wind, and it whacked Jenna on the nose. Lisa later said Jenna was the only one to shed blood for the fight.

The battle continued online as well. Michael found the e-signature of Shapiro & Fishman lawyer Anna Malone on documents signed months after she resigned from the firm. Lisa's law firm insiders passed her an instruction manual on how to manufacture affidavits for reasonable attorney's fees by cutting and pasting old signatures. And of course there were horror stories: banks breaking and entering into homes in the name of "property preservation," with one company even taking the ashes of a woman's late husband; families making all their loan modification payments and still getting foreclosed; a woman who paid off her house and *then* got a default notice; sheriff's deputies conducting an eviction and finding a dead body.

Finally Lynn got the call from *60 Minutes*. They actually ran two reports: one on children of foreclosure, focusing on a group from Orlando that lived in hotels and vans, and her segment, which aired on April 3, 2011.

"One thing weighing on the economy is the huge number of foreclosed houses. Many are stuck on the market for a reason you wouldn't expect:

banks can't find the ownership documents," began Scott Pelley. The story opened at a NACA event, the camera dollying across thousands of people in line to save their dreams. Pelley noted the irony that borrowers seeking relief needed to provide perfectly rendered financial information, but their lenders screwed up the paperwork on who owns their mortgage in epic fashion.

"In my mind, this is an absolute, intentional fraud," said Lynn in front of her poster boards, wearing a pink sweater, black slacks, and a bright aqua scarf, perhaps a subliminal nod to her friend Lisa Epstein. *60 Minutes* detailed Lynn's entire story: her foreclosure, her forensic experience ("she had trained FBI agents"), her research on BOGUS documents and Linda Green forgeries and officers of too many banks. "They were sitting in a room signing their name as quickly as they could to any nonsense document that was put in front of them," Lynn said bluntly.

60 Minutes even tracked down Linda Green in Georgia. She allowed herself to appear on camera but would not be interviewed. Pelley explained in a voice-over that she was a shipping clerk for an auto parts facility before becoming the vice president of twenty different banks. DocX, "a sweatshop for forged mortgage documents," chose Green for the assignment because she had an easy-to-spell name. Chris Pendley, the whistleblower who had reached out to Lynn, also appeared. "You're Linda Green?" Pelley asked Pendley.

"Yeah, can't you tell?" Pendley said he signed four thousand documents a day as Linda Green, alongside others spoofing their identity for $10 an hour.

"Not much for a guy who's vice president of five banks," Pelley said.

"Yeah, I was very underpaid for my status," Pendley concurred.

Neither DocX's parent company, LPS, nor the banks who used their services would publicly respond. In statements, the banks blamed the mortgage servicers; of course, big banks owned the largest mortgage servicing companies. LPS said that they shut down DocX when they discovered improprieties. The FDIC's Sheila Bair, Lynn's old pen pal, appeared at the end to express astonishment, agreeing that "millions" of documents could be involved. She suggested a "cleanup fund," like there would be in a natural disaster, compensating homeowners so they would accept the banks' ownership claims.

Forty homeowner activists gathered to watch that Sunday night at a house in West Palm Beach. They didn't think the cleanup fund sounded appropriate for an ongoing criminal enterprise. But they loved how the story so directly explained the fraud epidemic. It was obvious to them that a nationally televised exposé on an esteemed newsmagazine known for inspiring action would finally lead to justice.

19

WRIGGLING OFF THE HOOK

April 4, 2011

"The Next Housing Shock," the *60 Minutes* foreclosure fraud story, would later win the prestigious Loeb Award for excellence in business reporting. The day after it aired, Lynn had a hearing for the foreclosure case on her house. Her lawyer, Mark Cullen, passed on a message from the bailiffs: "Please tell Lynn we all support her." And with Michael Redman, Michael Olenick, and Lisa Epstein watching, Lynn got the case dismissed—without prejudice, of course, so Deutsche Bank could come back within thirty days and file again. But for a moment the hostility that normally greeted her arguments disappeared. That month homeowner activists praised Lynn at the foreclosure happy hour. Lisa and Michael passed out name tags: everyone had the name Linda Green.

Lynn frequently received emails and letters and calls because of her Internet postings, but after the story the phone rang constantly, day and night, from Maine to California. Over two thousand people contacted her within a week. Neighbors knocked on her door. The postman knocked, too, and not just to deliver mail; *he* had a foreclosure issue. Few people congratulated her for exposing the fraud; these were mainly cries for help. Some homeowners wanted an introduction to Scott Pelley so they could tell their stories. They sent so many documents by email, it crashed Lynn's computer. And they made Lynn their confessor, spinning tales of misery about seeing their life's work ground to dust. In the darkest moments, they spoke of the relief suicide might bring.

Lynn helped as many as she could, spending long nights talking down homeowners who were determined to shoot it out with sheriffs coming to evict them. But she couldn't deliver peace to everyone. The psychological burden of being perceived as a source of salvation nearly cracked her. Lynn believed it would soon be worth it, because the *60 Minutes* story would make it impossible not to bring indictments. Prosecutors would have to charge LPS, and then they would go up the chain, finding out who at the banks authorized LPS to produce false documents. But despite her certitude, in the days following the broadcast Lynn fielded only social calls from her law enforcement contacts. There were no major announcements.

Hidden observers began to pay attention to Lynn. During practically every phone conversation she heard clicks on the line, suggesting another presence listening in. Lisa and Michael heard them, too; sometimes in the middle of a conversation a voice would say, "This message is being recorded." An FBI agent from Atlanta grew angry after hearing the third party and demanded, "Are you recording my call?" Lynn said he must be the one recording it. The FBI agent suddenly changed his tone: "Hang up now."

Lynn had eight months of emails sucked dry, zapped from her inbox— from federal prosecutors, her lawyers, fellow researchers, friends. No data recovery specialist could ever find them. Her car was broken into in her own driveway, in a community with an iron gate and security guards. The burglars took only the GPS unit. One night Lynn heard a loud beep, like a fire alarm, every thirty seconds. She called a local security guard, and they spent a half hour digging through landscaping, trying to find the source of the noise. "I'm sure it's the pool warning system telling you that your leaf basket is full," the guard said. Lynn said she had no such system.

None of this was particularly unusual in the foreclosure fraud universe. Attorneys would tell Lynn about people burglarizing their offices and rifling through files. It was a throwback to her student radical days, when the FBI surveilled and tracked her across the country. But it didn't feel pleasant to be on the receiving end forty years later, and from private banks instead of the government.

Right around this time, Lisa received a bizarre-looking mechanical device in a package addressed to Michael. It smelled of kerosene and was shaped like a ray gun from a low-budget science fiction film. Lisa didn't remember Michael telling her anything about it. She called Lynn, who asked her, "Do you think it's a bomb? Is it ticking?"

When Lynn picked Lisa up for a previously planned meeting, Lisa had the contraption with her to give to Michael. Lynn didn't want it in the car and exclaimed, "Throw it out the window!" But it turned out the device was a used automotive fuel-sending unit, which Michael ordered on eBay. Michael didn't have a permanent residence, couch-surfing with friends after separating from Jennifer and moving out of the house. So he told Lisa he would mail the device to her place, and she forgot about it.

Lynn remembered a key element of the FBI's counterintelligence program: to make targets suspect infiltration in their networks. She guessed those psychological operations manuals hadn't changed.

Two officials buoyed by Lynn's TV appearance toiled as obscure custodians of public land records. John O'Brien, register of deeds of Essex County, Massachusetts, first elected in 1977, compared the sleepy task of maintaining his office to running the public library. But he took pride in his stewardship of one of the oldest land registries in America. O'Brien had loudly protested the corruption of the county records since 2008, when a forensic examiner named Marie McDonnell ran a pro bono audit of a sample of 100 files, finding the majority of the documents to be invalid. O'Brien contacted state attorney general Martha Coakley seeking funds for a full audit and demanding fees from MERS for unrecorded transfers. Coakley didn't respond for months.

O'Brien decided to go public, announcing he would no longer record fraudulent documents, making it nearly impossible to complete mortgage transactions. Banks started sending replacement documents to Essex County, with brand-new signatures and notarizations. O'Brien didn't buy it: "I believe the banks' actions speak louder than words and show their consciousness of guilt."

Down the Atlantic coast, Jeff Thigpen, a register in Greensboro, North Carolina (Guilford County), contacted O'Brien. They were a mismatched pair: O'Brien an irascible and boisterous Irishman, Thigpen a soft-spoken and deeply religious community activist who took the foreclosure crisis personally. When Thigpen was young, his father lost his leg in a farming accident; the same year his mother went temporarily blind. The community rallied to save the family home, and later he committed his life to repaying that debt.

When Thigpen watched Lynn on *60 Minutes*, he grew sick with terror. Those phony documents were infecting his office. Thigpen and O'Brien drafted an open letter, demanding all past and present MERS assignments be properly filed, to perfect chain of title and allow registers to collect lost fees. A few days later Lynn contacted them. She sent Thigpen fabricated documents from his own county, which led him to mobilize the office to search specifically for DocX/LPS files, the ones profiled on *60 Minutes*. Within a month they found 6,100 of them—processed for banks like Wells Fargo and Bank of America—4,500 of which had signature variations that suggested forgery. Some were dated after the Jeffrey Stephan revelations broke nationwide. In other words, the banks were *still* robo-signing, even while under investigation. Thigpen held a press conference, with Lynn and her poster boards at his side. He called it "a betrayal of public trust."

At a convention for county registers, Thigpen and O'Brien tried to get their colleagues interested in attacking fraud, with only scattered success. Most registers worked nine to five and just wanted to clock in and out without the burden of uncovering a national conspiracy. Thigpen sent his report to the attorney generals' fifty-state investigative committee; they never responded. All this damning evidence, millions upon millions of documents, was sitting around in courthouses and county offices. But nobody bothered to inspect the paper.

In fact, by February 2011 the media were eager to put a bow on a "global settlement" for foreclosure fraud. The *Wall Street Journal* said the whole thing would cost $20 billion to $30 billion, mostly going toward a fund for loan modifications for struggling homeowners. The head of Missouri's Consumer Protection Division told a community meeting the fifty-state investigation uncovered "a good deal of fraud" but found nobody to prosecute, an odd position to take amid negotiations. Critics noted there was already a $50 billion kitty for loan modifications, the government's HAMP program, and it wasn't working, because it relied on understaffed and venal mortgage servicers. The proposed settlement sounded like HAMP 2.0.

Iowa activists again asked Tom Miller if he would "put people in jail," as promised. He answered, "I really feel I shouldn't talk about what's going to be in the agreement." In March Miller delivered a twenty-seven-page "settlement term sheet" to the banks, featuring the modification fund and a series of standards for mortgage servicers to follow, mostly restating prohibitions that were already supposed to be illegal. There was no indication of what legal indemnification would be exchanged. Miller's fellow attorneys general didn't know about the term sheet until it was sprung on them at a scheduled meeting. At the time, no subpoenas had been issued, no depositions taken, no effort made to even talk to foreclosure fraud experts. The executive committee cobbled together unrelated reports about tiny samples of the mortgage market and extrapolated total liability from there. Nobody ever saw the underlying documentation from the reports, just the summaries. Michael posted the term sheet, commenting, "Without CRIMINAL INDICTMENTS, there is no settlement."

Activists found it difficult to acquire any hard information about the negotiations because the whole thing was run out of the White House, where officials believed a settlement could stabilize the housing market and remove uncertainty from mortgage servicers. They described a tension between doing something quickly for homeowners who had little time to save their homes and doing something commensurate with the scale of the problem. But all mortgages included mandatory default servicing for delinquent borrowers; the proposed "penalty" of mortgage modifications would just force servicers to live up to existing obligations. And since the financial crisis, Washington had been far more preoccupied with the safety and soundness of banks than of homeowners.

That vaunted interagency review, with hundreds of investigators crawling all over the banks, concluded that all the foreclosures were warranted because the borrowers were behind on their payments. Nobody tried to address *why* borrowers fell behind on payments, which could have been due to predatory servicing. They didn't bother to look at chain of title issues or the systematic lack of standing to foreclose. And the investigation involved only 2,800 loan files (and, FDIC's Sheila Bair admitted later, only 100 foreclosures), in most cases evaluated by the servicers themselves. Despite this narrow scope, the review found "critical deficiencies" in document preparation practices and "violations of state and local foreclosure laws." The alleged propriety of the foreclosures did not retroactively make criminality legal.

In February 2011 JPMorgan Chase admitted that they indeed wrong-fully foreclosed on active-duty military members, evicting them while they served in Iraq and Afghanistan. This violated the federal Servicemembers Civil Relief Act (SCRA), which carried jail time in the statute, but nobody ever suggested such a penalty. JPMorgan acted swiftly, firing the executive in charge of mortgages, David Lowman, and giving servicemembers back their homes, debt-free. Other banks who violated SCRA went above and beyond to make amends, even setting quotas to hire veterans. But while ser-vicemembers got justice, everyone else who suffered from similarly abusive treatment were on their own. Bloggers compared it to corporations who promoted environmentally friendly policies to engender public support. That was called "greenwashing"; this was "camo-washing."

In mid-April, a week or so after Lynn laid out the horrors on *60 Min-utes*, the Office of the Comptroller of the Currency and the Federal Reserve split from settlement talks and announced an enforcement action against ten mortgage servicers, LPS, and MERS. They ordered servicers to offer a single point of contact for homeowners and end the practice of "dual track-ing," pursuing foreclosures and loan modifications simultaneously. But mostly they just asked servicers not to break the law again. The regulators promised monetary penalties, based on an "independent review" of fore-closure files to determine borrower harm. Of course, the government just got done saying that everyone who experienced foreclosure deserved it. And the banks got to handpick and pay the reviewers. The orders, then, put guilty parties in charge of determining their own punishment.

Activists considered the orders a toothless ploy to undermine the fifty-state investigation. But at least it killed the global settlement, the one check for banks to pay. And Lisa found nuggets buried in the interagency review, released by the Fed in conjunction with the enforcement order. Page 3: "The reviews showed that servicers possessed original notes and mortgages," confirming that critical documents were never conveyed to the trustee's custodian. Page 7: "Examiners noted instances where documentation in the foreclosure file alone may not have been sufficient to prove ownership of the note at the time the foreclosure action commenced without reference to additional information." But then, sounding suspiciously like a cover-up: "When additional information was requested and provided to examiners, it generally was sufficient to determine ownership." On that point, Lisa noted "the financial sector's propensity to fabricate evidence." You could almost picture it: examiners found deficient documentation and asked the bank for an explanation, and the bank magically produced the original note, just like they did in courtrooms. And the examiners, ignorant of such practices, sighed in relief.

As 2011 wore on, courts across the country invalidated foreclosures. Louisiana bankruptcy judge Elizabeth Manger sanctioned LPS in a case, *In re Wilson*, for fabricating documents, saying, "The fraud perpetrated on the Court, Debtors, and trustee would be shocking if this Court had less experience concerning the conduct of mortgage servicers." In *Veal v. American Home Mortgage Servicing*, an Arizona bankruptcy court ruled that the assignor did not own the mortgage when they tried to assign it to the trust. Judges in Alabama (*Horace v. LaSalle*) and Michigan (*Hendricks v. U.S. Bank*) agreed that promissory notes never made it to the trusts in time, invalidating the sales and reverting the chain of title back to the original lender. A New York appeals court in *Bank of New York v. Silverberg* ruled that MERS had no right to foreclose on any homeowner or assign that right to anyone else if it never held the note. The Great Foreclosure Machine was perched on a cliff; anyone in power could tip it over. No one did.

That spring, though, David J. Stern gave up. The firm informed chief judges throughout Florida that they could no longer manage lawsuits and would withdraw from a hundred thousand cases statewide. They gave the courts four weeks' notice. A month later, Ben-Ezra & Katz, another foreclosure mill, shut its doors. This left foreclosures in limbo; Lynn's condo, a Stern case, would sit without docket action for a year. Stern ended up suing eight banks for breach of contract, and when Michael posted about that, a tipster who owned an employment agency revealed that Stern never paid him fees due for placing paralegals at the firm. Stern, ultimately, was the deadbeat.

The judicial system lost lucrative filing fees after the Stern implosion. Money began to dry up for the supersized rocket docket's retired judges; Governor Rick Scott granted the judiciary a loan to get through the fiscal year. In Palm Beach County, courts set up case management conferences for Stern lawsuits, hoping to find new counsel. Like any judicial proceeding, they were supposed to be open to the public. But Lisa and Michael were barred from entering because it was "too crowded."

Biases spilled into the regular case file. A friend of Lisa's told her defense attorneys were threatened with monetary sanctions for raising "frivolous" defenses about fabricated evidence. Chip Parker got a Florida bar complaint simply for making negative comments about the rocket docket to CNN. Matt Weidner was also investigated for talking to reporters; a judge pulled out the articles in court and admonished him. Bailiffs removed lawyer Mark Stopa from a courtroom after a judge ruled before hearing his argument. Broward County chief judge Victor Tobin showed his allegiances by quitting to work for the Marshall C. Watson foreclosure mill. Once the rocket docket went into overdrive, 140,000 foreclosure cases got cleared in nine months.

Of all the counties Larry Schwartztol and Rachel Goodman of the ACLU studied since coming to study Florida courts, Lee County, around Fort Myers, was the worst. Focused intensely on clearing cases, the county disposed up to two hundred a day. In an extreme example, Lee County judge James Thompson specifically exempted banks from filing verifications that foreclosure documents were valid, defying state supreme court orders. When caught, Thompson changed his order, but then allowed affidavits that didn't comply with the verification standard.

Schwartztol and Goodman sat in on cases and took testimony from defense attorneys. They hired their own court reporters and stationed them in Lee County courts. And they found a homeowner, Georgi Merrigan of Cape Coral, willing to sue the county. After Georgi's husband suffered a debilitating auto accident, she had to leave her job to become his caretaker. Because of the lost income they fell behind on their mortgage, and the ACLU argued they couldn't get a fair foreclosure trial from the Lee County rocket docket. They filed an emergency motion to intervene with the district court of appeals, supplemented with a five-hundred-page appendix of public records and court transcripts. The ACLU charged that whatever was happening in Lee County wasn't a court anymore. The appeals court didn't see it that way, denying the ACLU's request in a one-line order. With an adverse ruling, Schwartztol and Goodman saw no choice but to pull out of Florida. Their only solace was that rocket docket funding would soon run out.

That spring, Carol Asbury sold Lisa and Michael on a new idea. WDJA, a local radio station, allowed anyone to broadcast on their airwaves for $300 a week. The show would also stream over the Internet. Carol offered to

bankroll it; she called it Citizen Warriors Radio. Lisa and Michael checked
out the studio, just off I-95 in Delray Beach. They'd seen a lot of foreclosed,
vacant houses in disrepair over the years. This place looked worse. Their
car kicked up dust on the unpaved driveway as they pulled in. They had to
dodge broken glass to reach the door. The one-story bungalow wobbled as
they approached it, with overgrowth from a nearby thicket of foliage surrounding one side. Headshots from former guests dotted one wall of the
studio, and judging from the hairstyles, the station stopped collecting pictures in the 1970s. The production engineer, Byron Eggers, always wore a
pirate-themed bandanna. He would talk proudly about how hard he partied
the night before. Not surprisingly, Byron was also in foreclosure.

For some reason, Lisa and Michael agreed to come back every week.

Citizen Warriors Radio taped Saturday mornings at eight o'clock. Lisa
would book guests, either friends like Nye Lavalle or foreclosure defense attorneys. They discussed the latest news and court decisions, promoted rallies and street actions, took calls—whatever could fill the hour. There was
an outline, but Carol never followed it.

A couple of weeks into the radio show, Michael got a call while driving
to a barbecue with Lisa and some friends. It was Kim Miller at the *Palm
Beach Post*. "I'm calling for a comment about the indictment."

"Which banker got indicted?"

"No, I mean Carol Asbury."

"What?"

Federal authorities indicted Carol and two dozen others in a scheme to
defraud mortgage lenders. The group recruited straw buyers from poor
sections of Miami-Dade County who used phony income statements to
purchase luxury homes in an upscale real estate development called Versailles. The conspirators set up the sales as a double closing: one set of closing
documents with the real price went to the seller, and another set, with an
inflated price, went to the lender. The difference in prices represented the
profits, which got laundered through multiple bank accounts. The scheme
wrecked the community, as half the homes in Versailles fell into foreclosure and squatters moved into abandoned properties. According to the indictment, Carol's real estate brokerage and title company, which predated
her foreclosure defense work, prepared the double closing documents.

Michael told Kim Miller he didn't know anything about it, and rushed off the phone. He called Carol—"What the fuck is going on?"—but got no answer. Michael was panicked, not just because Carol represented his main source of income but also because his reputation would take a hit through association with a mortgage fraudster. It would give fuel to his critics.

At the barbecue, Michael couldn't relax. He thought about all those hints of surveillance on his phone line. "We always think somebody's coming after us and now it's happening," Lisa told him. So Michael called up Kim Miller. He gave her this comment: "I find it very disturbing that the government must use all their resources to attack the people that are exposing the fraud and corruption. Where are the indictments on all the known felonies committed by the banks, foreclosure mills and doc shops?"

The *Palm Beach Post* ran the story with Michael's quote. As predicted, critics had a field day. Foreclosure fraud blogger Steve Dibert gleefully recounted the news, adding that the Florida bar publicly reprimanded Carol in 2008 for failing to inform law enforcement about a fake escrow letter drafted by one of her employees. Carol listed *4closureFraud* as her personal law firm website with the bar, and Dibert intimated that soliciting donations, which Michael occasionally did to cover costs of events like the Rally in Tally, violated state law. Dibert didn't accuse Michael of being part of the scheme: "He's just trying to save his job and his credibility, both of which it appears just went out the window."

Carol finally told Michael the truth, or at least a version of it. During the housing bubble, both Carol's mother and her husband fell ill. So she entrusted the office to underlings while tending to family matters. Carol claimed her employees put together the phony double closings, not her. The FBI raided the office, and Carol cooperated while understanding that there would be no immunity. Carol told Michael the feds were making an example of her because she defended homeowners. But Michael believed the foreclosure defense work could have been a public relations ploy, to cast her as a victim of retaliation for challenging foreclosure fraud. He felt foolish for initially defending her, even as he considered her crimes insignificant compared to the banks'.

Carol pleaded guilty in October. She reiterated the story she told Michael to the *American Bar Association Journal*, framing her aid to homeowners as a way to make amends. "If the worst happens, I've still done the best I can," she said. The judge gave her two and a half years in prison.

One Friday in late May, at the Economic Crimes division offices in Fort Lauderdale, June Clarkson was poring through a pile of Lender Processing Services documents, as she had been doing all month long. LPS was one of the only cases June and her partner Theresa Edwards were allowed to keep. After the new regime took over in Tallahassee, they split up the foreclosure fraud investigations, farming them out to five different offices, to prosecutors unfamiliar with what June and Theresa had been tracking for over a year. June and Theresa weren't even allowed to provide transition notes.

One case quickly reached conclusion. Attorney general Pam Bondi settled with foreclosure mill Marshall C. Watson for just $2 million, along with promises to foreclose properly in the future. Bondi did not require Watson to admit that they engaged in anything illegal, even though the background facts in the case included such illegal practices as document forgery, false affidavits and notarizations, and process service to imaginary defendants. Watson effectively paid a small percentage of their foreclosure-based profits as hush money. June thought Bondi settled cheap.

It wasn't the first hint of whitewashing from Bondi, who publicly endorsed a fifty-state settlement without monetary penalties. She argued that forcing banks to lower loan balances for underwater homeowners would create "moral hazard," as homeowners would stop paying their mortgage to get a principal reduction. Homeowner deception weighed more heavily on her mind than deception by the banks.

June and Theresa got a commendation for "triggering a nationwide review" of foreclosure practices, and their presentation to county clerks was used as evidence in a New York case. But when it came to prosecuting wrongdoing, June and Theresa couldn't sneeze without asking Tallahassee. Whenever June found something notable in the LPS files, she'd have to walk down to her supervisor, Bob Julian, and show it to him. That Friday, every time June entered the room, Julian's face sank. He finally just shut the door. Theresa Edwards stopped by June's desk at three-thirty that afternoon. "Bob wants us both to come into his office."

Julian, who had known Theresa since law school, sat the two prosecutors down. "You're both done at the end of today. You can either quit or be terminated."

"Why are we being let go?" Theresa asked.

"It came from the top. Tallahassee didn't give me a reason."

June and Theresa hurriedly wrote resignation letters and turned in their security cards. They had to go back over the weekend for their personal items.

Within weeks of June and Theresa leaving, Joe Jacquot, a former deputy attorney general, became senior vice president of government affairs at LPS. Mary Leontakianakos, director of the Economic Crimes division under former AG Bill McCollum, went to work for Marshall C. Watson, the same foreclosure mill to which Bondi gave the sweetheart deal. Erin Cullaro, who moonlighted as a robo-signer while working for the attorney general, was also let go, more than a year after Lisa informed the office of her activities. But she landed with foreclosure mill Shapiro & Fishman. In Florida, there were rewards for those who played ball, and consequences for those who didn't.

The story didn't get out for a couple of months. Lisa knew something was wrong when emails to June and Theresa started to bounce back. When she heard the news, she felt sick. June and Theresa were the first prosecutors in America to actually investigate foreclosure fraud. They courageously trusted Lisa's wild theories, which were eventually proven true. It looked like the industry was busy tying up loose ends, making plans for its eventual impunity.

Bondi said nothing for a week after the story broke. Then her spokesperson issued a statement smearing June and Theresa's poor judgment and lack of professionalism. But Andrew Spark, a former lawyer in the Tampa Economic Crimes unit, released a letter that backed up everyone's suspicions. "As Clarkson and Edwards found out, and as I have found out in 7½ years of having one effort after another squelched, bold action is rare," Spark wrote, describing an Economic Crimes office that too often ceded ground to bullying corporate lawyers and wealthy contributors. It only grew worse, Spark said, under Pam Bondi.

Lisa requested a formal review of the firings by the state inspector general. Public interest group Progress Florida echoed that demand. As the scandal grew, June and Theresa granted several media interviews, including on Citizen Warriors Radio with Lisa and Michael. After days of pressure, Bondi agreed to have the inspector general for the state's chief financial officer conduct an investigation.

Deutsche Bank did refile for foreclosure against Lynn Szymoniak, naming her son Mark Elliot as a co-defendant, though he was still taking poetry classes in New York City and hadn't lived regularly in Palm Beach Gardens for seven years. A lawsuit on his record could hurt his credit and job prospects. It was a petty tactic to harass the family into silence. The case dragged on, three years after the initial filing.

Lynn knew *60 Minutes* was the last card she could play to force criminal investigations. She could write *Fraud Digest* articles and appear at happy hours until the end of time and wouldn't get the audience she had on CBS. But Jacksonville didn't budge. The U.S. attorney's office in South Carolina gave her conflicting signals. One day they'd say they were definitely filing criminal charges over the assignments. Then they'd say no, suing Chase for violations of the SCRA would play better with a jury. Then they'd change their minds again and focus on the mills. The indecision seemed to be a pretext for never moving forward.

Lynn wondered if *60 Minutes* could kick-start an IRS investigation. If mortgages were never conveyed to the trusts, with nonperforming loans stuck into them after the fact, they violated REMIC tax laws, which should trigger a 100 percent penalty. Reuters actually reported on this a few weeks after Lynn's story aired, with the IRS acknowledging an "active review" of REMIC practices in mortgage-backed securities. But Lynn heard from *Naked Capitalism* blogger Yves Smith that the fix was in. A senior IRS officer initially seemed interested but then dropped the issue when the White House sent word that they would not use tax laws as a tool of policy. When Yves broached REMICs at a meeting with top Treasury officials, they quickly changed the subject. The threat of trillions in tax penalties to induce a resolution was off the agenda. Georgetown professor Adam Levitin described failing to prosecute the REMIC issue as a "backdoor bailout of the financial system." Lynn decided not to call the IRS.

Instead of issuing press releases announcing indictments, or photos of top executives led away in handcuffs, Jacksonville only asked Lynn for more documents. Get me two hundred examples of this law firm signing mortgage assignments after they filed their foreclosure case, or thirty Linda Greens in this region of the country. Lynn spent hours on these projects, feeling like she couldn't say no. At one point the assistant U.S. attorney requested a set of files that Lynn knew would take fourteen hours to assemble. She emailed her friend Henry "Tommy" Clark, the old insurance fraud specialist who partnered with the FBI, telling him about it. Tommy called her within a few minutes, and didn't even say hello. "Don't waste your time," he said. Lynn was stunned.

Tommy was in the same position as she was—an outsider the office would employ for grunt work, like looking through ten thousand emails, searching for a smoking gun. Tommy worked with his Jacksonville friends for a long time, and saw them as honorable people willing to follow the evidence wherever it led. But he also recognized the pressure imposed on that office from above. So when he said, "I'm not working on it anymore, I've got a whole lot of other cases where I can file," to Lynn that meant everything. A friend was telling a friend to stand down. It was all over.

As the months went on, Lynn got bits and pieces of the story, always in the roundabout manner Tommy or her other friends used when discussing active investigations. The Justice Department stonewalled the case, refusing requests for additional resources and micromanaging the grand jury probe. She heard one emblematic story, where DoJ sent a young lawyer to south Florida to sit in on an FBI deposition with Cheryl Samons, from the now-defunct Stern law firm. The lawyer obstructed the investigation, filling time with dubious, irrelevant questions and stopping the agent from properly deposing the witness.

People threatened to quit, waved critical pieces of evidence in front of their superior's face, thundered that letting this fade would violate the cause of justice. But it didn't matter. Maybe the office would find a patsy, a sacrificial lamb, and plant everything on them. But it wouldn't be anything close to what Lynn expected in those frantic days thirty months earlier when she stayed up for seventy-two hours straight and made all those discoveries. Those documents in her front room now symbolized a pile of disappointments.

20

THE FINAL WHITEWASH

September 17, 2011

The heat finally subsided in south Florida, cooling the Intracoastal's waters and shaking the palm tree fronds as the winds returned. That summer Michael moved into Lynn's downtown condo, from one foreclosure to another. He insisted on paying the homeowner's association fee out of the cash he held back for the mortgage in Port St. Lucie. With the *4closureFraud* sponsorship in limbo, it was practically all Michael had left. During child support hearings with Jennifer, her lawyer alleged that Michael must have hidden assets. After all, he was a celebrity, featured in newspapers and magazines. He even had his own radio show. "We pay $300 a week for that radio show!" Michael shouted at the hearing. The lawyer couldn't understand that; radio stations paid the hosts, not the other way around.

A liberal group in Washington State contacted Lisa about Dixie Mitchell, a seventy-one-year-old cancer survivor facing foreclosure, whose mortgage servicer, Ocwen, perpetually lost her loan modification paperwork. Ocwen's headquarters were near Lisa's co-op, in a West Palm Beach office park. Lisa and Michael printed T-shirts for a fictional company called Bermuda Triangle Recovery Services, specializing in finding missing documents. On a rainy fall day they hand-delivered Dixie's documents to Ocwen, camera crew in tow, along with a petition from 7,400 Washingtonians supporting Dixie. A man in the lobby, who had been waiting all day to see someone about his mortgage, remarked, "Boy, I wish I could've done that!" After some media attention, Dixie did get a modification, showing that servicers could help their customers—at least if they needed to protect their reputations.

Soon the foreclosure fighters had new allies. On September 17, Occupy Wall Street, born from a suggestion in the Canadian magazine *Adbusters*, set up camp in Zuccotti Park in lower Manhattan. Protesters expressed widespread frustration that the economy served the interests of the wealthiest 1 percent. Everything foreclosure bloggers documented about the bubble and the crash drove the unrest in New York. Eventually some protesters figured that out; in the beginning they searched for answers.

Occupy spread nationwide, including to Palm Beach. A throng gathered at the Bryant Park clamshell and pitched tents. The first general assembly drew four hundred attendees. Lisa went down and saw nothing like the hordes of violent youths the media were hyping. This group was older, people touched by the financial crash's impact who feared for their kids' futures. Lisa thought she could finally match her knowledge of fraud with enough bodies willing to lie in the street and demand action. She took the floor and started by saying, "If your neighbor is in foreclosure and you call them a deadbeat, you're hurting yourself. Let me explain why." She tied foreclosures to the accumulation of mortgage-backed securities in public pension funds. Mass foreclosures hurt investors, who would make more money keeping people in their homes at a reduced payment. In fact, preventing foreclosures was preferable for just about everyone. But instead investors paid for delays, fraudulent document production, and legal work, exacerbating losses. The public pension crisis had an antecedent in the foreclosure crisis; people hadn't put that together.

Over time, the Occupy Palm Beach crowds thinned out. But Lisa spent a lot of time at the encampment, bringing Lynn over to run teach-ins on fraudulent documents and vacant properties. The core Occupiers reacted strongly to the message. It gave them an explanation for the rigged system they were condemning.

Occupy's founding coincided with another potential bailout; the fifty-state settlement had been described as "imminent" for at least six months. That summer New York attorney general Eric Schneiderman told a local paper he was "stunned" by the lack of investigative work from the executive committee, declaring, "We have no leverage." He announced he would not sign any settlement if it immunized banks for violating New York law. Instead, he opened a new investigation into the validity of mortgage-backed securities transfers involving Bank of America, as well as leading trustees Deutsche Bank and Bank of New York Mellon. Delaware attorney general Beau Biden, the vice president's son, joined Schneiderman on the probe; between them, they represented states where all mortgage-backed trusts incorporated themselves, the beating heart of securitization FAIL. At *4closureFraud*, Michael posted graphics portraying Schneiderman in a white hat, like the lawman coming to clean up the town. "Please everyone, we must support this man," Michael wrote. "He is our last hope on a national level."

In response, Tom Miller booted Schneiderman off the fifty-state executive committee, saying he "actively worked to undermine" settlement efforts. The White House pressured him to support the deal he was just barred from negotiating. Kathryn Wylde, chief executive for the business-friendly Partnership for New York City, even accosted Schneiderman at the funeral for former New York governor Hugh Carey, urging him to back off the banks because "Wall Street is our Main Street." Housing and Urban Development secretary Shaun Donovan, who spent months hosting tea-and-cookies settlement talks with banks in his conference room, didn't deny the effort to rein in Schneiderman, telling the *New York Times* that everyone would benefit from a speedy resolution. But the fifty-state probe had launched a year earlier; all this time spent crafting deals could instead have been spent on investigating.

As chants of "We are the 99 percent" reverberated, attorneys general chose sides. Delaware's Beau Biden, Massachusetts's Martha Coakley, and Nevada's Catherine Cortez Masto stood with Schneiderman; all had active foreclosure investigations in their states. On September 13, Lori Swanson of Minnesota released a letter rejecting a settlement over conduct "that has not been investigated." Kentucky's Jack Conway announced on September 22 that he opposed "immunity against the banks." The big holdout was California's Kamala Harris. Her brother-in-law Tony West, a top Justice Department official, was helping negotiate the settlement, and she served as a key surrogate in Barack Obama's 2008 election. Like almost all attorneys general, she viewed the office as a stepping-stone. But she represented the nation's biggest state, one of the hardest hit by the foreclosure crisis. Without her participation, the settlement would be incomplete.

Practically everyone who helped get Harris elected, from community and labor groups to the half-million-strong California Courage Campaign, started encouraging her to abandon the talks. Phone lines at the attorney general's offices, unused to constituent calls, jammed several times. Gavin Newsom, lieutenant governor and Harris's biggest potential rival in California politics, joined a coalition opposing the emerging deal called Californians for a Fair Settlement. This presupposed a settlement at some point, instead of civil lawsuits or criminal prosecutions. But it got Harris to abandon Tom Miller. After spending a full day with bank executives trying to hammer out a deal, Harris announced on September 30 that the proposal was "inadequate for California homeowners" and that she would forge "an independent path forward to resolution."

A lack of accountability characterized the first decade of the new millennium, from the 2000 election onward. Torturers and warrantless wiretappers and commanders in chief lying America into war received free passes for their crimes with such regularity that upholding the rule of law felt like an anomaly. Banks already got away with breaking the U.S. economy, and for a time it looked like they would obtain the same privilege for the biggest consumer fraud in history, in exchange for a meaningless dollar amount plucked out of thin air. Grassroots activists, joined by scattered leaders disinclined to facilitate a crime spree, put a pause to it. But it was only a pause.

In the foreclosure devastation, community organizers saw kindling for a mass movement wildfire. For years national groups held public protests, like when activists in Robin Hood outfits crossed a moat and stormed JPMorgan Chase's headquarters in Columbus, Ohio (in true medieval fashion, JPMorgan Chase's headquarters has a moat). But smaller organizations like No One Leaves in Springfield, Massachusetts, specialized in post-foreclosure eviction defense. They combined legal resources for homeowners and mass resistance to make it painful for banks to toss people into the street. More radical groups like Take Back the Land broke evicted residents back into their vacant homes, a tactic they called a "live-in." It was a throwback to farm communities banding together in the Depression to prevent foreclosures and stabilize neighborhoods.

Foreclosed properties stolen by banks with false documents were contested spaces, like the city parks and sidewalks Occupy commandeered.

Matt Browner-Hamlin, who organized the Where Is the Note? campaign for the Service Employees International Union, thought he could convert disorganized Occupy protests into meaningful action. To his surprise, he found it happening organically. In Atlanta, Minneapolis, Cleveland, and Los Angeles, foreclosure victims asked for help at Occupy general assemblies, and Occupiers mobilized to defend those homes. Browner-Hamlin supported this with a toolkit of resources and links to larger community groups. Occupy Wall Street activists got involved, and soon they announced Occupy Our Homes, a national day of action on December 6, 2011. Organizer Max Berger enthused, "This is a shift from protesting Wall Street fraud to taking action on behalf of people who were harmed by it."

With her new friends at Occupy Palm Beach, Lisa organized two events. One was a program called Foreclosure Watch, based on the efforts of Mothers Against Drunk Driving in the 1980s. In the morning, activists in Foreclosure Watch T-shirts sat in the courtroom and bore witness to hearings, their presence a signal that rulings affecting homeowners would be monitored and remembered. Judges seemed to take more care when Foreclosure Watch arrived.

In the evening, protesters lit candles at a Deutsche Bank–owned foreclosed property on North B Street in Lake Worth, to "mourn" lack of prosecutions of bank executives. Lisa previously participated in two previous vigils at this same white-and-yellow house, which had been boarded up for years without Deutsche Bank spending a dime to maintain it. Lynn and Michael and Jenna were there, too, along with dozens of others.

Other Occupy Our Homes groups were more aggressive. Protesters formed a human chain around foreclosed homes, keeping residents safe inside. Activists in Atlanta camped in the front yard of a police officer facing eviction. Families reclaimed vacant homes. In Brooklyn, Occupiers disrupted a foreclosure court by loudly singing; other demonstrators "mic-checked" foreclosure auctions.

These tactics worked. Los Angeles homeowner Rose Gudiel, who occupied her foreclosed home, got a loan modification offer from Fannie Mae. Beth Sommerer of Cleveland won a thirty-day stay of eviction. One-hundred-three-year-old Vita Lee of Atlanta got a reprieve from JPMorgan Chase. In Minneapolis, an ex-Marine named Bobby Hull had 150 people rally on his front lawn in front of television cameras, refusing to leave. Bank of America made him a deal.

Even after local police dismantled Occupy encampments, evicting protesters the way they evicted homeowners, Occupy Our Homes lived on. Homes became community hubs, with round-the-clock patrols so that homeowners could leave for work without threat of repossession. Occupy Homes Minneapolis placed heavy concrete barrels on front porches and chained themselves to them, making it difficult for law enforcement to remove them. They created an emergency text blast system that could bring a hundred activists to homes within thirty minutes. Occupy Fights Foreclosures in Los Angeles descended on foreclosure auctions, warning that banks had no proof of ownership in the homes they were selling. One thousand Los Angeles protesters prepared a Rose Parade float, a seventy-foot octopus made from plastic bags, symbolizing the financial industry.

Behind the resistance, Occupy Our Homes facilitated negotiations with mortgage servicers, with the protests creating leverage. Organizers recognized the value in creating a cost for evictions, throwing sand in the gears of the Great Foreclosure Machine. Victims telling their stories humanized the crisis and brought media attention that no bank wanted. Occupy Our Homes neutralized the greatest weapon the financial industry employed: shame. If you could convince homeowners that they did nothing wrong, you could get them to defy an unjust process, and build political power.

Evidence of false documents underpinned the movement and tore the veneer off the industry's schemes. Occupy Our Homes members knew about Linda Green. They understood securitization FAIL. If law enforcement would not arrest the perpetrators of an industry-wide crime spree, protesters would enforce the law through confrontation.

As protesters took action, Lynn found another inside game in Nevada, where three out of every five homeowners were underwater. Before their firing, June and Theresa worked with Nevada investigators on LPS. So Lynn sent files over and connected with Helene Lester, an assistant to John Kelleher, chief deputy of the Criminal Fraud Unit. When Kelleher was chosen to lead Nevada's Mortgage Fraud Strike Force in 2007, there wasn't even a crime called "mortgage fraud" in the state code. But after educating himself and hearing thousands of consumer complaints, he recognized the depth of the problem. With assistance from Lisa, Lynn passed along numerous documents to the strike force that summer, explaining to Lester in strategy sessions how they could locate fraud in county records. Lynn became their go-to consultant.

Catherine Cortez Masto, Nevada's attorney general, told Kelleher to follow the evidence wherever it led, and prosecute whomever was responsible. In August 2011, Masto sued Bank of America for promising to modify mortgages in a prior settlement but deceiving homeowners instead. In an amended complaint, Masto pulled out a bazooka:

> Bank of America misrepresented, both in communications with Nevada consumers and in documents they recorded and filed, that they had authority to foreclose upon consumers' homes as servicer for the trusts that held these mortgages. Defendants knew that they had never properly transferred these mortgages to those trusts, failing to deliver properly endorsed or assigned mortgage notes as required by the relevant legal contracts and state law. Because the trusts never became holders of these mortgages, Defendants lacked authority to collect or foreclose on their behalf and never should have represented they could.

Lynn's arguments helped to shape that language of securitization FAIL. Masto even quoted from *Kemp v. Countrywide*, where Bank of America executive Linda DeMartini admitted that mortgages never made it to the trusts. It wasn't just that Masto was suing over Bank of America's failure to honor a settlement, at a time when the Justice Department and other AGs wanted to clinch *another* settlement. Rather, her office understood the core issue, which many colleagues still regarded with bemusement. "These are not mere technicalities," the complaint stated. "The PSAs spelled out a specific procedure in order to ensure a proper transfer."

By September, investigators found repeated patterns in the Clark County recording office on notices of default, which inform Nevada homeowners that they face foreclosure. Two names kept showing up on the notices as representatives of multiple different banks: Gary Trafford and Gerri Sheppard. Prosecutors traced the documents to a Lender Processing Services branch office in Las Vegas. But Trafford and Sheppard actually worked in Orange County, California. The notary stamps came from Nevada, but the individuals who purported to sign documents in the notary's presence lived one state over. Investigators pulled Trafford and Sheppard's driver's licenses from the California DMV, and the signatures didn't match the Clark County notices of default. Tens of thousands of documents appeared forged. The strike force tracked down employees from the Vegas LPS office, including Tracy Lawrence. Tracy entered the real estate business in her twenties with only a high school education. A month into her new job at what would become LPS (the company went through five different names during this period), her bosses asked her to become a notary. Actually, they strongly implied that her continued employment depended on her becoming a notary. So she filed an application and got a stamp.

Within a year Tracy became assistant title officer to Gary Trafford. The office processed notices of default for entities foreclosing in Clark County, including Bank of America, Washington Mutual, and Fannie Mae. Trafford had a system: Tracy would receive the documents, sign Gary's name, notarize in her own name, and send the notice to the recording office. When this began, there weren't many notices to forge, but after the bubble popped, the numbers grew to three hundred a week, every week, for five years.

Tracy said Trafford rarely visited Las Vegas. But there was his name, all over Clark County land records. Tracy forged Gary Trafford's name, and other employees forged Gerri Sheppard's. At some point Sheppard apparently recognized the fraud inherent in the workflow, but only tried to make the forgery less detectable. She told employees in an email: "Regarding the signature of my name . . . please have someone other than the person that is notarizing it sign it. Thanks everyone—Gerri." Tracy didn't want to be blamed for following orders, so she checked with her boss via email: "Per your instructions, I will continue treating our docs as I have all along, i.e. signing your name and notarizing myself. If there are any further changes, let me know." Trafford replied affirmatively. And like a good employee, Tracy did as she was told until getting laid off in 2010.

But when state investigator Todd Grosz stopped by her home a year later, she was given a choice: testify against Gary Trafford or face arrest. So Tracy, again following instructions, agreed to testify in exchange for leniency. Before the grand jury, she nonchalantly explained the institutionalized fraud that occurred at 500 North Rainbow Boulevard every day for five years. It sounded like any office in America: employees covering their ass to avoid blame, stressed out by superiors squeezing more productivity from everyone. "Did you ever have any feelings that what you were doing may be illegal?" Kelleher questioned.

"I didn't really think about it," Tracy said. "They said, 'Oh yeah, it's OK, you can sign our names.'" Submitting to authority was so ingrained in office culture, it never occurred to robo-signers to question the system.

Tracy Lawrence wasn't the mastermind behind the destruction of America's mortgage market, just a tiny pin in the Great Foreclosure Machine, a line worker. Even Gary Trafford and Gerri Sheppard were only slightly larger pins. But they represented a way to get to executives at LPS who authorized the forgery factory, and then the servicers who hired them. It was Criminal Justice 101: flip the small fry to get to the big fish. Kelleher was itching to indict a director at one of the major banks, and the strike force was deliberately climbing toward their target.

On November 16, 2011, a week after the grand jury wrapped testimony, Masto announced a criminal indictment against Trafford and Sheppard on 606 counts of signing documents without a notary present, offering false documents for recording, and abetting the false certification of those documents. Trafford and Sheppard pleaded not guilty, and LPS, while admitting that "the signing procedures on some of these documents were flawed," brushed it off, saying they were "properly authorized and their recording did not result in a wrongful foreclosure." In other words, LPS admitted to the counts of the indictment but argued they should be overlooked because deadbeats didn't pay their mortgages.

Tracy was the only publicly named witness, and the only one with authorization in writing from her boss to forge his name. In exchange for her testimony, prosecutors reduced her charges to one misdemeanor for falsely notarizing a signature, which could lead to a $2,000 fine and one year in prison. Because she was a cooperative witness in a major fraud case, actual time served was expected to be far lower. Tracy faced sentencing on November 29. As Lisa and Lynn heard later, friends who talked to her the day before described her as upbeat, at peace with her decision, and ready to face the consequences. She talked about going back to college when it was all over.

On November 29, Tracy failed to show up for the hearing. When police reached Tracy's apartment, they found her dead. She was forty-three.

John Kelleher rushed to the scene as medical personnel were removing Tracy's body. She had uningested pills still in her mouth. A drape was flung up over the valance atop the living room window. There were sixty bottles of pills on the kitchen table and a powdery substance on the carpet below the sink. To Kelleher, the scene looked staged. But detectives immediately ruled out homicide; they never tested the powder or the curtains. After an autopsy, the coroner listed the cause of death as suicide through intoxication, from Xanax and two antihistamines.

Nevada tried to salvage the case; they had other notaries from the Vegas office who took the plea deal. The strike force even followed the script by suing LPS for document fraud, going up the chain. But Tracy Lawrence's death was a huge blow, and a chilling signal for anyone thinking of turning on the Great Foreclosure Machine.

Lisa heard the news in a phone call from Helene Lester, who said, "I'm calling to tell you that you need to be very careful. Our witness died; they say it's suicide, but we don't think it is." Lester gave Lynn the same warning. There was no way to know the truth. But to this day, Lisa and Lynn don't believe the official story. After Tracy's death, they shut their doors a little tighter and pulled their window shades down a little further.

After Kamala Harris backed out of settlement talks, everything went silent for a few months. By this time Lisa had sent packages of documents to the offices of thirty-odd attorneys general, but she rarely heard anything back. Calls with Laurence Tribe's Justice Department deputy unceremoniously ended. The Florida Department of Law Enforcement wouldn't respond. Other leads fizzled. Lynn wasn't even calling Jacksonville anymore. Michael, Lisa, and Lynn were stuck on an island, having proven a far-reaching fraudulent scheme but unaware of how that proof was being used. They had allies—some registers of deeds, scattered judges willing to invalidate foreclosures, and a couple of journalists exposing it all. But they had no vantage point on the endgame, no way to impact the process. They always talked about giving their information to someone in power to generate a reasonable solution. But what if that solution wasn't reasonable?

All the foreclosure fighters could do was fill the Internet with truth and give comfort and resources to homeowners. They could highlight the horror stories ("Sharon Bullington may lose her home because she paid her mortgage a week early") and call out the shenanigans. They could cheer heroes and jeer villains. They could hold happy hours; Tim Miller, a musician who wrote a song about foreclosures called "Love, Your Broken Home," gave a live performance at one.

That fall, state organizations under the umbrella Campaign for a Fair Settlement began to flood the inboxes of reporters and state and federal law enforcement with nearly identical talking points. "It is premature to sign an agreement before there is a full investigation into the foreclosure crisis," claimed Nevadans for a Fair Settlement. "We cannot accept a settlement without a full investigation," Pennsylvanians for a Fair Settlement agreed. It seemed like a spin-off of Californians for a Fair Settlement, which dislodged Harris from the fifty-state talks. But something was off about it. Why did they assume a settlement, with the only question being whether that settlement was fair? What investigation were they referring to? What happened to sending perpetrators to jail? Other than Catherine Cortez Masto, nobody seemed to be making the leap from robo-signing and document fraud to implicate the banks that authorized it. A settlement would break the path up the chain, tossing aside a mountain of documentary evidence. The mortgage industry didn't create phony documents because it was quicker but because they had no other alternative.

On December 1, 2011, Massachusetts attorney general Martha Coakley filed the kind of lawsuit activists wanted. She sued five big banks—Bank of America, JPMorgan Chase, Citi, Wells Fargo, and GMAC—for "conducting foreclosures when the defendants lacked the right to do so." This lawsuit effectively accused banks of stealing homes. Because of the *Ibanez* case, Massachusetts had the legal basis for charges about improper proof of mortgage ownership. But JPMorgan Chase's reaction to the Coakley lawsuit was ominous: "We are disappointed that Massachusetts would take this action now when negotiations are ongoing with the attorneys general and the federal government on a broader settlement that could bring immediate relief to Massachusetts borrowers rather than years of contested legal proceedings." Chase floated the prospect of quick homeowner aid to try to shut down a comprehensive inquiry into their practices. They sounded exactly like the White House officials pressing for a global settlement.

After New Year's, Lisa and Lynn had something new to worry about. The inspector general for Florida's chief financial officer released his report about the firing of June Clarkson and Theresa Edwards. It not only absolved Pam Bondi and her underlings of wrongdoing but also gratuitously accused June and Theresa of gross misconduct. They had "messy desks" and sloppy case files, which was true, mainly because the public delivered millions of mortgage documents and they had no legal secretaries to handle them. They were unprofessional, Economic Crimes unit director Richard Lawson told the inspector general, citing a letter from a corporate lobbyist complaining of aggressive treatment. They spun wild theories about mass fraud without evidence, even though these theories were confirmed by Florida court rulings. They threw around terms like "forgery" in their PowerPoint presentation, in contrast to how Lender Processing Services claimed to have internal "surrogate signing" policies whereby individuals would delegate signing authority. Why LPS internal policy mattered more than state law was unclear. Lawson accepted the opinions of investigation targets and their corporate lawyers over his own prosecutors.

According to the report, Lisa and Lynn leveraged their personal relationships with June and Theresa to dictate the investigations ("[Clarkson] was just listening to Lisa Epstein and following her instructions"). The foreclosure fighters had no opportunity to rebut this because they were never interviewed. Lisa, described as "a blogger who is being foreclosed on," was in Lawson's view using the Economic Crimes office to "extort a better result out of her own foreclosure case." The "last straw" was June and Theresa leaking a confidential multistate draft subpoena against LPS to Lisa. But Lisa made a public records request for that document and never published it or circulated it to the media, though the report claimed otherwise.

It was the only day since getting her foreclosure notice that Lisa felt afraid. She had no relationship with June and Theresa except as a source of publicly available documents. She certainly had no power to force them to do her bidding. Yet in an official report that she requested, the state smeared her as a conniving deadbeat looking for a free home. Not only did it legitimize the fraud, but no whistleblower would ever approach the state with information again. That week Lisa's hair came out in clumps from the stress.

Lynn had a greater disrespect for authority than Lisa and took the report in stride. But she found criticisms of the PowerPoint presentation ridiculous. The allegedly "sensitive" documents in there were on Lynn's website for a year. Assistant attorney general Trish Conners gave the same presentation to the Florida Senate. When Lisa met with Conners and Richard Lawson at the 2011 Rally in Tally, Conners personally thanked Lisa and other "citizen whistleblowers" for their work. Yet in the report, Conners seemed to develop amnesia: she "may have used a couple of slides" from the presentation but couldn't remember which.

The fact that the Florida attorney general's office hadn't issued a subpoena to any foreclosure fraud target since June and Theresa left suggested that they weren't committed to hard-charging prosecutions. In fact, Richard Lawson told Scott Maxwell of the *Orlando Sentinel* that he'd rather work with companies to change their internal culture than penalize them.

Days after the release of the inspector general's report, Lisa obtained confidential communications between LPS lawyers and the attorney general's office through a public records request. In June 2011 several states were discussing a civil suit against LPS, but Michigan had issued more damaging criminal subpoenas. Joan Meyer, a partner with LPS's law firm Baker and McKenzie, emailed Victoria Butler in Tallahassee to "catch up" about the Michigan subpoenas: "These public announcements can deeply impact LPS's business operations and stock price. . . . Wondering if there's anything we can do," Meyer wrote. Later that day, Meyer followed up: "Sue Sanford from the Michigan AG's Office is going to call you about the State AG meeting with LPS. She may ask about converting her investigation from criminal to civil. If you are comfortable, please encourage her to join the civil group."

So a month after June and Theresa's dismissal, LPS lawyers were encouraging Florida officials to lobby Michigan to reduce charges, even as LPS was under active investigation in Florida.

On Citizen Warriors Radio that weekend, Lisa summed it up. "It's a simple cover-up of the fact that these attorneys were ousted because the targets and their attorneys are very powerful, and they did not like the investigations." From Tallahassee to Washington, the power elite seemed to want to put this sad chapter in American history to bed.

On January 24, 2012, President Obama delivered the final State of the Union address of his first term. The First Lady's box always included dignitaries, from public officials to ordinary Americans the president planned to highlight in the speech. This year one of the guests was Eric Schneiderman.

"Tonight, I'm asking my attorney general to create a special unit of federal prosecutors and a leading state attorney general, to expand our investigations into the abusive lending and packaging of risky mortgages that led to the housing crisis," Obama announced to applause. Schneiderman stood and clapped as the president winked in his direction. "This new unit will hold accountable those who broke the law, speed assistance to homeowners, and help turn the page on an era of recklessness that hurt so many Americans."

Across town, in a dimly lit hotel room, Kamala Harris, attorney general of California, looked out the window, the address on TV in the background. She wanted to be the "leading state attorney general" in the First Lady's box that night. But Schneiderman had outmaneuvered her.

The Residential Mortgage-Backed Securities (RMBS) working group was the culmination of a strategy Schneiderman and his top officials had crafted for months. They believed a settlement was inevitable; the president was desperate to make a show of force against the banks as he headed into his reelection campaign. So Schneiderman's chief of staff, Neal Kwatra, created the Campaign for a Fair Settlement, in association with longtime allies from New York's Working Families Party, to build outside pressure for a better deal.

Many coalition partners in the campaign had memberships of struggling homeowners needing immediate assistance. They weren't focused on the consequences of elites being allowed to break the law while merely paying back a sliver of their profits as a penalty. Schneiderman's team didn't think robo-signing and false document submissions were big enough transgressions to get homeowners what they needed. They covered up what he considered the real crimes of mortgage origination and securitization—"the lending and packaging of risky mortgages," as Obama put it. So Schneiderman's team negotiated a two-step process: first get federal buy-in for an investigation of pre-crisis conduct, where he could pull from multiple state and federal agencies to exert maximum pressure on Wall Street; then reach a narrow settlement on false documents and servicer abuse, securing relief for homeowners in the process.

Schneiderman was one of five co-chairs of the RMBS working group, housed inside a Financial Fraud Enforcement Task Force that had done little in two-plus years. Other co-chairs included federal officials who previously worked for banks, including Lanny Breuer (Justice Department/corporate law firm Covington & Burling) and Robert Khuzami (Securities and Exchange Commission/Deutsche Bank). In fact, Breuer and Khuzami were already on the task force and authorized to investigate bank misconduct for years; why would they do it now? But Schneiderman's advisers vowed to critics that if the government tried to kill or slow-walk the investigation, he would bolt in the showiest, most public way possible, letting everyone know who was responsible for the lack of prosecutions.

The Campaign for a Fair Settlement front organization fell in line, praising the working group. For some reason, everyone claiming to want to hold banks accountable was thrilled with the foreclosure fraud investigation resulting in little more than a *second* investigation. The attorneys general Schneiderman led in opposition had no leverage once he made his deal. Nevada's Catherine Cortez Masto asked her strike force to review the release of liability, and John Kelleher recommended she reject it, calling it overbroad and vague, arguing it would harm their ability to bring criminal prosecutions. The next day Masto signed on, despite the recommendation. As for California's Kamala Harris, the White House told her they were fully prepared to move on without her; holding out would only hurt her constituents. Michael changed his Schneiderman graphic, replacing the white hat with a black hat. The sheriff had become the villain.

On February 9, 2012, state and federal regulators announced the National Mortgage Settlement with the five largest mortgage servicers: Bank of America, JPMorgan Chase, Citigroup, Wells Fargo, and GMAC. Forty-nine states joined, all but Oklahoma, which didn't believe the banks should pay any penalty. In exchange for releases from liability on robo-signing and other forms of foreclosure fraud, along with numerous servicing practices like fee pyramiding and driving homeowners into default—components of the largest consumer fraud in history—the banks agreed to pay $25 billion. That was the same number offered a year earlier, which Eric Schneiderman said at the time would let the banks off cheap.

Only $5 billion was in cash, with $3.5 billion of that going to the federal government and state-based mortgage relief programs. The remaining $1.5 billion in cash would go to victims of foreclosure in an estimated $2,000 "sorry you lost your home" check, a paltry compensation for the wrongful seizure of their property. Officials earmarked $3 billion for refinancing underwater homes, and the other $17 billion would get paid out through consumer relief credits. For every dollar of mortgage principal reduction, banks would get a dollar of credit. But they could also get partial credit for short sales (where banks agree to allow homeowners to sell for less than the price of the mortgage), post-foreclosure housing assistance, and even anti-blight measures like donating homes to charity or bulldozing properties. Banks performed these activities routinely, and none of them helped save homes. Yet they could comprise over one-quarter of the penalty; principal reduction only had to come to $10 billion.

Banks could also get credit for modifying loans in mortgage-backed trusts owned by investors, paying their penalty with other people's money. They could route loan modifications through HAMP, and take HAMP incentive money *with* their punishment. Homes owned by Fannie Mae or Freddie Mac, the majority of the market, would be ineligible, because the government didn't want those agencies taking more losses. Homeowners benefited from the settlement only if they met random criteria beyond their control. The five servicers would also have to comply with a variety of new standards, but the Consumer Financial Protection Bureau was readying similar standards for industry-wide adoption anyway.

Headlines touted the largest corporate payout since the tobacco settlement. HUD secretary Shaun Donovan said one million borrowers would get mortgage balances cut. But at the time there was $700 billion in negative equity in the country, and this deal wouldn't cover more than a sliver of that. In fact, the Treasury Department had twice as much money designated for mortgage relief in HAMP as there was in the settlement.

Banks had been caught red-handed submitting false documents to courts, with millions of documented examples, and law enforcement treated it like a man catching a too-puny fish and throwing it back. No one bothered to investigate the misconduct, instead charging banks $2,000 for every family they threw into chaos and leaving it at that. That evidence would be unusable in future cases; Nevada couldn't go up the food chain from LPS and nail servicers for fraudulent documents. Ongoing foreclosure fraud using previously submitted forgeries and fabrications would be effectively legalized, or at least beyond the reach of state and federal prosecutors. And nobody would see a jail cell. Sure, officials swore that they still reserved the right to pursue criminal charges, but the reaction to that varied between chuckles and hysterical laughter. Individual borrowers could still challenge their cases, but their resources were far smaller than those of the banks. This is why attorneys general existed, but in this case they abdicated their responsibilities, knuckling under to those who really wielded power in America—Washington and Wall Street.

Amid the morass, there was one silver lining. The government folded a bunch of lawsuits into the deal, relieving banks of as much liability as possible. Among them were five whistleblower cases: appraisal fraud at Countrywide, fair lending violations, underwriting inaccuracies, and more, all lumped in as violations of the False Claims Act. One of those cases came from Lynn Szymoniak. Her *qui tam* suit retrieved $95 million for the U.S. government, and under the law, she would receive $18 million of that herself.

21

LISA'S LAST STAND

Lynn learned about the $18 million from her lawyers, but the news didn't go public until National Mortgage Settlement term sheets were released in March 2012. Everyone offered congratulations: Lisa, Michael, Damian, Matt Weidner. She was officially gracious—"It's very satisfying to recover this money for the government," she told the *Huffington Post*—but privately, she wished the payout would go to homeowners who needed it. The situation was almost farcical: five banks paid the government $95 million for filing FHA insurance claims based on false documents, but those documents could still be used to remove people from their homes.

Lynn's own mortgage company proved this. Deutsche Bank removed Mark Elliot from the case, but a new law firm, corporate giant Akerman Senterfitt, decided to depose Lynn again. The meeting featured nine plaintiffs' lawyers and two armed guards, as if Lynn presented a threat. Though Lynn's original allonge was supposed to be affixed to the note, she discovered years earlier that it had no staple holes or signs of attachment. But during the deposition, Akerman's lead lawyer pulled out the allonge, and it did have staple holes. Days earlier Akerman filed an order to release the allonge from the court file; not being idiots, Lynn and her lawyer, Mark Cullen, went to the courthouse and took close-up photos of the allonge, in case Akerman tried to doctor it. Which they did.

"I knew you would do this, you lying cheats!" Lynn bellowed as the camera videotaping the deposition rolled.

"Who do you think did what?" the lawyer answered with mock surprise.

"You did it, you counterfeits! But guess what, we took photos of this, so you're caught!"

The Akerman lawyer pulled back and stuttered, "Well . . . why didn't you disclose ahead of time that you took photos of the allonge?"

"*That's* your question? I don't believe this."

Reuben Guttman, the lawyer from the *qui tam* case who watched the deposition, told Lynn it was his all-time favorite.

In that same deposition, Akerman asked Lynn to identify everything she remodeled in the home. The application for Lynn's original refinance stated the purpose of the loan as "home improvement." It did not obligate her to any dollar amount for that purpose. But Lynn answered the question: she reconfigured the bathroom for her late mother, installed new floors, and did pool and lawn maintenance. Within a few days, Akerman said they wanted to depose pool maintenance staff, landscapers, contractors, and plumbers. Mark Cullen filed a motion for protective order, calling it a frivolous attempt to harass the defendant. But Diana Lewis, the notoriously pro-bank judge, accepted the argument that Lynn potentially lied about home improvements on her loan application.

Everyone drove ninety minutes west to depose Lynn's contractor, a personal friend who installed her floors. Akerman's lawyers demanded information about every job the contractor held since high school and every detail about the installation. "Was Lynn Szymoniak ever late paying her bills?" The contractor replied that he lost past invoices in a hurricane.

"Isn't that convenient!"

"Look," spat back the contractor, a big ex-firefighter, slapping the table. "If you want to call me a liar, say it to my face! Don't do this chicken-shit stuff!"

The Akerman lawyer started shaking so much he dropped his list of questions.

Lynn didn't want to validate these tactics by paying off her house, but she saw no other options in the Palm Beach County court system. If anything, the courts had grown *more* hostile to homeowners after revelations of robo-signing and false document pleadings. You couldn't walk into a courtroom, assert that evidence had been falsified, and expect anyone in authority to care. So Lynn mentally set aside a big chunk of cash to buy peace.

The National Mortgage Settlement waived so many predatory servicing practices that a lot of people were astounded that such companies remained in business. Beyond the illegal fees, force-placed insurance scams, dual tracking, lies to borrowers seeking loan modifications, and lost paperwork was a basic inability to perform, euphemistically described as "failing to maintain accurate account statements." A HUD inspector general report released with the settlement documents reviewed a sample of thirty-six JPMorgan Chase foreclosures and found incomplete or incorrect information on what borrowers actually owed in thirty-five of those cases. That report was among the most extensive federal investigations of mortgage servicing, and it still only examined a handful of files. But managers who oversaw the 97 percent error rate didn't have to resign in disgrace. In fact, no servicer had to admit wrongdoing. Falsifying documents and stealing from customers are serious criminal offenses in any other legal context, unless you're a bank.

GMAC, which by then changed its name to Ally Bank, succeeded in cutting its fine in half based on "an inability to pay it," Reuters reported, making the National Mortgage Settlement one of the first "pay what you can" corporate penalties in American history. Ally doled out dividends to the U.S. government on its Troubled Asset Relief Program funds while crying poor to settlement negotiators.

Negotiators never mandated that cash awards to the states had to go to mortgage relief. So, one by one, states started using the money to fill holes in their budgets, from Wisconsin to California to, of course, Florida. By the end, nearly half the penalty—over $1 billion—got sucked into state budgets, leaving homeowners expecting free counseling or modification programs with nothing.

The most shocking wrinkle in the term sheet concerned "threshold error rates." Servicers received indemnity for a certain amount of violations of settlement standards, including illegally taking someone's home. For most standards, the threshold error rate was 5 percent. So servicers could break the law on one of every twenty mortgages they serviced, or 90,000 of the 1.8 million foreclosure filings throughout 2012, with nobody able to do anything about it. Since servicers self-reported their own errors and could appeal findings of noncompliance, far more fraudulent foreclosures could be made undetected. The settlement codified predatory servicing.

Many state lawsuits, including Ohio's against GMAC and Nevada's against Countrywide, were folded into the settlement. But justice didn't roll down from the other lawsuits carved out. Eric Schneiderman filed a last-minute suit against MERS and three banks but quickly settled the case for $25 million. After years of litigation, Massachusetts's Martha Coakley got only $2.7 million from banks who foreclosed on homeowners without standing. Illinois's Lisa Madigan agreed on a $350,000 settlement with Nationwide Title Clearing. Delaware's Beau Biden settled with MERS for $0 and promises that the company would no longer sue for foreclosure in their name and record assignments prior to foreclosure—things MERS already voluntarily agreed to do.

Catherine Cortez Masto's case against LPS had perhaps the most humiliating outcome. In May 2012 John Kelleher was abruptly taken off the Mortgage Fraud Strike Force, in what Masto called a "realignment." Within a month he left. The facts came out in an affidavit provided to the court. Kelleher was himself a foreclosure victim; just like Lisa Epstein, his servicer told him to miss payments and put him into foreclosure after he did. Saxon Mortgage served him with papers in January 2011, before the criminal fraud case against Gary Trafford and Gerri Sheppard. Kelleher alleged in his affidavit that he was being considered for a loan modification the entire time, but the defense found a notice of default taped to Kelleher's door on September 7, 2011. The notice came from LSI Title, one of the many names used by Trafford and Sheppard's document processing company. Defense attorneys argued that Kelleher, in a vindictive rage, bullied Tracy Lawrence into testifying before the grand jury and accepting the plea bargain. Kelleher claimed that he never saw the notice from LSI Title until after Tracy Lawrence's death, and when he did, he informed the attorney general and recused himself from the case. But it was too late. The judge dismissed the charges against Trafford and Sheppard entirely.

John Hueston, Trafford's lawyer, who previously represented Ken Lay and Jeffrey Skilling in the Enron trial, called the defeat a "complete embarrassment." But he made more revealing comments to Law360 about the impact of Tracy Lawrence's death. "When we first got involved in the case we realized the critical witness was no longer with us," Hueston said.

Kelleher believes he was pushed off the strike force for getting too close to prosecuting the banks, like June Clarkson and Theresa Edwards in Florida. After he left, former colleagues were told not to speak to him. His replacement closed all pending mortgage investigations. Kelleher ended up running a martial arts studio for three years before finding another lawyer job.

Lisa had almost run out of financial reserves, so within months the full-time activism would have to stop. And yet she didn't feel she was through pursuing a justice that never seemed further away. She would tick through scenarios for possible redemption. Maybe the Schneiderman task force could devise some fertile prosecution strategy. Maybe judges would suddenly sanction the fraudsters. Maybe some media exposé could awaken the dormant conscience of a nation. Or maybe there were just a few homeowners left to help; even that would be worth it.

A lot of her activism filtered through Occupy Palm Beach; she and Lynn ran several "teach-in" events on foreclosure fraud. One day in March 2012, Tom Conboy, a local Democratic Party activist, attended their presentation, and grew furious: "What is our clerk of courts doing about this?"

Since 2004 the Palm Beach County clerk of courts was a Democrat named Sharon Bock, a bleached-blond doyenne with a plastic smile. Bock told the *Palm Beach Post* she had no authority to reject fraudulent documents, despite the clerk's responsibility to maintain integrity of public records. Other land records officials, like John O'Brien in Massachusetts and Jeff Thigpen in North Carolina, loudly publicized the crime scenes in their offices. Curtis Hertel, a register of deeds in Oakland County, Michigan, sued Fannie Mae and Freddie Mac for failure to pay recording fees on property transfers; Thigpen had just sued MERS. But Bock viewed her job narrowly; in fact, in all the time Lisa had been going to the courthouse, she never saw Bock there. "I've practiced law here for thirty-two years and I can't get a fifteen-minute meeting with Sharon Bock," Lynn said.

"Well, we need someone to run against her," Tom Conboy replied.

Lynn smiled. "I nominate Lisa!"

Lisa thought they were nuts. She had spent years learning about foreclosures and securitization and the judicial system, and now they wanted her to learn about election laws and fund-raising and campaigning? And though she'd grown more comfortable in the spotlight, the idea of running around seeking votes filled her with unease.

Yet something about it also appealed to her. She relished getting control of the fraudulent evidence, joining the activist clerks resisting more powerful officials who wanted to put this tragedy in the past. And it wasn't just about foreclosures: fabricated assignments and satisfactions put all real estate transactions at risk. It would be enormously challenging—Palm Beach County had 1.3 million residents, stretching an hour east to Belle Glade and back. Lisa knew she would have a slim chance against an entrenched incumbent. But somebody had to keep up the fight. Something inside Lisa kept whispering, *You're not done.* So she announced her intent to run in the Democratic primary.

Lisa's first priority was to figure out what a clerk of courts actually did. Through foreclosure work, she knew a defense attorney in the Jacksonville area whose husband was a deputy clerk of courts. Michael and Lisa went to his office and shadowed him for two days, learning everything about how land records were kept, stored, and distributed. Lisa soaked up information about file management systems and digital document retrieval strategies. In Palm Beach the clerk of courts also served as the county's chief financial officer. So Lisa researched county investments and accounting practices. But days after filing her intent to run, Lisa heard from Mark Alan Siegel, chairman of the Palm Beach County Democratic Party. Sharon Bock wanted to meet.

They planned lunch at the Broken Sound Club in Boca Raton, a posh golf and tennis resort where Siegel was a member. Tom Conboy attended as a go-between, along with Lisa, Lynn, and Michael. They entered the main lobby, a four-story rotunda dominated by an undulating pink sculpture that looked like stacked seashells. Siegel greeted them and took one look at Michael. "Blue jeans in the dining room," he said with clear disdain. "That's going to be a problem."

"Okay, we can eat on the patio!" Lynn offered cheerily.

"No, I'll take care of it," Siegel interrupted.

As they walked into the fancy dining room, they saw ladies in casual tennis outfits and bikinis with sarongs. "Some dress code," Michael snickered.

The group reached the table. Sharon Bock, seated between two deputies and wearing a sharp white suit, stood up and smiled broadly. Lynn thought this lady had on more makeup than she had ever seen on a human being.

"It's nice to see you, Sharon," Lynn said, "I've been trying to meet with you for four years."

"No," Sharon replied with deep sincerity, "I would have known."

Everyone got settled, with Sharon fishing lipstick out of her purse and laying it on the table. As the meeting began, Sharon reapplied her lipstick carefully, and continued to do so after almost every bite of lunch. It was like she would melt away into a puddle without a full plastering of ruby red.

Mark Alan Siegel, who represented Manhattan in the New York State Assembly in the 1970s and 1980s, laid on the charm as thick as Sharon's makeup. "You've all raised so many important issues. How can we be helpful?" he asked. The implication was clear: what would it take for Lisa to go away?

Lisa and Lynn came prepared with several ideas to improve the clerk of courts office. By this time, word had spread about Lynn's $18 million judgment, which Sharon seemingly saw as a key funding source for the primary. So Lynn was uniformly celebrated as the smartest person in the room. "If you recorded assignments under the homeowner's name, people could find their own records easier," Lynn said.

"Great point, Lynn!" Sharon Bock shouted enthusiastically between lipstick applications. "Write that down," she said to her deputy. "Keep a list so we can implement these fine suggestions."

Lynn asked if Sharon had ever been to foreclosure hearings, which occurred three doors from her office. Sharon said no. Then Lisa asked about the county signing a case management contract with a division of LPS. "They're still under investigation by the Florida attorney general's office. Don't you see this as a concern?"

"Well, LPS is a respected company," Sharon replied. "We don't expect any problems." Lisa would later learn that LPS gave Sharon a maximum-level contribution for her reelection three days before the meeting. Sharon eventually returned the money.

Lisa brought up the $1.4 billion county investment fund, over half of which was tied up in funds exposed to mortgage-backed securities. Sharon Bock didn't fret about that, either. She leaned back in her chair and said, "Those were all AAA-rated!" Lynn almost spat out her salad.

It went back and forth for a while. Siegel and Bock offered Lisa and Lynn plenty of inducements, from better access to files online to a citizen task force. "The party needs you," Siegel said, horse trading like he was negotiating a highway bill. Lisa committed to nothing, but tried to stay positive.

As they wrapped up, Tom Conboy thanked everyone for coming, adding, "We've accomplished a lot today."

After a final splash of lipstick, Bock's smile turned stern. She leaned toward Lisa. "But if you go forward with this campaign, this will be the last time we accomplish anything. We'll be enemies."

If it was intended as a threat, Lisa didn't pick up on it. "Oh, I don't think so, Sharon. I think we can still work together!"

Candidates in Palm Beach County needed to complete two steps to make the ballot. In March they filed an intent to run. In June candidates could file a petition signed by 5 percent of the county's voting population—about ten thousand names—or pay a filing fee of $9,300 out of campaign contributions. Lisa just started her campaign and saw no reasonable way to amass ten thousand signatures in ninety days. So the first few months mostly involved dialing for dollars.

Every call Lisa made, people responded the same way: "Why don't you ask Lynn Szymoniak?" She'd have to explain that individuals could only donate a maximum of $500. "She's already given that, so now I'm calling you!" Sharon Bock fueled that misimpression, telling supporters that Lisa had millions of dollars behind her. Lynn hadn't even received her money yet, but that didn't matter; Bock raised more off her than Lisa did.

The first non-Lynn contributor was David Weck, head of the Boca Raton Investment Club, a group of local real estate investors that Lynn and Lisa spoke before every year. Many others gave what they could, sometimes just a few dollars. Lisa's ex-husband, Alan, even donated. Grace Rucci, a *Foreclosure Hamlet* member, became campaign treasurer. Tom Conboy stayed involved. And other activists, inspired by her run, started their own campaigns, like Ron Gillis's wife, Deb Lilley, in Charlotte County, and writer Matt Gardi in Monroe County. Grubbing for money never got comfortable for Lisa, but she managed to make enough for the filing fee.

Publicly, Democratic leaders dismissed Lisa's challenge as a trivial sideshow. Behind the scenes, Mark Alan Siegel tried relentlessly to dissuade Lisa from running. They held meetings over the phone, at Democratic club meetings, at a local Cracker Barrel. Siegel once took out a map of Florida and suggested Lisa should pursue a state House seat instead. "We need your voice in Tallahassee," Siegel said. He set up calls with the head of the state Democratic campaign committee.

Lisa asked Lynn how she could travel back and forth to Tallahassee, with Jenna about to start kindergarten.

"Why would you be going to Tallahassee?"

"Well, maybe I want that job instead of clerk of courts."

"What job?"

The night before the filing deadline, Siegel and Sharon Bock met with Lisa until ten o'clock. Lisa brought a strategy document full of initiatives, from publishing a list of known robo-signers to working with other clerks to ensure accuracy of the land records. After insisting to the media that clerk of courts was merely a ministerial position without the capacity for activism, Sharon shifted course and vowed to turn her office into a crime-fighting unit. "You've brought this to our attention now," she said to Lisa. "Lynn can write up an action plan. And you can be in charge of it, as long as you drop out."

They were convincing Lisa of something she already wanted to do. All the stress of campaigning would go away. Maybe she and Sharon could even make progress. But one of Lisa's key backers was an activist named Maria Cole, who sold her dental practice to get involved in politics full-time. Maria's mother, whom Lisa only knew as Mama Cole, wouldn't abide by Lisa's wavering, telling her, "You cannot back out, you raised this money, you told people you were going to run."

On deadline day, Lisa and Michael arrived at the county elections office, across from a shopping mall at the corner of Military Trail and Gun Club Road, a quintessentially Floridian destination. She entered the office with her paperwork and filing fee. Mark Alan Siegel accosted Lisa in the lobby, physically blocking her path to the filing window. It was 10:30 a.m.; the deadline was noon.

Siegel, normally a grandfatherly figure, berated Lisa for forty-five minutes, his tactics shifting from charm to intimidation, carrot to stick. "You don't want to do this," he warned. "You don't know what political campaigns are like. We're going to make sure you regret this. We're going to tear you apart. In politics, anything goes, and you're not up for it."

"Please, Mr. Siegel, I've made my decision—"

"All those supporters who want you to run for office? They're like spectators in the Colosseum and they're going to applaud when you get thrown to the lions!"

Finally an employee of the supervisor's office rescued Lisa, escorting her back to pay the filing fee. Lisa was amazed at how far Palm Beach County Democrats would go to snuff out challenges to their power. They didn't call it "Corruption County" for nothing. After leaving the office Lisa gave a brief interview to awaiting news cameras—"our public land records have been defiled and unauthenticated with massive fraud by the banking industry"— and then, as a courtesy, called Sharon Bock to let her know she was running. Sharon was at the airport, about to leave for vacation. And she started screaming. The CBS affiliate captured the animated conversation on camera. In one ear, Lisa heard Sharon ranting; in the other, she could hear the news team whispering, "We believe she is talking to her opponent." They tried to get Lisa's "campaign representative"—Michael—to give a statement. He kept quiet.

Siegel told the *Palm Beach Post* that the primary would "damage Lisa Epstein as the voice of the dispossessed. Now she's just another candidate for office."

One sultry May morning, Lynn Szymoniak checked her bank account balance and noticed several extra zeroes. She called out to Zach and Molly, "You know that money I told you about? It's here."

Lynn had to pay her lawyers as well as taxes. The net result was $5.5 million. She was never in this to make money; banking on profiting from two years of researching fraudulent mortgage documents would have been the worst get-rich-quick scheme imaginable. But after not knowing whether she could pay the light bill, Lynn was happy to get some peace of mind. She took the family to Maui, a pause from the fight. When they got back, she told her kids that each of them could have a car, but only something sensible, "not something that ends in a vowel like Lamborghini." Lynn bought a Buick.

Lynn began talking to Lisa and Michael about a nonprofit organization, something that would enable them to influence housing issues. Lynn could oversee it and Lisa and Michael could run it. Michael had no cash flow except for *4closureFraud* Google ads, so he was all for it. But it never progressed past initial discussions.

The first money Lynn donated was a quiet tribute to her father, who'd shuttled between mental hospitals most of his adult life after serving in the Marine Corps. Angel Fire was a local organization that worked with disabled veterans, taking them hunting and fishing. She gave them $220,000. Plenty of people had ideas for the remainder. Because the National Mortgage Settlement immunized document fraud from prosecution, it unclogged the drain of foreclosure cases in many state courts. Foreclosure filings rose 85 percent in south Florida in March 2012 alone. And those desperate homeowners found Lynn. They used to ask for help; now they just asked for money. Lynn did quietly fund relocation expenses for a handful of homeowners. But people usually wanted more—a house, a car, a job. And because the entire world knew the contents of Lynn's bank account, any attempt to say no would be met with rage. They called her selfish, ignorant, merciless, and crude. Lynn had a bleeding heart, but not enough resources to help everyone with a story.

A woman emailed Lynn one day asking for $50,000 for a documentary that would blow the lid off bank malfeasance and save democracy. Lynn declined, and the woman demanded to know how she was spending her money. Then she threatened to have her crew call Lynn every day, tying up her phone lines and making her life miserable. The accelerated evolution from contrition to anger was a feature of Lynn's post-settlement correspondence.

Lynn's biggest expenses involved putting to rest her everlasting legal battles. The condo was relatively easy: it sat dormant since David J. Stern dropped the case, so she just paid it off. But the house on Man O' War Road was more of a challenge. In February, before the settlement news leaked, Lynn requested a payoff figure from Deutsche Bank, and attorney's fees were $12,000. But a month later, after the press release, suddenly Akerman Senterfitt demanded $267,000. Lynn disputed the charges; she wanted the law firm sanctioned for tampering with the allonge, not granted a windfall. The Akerman lawyers argued that the complexities of the case required hundreds of man-hours. The retired judge at the hearing seemed bored until he looked at Lynn for a minute, finally exclaiming, "Oh, this is that *60 Minutes* woman! No wonder they want a lot of money!"

After watching Lynn resist their extortion attempt, Akerman offered to drop the claim if Lynn included a non-disparagement provision. Mark Cullen told Lynn, "You can't do that; you're incapable of not opening your mouth!" Finally Akerman and Lynn agreed to an undisclosed settlement to pay off the mortgage. It was the 274th and final docket entry in the case of the home on Man O' War Road. Four years after it began, it was all over.

The Democratic machine in Palm Beach County didn't have to worry so much about Lisa Epstein's clerk of courts challenge. They had incumbency, most of the money, most of the endorsements, and party stalwarts who did as they were told every election. Lisa had $25,000 in donations, a handful of volunteers, the energy to crisscross the county for multiple events every day, and Jenna, now five years old and a junior campaign manager. Lisa would take Jenna along to candidate meet-and-greet events, and Jenna would push her: "Go talk about foreclosure fraud Mama!" One night Lisa was trying to get her daughter into the bathtub. Jenna stood up, put her hands on her hips, and said, "If you make me take a bath, I'm going to vote for Sharon Bock!"

Through campaigning, Lisa enjoyed a behind-the-veil glance into the smallness of American politics. A man at the Palm Beach Chamber of Commerce in a $3,000 suit yelled at her for thirty minutes that the foreclosure crisis was "all Barney Frank's fault." The local chapter of the National Organization for Women asked for Lisa's position on parental notification for sixteen-year-olds wanting an abortion, and when she meekly mentioned that the clerk of courts had no jurisdiction over reproductive policy, the ladies shouted at her, too.

All the candidate meetings, debates, endorsement lunches, media appearances, door-to-door pleading, and retail campaigning only reached a sliver of the population. Most people had little interest in an end-of-the-ballot primary, except for the community of online foreclosure activists. Steve Dibert trashed Lisa as "a joke" who believes that "everyone is entitled to a free house and that the American banking system must be destroyed." Even at *Foreclosure Hamlet*, where frustration at the lack of action against banks boiled over, members created a splinter site, accusing Lisa of taking too much credit and abandoning the cause. Lisa wondered where these people got the time to worry about her. It was the kind of down-and-dirty stuff Mark Alan Siegel warned her about, but it didn't come from the Democratic Party; it came from her own community.

Late in the campaign, someone approached Lisa at a campaign event. "You should check out what's happening in the evidence room," the person said, and then quickly walked away. As clerk of courts, Sharon Bock ran the evidence room at the county courthouse. Lisa heard rumors about missing evidence, but nobody could confirm anything, so she never acted on it. A week after Election Day the *Palm Beach Post*, which had endorsed Sharon Bock, ran the story. Three clerks were under criminal investigation for stealing more than a thousand oxycodone pills from the evidence room and selling them on the black market. Bock knew about the case, having suspended the employees two months earlier. Michael accused the *Post* of sitting on the story.

Lisa got the news at her election night party, August 14, 2012, at Brogues Boomerang Bar in Lake Worth, an Irish pub owned by Australians. Sharon Bock won, 76 percent to 24 percent. But Lisa was proud to have received 27,003 votes from people from all over the county who heard her message. In a short speech Lisa thanked campaign staff and volunteers, everyone who helped and supported her. She could barely conceal her excitement that the race was ending.

A couple of days after Election Day, Lisa was on the phone about some foreclosure-related issue, and Jenna tugged at her shirt. "Why are you still talking about foreclosure fraud, Mama? Sharon Bock won!" Lisa had to admit that Jenna was right. She was exhausted, not just from campaigning but from living on three hours of sleep a night for years. She sacrificed everything—her job, her personal life, even motherhood—for this mission. It was time to pass the baton. She made the decision with serenity. She could answer that inner voice and finally say she was done.

As Lisa stepped away, Lynn sent in her check to Deutsche Bank, closing a chapter in her life, too. A year later, on July 22, 2013, Akerman Senterfitt finally executed an official release of mortgage lien, filing it with Sharon Bock at the office of the clerk of courts, Book 26197, Page 1091. Signing for Deutsche Bank National Trust Company, as trustee for the certificate holders of Soundview Home Loan Trust 2006-OPT2, was a vice president named Leticia Arias. Lynn smiled. Leticia Arias was a known robo-signer.

EPILOGUE

On the alphabet streets in Lake Worth, houses are dotted with black mold. Others have buckled roofs, interiors gutted by fire, or stripped wiring. Pests and critters move in as people move out. Half the homes have busted windows, and No Trespassing/No Traspasar signs in English and Spanish are ubiquitous. "Those are to keep the drug sales out," says my tour guide, Lynn Szymoniak. "I've been stopped doing these tours. Cops have told me, 'You're not supposed to be here.'"

Lynn runs this circuit for journalists, filmmakers, or anyone interested in battered monuments to the foreclosure crisis; sometimes she drives by herself. She checks on that yellow Deutsche Bank house, the site of all those protests; it's still boarded up. Homes in this neighborhood went for $300,000 at the top of the bubble. Prices are now one-third of that, and some will never be sold again; Lake Worth recently got funds to bulldoze the worst of the worst. "You can find whole blocks gone here," Lynn told me. "It's like a flu spread and everybody had to leave."

Back at the Intracoastal Waterway, we reach the thirteenth-floor offices of Lynn's organization, the Housing Justice Foundation. The same high-rise houses the local headquarters for SunTrust, a regional bank that paid fines for robo-signing and servicing abuse in 2014, as well as local offices for the FBI. Lynn figures the FBI's presence makes it secure from break-ins. She has a spectacular view of downtown Palm Beach, but it's only twelve hundred square feet for four employees and all the files.

Lynn runs the foundation with her two sons, Zach and Mark Elliot, and Mark Elliot's wife, Rachael. They call it a research and education nonprofit, dedicated to investigation and awareness of foreclosure fraud. Even after the settlements, there's plenty to be aware of, because every day in America, families get thrown out of their homes based on false documents. And no regulator, politician, public prosecutor, or federal judge manages to care. They've collectively decided to pretend the ruination of a three-hundred-year-old property records system never happened. Like the Amazing Mystico and the block of flats, everyone believes in the Great Foreclosure Machine again.

Exhibit A: Brent Bentrim of Charleston, South Carolina, hit with foreclosure actions from multiple servicers since 2008, despite never missing a payment. Wachovia and then Wells Fargo repeatedly misapplied payments, illegally charged penalty-rate interest, force-placed insurance, and altered the principal balance. Wells Fargo filed a lost note affidavit, then found the "original" note, which showed a completely different bank as the lender, without a chain of title extending to Wells Fargo. Bentrim is still in court; the most recent docket item was March 2015, seven years from the initial filing.

Exhibit B: An email conversation accidentally filed in the case of Abby Lopez, Lisa Epstein's former neighbor from Gazetta Way. In the email, LPS employee Nicolas Leonhard tells his supervisor that the plaintiff on the complaint, HSBC, doesn't match the name in their loan system, Bank of America. Instead of stopping the foreclosure, the supervisor tells Leonhard to simply deed the house over to Bank of America after the foreclosure sale to HSBC. Problem solved. Lawyers for HSBC tried to have the email records purged, but failed.

Exhibit C: *Phoenix Light v. JPMorgan Chase*, a 2013 case where investors surveyed the transfer history for 274 loans in JPMAC 2006-WMC4 mortgage-backed trusts, finding that none of the mortgages and notes were conveyed properly before the closing date, making the trust not backed by mortgages (securitization FAIL) and liable for a 100 percent penalty for violating REMIC tax status. A 2012 case against Barclays Bank looked at three other securitizations, similarly discovering that 99 percent of the mortgages were either unassigned to the trusts or assigned improperly.

And so on.

Lynn was actually cited in the *Phoenix Light* case. At the Housing Justice Foundation, she showed me thousands of files in pull-out stacks, cross-referenced by bank and trust. More get added every day, projects documenting bankrupt mortgage trusts and abandoned homes and phony note endorsements. If someone were doomed to an eternity of meticulously accounting unpunished crimes, the work product would resemble the contents of this room.

I got to see the famous poster boards, and two pictures of Lynn, one with President Obama and the other with Vice President Biden. During the 2012 election, she got to meet both of them, thanks to her lawyer and Democratic power player Dick Harpootlian. "This is the woman who sues the banks," Harpootlian said, introducing Lynn to Biden. Lynn mentioned Biden's son Beau, the Delaware attorney general, and the vice president beamed, saying, "You know you're a success when your children are better people than you are." Beau Biden died of brain cancer three years later.

Lynn paid her way into the Obama meeting, a small fund-raising lunch in Atlanta. The president, who told *60 Minutes* eight months after Lynn's appearance on that show that "some of the least ethical behavior on Wall Street wasn't illegal," greeted everyone in the room warmly. Lynn expressed her disappointments on the failure to prosecute. Obama, like all great politicians, said what Lynn wanted to hear, stressing the need for more principal reductions and an end to predatory mortgage practices. After the lunch, Atlanta mayor Kasim Reed thanked Lynn for asking her question, telling her about all his city's foreclosure problems. Lynn thought, *Well, why didn't you say anything?*

In addition to research, the Housing Justice Foundation issues grants to organizations focused on foreclosures, from the Florida First Amendment Foundation to Occupy Our Homes, which sprouted nearly a dozen chapters focused on eviction defense. In 2013, with help from Lisa and Michael, Lynn convened a nationwide Occupy Our Homes conference at the foundation offices, empowering them with detailed information about fraud. Through direct action, Occupy Our Homes saved and continues to save hundreds of homeowners from eviction. They never reached a scale to truly pressure the banks, but they haven't relented.

Nearly every day, homeowners plead with Lynn for help, praising her like she was Mother Teresa. When she informs them there isn't much she can do, they conclude she's as bad as Jamie Dimon, JPMorgan Chase's CEO. Enduring a daily barrage of inchoate rage exposed Lynn to the depths of human desperation, and she started blaming herself for snuffing out people's hope, closing off avenues of escape. The vitriol would have dimmed her view of human nature if it wasn't already pretty low.

The foundation's biggest project was the *qui tam* case, which didn't end with the $95 million federal settlement. That only involved the five leading mortgage servicers; Lynn sued thirteen other parties, from servicers to trustees to document manufacturers like Lender Processing Services. In August 2013 the case was unsealed, along with one remarkable document: a mortgage assignment dated February 9, 2009, *after* the foreclosure of the mortgage in question. Typed on the right-hand side of the assignment was this note: "This Assignment of Mortgage was inadvertently not recorded prior to the Final Judgment of Foreclosure . . . but is now being recorded to clear title." You could not find stronger evidence of a mass document production scheme to fabricate ownership.

Though the behavior of the five servicers in the settlement and the behavior of the remaining defendants were identical, the Justice Department declined to intervene in the second half of the case, leaving Lynn and her lawyers to cover expenses. When the seal was lifted, Lynn discovered that all those confidential information disclosures, which she spent hundreds of hours crafting for DoJ, were never served to the banks to force disclosure of documents. All that drafting was just a D.C. smokescreen.

Lynn kept returning to federal court in Columbia, South Carolina, for *qui tam* hearings. She would hear whispers from prosecutors: "Why doesn't she just take her money and go home?" The banks drew out the case, resisting every discovery request, making frivolous arguments and abruptly dropping them, and bringing in dozens of lawyers—at least three for each bank—to argue each point separately. A lawyer for American Home Mortgage Servicing tried to explain away forgery by saying, "You know how it is sometimes when you're married, judge, and you sign your wife's name to a check. And sometimes she knows . . ." He paused dramatically, then concluded, "And sometimes she doesn't!" He sat down with a big grin on his face.

But no matter how many bank lawyers embarrassed themselves, they simply wore out the system. In spring 2014, in what felt like a bloodletting, Judge Joseph Anderson threw out most of the case. Lynn trudged on for another year, filing appeals and motions out of some warped sense of duty to the truth. But she reached an undisclosed settlement on the lion's share of the claims on April Fool's Day 2015. On June 26, Lynn kept alive a sliver of the case, appealing to the Fourth Circuit on HUD claims against three trustees, two mortgage lenders, and LPS. If that fails, all that's left is the Supreme Court. But even if it succeeds, Lynn won't send Wall Street tumbling to the ground. She won't even make them hand back all their illegally gained profits.

One other case remains. On March 4, 2013, Damian Figueroa, the *Stop Foreclosure Fraud* blogger who was once Lynn's client, sued her for breach of fiduciary duty and unjust enrichment. Damian said Lynn stole his research, to be used in a jointly filed *qui tam* case, and filed the suit on her own. And he submitted hundreds of emails between him and Lynn to prove it.

When I asked Lynn about this, she dismissed it as a lie. She did represent Damian in a class action suit against the David Stern law firm and MERS, as specified in the retainer. She actually disclosed to Damian, confirmed by his emails, that she had a False Claims Act case going, with her as the relator. Many of Lynn's articles describing fraud, along with her letters to regulators, predate ever meeting Damian. They collaborated later, but everybody was helping everybody research public documents. Lynn added that Damian congratulated her after learning of the settlement, and they even went to lunch together. He never said he was the "real relator."

Damian, whose class action suits against the banks were all dismissed, declined to speak to me, on the advice of his lawyers. But in his complaint, he says he initiated talk of a *qui tam* on February 9, 2010, at the foreclosure happy hour where he and Lynn met. A week later, over email, Lynn did say she had a *qui tam* going, though she expected nothing to come of it. "But if you want to try this too, let me know and we will file together both knowing that this is a real long-shot," Lynn's email added. That line is the essence of Damian's argument.

For months they continued corresponding, with the *qui tam* offer never again made explicit. Lynn occasionally asked for research and Damian would supply it. At one point Damian found a list of LPS signers and shared it with Lynn. The names ended up in the complaint, though lists of robosigners were also compiled elsewhere. After filing the *qui tam*, Lynn complied with the seal order by denying to Damian that she had her own case going. Lynn specifically says that Damian should consider a *qui tam* against the Stern law firm and IndyMac, who were never defendants in her case.

Damian wasn't the only one claiming that Lynn stole his work; people habitually called up the office with such charges. But nobody else acted on the impulse. The case remains in the courts, and Lynn thinks it'll just go on forever. You can parse the evidence on either side. But it's really a textbook example of what happens when movements falter. Before long everyone starts turning on each other, and the cause itself becomes secondary, making it easier for perpetrators to steal away into the dark.

Housing and Urban Development secretary Shaun Donovan insisted the National Mortgage Settlement would deliver principal reductions to one million struggling homeowners. In the end, according to reports filed by the settlement's oversight monitor, just 83,000 homeowners received a first-lien principal reduction, over 90 percent fewer than promised. The banks issued almost exactly the $10 billion in principal reduction listed in the settlement as the minimum requirement. Donovan touted over $50 billion in tangible benefits, but much of it came in the form of short sales, where homeowners sell their homes for below the mortgage balance, without having to make up the difference. Short sales can be helpful for families, but they represent the polar opposite of keeping people in their homes, the intended goal. Far more Americans lost homes in transactions via the National Mortgage Settlement than got principal reductions to save them.

Servicers received credit for "forgiving" debt already discharged in bankruptcy, for extinguishing second mortgages deemed uncollectible, and for modifying loans held by investors (paying for the settlement with other people's money). They satisfied their penalty by donating some homes to charity and bulldozing others, routine activities to establish community goodwill. And in perhaps the most devious maneuver, nearly one-quarter of the gross consumer relief value, $11 billion, came from short sales in "non-recourse" states like California, where lenders are prevented by law from seeking money from borrowers if the sale price comes in lower than the price of the mortgage. In other words, this supposed "gift" to homeowners had no material value whatsoever.

Cash payouts for families illegally kicked out of their homes ended up as an insulting $1,480, less than two months' rent. Oklahoma, the one state that didn't join the settlement, set up a mortgage fund for foreclosure victims that granted over seven times as much cash per homeowner.

The other big settlement, the Independent Foreclosure Review from the Federal Reserve and the Office of the Comptroller of the Currency, was neither independent (banks hand-picked their own reviewers) nor an adequate review (whistleblowers alleged that reviewers deliberately minimized evidence of borrower harm). In the end, regulators aborted the mission, with banks instead paying $3.6 billion in cash to all 4.2 million families put into foreclosure in 2009 and 2010, divided into broad and seemingly random categories. People approved for a loan modification who illegally lost their homes anyway got $300 for their trouble. Most homeowners received under $1,000; some were so insulted that they sent the checks back. Lisa Epstein got a check for $600.

Aside from the woeful consumer outcomes, the basic architecture of a law enforcement settlement presumes that the activity being settled stops. But robo-signing, document fraud, and predatory servicer abuse continue unabated. All the foreclosure fighters got out of years of fraud exposure was another weak investigation.

One thousand FBI agents and prosecutors brought bank executives to justice after the savings and loan scandals of the late 1980s. By contrast, months after the inauguration of the vaunted securitization task force co-chaired by Eric Schneiderman, the New York *Daily News* noticed that it had no executive director, no offices, no phones, and no staff. In congressional testimony, Securities and Exchange Commission enforcement chief Robert Khuzami let slip that "most of the investigative work . . . is not really being done by a staff that belongs to the task force, it's being done by the individual investigative groups that make up the task force." In other words, the task force didn't exist; it was a repository for press releases about existing cases.

In 2013 and 2014, the task force secured several headline-grabbing settlements with big banks like JPMorgan Chase, Bank of America, and Citigroup, all of which knowingly sold to investors mortgage-backed securities that failed to meet prescribed underwriting guidelines. Investors, the actual party harmed by securities fraud, saw none of the benefit; the top beneficiary of the cash awards was the Justice Department. The settlements netted nearly $37 billion, but they had what writer Yves Smith called a high "bullshit-to-cash" ratio. For one, they were tax-deductible, meaning that ordinary taxpayers effectively paid part of the fine. "Consumer relief" portions of the settlement allowed banks to get penalty credit for loan modifications they were already doing, and even for making loans in low-income communities, a profit-generating activity. It was like sentencing someone convicted of stealing to opening a lemonade stand. When you weeded out the bullshit, the $37 billion fine looked more like $11 billion.

Schneiderman's lieutenants vowed that the task force investigations would result in outcomes "an order of magnitude" bigger than the National Mortgage Settlement, but they simply didn't. Chain of title issues or REMIC tax fraud—the biggest sources of exposure on securitization, both of which Schneiderman talked up before the task force got started—were never on the menu. And despite swearing that all options remained on the table, the task force never issued one criminal subpoena. The banks bought their way out of the problem cheaply, and those paying the penalty were the shareholders, not the executives who helped generate the largest destruction of wealth in American history.

The Obama administration has ignored banks that lie to people, and prosecuted people who lie to banks. Theresa and Joe Giudice, stars of the *Real Housewives of New Jersey*, obtained mortgages with fraudulent applications, and they went to jail. Four different federal agencies worked on that case. Meanwhile, Lanny Breuer and Eric Holder, the Justice Department leadership who presided over this disparity, went right back to the corporate law firm, Covington & Burling, from which they came. The firm even held open a corner office for Holder while he was attorney general, as he negotiated settlements with banks that were Covington & Burling clients.

America is a punitive nation, the most incarcerated nation on earth. If you're caught stealing a soda or smoking a joint, we'll put you away for way too long. But if you commit systemic crimes—if you hand out millions of fraudulent mortgages, package them into fraudulent securities, fail to complete fraudulent securitizations, engage in fraudulent servicing, and evict homeowners with fraudulent foreclosure papers—you can get away with it. Many have theorized why the banks would be so cavalier as to break the housing market just to make a few extra dollars. And the answer is proven by the outcome: because they knew they *could*, without serious consequences. We don't have a justice system with the will to convict everyone, regardless of wealth and power. And that ensures that the wealthy and powerful will keep committing crimes.

In Jacksonville, determination against concerted resistance from Washington led to the only major prosecution for foreclosure fraud. Lorraine O'Reilly Brown, founder and CEO of DocX, which produced over a million fraudulent assignments and affidavits for mortgage companies, was indicted in November 2012 on conspiracy to commit mail and wire fraud. Apparently this was a conspiracy of one, because the indictment claimed Brown directed the document forgery and fabrication scheme "unbeknownst to DocX's clients." In other words, mortgage servicers contracted Brown to fake evidence so they could prove standing to foreclose, but they were shocked that she would, you know, fake the evidence. Servicers may not have known the precise mechanics of the DocX fraud, but that's because they wanted a layer of plausible deniability.

LPS wiggled out of criminal indictments by paying $35 million in a non-prosecution agreement and cooperating in the Brown conviction. According to the complaint, LPS was unaware of this DocX scheme and fired Brown when they discovered what was occurring, despite performing the same fraud at multiple other facilities. It's not like Brown invented robo-signing. In fact, the indictment confirmed that "surrogate signing," authorizing temps to forge the names of senior employees on foreclosure documents, was illegal, though LPS defended it as legitimate for years.

Brown's biggest sin was lying to Jacksonville FBI agents and being expendable after LPS cut her loose. She pleaded guilty, with concurrent convictions in Missouri and Michigan. John O'Brien, the register of deeds in Essex County, Massachusetts, received a call from assistant U.S. attorney Mark Devereaux asking him to testify at the sentencing hearing. O'Brien tried to recoup $1.28 million from Brown, to clean up the 10,567 polluted DocX land records filed with his office. Devereaux called him back, saying the judge wouldn't accept the claim, because registers were not victims. "What do you mean, we're not a victim?" O'Brien exclaimed. "We're the ones with all these false documents!"

"No, the bank is the victim," Devereaux replied.

Lynn went to Brown's sentencing hearing. Jeff Thigpen, register of deeds from Guilford County, North Carolina, testified. Judge Henry Lee Adams asked Jeff if he sought restitution, and he replied, "I'd like it but I realize I'm not going to get it." The judge asked Devereaux who would replace all these false documents in registers' offices. "Well, that's where we—that's where we get a lot of issue here," Devereaux stuttered. "I don't know how you fix that."

Prosecutors revealed that the FBI interviewed over seventy-five DocX employees in the case, with forty-five agents taking statements from homeowners who lost homes via DocX assignments. Jeff could sense the frustration that all that work amounted only to putting Lorraine Brown in jail; everyone else was protected. Brown cried in court, apologizing repeatedly. Her lawyer argued that the government was prosecuting his client for activities the banks did on a regular basis. But the judge showed no leniency. Brown got five years, the maximum sentence.

Lynn told Devereaux after the guilty plea that she still watched people lose their homes to DocX documents, because nobody required the courts to be notified. Devereaux replied that he hoped bank lawyers would disclose that information. "I hope you're kidding," Lynn said. At the hearing, Devereaux wouldn't look her in the eye. But Lynn decided to feel relief instead of frustration. At least someone went to jail for falsifying mortgage documents, proving they were real crimes punishable by prison time, not "sloppy office work." But Brown was a convenient scapegoat, the PFC Lynndie England of foreclosure fraud. Nobody else went to jail because the misconduct was so pervasive that the entire banking industry would have to pay the price, and Washington couldn't let that happen.

After it ended, Lynn called up one of her FBI friends and thanked him for convicting Lorraine Brown. There was a long pause. When the agent finally broke the silence, he said, "I don't think the taxpayers were well served."

In a lush backyard surrounding a swampy south Florida lake, prehistoric-looking birds periodically dive-bomb the water in search of food. Every few minutes, planes roar upon takeoff at the nearby West Palm Beach airport. Michael Redman tosses some shrimp on the grill and lights citronella candles to keep the mosquitoes away.

Michael started renting the renovated back house on this lot a couple of years ago. It's just one room with a bed and a couch and a kitchen, but it's adequate for him, and for his daughter, Nicole, when it's his turn to take care of her. He likes the backyard oasis, hiding out in the shadows, where he wants to be. He has no mortgage and expects to never have one again.

A few months back, a new family moved into the main house. Michael said hello to the wife and asked what she did. She said she represented banks in foreclosure cases. "Some of this stuff, I can't make it up," Michael tells me. "She's doing exactly what I'm doing, only the opposite."

Every day Michael travels an hour to Fort Lauderdale, to work at the law offices of Evan Rosen. Evan was the only attorney who showed up at Lisa and Michael's rained-out Homeless for the Holidays protest, something Michael never forgot. Lisa hooked on with Evan first, doing side research and docket checks. Evan later reached out to Michael and they made a deal over lunch. Michael handles client intake, along with preparing discovery requests and depositions. Of course, Michael runs Evan's website; sometimes he'll cross-post stories to *4closureFraud*, which remains online, though not as active.

West Palm Beach is about halfway between his job in Fort Lauderdale and where his ex-wife, Jennifer, lives. In 2014 she executed a short sale on the property in Port St. Lucie, the dream house that started Michael down this path. Jennifer stayed around Port St. Lucie, and Michael won't move closer to work, because he'd be too far away from his daughter. So he logs a lot of hours on I-95. He joked about applying at Ocwen, the mortgage servicer headquartered up the street: "I've wanted to go undercover for so long."

Michael expected to be co-directing the Housing Justice Foundation with Lynn and Lisa. The three foreclosure fighters talked about the nonprofit a lot; Lynn even supplied details like the building site and insurance status, things Michael would never care about if he wasn't part of the team. Even when Mark Elliot and Rachael moved into Lynn's condo and Michael had to move out, he found another place downtown, close to the offices. But the partnership never materialized. I ask Michael if he felt strung along. He would only reply, "Things ended up working out for the best."

Michael attributes the decline of *4closureFraud* to the death of Google Reader. All his keyword searches and news feeds were wiped out, and he never quite figured out how to replace them. Plus there was less urgency to cover every detail of foreclosure nation anymore: after a while it just felt pointless. The site still looks the same, the Carol Asbury ad replaced with a bigger one for Evan Rosen. But he can go weeks without writing, unlike the daily grind of the activism years. Instead of trying to save the nation, Michael has pulled back, trying only to save one Florida homeowner at a time.

It can be difficult. Too many judges in Florida, and really nationwide, aren't willing to enforce the full panoply of the nation's property laws. A securities lawyer put it to me this way: Judges like to avoid big legal issues whenever possible. Why bring foreclosures to a standstill if they can find an escape route? Besides, the judges come from the same class as the plaintiff lawyers, not the homeowners. Even when those lawyers openly lied to them and defiled their courtrooms, they couldn't bring themselves to sanction them if it meant giving some deadbeat a free house.

I attended a mock court session Evan Rosen coordinated to teach sixteen defense lawyers in Fort Lauderdale. Rosen played the bank attorney and his colleague played the judge. The biggest innovation banks have made in judicial foreclosure states has been to bring the fraud into the courtroom. Instead of having a robo-signer create an affidavit attesting to the validity of the foreclosure, a professional "robo-witness" walks into court and testifies to the accuracy of the records. For the mock court, Lisa and Michael were the robo-witnesses.

The robo-witness knows as little about the case as the robo-signer, having read the documents a moment before testifying, if at all. They are hired from low-skill temp jobs, with no record of bank employment. They have no firsthand knowledge about how the payment history was generated, whether the note was properly endorsed, or whether the plaintiff has a complete chain of title. The only difference between them and robo-signers is that they look the part. "The witnesses are actresses," Michael told me. "They hire somebody to parrot a script. If you actually trained them to know anything, it would cost money."

The strategies Rosen taught didn't hinge on fraudulent evidence or standing to foreclose. Those crimes are off-limits in Florida courts these days. You may get a win on a missing delinquency letter—April Charney's old defense, nailing servicers for failing to inform borrowers how to cure a default. You could maybe hit the plaintiff for not presenting documents as evidence before trial, or violating another courtroom procedure. You could argue that the account statement provided was a summary and not a full loan history. You had to play around the edges to find something the judge would accept, to make them think they'll look smart if they align with the defense.

The mock judge kept overruling defense objections. "This trial is going on no matter what," she said, smacking down a challenge. It was an accurate depiction. Florida judges are mostly plumbers now, flushing through cases to clear the clog. Banks convinced judges that the only path out of the crisis was to throw people out of their homes. And they convinced the legislature to help make that a reality. After years of false starts and Rallies in Tally, the state did pass a law to speed up the foreclosure process, though it was so poorly written that it actually slowed foreclosures down at first. But in a bizarre irony, Florida allocated $36 million from the National Mortgage Settlement, intended to aid homeowners, to fund high-speed foreclosure courts for another three years. Bank penalties finance homeowner evictions. The new rocket docket has a mandate to clear 256,000 foreclosure cases a year. One judge in Broward County closed 786 cases in a single day, mostly final judgments against homeowners. Florida homeowners in foreclosure have two adversaries: their lender and their government.

Law enforcement in Florida hasn't batted an eye at this seeming destruction of due process. A judge allowed one foreclosure mill law firm under investigation by attorney general Pam Bondi's office, Shapiro & Fishman, to quash a subpoena for records, on the grounds that only the Florida bar could discipline law firms. Michael was at the trial and said it was incompetently argued. When an appeals court upheld the ruling, Bondi threw up her hands, saying that she could no longer do anything to stop unfair practices by foreclosure mills. The ruling, according to attorney Tom Ice, left the door open for Bondi to use other statutes to discipline foreclosure mills. But Bondi let it all go, closing the investigation opened by June Clarkson and Theresa Edwards years before.

The Florida bar belatedly disbarred David Stern in 2014. Marshall C. Watson agreed to a plea deal in 2013 that forced him to shut down his firm. But he reopened it under a different name, Choice Legal Group, and went on representing banks. The mill lawyers mostly haven't changed; Lisa Epstein told me she once saw an attorney stamping final judgments with the judge's signature.

Tom Ice and his colleagues have reversed cases on appeal, a better wager than rocket docket judges. They've built up significant appellate court case law imperiling the use of robo-witnesses who have no personal information about the authenticity of the documents. Evan Rosen started going after "robo-verifiers," servicer employees who signed verifications attesting that the company made every effort to confirm the facts of a particular foreclosure case. They deposed Lona Hunt, robo-verifier for Seterus, a servicer for many loans owned by Fannie Mae. In the deposition, Hunt admitted twice that she never read the complaint before she signed a verification. Off that deposition, Rosen won the case.

But even when banks lose, the plaintiffs can always voluntarily move to dismiss, fix up the paperwork, and try again. This came to a head in the 2013 *Pino* decision. Ice Legal tried to force the court to reopen a voluntary dismissal and impose sanctions for fraud. A favorable ruling could have made all Florida mortgages soiled by false documents unenforceable. But the state supreme court ruled that voluntary dismissal was fine. "It's happening every day," Tom Ice told me, "and the world doesn't care."

Servicers can afford to lose one case if another twenty go through because homeowners don't have the resources to contest the eviction. Defense attorneys amount to nuisances, not a real impediment to the business model. But for now, it's all Michael can achieve. When he succeeds—and he often does—it's thrilling. "We do it home by home and client by client," he tells me over drinks. "It's amazing what we can do for people."

"The plaintiff does not have standing, your honor," says the defense counsel in the case of *U.S. Bank as Trustee for Citigroup Mortgage Loan Trust v. Mara Papasoff*. He's holding a note with a special endorsement to Bishop's Gate Mortgage Trust, not U.S. Bank. Bishop's Gate was some middleman link in the securitization chain. But the endorsement in its name made the case problematic.

"If the endorsement identifies a party, it's only payable to them," the defense attorney continues. "Only Bishop's Gate can sue on this note. The case has to be dismissed." This was exactly the same issue in Lisa Epstein's case, six years earlier: a note endorsed to a party other than the plaintiff, making it impossible for the plaintiff to enforce. The trustee was even U.S. Bank in both cases. And Lisa Epstein is sitting next to me, watching this transpire in courtroom 4A in the Palm Beach County Courthouse.

The plaintiff's lawyer insists that U.S. Bank has standing because the assignment indicated its acquisition of the mortgage. So instead of the long-time industry assertion that the mortgage follows the note, in this case the bank argued that the note follows the mortgage. "This is what you call a shuck and jive," Lisa says.

Judge Roger Colton, a retired judge paid with rocket docket funds, looks perturbed that he must make an actual decision. He tells the parties he will take the case under advisement. A week later he did affirm final judgment of foreclosure and set a sale date, despite the evidentiary problems. But then the parties filed a joint motion to vacate the judgment, and Judge Colton put the sale on hold, pending another hearing. The case remains in limbo.

Lisa and I head to the courthouse commissary to chat. After losing the race for clerk of courts, Lisa took a year off for rest and self-preservation. She handed *Foreclosure Hamlet* to KT, the foreclosure fighter from Maine, who told me that she stayed on the site sixteen hours a day, drawing purpose from confused homeowners seeking help. Tragically, KT died of a recurrence of breast cancer in June 2015, so the future of *Foreclosure Hamlet* is unknown. KT and Lisa never had the chance to meet.

Lisa also works for Evan Rosen, but she doesn't go to Fort Lauderdale every day, telecommuting from her tiny apartment in the Royal Saxon, on the Intracoastal. Lisa works during the day, while Jenna is at school, and picks her up in the afternoon. They get to talk, read together, and bond. Distracted by foreclosure fraud, Lisa missed three critical years as her child grew up. She would have done her best as clerk of courts, but in losing, Lisa won back the semblance of a normal life.

On the weekends Lisa and Michael and the kids sometimes get together. Jenna and Nicole play while the adults sit in the backyard, talking shop or reminiscing. They were strangers, became partners, and are now best friends. I spent a night with them in the backyard, and they excitedly overlapped each other's sentences, laughing about the old days. They prefer to remember the good parts.

Lisa still hears from homeowners and the media. People she doesn't even remember come up to her and say, "I think about you all the time." Lisa usually doesn't respond to the emails; she finds it too harsh to tell them to consider moving on with their lives. Everyone assumes the pioneers of the movement to fight foreclosure fraud must have the answer that unlocks the key to saving homes. To Lisa, there is no answer.

The house on Gazetta Way that Lisa never wanted, the one she bolted from the first chance she could get, remains in foreclosure. A new debt collector pursued final judgment a while back, but canceled the hearing at the last minute. One of Alan's cousins lives there now. Lisa and I go over to check the place out. It did have a feeling of randomness to it, an artifact of its rush to market. The trees are a bit bigger now, but one of them was slumped over, half dead. There's still a picture of an infant Jenna on a table in the enormous front room. Lisa flips through a stack of late notices, urging her to cure her debt. The co-op, meanwhile, is fully paid off.

Lisa looks back on those years of activism as if remembering a distant dream. "It's like an intense romance in your teens. You can't picture that person now, but he meant the world to you then." She doesn't recognize the woman in hospital scrubs who ran from courtrooms to protests to meetings to research sessions, leaving cartoon hairpins flying behind her, feeding off the energy that comes from deep focus. When we talk about what she did, Lisa shakes her head at how crazy it all was, how all-consuming. For all the criticism about "hogging the spotlight," Lisa was a reluctant warrior. She's relieved to get to read a book again or spend time with her daughter without jumping to the computer for the latest foreclosure fraud news. "It's done now. And I'm glad it's done."

The activists who helped expose foreclosure fraud did everything civics classes teach us will create effective change. They found patterns of systematic criminality. They coordinated and gathered evidence. They organized, using old-fashioned protests and new media tools, paralleling the pamphleteers of the American Revolution and the muckrakers of the Progressive Era. They built a movement of similarly situated followers, and publicized their cause through the media. With persistence, they enlisted support from figures of authority. They helped file lawsuits against the perpetrators. They ensured that the whole nation, from a circuit court judge to the man seated in the Oval Office, would know what happened. They did all this while simultaneously fighting their own foreclosures.

Their tactics weren't always perfect. They put too much faith in a justice system dismembered by collusion between Washington and Wall Street. The motivation to try anything to expose the truth led to some unwise decisions. Critics accused them of taking too much credit. The worst charged they just wanted a free place to live. They were at times stubborn, naive, and self-destructive. In other words, they were human.

But what Lisa Epstein, Michael Redman, and Lynn Szymoniak learned, through triumphs and stumbles, is that this democratic ideal of grassroots action doesn't work the way it's described in history textbooks or Frank Capra narratives. At least, it doesn't work when you go up against banks, even if you have the truth on your side. "I believed there would be a resolution for everybody," Lisa told Michael and me at a recent dinner. "I don't believe it anymore."

Grassroots movements can succeed in America. Recent civil rights advances for gays and lesbians owe much to ACT UP holding die-ins in the streets in the 1980s. The nation now believes the Iraq War was a mistake, largely because liberal bloggers made that case daily. Even economic movements, like the low-wage worker Fight for $15, can post victories. Why does Wall Street benefit from a protective bubble, preventing accountability at every step? What's become of our system, that policy makers can ignore millions of pieces of false evidence used to dispossess Americans to this very day?

Those are difficult questions to answer. But the easiest way to discourage dissent is to cast it as hopeless; that robs the purpose from fighting. It's a testament to the innate desire for human understanding and the power of the Internet that, despite so many hurdles—from a desiccated public square to an ignorant media to a massively powerful financial sector to a law enforcement elite acting as their servants—the foreclosure fraud story got so far. And the story of movements in America is that they crash onto the shore like waves of the incoming tide, each one progressing a bit further than the last.

Crooked banks rely on isolation and shame. The isolation renders the prospect of individual homeowners fighting big banks impossible; the shame makes no level of misconduct from Wall Street as critical as missing a mortgage payment. The foreclosure fighters created community spaces to disarm isolation and shame, giving struggling homeowners a voice and a chance. Without the foreclosure fraud movement there is no Occupy Wall Street; there is no Elizabeth Warren wing of the Democratic Party; there is no student debt movement, or low-wage worker movement, or movement to transfer money to credit unions and community banks. Lisa and Michael and Lynn, and all the bloggers and lawyers and activists who put their heart into this issue, raised public consciousness so that mega-banks have lost just a hint of their aura of invincibility.

There are new rules against predatory lending and servicing, courtesy of the Consumer Financial Protection Bureau, a rare example of grassroots energy forging a regulatory agency. The crisis in Minneapolis created by the successful eviction defense arranged by Occupy Our Homes set the stage for a statewide foreclosure prevention law called the Homeowner's Bill of Rights; a similar bill rose from below and passed in California. Lisa Epstein's Skype session to the Hawaii legislature helped turn the island into a judicial foreclosure state. State and federal officials told me that without the passion of people like Lisa and Michael and Lynn, the admittedly meager outcomes in the litany of big bank settlements over the past several years would have been markedly worse.

In his office in St. Petersburg, Matt Weidner offered an optimistic take, an anomaly for him: "When you look at the vast amounts of legal and advocacy work that was done, it was extraordinarily successful. If you decided that you were going to fight this, you're likely still in your home today." He believes banks did change their behavior, partially out of reluctance to duke it out for years with experienced defense attorneys. "The default model of foreclosure litigation doesn't exist anymore because people fought. If everyone shut their mouth, David Stern would still be in business."

We should temper the shouts of triumph. It's an enormous failure of public policy that we don't know precisely how many families lost their homes in the foreclosure crisis. But the best estimate is close to six million. And that doesn't include millions more who gave up their homes in short sales or "cash for keys" trades. Repeated studies show that people living in areas with high foreclosures suffer elevated physical and mental health ailments. A 2014 report in the *American Journal of Public Health* linked high foreclosure rates with increased suicides. The foreclosure crisis generated the largest ruination of middle-class wealth in nearly a century. Former congressman Brad Miller calls it "an extinction event" for the black and Latino middle class. It contributed massively to the soaring inequality of what some call the new Gilded Age. Amid the carnage, people became wary of volatile assets like mortgages, stunting future economic growth.

Perhaps most important, homeowners and municipalities must deal with corrupted property records, questions of true ownership, and "clouded title" for years to come, if not decades. There's a respected Florida lawyer named Henry Trawick who practically wrote the rules for legal practice and procedure in the state. He worked as a title officer in the 1950s, struggling to reconcile Depression-era mortgages with pervasive flaws, and he sees the same mess now. It took a long time after the Depression to scrub the rot out of the system. It may take longer today.

But even among those who most deeply internalized the pain of this scarred American landscape, the hope hasn't been snuffed out. In fact, Lisa, Michael, and Lynn got back together in 2014 to take on Diana Lewis, the rudest, most loathsome foreclosure judge in Florida, who heard several of the cases described in this book. Lewis's father, Philip, was a powerful state senator whose name is stamped on a homeless intervention facility in Palm Beach County, and the joke is that his daughter kept it well stocked.

When Lewis came up for reelection, Jessica Ticktin, a thirty-five-year-old foreclosure defense attorney who argued cases in her courtroom, decided to challenge her. Lawyers across the state contributed to Ticktin's campaign. And the foreclosure fighters did their part. On a hot August Election Day, Lisa and Michael stood on their feet for hours, encouraging voters to dump Lewis. It worked—Diana Lewis lost 54 percent to 46 percent, becoming just the fourth Palm Beach County circuit judge to be booted in the last thirty years. Lynn went to court the next day, just to observe. Judge Lewis was unusually peevish.

One election does not make up for the outrage and human tragedy of the foreclosure crisis. But to Lisa, it felt so gratifying. And it showed that the spirit of the movement that gave its best shot at forcing accountability remains alive. They may have gone local, but they can still pack some force.

And they won't stop for generations. Lisa's daughter, Jenna, is now eight. One day her teacher gave a lesson, explaining how you can save money by putting it in a bank. Jenna raised her hand and said, "No, don't you know? The banks steal money! If you put it in a bank it'll be gone forever!" The teacher sent Jenna home that day with a note, telling Lisa that her daughter didn't understand the concept of banking. Jenna told her mother, "Mama, that teacher's crazy! She told us to put our money in a bank today!" Lisa just smiled.

AFTERWORD

Two days after Donald Trump's election, I was strolling aimlessly through a mostly empty outdoor mall in Coral Gables, Florida, when my cell phone rang. It was Lisa Epstein, and two seconds into the conversation she unburdened her thoughts. "I really think Trump won because the Democrats did nothing to stop foreclosures and the fraud that went on," she said.

A variant of this argument has subsequently raged among liberals for months: did Trump triumph due to thinly coded racism and xenophobia, or did he tap into a broader economic anxiety in small towns and cities left behind by globalization? The answer doesn't need to be one or the other; people are complicated and their political decisions are often irrational, and anyway cultural and economic discontent cannot be neatly disaggregated. But few debaters ever raise the points Lisa Epstein did on that phone call with me, that the failure to protect homeowners and hold accountable their tormentors tore holes in a fragile social fabric. "The people did not see their government helping them in a time of need," Lisa said. And they revolted, kicking the party too reluctant to stop the carnage out of office.

If you try to explain this history in 2017, you're immediately admonished by the anti-Trump resistance not to contemplate how the fire started until it's put out. There are simply more pressing concerns: the next erosion of political norms, the next ethically dubious personal enrichment, the next early-morning tweet. But it's a mistake to bury history and ignore its lessons; we should instead recognize what failure can unleash. And you can easily measure the impact of never exacting justice for foreclosure

fraud, simply by tracking the recent career trajectory of the engineers of
the Great Foreclosure Machine.

Weeks after the election, Trump selected his campaign finance chair, Steven
Mnuchin, for secretary of the treasury. The pundits immediately brought up
Mnuchin's seventeen years at Goldman Sachs, following in the footsteps of
his father, *also* a partner at the firm. But that was the least distressing part of
his résumé.

After spinning off his own hedge fund in 2004, Mnuchin led an investment team that purchased failed subprime lender IndyMac. They changed
the name to OneWest Bank and made Mnuchin CEO (later chairman of
the board). Among the bad actors in the mortgage industry, OneWest
stood out as uniquely sleazy, partially because of the sweetheart deal they
struck with the Federal Deposit Insurance Corporation, which controlled
IndyMac after the company collapsed. The FDIC gave OneWest a backstop:
they would cover all losses on loan defaults after the first 20 percent. Mortgage servicers make money on foreclosures through late fees and inspection
fees and appraisal fees. But OneWest couldn't lose more than a minimum
amount on the actual loan. While the FDIC lost $13 billion on IndyMac,
OneWest turned a $3 billion profit before selling the bank to CIT for double
the initial investment.

OneWest foreclosed on over 36,000 families in California alone, with
68 percent of those evictions occurring in non-white zip codes. Leslie Parks
of Minneapolis, Minnesota, was negotiating a loan modification with One-
West when she came home in a blizzard one December night to find her
locks changed. Heather McCreary of Sparks, Nevada, had her payment denied because it wasn't a certified check, a requirement not cited in any of her
paperwork. OneWest foreclosed a few months later. Tim Davis of northern
Virginia had a mysterious $14,479 charge added to his loan's escrow bal-
ance that kept reappearing, even after a bankruptcy court ordered it removed. Myrtle Lewis, 103, of north Texas, got a foreclosure notice after her
insurance lapsed, one of numerous "widow foreclosures" that led to an $89
million settlement with the Justice Department. Teena Colebrook, a Trump
voter from Hawthorne, California, was told she could only get help from
OneWest if she fell ninety days behind on her payments. Then they foreclosed, in a familiar bait-and-switch. Colebrook started an online com-

plaint group to share stories about OneWest, just like Lisa and Michael and Lynn.

None of these tales were unique, but Mnuchin's nomination refocused the spotlight on a forgotten deception. Senate Democrats brought four homeowners to Washington to testify, in what may have been the first congressional forum of foreclosure victims since the crisis began. Rose Mary Gudiel, who camped out on the lawn of Mnuchin's Bel-Air mansion in 2011 in a protest to save her home, led a march back to the residence the day before Mnuchin's January 19 confirmation hearing. Activists placed furniture on the driveway before police dispersed them. On the other side of the country, demonstrators sat down in front of Goldman Sachs's Manhattan headquarters for days.

A couple weeks before the hearing, I delivered my contribution to the debate. A few months earlier, I'd received a brown envelope in the mail with no return address. Inside was a 2013 "package memo" from investigators in the consumer law section of the California attorney general's office. In twenty-two pages, the memo presented evidence appearing to show that OneWest engaged in "widespread misconduct," systematically violating state foreclosure laws. The bank, investigators alleged, ignored notice and waiting period statutes meant to give homeowners time to cure their defaults; gamed foreclosure auctions by making unlawful bids that freed them from paying taxes and chilled competitors; and backdated documents to make it look like they complied with key elements of the foreclosure process when they hadn't.

That last one was particularly easy to spot. Investigators working through county records found eighty-six documents dated before March 19, 2009, the day OneWest opened for business. In another set of electronic documents obtained through a third party, they checked the metadata on when the document was created and compared it to the execution date written on the page. Of the 913 documents in this set, 909 had dates on the documents earlier than the date in the metadata.

The investigating attorneys wanted the state attorney general, Kamala Harris, to sue OneWest for these violations, detailing the bank's misconduct for the public and enhancing the deterrent to violating state law. But Harris chose not to prosecute. She never even brought in OneWest executives for a meeting to discuss it. Pressed to explain why, Harris called it "a decision my office made," as if the office walls had the ability to make assessments instead of its leader.

Harris had been criticized throughout her attorney general tenure for weak enforcement of consumer fraud. She habitually took credit for cases pursued by multi-state coalitions where she had little input. And political staff appeared to dominate the office, prioritizing how a case might look if it failed rather than the importance of enforcing the law. But fate would now force Harris to confront her disinterest in going after Wall Street. As a senator, she would have to vote on Mnuchin's treasury secretary confirmation. (For the record, she voted no.)

At the confirmation hearing, Mnuchin grew prickly when asked about the leaked memo, calling its release "highly inappropriate." It was one of the few moments that shook him up. Mnuchin insisted that OneWest was a good corporate citizen that tried to help homeowners, issuing over 100,000 loan modifications. But the statistic actually referred to "trial plan offers extended." In other words, they were merely proposals to homeowners of loan modifications, not approved permanent mods. Only 36,000 of them were made active, and even that doesn't count loans that later re-defaulted. So of all the modifications Mnuchin touted, two-thirds of them didn't go through, and many more ended in foreclosure.

"Extended is not the same as a modification," Senator Bob Casey admonished Mnuchin.

"They were offered," he replied wanly.

Mnuchin followed up his public testimony by giving written answers for the record about OneWest's long history of robo-signing that varied from known facts. In this book, you can read about Erica Johnson-Seck's deposition, how she spent thirty seconds reviewing foreclosure files before swearing in affidavits that she verified all the facts. The *Columbus Dispatch* later found dozens of other clear examples of robo-signing. But Mnuchin wrote in response to questions submitted after the hearing that "OneWest Bank did not robo-sign documents," denying objective reality to such a degree that a watchdog group called the Campaign for Accountability asked the Justice Department to investigate him for making false statements to Congress.

Senator Casey demanded Mnuchin correct the answer about robo-signing. Mnuchin responded by insisting that the Obama-era Independent Foreclosure Review cleared his bank's name. But OneWest, like all banks, handpicked the not-so-independent reviewers, and laid out the manner in which they reviewed. If the review doesn't say specifically that OneWest robo-signed, that's because OneWest created the categories and hid its past behind vague language. It was another example of how a lack of accountability boosted bank executives. Regulators designed flawed foreclosure reviews that did not reveal the extent of borrower harm. And then Trump's treasury secretary nominee employed it to whitewash his bank's legacy.

It worked. Mnuchin became treasury secretary, earning the vote of all fifty-two Republicans; making false statements to Congress was obviously not an obstacle. At the Treasury Department, he hired Craig Phillips, who while at Morgan Stanley packaged garbage mortgages into securities and sold them to unwitting investors. Phillips headed up the Trump administration's bank deregulation plans. Former OneWest vice chairman Brian Brooks also got a top job at the Treasury Department. In June, President Trump chose Joseph Otting, Mnuchin's OneWest colleague who succeeded him as CEO, as the comptroller of the currency, OneWest's chief federal regulator. Every chief executive in the short history of that bank was now in the government. Meanwhile, Wilbur Ross, Trump's commerce secretary, owned American Home Mortgage Servicing Inc., the corrupt company that mishandled Lynn Szymoniak's loan and forged countless foreclosure documents.

It wasn't just executives at the top who prospered. A June 2017 study from academic researchers found that 85 percent of bankers involved in the mortgage-backed securities market remained in the industry a decade later, and 63 percent of them got promoted, a ratio virtually indistinguishable from that of their colleagues in the finance sector. But the elevation of Mnuchin and his cronies stung even more. Top financial executives defied the country's foreclosure laws, and then rose to become in charge of enforcing the same laws. The unwillingness to prosecute financial wrongdoing went from tragic to toxic.

By protecting the balance sheets of banks instead of homeowners, the Obama administration taught the public that the rules don't apply to the wealthy and powerful. They sapped faith in institutions when they could have restored it. They rehabilitated the reputations of bankers who stole homes. And the public responded with blind rage, sweeping into the White House a reality game show host who then put the very people who profited from foreclosures and benefited from de facto legal immunity in charge. The rot at the heart of our democracy would only spread; the moment to repair it was lost.

I was in Florida after the election for events to tie in with the hardcover publication of *Chain of Title*, but I also wanted to check in on Lisa, Michael, and Lynn. I hadn't seen them since the book's release. I first visited Lynn at the house on Man O' War Road in Palm Beach Gardens, which she paid off with the proceeds from the whistleblower payout.

Lynn greeted me at the door wearing a small skullcap. She suffered a relapse of cancer in late 2015 and, after beating it, her original breast cancer from over a decade ago recurred. She underwent a double mastectomy and aggressive chemotherapy treatments. It became too tiring to leave the house; life became consumed with diagnoses and procedures. With the offices of the Housing Justice Foundation mostly sitting empty, Lynn decided to shut them down.

But though she looked a little gaunt and punctuated her sentences with pauses that I took as a chance to catch her breath, the glint in her eye remained undiminished, especially when the conversation turned to activism. She told me about an email list of lawyer friends, all of them chattering about how to survive the Trump era. She talked about her case in federal court—it was still alive on appeal—and how she hoped to get well enough to honor a request to testify in an upcoming securities lawsuit in Ohio. She threw out legal strategies and opportunities to get at the banks. The thirst for justice wasn't yet quenched.

One case in particular couldn't be filed away. In 2014, Lynn began an effort to liberate documents from the FBI. She was always curious about what happened to the case she initiated, the case that revealed DocX as a serial manufacturer of false evidence, the case that sent Lorraine Brown to jail and nobody else. Using the Freedom of Information Act, she requested documents pertaining to the investigation. The FBI gave Lynn two choices: pay $8,000 for all 300,000 pages on a CD, or take the main file—about 600 pages—for free. Lynn asked for both; so far only the main file has been released.

It was damning enough. According to the files, the FBI and the U.S. attorney's office in Jacksonville, Florida, called in dozens of agents and forensic examiners, impaneled a grand jury, conducted seventy-five interviews, issued hundreds of subpoenas, and reviewed millions of pages of documents. The agents gained a detailed understanding of how and why mortgage companies enlisted third parties like DocX to create false documents to be used in courtrooms. They visited Alpharetta, Georgia, and heard about what one DocX employee called a mortgage document "sweat shop." They learned of managers pushing subordinates to forge mortgage assignments, warning to keep any legal concerns quiet "for the good of the company." And they picked up on how the false documents papered over a larger fraud, the failure to maintain accurate ownership records on millions of loans.

The Jacksonville FBI sought reinforcements, asking their superiors for an investigative team to help conduct interviews across the country and review documents. On June 24, 2010, the FBI's Criminal Investigative Division partially granted their request. "If evidence collected shows intent to defraud investors by the real estate trusts, this matter has the potential to be a top ten Corporate Fraud case," the reply read. In other words, the FBI saw the potential of going beyond DocX, traveling up the chain of mortgage securitization, and scrutinizing why trustees and servicers needed this phony evidence. That could have implicated most of America's biggest banks.

The Jacksonville office made another request for resources in early 2011, noting that the local U.S. attorney was considering indicting officials at third-party facilitator Lender Processing Services, and perhaps others at Deutsche Bank, a trustee whom they felt "made material misrepresentations to the SEC and the investing public." But the trail went cold. Despite accumulating a mountain of evidence, the investigation never ranged beyond DocX. "The field agents did their jobs," Lynn concluded. "The betrayals came from the highest levels."

Even Lorraine Brown, the DocX CEO who was sentenced in 2013 and remains the only individual ever jailed for foreclosure fraud, was paroled into federal custody after serving her minimum sentence. Her final release date was expected sometime in summer 2017. "Lorraine Brown was a very small cog in a giant machine," Lynn told me. "To me she deserved to spend time in prison because of the choices she made and the people whom she hurt. I am only sad that the thousands who made similar choices did not have similar fates—but their time will come."

After surgery to remove the cancer, Lynn started to slowly heal. And she didn't cower from what seemed an impossible task of justice. Two weeks after the election she wrote an exposé of Wilbur Ross, Trump's commerce secretary choice, whose company American Home Mortgage Servicing started her down this road. She delivered that testimony in Ohio, in a securities fraud case against Bank of New York Mellon; she said it felt great to be back in the fight. Lynn's own case ended after seven years when the Fourth Circuit Court of Appeals ruled against her in February. But she didn't despair, spending hours knitting pink pussyhats for the Women's March, an echo of her old life in the antiwar movement.

Every so often Lynn fires up her computer and unearths more examples of the degradation of America's property records system. Her favorite was a mortgage assignment from February 2007 for a condo in central Florida. The assignor was MERS, Mortgage Electronic Registration Systems, as nominee for a wholesale lender. Or at least it was supposed to be. In four different places on the document, the name is spelled, with impish accuracy, "Mortgage Electronic Registration Sidesteps." When Lynn saw the document for the first time, she had to take a walk to cool down.

Intellectually, Lynn knows the battle is over. But she can't stop assembling facts for a record few will discover, a testament to the depths of the crimes she witnessed. Someday, Lynn believes, someone will find that record and face down the perpetrators. "I am one of those people who still believes in heaven and hell and Judgment Day."

I met Lisa, Michael, and their kids at a family restaurant in Lake Worth, near Lisa's condo. Michael had picked up on Lisa's thesis that the foreclosure mess presaged the rise of Trump, and he somehow labeled himself personally responsible. "We were the ones who exposed this, it's our fault," he said, and I couldn't be sure if he was kidding.

Michael returned to his roots when the book released. In May 2016 he restarted *4closurefraud*, for a while writing at the same frequency as he had in the critical years of the crisis. At first he just posted reviews about *Chain of Title*, but he quickly discovered that there were still many nightmares to catalog: Wells Fargo trying to evict an eighty-five-year-old woman with Alzheimer's; a Michigan woman's property foreclosed on over a $7 late fee;

a fabricated set of documents in a foreclosure in Massachusetts. He increasingly felt like nothing had changed.

Within a month, Michael hit on a little scoop. He found a job description at a recruiting board for a "Chain of Title specialist." Select Portfolio Servicing needed someone for "assistance in demonstrating the Investor has the appropriate legal authority to initiate" foreclosure actions, "by recognizing and preparing the required documents to complete the Note with applicable Endorsements." All these endorsements should have been prepared and recorded within days of the transfer of sale—the failure to do so ruptured the chain of title. So Select Portfolio Servicing was really looking for time travelers to fix their broken ownership records.

Michael posted the job listing at *4closurefraud*. A few days letter, attorney April Charney sent him another one: a third-party recruiter looking for a "default breach specialist," to "identify missing assignments needed to complete the chain of title prior to foreclosure referral." Michael archly noted that at least the pay was better: mortgage companies used to offer $10 an hour for this work, but now they boosted it up to $22. A little later, *Living Lies* tracked down the profile of a "chain of title specialist" at mortgage servicer Ocwen, who listed her current duties as "researching Mortgage Documents to verify a full Chain of Title is present . . . if it is not create the needed Documents."

Michael also wrote about Ocwen, the mortgage servicer whose offices were a few blocks from his house. Servicers now used "robo-witnesses" in their foreclosure trials; they were supposed to be independent third parties that could verify the amounts owed and business practices involved. Michael found and published a letter showing Ocwen lawyers coaching the witnesses and spoon-feeding them answers. In April 2017, the Consumer Financial Protection Bureau and two dozen states charged Ocwen with a complete inability to execute the basic functions of mortgage servicing. A few states actually banned the company from servicing mortgages within their borders. Of course, CFPB fined Ocwen for this same dysfunction four years earlier, but inexcusably let them stay in business, to pulverize tens of thousands more customers.

When you fail to hold companies or their executives accountable, they have no reason to mend their ways. In fact, the rot has spread: dozens of cases involving National Collegiate Student Loan Trusts have been dismissed in court, because the company could not prove they actually owned the debt. It's *Chain of Title*, student loan edition.

Michael kept up his blog for about six months before tapering off, though he still posts now and again. He's getting by on the periphery of Florida's still-robust foreclosure defense industry. Like Lynn, he exhibits almost a split personality: harboring no illusions about the prospects of accountability for fraud, yet insistent on trying to move the ball forward and help homeowners.

Lisa had turned fraud research from a hobby into a career, too. At the time of the release of *Chain of Title*, both she and Michael were out of work; the jobs they held with a foreclosure attorney had wrapped up. While Michael sought out more foreclosure work, Lisa found a role with The Capitol Forum, an investigative website that covers government contracting, market competition, and consumer protection. The subscription-based site's in-depth coverage has earned a following from policy makers, investors, law firms, and think tanks.

As a correspondent covering consumer protection issues, Lisa had to adapt her freewheeling blogging style to a more buttoned-down journalism. She felt uncomfortable at first and solicited my advice. I told her that she knew better than anyone how to find unscrupulous behavior lurking beneath the surface. Relaying those stories to her new audience would take time, but she'd get the hang of it.

Before long, Lisa was detailing rip-offs by a subprime auto lender and a company that offered fuel discounts for small businesses. Her training observing the Great Foreclosure Machine served her well. She had no problem cold-calling victims and former employees, and speaking to them for hours. People just wanted to unburden themselves to Lisa. Her boss at The Capitol Forum, Teddy Downey, sung her praises to me, wondering, "What's the over-under on the number of years it takes Lisa to win a Pulitzer?"

Lisa still kept an eye on foreclosures. When the Justice Department announced settlements with Deutsche Bank and Goldman Sachs for selling bad mortgage securities to investors, they directed some of the settlement funds to consumer relief. But there was a problem—as trustees and securities arrangers, Deutsche and Goldman didn't own or service any actual loans, and therefore couldn't assist struggling homeowners. So Goldman started buying up distressed loans on the cheap from Fannie Mae and other mortgage holders. When it modified loans for borrowers, it satisfied obligations under the settlement. But Goldman didn't cut the balances to the level at which they bought the mortgages. As the modified payments rolled in, the bank would earn a profit. In other words, the government sentenced Goldman Sachs to make money.

Deutsche Bank's strategy was even loopier. It invested in hedge funds, which then bought up delinquent mortgages. Deutsche couldn't really lose on the investment, and homeowners were not guaranteed to benefit. If a homeowner suffered foreclosure but got a secondary loan canceled that Deutsche helped to purchase, the bank would earn credits in the settlement.

CBS MarketWatch quoted Lisa in their story about this treachery. She described how Deutsche Bank, a trustee for mortgage-backed securities, could have been forced to direct the servicers it worked with to modify the loans and cover the losses for investors. Homeowners and prospective buyers would get the same outcomes, but the offending bank would actually pay the price, instead of earning a reward. "The devil himself couldn't have thought up a better end run around the settlement," Lisa said.

After dinner, we walked over to the Lake Worth beachfront, site of a monthly bonfire attended by hundreds of locals. Lisa and Michael actually deemed one of these bonfires in 2011 "Torch the Fraud," tossing fraudulent documents into the blazes in a symbolic protest. We strolled the boardwalk and got some ice cream. We talked about Lisa and Michael's lives, and how friends and colleagues reacted to seeing their story memorialized. They seemed happy and content.

As I said my goodbyes and prepared to leave, Michael was still feeling remorseful about the election outcome. "We did it! We caused Trump!" I told him that he and Lisa only gave voice to what was happening across the country. It's not like they signed false documents or failed to prosecute wrongdoers. Michael just shook his head; I still don't really know if he was putting me on. I got in my rental car and crossed over the Intracoastal Waterway and into the night.

The foreclosure crisis has yet to abate for those unlucky enough to buy a home at the wrong time. According to the freshly named Black Knight Financial Services (formerly the notorious LPS), an industry source that would be thrilled to present positive numbers, in March 2017, loans ninety days delinquent or more were still 25 percent—and active foreclosures 45 percent—above historical norms. That translates into 250,000 more loans either seriously delinquent or in foreclosure than what we would see in a healthy market.

This isn't a month or a year after the financial collapse, but more than a *decade*. Despite an improved job market and a consistently growing economy, despite increasing housing prices that have some experts wondering whether another bubble is inflating, foreclosures continue to pile up at a level that at any other point in history would be rightly called a crisis. That's what gives loudmouths shouting about the failures of Washington staying power; the No Trespassing signs and boarded-up windows speaking to a permanent decline, a slow rolling of inequity.

Curiously, this perpetually enlarged foreclosure stock isn't coming from newly originated loans, which have performed exceedingly well since new standards from the Consumer Financial Protection Bureau went into effect in 2014. The elevated delinquencies and foreclosures come from vintage loans from the bubble era, toxic waste never cleaned up by government programs or judicial action. The extreme dysfunction of the Great Foreclosure Machine, the inability to clearly determine ownership with even a semblance of accuracy, has stretched out court cases further than anyone could have imagined, putting Americans in a battle for their homes lasting longer than most of this country's wars. It's like a powerful tide, with hundreds of thousands of families caught in its undertow, unable to claw back to shore.

As I learned in the months after *Chain of Title*'s publication, foreclosure victims no longer really petitioned their government for help. They lost confidence that their leaders could provide assistance or even fair arbitration. They instead turned to people like me. In a punishing echo of the letters and emails Lisa, Michael, and Lynn had become accustomed to receiving, they started to flow my way in greater numbers than ever before. Nearly every morning I awoke to another horror story.

"I lost my home of thirty years to fraudclosure."

"No such person, no matter how much power they hold, should have the right to take or rob a family from their home without any just reason."

"I mean am I the only one fighting who is so alone? No family, I lost everyone and everything over this."

They tell me about banks breaking into their homes and changing the locks. They tell me about losing their grip on their home despite never missing a payment. They tell me about magically appearing affidavits purporting to fix defective documents several years into a foreclosure. They tell me about signatures on mortgage documents signed six different ways. They tell me about bad attorneys and unfair trials and courtrooms so crooked I'd consider them tales of conspiracy theorists if I didn't know the dark history. They tell me about being weeks away from living on the street, of the shame of failing their children, of the sicknesses befalling them from a combination of stress and despair.

In Lincoln, California, Erik and Renee Sundquist, two athletes who had excelled on the soccer field and the ice rink, were physically and emotionally damaged after Bank of America drove them into foreclosure, lost their loan modification paperwork on twenty separate occasions, illegally violated a bankruptcy stay, sold their home, hired contractors to stalk the family, and eventually took control of the property. By the time the error was corrected and the Sundquists got back in the home, they found all furnishings and appliances removed and the trees dead. Bank of America refused to take responsibility; in fact, they were still threatening to foreclose. Erik attempted suicide with pills. Renee routinely cut herself with razors. "All I do is cry," she wrote in a journal documenting the six-year ordeal.

The judge in the case ordered a million-dollar verdict for the Sundquists for housing expenses and distress. But he found that scarcely enough to matter to the bank. So he awarded another $45 million in punitive damages to public law schools and consumer groups, so anyone else going through such nightmares would have a well-funded advocate in their corner. "Franz Kafka lives," the judge wrote. "He works at Bank of America." The bank is appealing the verdict.

These moments of mortgage industry comeuppance have been far too rare. Yet the testimony continues to pour in from across America, from homeowners with different social, economic, and racial backgrounds. They are Democrats and Republicans and independents. Sometimes they find legal assistance for their battle against the most powerful institutions in this country. Most of the time they don't, and are left to pick through the rubble on their own.

And these people are meticulous. They've kept every scrap of paper related to their cases. They can recite the vagaries of the chain of title, the signature on their note, the lady they talked to a year and a half ago who gave them some scrap of information that helps prove their case. They share that perseverance Michael, Lisa, and Lynn once had, that belief that the truth is enough to set things right.

One interaction stands out. I gave a talk about my book in St. Louis last summer. The skies erupted minutes before the event and few battled the rainstorm to join the audience. But when I opened it up for questions, Andy Williams Jr., dreadlocks scraping his shoulders, stood up and said, "David, you are a hard man to find."

Williams drove five hours that day, from Chicago to St. Louis, to tell me about an eleven-year foreclosure ordeal. He said his servicer misapplied his payments, charged illegal fees, and unlawfully placed him into homeowner's insurance when he already held it. His case goes on—it's still in federal court—but he compiled horror stories from borrowers in the Chicago area, and also helped to build six law firms to protect others at risk of dispossession. "When I read your book, I thought I was reading about me!" he said.

These odysseys all happened in parallel, separate foreclosure fights in separate cities. In the end, I became the connective tissue bringing them together. So they ask me, a non-lawyer who has only observed and not participated directly in their struggle, for answers I mostly don't have, for a solution I mostly cannot provide. I cannot convince a judge inclined only to clear their case from his desk, or a bank executive inclined only to see them as a financial asset to be plucked, to change their minds. I cannot fix what life has decided to pile upon their shoulders. I answer as many people as I can, but mainly to express sympathy that the massive netting of fraud laid by the mortgage industry over a decade ago continues to trip people like them.

But when I respond in this totally ineffectual fashion, they do the most amazing thing: they thank me. Just by giving voice to similar terrors, I have instilled in them hope that they aren't utterly alone in their misery, that they haven't been singled out by a vengeful nation, that somewhere out there they have an ally and a confidant. I wish I had more to offer than mere recognition and an apology that their government, their legal system, the American promise of liberty and justice, failed them. But in sharing this struggle for so long, I've come to understand how acknowledgment can be a gift.

David Dayen
September 2017

ACKNOWLEDGMENTS

In summer 2010 a family friend asked me, apropos of nothing, "Why was President Obama's plan to help those struggling with their mortgage written to favor the banks instead of the people?" His story of mistreatment by his mortgage servicer sparked an interest I didn't know I had into a subject I hadn't previously bothered to understand. Six years later you're holding the end result.

I have an inordinate number of people to thank, starting with my editor Carl Bromley and all the staff at The New Press. Carl took a chance on a first-time author for reasons that are still obscure to me, and yet he was generous, gracious, and wise from beginning to end. It was a great pleasure working with him and his team.

Jane Hamsher, the founder of the dearly departed, groundbreaking political blog *Firedoglake*, where I worked from 2009 to 2012 as a news writer, was the first to suggest that I turn this story into a book, and I am eternally grateful for not only that but everything else. Gregg Levine, Cynthia Kouril, and the late John Chandley got me interested in foreclosure fraud and nurtured my years of reporting on it at *Firedoglake*. After that, Blake Zeff, David Daley, Ben Crair, Ryan Kearney, Heidi Moore, Ryan Cooper, Robert Kuttner, Jan Frel, Yuval Rosenberg, Steven Mikulan, Blake Hounshell, Dan Froomkin, and many other editors I'm sure I'm forgetting gave me the gift of placing my scribblings at their publications, to say nothing of their expert editorial support. All of that work informed this book, which I feel like I've been writing in a Dickensian serial format for years.

So many offered critical advice and encouragement as the book moved forward, including but not limited to Binky Urban, Daniel Conaway, Peter Richardson, Marcy Wheeler, Rick Perlstein, and Helaine Olen. My agent Andrew Ross recognized the possibilities of getting this made at a time when I was filled with doubt, after years of fits and starts. Without the passion he brought to the project, I don't think it would have happened. Heather "Digby" Parton, Jeff Connaughton, Mehrsa Baradaran, and Jared Blank read the manuscript during various drafts and were extremely insightful with their comments.

I am indebted to my fellow writers, reporters, and academics on the foreclosure fraud beat, whose work I drew upon constantly. Michael Lewis, Neil Barofsky, Matt Taibbi, Michael W. Hudson, Jennifer Taub, Joe Nocera, Bethany MacLean, Shahien Nasiripour, Zach Carter, Ryan Grim, Mike Konczal, Yves Smith, Matt Stoller, Abigail Field, Kimberly Miller, Paola Iuspa-Abbott, Gretchen Morgenson, Damon Silvers, Joshua Rosner, Adam Levitin, and Katherine Porter stand out. But there are dozens of others, especially those from small local papers and broadcast affiliates, who related foreclosure nightmares of people in their areas. This often thankless—and, in an age of newspaper cutbacks, rapidly diminishing—work was immensely helpful in revealing a pattern of widespread abuse, and these reporters deserve the thanks of not only me but the whole nation. If you flip through the footnotes, you'll see I tried to recognize all of their contributions.

I spoke with several dozen lawyers, activists, bloggers, and foreclosure victims to put together this book. Special thanks go out to Matt Weidner, Tom and Ariane Ice, April Charney, Max Gardner, Nye Lavalle, Thomas Cox, Jim Kowalski, June Clarkson, Theresa Edwards, Jacqulyn Mack, Harley Herman, Mark Cullen, Evan Rosen, Dick Harpootlian, Ruben Guttman, and the foreclosure defense community in Florida and across the country, whose work persists to this day. James Elder, James Chambers, Alina Virani, Grace Ricci, Ronald Gillis, Andrew "Ace" Delany, Dan Junk, Eric Mains, Bill Paatalo, Nick Espinosa, Shabnam Bashiri, Malcolm Cho, Carlos Marroquin, and their many fellow foreclosure activists all inspire me. Kim "KT" Thorpe, who sadly did not live to read this story, gave practically her whole life to this cause and will be sorely missed. Thanks also to Larry Schwartztol, Rachel Goodman, Barbara Petersen, Steve Dibert, Matt Lockshin, Matt Browner-Hamlin, Daniel Mintz, Jeff Thigpen, John O'Brien, John Kelleher, Sheila Bair, Damon Silvers, Jennifer Brunner, and Tim Miller. There's a scene in November 2010 when Lisa Epstein, Michael Redman, and Lynn Szymoniak visit Washington, D.C., for a meeting about foreclosure fraud. That's where I first met these extraordinary people, who humble me with their dedication, their knowledge, and their spirit. I was honored to be entrusted with their story, and I hope that they now get the proper credit and respect they deserve for taking on the most powerful entity in American life armed with only their wits, a sense of justice, and the truth. During my weeks of research in south Florida, Lisa, Michael, and Lynn were way too hospitable to me while I retraced years of their lives down to the smallest detail, and with all of them being generally private people I understand how difficult that was. Thanks for being my tour guides.

My parents, Neil and Dara, and my sister, Jessica, should know that they are integral to who I am today. I'm so fortunate to have such a great family in my corner.

I told my wife, Mary, that I wouldn't express my appreciation to her by using a clumsy metaphor tangentially related to the topic of the book ("to Mary, who foreclosed on my heart"), but I appear to have now broken that promise. So I'm sorry. Also I love you.

NOTES

Preface

vii No high-ranking Wall Street executive has gone to jail: Jed S. Rakoff, "The Financial Crisis: Why Have No High-Level Executives Been Prosecuted?" *New York Review of Books*, January 9, 2014.

1. A Knock at the Door

1 Home prices in Florida, Arizona, California, and Nevada surged: Federal Housing Finance Agency, purchase-only index data for Q1 1998 to peak, www.fhfa.gov /DataTools/Downloads/Pages/House-Price-Index-Datasets.aspx.

1 half of all subprime mortgages: Shayna M. Olesiuk and Kathy R. Kalser, "The Sand States: Anatomy of a Perfect Housing-Market Storm," *FDIC Quarterly* 3, no. 1 (April 2009).

2 one in twenty-two Florida homeowners: Les Christie, "Foreclosures up a Record 81% in 2008," CNNMoney.com, January 15, 2009.

2 "sewer service": "Super Sewer Service—I Feel Bad for All the People Who Lost Their Homes and Were Obviously Not Served," 4closurefraud.org, October 3, 2010.

3 fake recipients of foreclosure papers: Shannon Behnken, "Judge Wants Answers to Foreclosure Document Fees," *Tampa Tribune*, November 18, 2010.

6 Instead of obtaining a mortgage, purchasers take out loans to buy shares: HSBC, "Owning a Co-Op: 10 Questions to Ask Before You Buy," https://www.us.hsbc .com/1/PA_1_083Q9FJ08A002FBP5S00000000/content/usshared/Personal%20 Services/Home%20Loans/Mortgage/FYI/Shared/Coop%20Guide.pdf.

8 Ameriquest, one of the biggest mortgage lenders: Kathy Kristof and David Streitfeld, "Ameriquest Plans to Cut 3,800 Jobs," *Los Angeles Times*, May 3, 2006.

8 New Century Financial, another giant: Julie Creswell, "Mortgage Lender New Century Financial Files for Bankruptcy," *New York Times*, April 2, 2007.

9 As Federal Reserve chair Ben Bernanke testified: Ben Bernanke, "The Economic Outlook," testimony before the Joint Economic Committee, March 28, 2007, www.federalreserve.gov/newsevents/testimony/bernanke20070328a.htm.

11 As prominent financial analyst Josh Rosner said: Joshua Rosner, Graham Fisher & Co., "Housing in the New Millennium: A Home Without Equity Is Just a Rental with Debt," June 29, 2001, http://papers.ssrn.com/sol3/papers.cfm?abstract_id =1162456.

12 government officials solicited Chase to buy it: Andrew Ross Sorkin, "JPMorgan Pays \$2 a Share for Bear Stearns," *New York Times*, March 17, 2008.

14 banks like Chase received hundreds of billions of dollars: JPMorgan Chase received \$25 billion on October 28, 2008, through the Capital Purchase Program. Information from Pro Publica, "Eye on the Bailout," https://projects.propublica.org/bailout/programs/1-capital-purchase-program.

2. The Dark Side of the American Dream

16 CNBC host Rick Santelli shouted: Rick Santelli, CNBC, February 19, 2009, https://www.youtube.com/watch?v=bEZB4taSEoA.

17 around 95 percent of the cases went uncontested: Virtually everyone involved with foreclosures on either side has made this assertion, though statistics on foreclosures nationwide can be hard to find. Monroe County, Florida, circuit judge Luis Garcia (http://floridakeyswaterfrontexpert.blogspot.com/2008/12/judge-offers-foreclosure-help.html) and New Jersey chief justice Stuart Rabner (www.judiciary.state.nj.us/superior/press_release.htm) have said this on various occasions.

18 "J. P. Morgan Acceptance Corporation I (the 'Company')": Securities and Exchange Commission 8-K form, June 15, 2007, www.sec.gov/Archives/edgar/data/1400186/000116231807000671/m0665form8k.htm.

18 That's how many Americans lost their homes each *day*: David Wheelock, "The Federal Response to Home Mortgage Distress: Lessons from the Great Depression," *Federal Reserve Bank of St. Louis Review*, May/June 2008, Part 1, 138.

18 the Home Owner's Loan Corporation (HOLC) bought defaulted mortgages: Jennifer Taub, *Other People's Houses: How Decades of Bailouts, Captive Regulators and Toxic Bankers Made Home Mortgages a Thrilling Business* (New Haven, CT: Yale University Press, 2014), 40–41.

19 HOLC generated confidence in the long-term, fully amortized mortgage: Richard K. Green and Susan M. Wachter, "The American Mortgage in Historical and International Context," *Journal of Economic Perspectives* 19, no. 4 (Fall 2005): 93–114.

19 Roosevelt established the Federal Housing Administration: Ibid., 95.

19 In 1938, the Federal National Mortgage Administration: Ibid., 95.

19 The FHA loosened standards: Ibid., 96.

20 In 1940, 15 million families . . . ; by 1960 that number: Taub, *Other People's Houses*, 41.

20 Savings and loans found the formula: Ibid., 42.

20 State laws initially restricted savings and loans: Ibid., 40.

20 The annual foreclosure rate from 1950 to 1997: Peter J. Elmer and Steven A. Seelig, "The Rising Long-term Trend of Single-Family Mortgage Foreclosure Rates," Federal Deposit Insurance Corporation, Division of Research and Statistics, 1998.

20 By 1980 there was more money sloshing around: Taub, *Other People's Houses*, 45.

21 four suits, all of them polyester: Michael Lewis, *Liar's Poker: Rising Through the Wreckage on Wall Street* (New York: W.W. Norton, 1989), 142.

21 "the wild and woolly genius": Ibid., 96.

21 The GSEs would pool hundreds of these loans together: Taub, *Other People's Houses*, 43–44.

21 Salomon Brothers and Bank of America attempted to bypass Fannie and Freddie: Lewis, *Liar's Poker*, 111; Taub, *Other People's Houses*, 45.

22 This hurt S&Ls on every level: Lewis, *Liar's Poker*, 124–25; Taub, *Other People's Houses*, 50–53.

22 and Salomon made a killing: Lewis, *Liar's Poker*, 130–32.

22 Ranieri then got Freddie Mac to help with a bond deal: Taub, *Other People's Houses*, 68–69.

22 CMOs created different classes for investors with different risk profiles: Neil Barofsky, *Bailout: How Washington Abandoned Main Street While Rescuing Wall Street* (New York: Simon and Schuster, 2012), 81–87.

23 "If Lewie didn't like a law, he'd just have it changed": Lewis, *Liar's Poker*, 125.

23 President Reagan signed SMMEA in October: Taub, *Other People's Houses*, 74–75.

23 real estate mortgage investment conduit (REMIC): Bethany McLean and Joe Nocera, *All the Devils Are Here: The Hidden History of the Financial Crisis* (New York: W.W. Norton, 2010), 15–16.

23 The mortgage-backed securities market reached $150 billion: Lewis, *Liar's Poker*, 142.

23 It probably accelerated the demise of the S&L industry: Taub, *Other People's Houses*, 76.

24 He was a dream salesman: Lewis, *Liar's Poker*, 141.

24 But homeownership rates rose nearly twenty points: U.S. Census Bureau, Historical Census of Housing Tables, https://www.census.gov/hhes/www/housing/census/historic/owner.html.

24 Wall Street investment banks staffed up: Lewis, *Liar's Poker*, 184–86.

24 "I wasn't out to invent the biggest floating craps game": Shawn Tully, "Lewie Ranieri Wants to Fix the Mortgage Mess," *Fortune*, December 9, 2009.

25 By 2009, one out of every four Floridians: David Streitfeld, "U.S. Mortgage Delinquencies Reach a Record High," *New York Times*, November 19, 2009.

26 "I believe that the mortgage crisis has produced manifest evil": Mission statement, *Living Lies*, https://livinglies.wordpress.com.

26 the site had jumped from 1,000 hits per month: Mike Stuckey, "The Home You Save Could Be Your Own," MSNBC.com, January 28, 2009.

27 "If they can fog a mirror, we'll give them a loan": David Dayen, "Wall Street's Greatest Enemy: The Man Who Knows Too Much," *Salon*, August 28, 2013.

28 Depository Institutions Deregulation and Monetary Control Act (DIDMCA): McLean and Nocera, *All the Devils Are Here*, 29.

28 Alternative Mortgage Transaction Parity Act: Taub, *Other People's Houses*, 69–71.

28 "subprime lending could not have flourished": Ibid., 70.

28 Investment banks made the securities attractive with credit enhancements: McLean and Nocera, *All the Devils Are Here*, 31.

28 warehouse lines of credit: Ibid., 23.

28 Brokers were given "yield spread premiums": Center for Responsible Lending, "Yield Spread Premiums, a Powerful Incentive for Equity Theft," June 18, 2004.

29 Another industry creation was the cash-out refinance: McLean and Nocera, *All the Devils Are Here*, 35.

29 "redlining": Ta-Nehisi Coates, "The Case for Reparations," *Atlantic Monthly*, June 2014.

29 Federal Reserve statistics show that subprime lending increased: Liz Laderman, "Subprime Mortgage Lending and the Capital Markets," *Federal Reserve Bank of San Francisco Economic Letter*, December 28, 2001.

29 The Clinton administration wanted to increase homeownership rates: McLean and Nocera, *All the Devils Are Here*, 32.

30 collateralized debt obligation (CDO): Ibid., 120–22; Barofsky, *Bailout*, 86.

30 Commodity Futures Modernization Act: McLean and Nocera, *All the Devils Are Here*, 109.

30 "Synthetic" CDOs: Ibid., 263–84.

31 second wave of subprime mortgages dwarfed the first wave: Ibid., 125–37.

31 a man coordinating dances at a Mexican restaurant: Michael W. Hudson, *The Monster: How a Gang of Predatory Lenders and Wall Street Bankers Fleeced America—and Spawned a Global Crisis* (New York: Times Books, 2010), 4–9.

31 Some brokers used light-boards: McLean and Nocera, *All the Devils Are Here*, 130.

31 Others presented borrowers with a loan at closing: Hudson, *The Monster*, 3.

32 It was clear securities fraud: Felix Salmon, "The Enormous Mortgage-Bond Scandal," Reuters, October 13, 2010.

32 "Good find on the fraud :)": Nathaniel Popper, "Court Filing Illuminates Morgan Stanley Role in Lending," *New York Times*, December 29, 2014.

32 "If fraudulent practices become systemic": Financial Crisis Inquiry Commission, *The Financial Crisis Inquiry Report* (Washington, DC: Government Printing Office, 2011), 161.

32 when Georgia tried to protect borrowers: Hudson, *The Monster*, 165–81.

32 Banks issued $1 trillion in nonprime mortgage bonds: Adam B. Ashcraft and Til Schuermann, "Understanding the Securitization of Subprime Mortgage Credit," Federal Reserve Bank of New York staff report no. 318, March 2008.

32 Subprime mortgages made up nearly half: McLean and Nocera, *All the Devils Are Here*, 216.

32 Total mortgage debt in America doubled: Neil Bhutta, "The Ins and Outs of Mortgage Debt During the Housing Boom and Bust," staff working paper 2014-91, Divisions of Research and Statistics and Monetary Affairs, Federal Reserve Board, 2014.

32 loan brokers right out of college made $400,000 a year: McLean and Nocera, *All the Devils Are Here*, 125.

32 Home prices appreciated rather slowly for fifty years: Barry Ritholtz, "Classic Case Shiller Housing Price Chart, Updated," *Big Picture* (blog), December 30, 2008, www.ritholtz.com/blog/2008/12/classic-case-shiller-hosuing-price-chart-updated.

32 In several states, *annual* **price increases hit 25 percent:** Federal Reserve Bank of St. Louis, All-Transactions House Price Index for Arizona, accessed at https://research.stlouisfed.org/fred2/series/AZSTHPI. All-Transactions House Price Index for Florida, accessed at https://research.stlouisfed.org/fred2/series/FLSTHPI. All-Transactions House Price Index for California, accessed at https://research.stlouisfed.org/fred2/series/CASTHPI. All-Transactions House Price Index for Nevada, accessed at https://research.stlouisfed.org/fred2/series/NVSTHPI.

33 Even Fannie Mae and Freddie Mac, locked into buying: Taub, *Other People's Houses*, 178–80; McLean and Nocera, *All the Devils Are Here*, 183–84.

33 even amid rising prices, homeownership rates rose: U.S. Census Bureau historical homeownership rates, www.census.gov/housing/hvs/files/currenthvspress .pdf. Homeownership rates peaked in the fourth quarter of 2004 at 69.2 percent, and remained within three-tenths of a point of that number until the end of 2006, the peak of the housing bubble.

33 skyrocketing early payment defaults: McLean and Nocera, *All the Devils Are Here*, 251.

33 Foreclosures started to occur in large enough numbers: Al Yoon, "Foreclosure Rates Almost Doubled in 2007: Report," Reuters, January 29, 2008; Les Christie, "Foreclosures Up a Record 81% in 2008," CNN Money, January 15, 2009.

33–34 Garfield called them "pretender lenders": Sample complaint template, *Living Lies*, https://livinglies.files.wordpress.com/2008/11/template-complaint1.pdf.

34 "The reality is that nearly all securitized mortgage loans are worthless": Neil Garfield, "NY Times Says It All—Almost—Foreclosures: No End in Sight," *Living Lies*, June 2, 2009.

34 "The ONLY parties seeking foreclosures": Neil Garfield, "A Reality Check on Mortgage Modification—NYTimes Gretchen Morgenson," *Living Lies*, April 26, 2009.

34 "Democracy is not supposed to be efficient": Wendell Sherk, "Why Show Me the Note Matters," Bankruptcy Law Network, March 17, 2009.

3. Securitization FAIL; or, Cirilo Codrington and the Panama Doc Shop

35 Home Affordable Modification Program, or HAMP: "Remarks by the President on the Mortgage Crisis," Dobson High School, Mesa, Arizona, February 18, 2009.

37 This desire for "bankruptcy remoteness" drove securitization transfers: Mike Konczal, "Foreclosure Fraud for Dummies, 1: The Chains and the Stakes," *Rortybomb* (blog), October 8, 2010, https://rortybomb.wordpress.com/2010/10/08 /foreclosure-fraud-for-dummies-1-the-chains-and-the-stakes.

37 "On the Closing Date, the Depositor will transfer": Prospectus, Soundview Home Loan Trust 2006-OPT2, June 18, 2007, www.sec.gov/Archives/edgar /data/1356081/000088237706000772/d454063_fwp.htm.

38 And under New York law, there was no mechanism: Professor Adam Levitin, Georgetown University, testimony in hearing before the House Financial Services Committee, Subcommittee on Housing and Community Opportunity, November 18, 2010, 56–57, www.gpo.gov/fdsys/pkg/CHRG-111hhrg63124/pdf/CHRG-111hhrg63124.pdf.

38 There are tax consequences associated with this failure: 26 U.S. Code § 860F (a).

39 "There is an 18-minute Nixonian gap": Neil Garfield, "Ohio Slam Dunk by Judge Morgenstern-Clarren: US Bank Trustee and Ocwen Crash and Burn," *Living Lies*, June 29, 2009.

39 a November 2007 report by law professor Katherine Porter: Katherine Porter, "Misbehavior and Mistake in Bankruptcy Mortgage Claims," *Texas Law Review* 87 (2008).

40 This was the "re-establishment of lost note" count: Florida Statute § 673.3091.

40 filed a motion to dismiss for lack of standing: *US Bank N.A. v. Lisa Epstein*, Case No. 50-2009-CA-005542XXXXMB, docket report at http://courtcon.co.palm -beach.fl.us/pls/jiwp/ck_public_qry_doct.cp_dktrpt_frames?backto=P&case_id =502009CA005542XXXXMB&begin_date=&end_date=.

41 Florida Default Law Group (FDLG): Ibid.

41 The newly found note was not endorsed in blank: Copy of note in possession of author.

41 Furthermore, the mortgage assignment went directly: Assignment of Mortgage for Lisa and Alan Epstein, dated May 21, 2009, Public Records of Palm Beach County, Florida. File No. F09015624.

42 "**Chase Home Finance LLC as-attorney-in-fact-for" affidavit: Can be found in Lisa Epstein comment to Florida Supreme Court, October 7, 2009, www.floridasupreme court.org/pub_info/documents/foreclosure_comments/Filed_10-07-2009_Epstein.pdf.

42 U.S. Bank's address was listed: https://www.chase.com/home-equity/contactus.

42 JPMorgan Chase had had a ninety-day closing window: Available at SEC website, http://google.brand.edgar-online.com/DisplayFilingInfo.aspx?Type=HTML &text=%2526lt%253bNEAR%252f4%2526gt%253b(%22MATTHEW%22%2c%22WO NG%22)&FilingID=5245705&ppu=%2fPeopleFilingResults.aspx%3fPersonID%3d29 64553%26PersonName%3dMATTHEW%2520WONG.

43 One screenshot showed that DHI Mortgage: Copy of screenshot in possession of author.

43 The mortgage assignment, dated three months: Assignment of Mortgage for Lisa and Alan Epstein, dated May 21, 2009, Public Records of Palm Beach County, Florida. File No. F09015624.

43 When she typed in Cirilo Codrington: https://www.facebook.com/cirilo.codrington.

44 "the premier legal and financial support services provider in Panama": Firm Solutions Panama corporate website, http://fspanama.iapplicants.com.

44 Lisa found one Facebook page where Firm Solutions: https://www.facebook.com/pages/Firm-Solutions-Panama-Florida-Default-Law-Group/107309169302890.

45 Mortgage originators sold $1.9 million worth: Adam B. Ashcraft and Til Schuermann, "Understanding the Securitization of Subprime Mortgage Credit," Federal Reserve Bank of New York staff report, March 2008. The data show $1 trillion in subprime and Alt-A mortgage originations in 2005 and 2006. That calculates to a per-minute rate of approximately $1,902,587.

45 Property recordation: Jill E. Martin, *Hanbury and Martin: Modern Equity*, 19th ed. (London: Sweet and Maxwell, 2012), 9.

46 The Statute of Frauds: Statute of Frauds, 1677, accessed at www.languageandlaw.org/TEXTS/STATS/FRAUDS.HTM.

46 "What creates capital": Hernando de Soto, *The Mystery of Capital: Why Capitalism Triumphs in the West and Fails Everywhere Else* (New York: Basic Books, 2000), 46–47.

46 The Massachusetts Plymouth Bay Colony established: George L. Haskins, "The Legal Heritage of Plymouth Colony," *University of Pennsylvania Law Review* 110 (1962): 856–57.

46 They created land registration offices: Christopher L. Peterson, "Foreclosure, Subprime Mortgage Lending, and the Mortgage Electronic Registration System," *University of Cincinnati Law Review* 78, no. 4 (Summer 2010): 1364–65.

47 the Mortgage Electronic Registration Systems (MERS): Ibid., 1368–70.

47 MERS as the "mortgagee of record": Ibid., 1362.

48 Law professor Alan White: Michael Powell and Gretchen Morgenson, "MERS, the Mortgage Holder You Might Not Know," *New York Times*, March 5, 2011.

48 In re Hawkins: United States Bankruptcy Court, D. Nevada, March 31, 2009, Case No. BK-S-07-13593-LBR.

49 "To grant MERS standing based on legal title": Peterson, "Foreclosure," 1384–85.

49 MERS sold their corporate seal: Ibid., 1392.

50 based on the principle of privity: Jesse W. Lilienthal, "Privity of Contract," *Harvard Law Review* 1, no. 5 (December 15, 1887).

4. The Originator

51 a consultancy and research firm called the Sports Marketing Group: "NBA Booming, but Football Is America's Favorite Sport," Associated Press, February 21, 1991.

51 He called the rise of figure skating: Shannon Brownlee, Katia Hetter, and Karen Nickel, "The Value of Grace, the Price of Spunk," *U.S. News and World Report*, January 16, 1994.

52 SOA would tack on a late fee anyway: Nye Lavalle, "Predatory 'Grizzly Bear' Attacks Innocent, Elderly, Poor, Minorities, Disabled and Disadvantaged," 23–25, www.msfraud.org/Articles/predbear.pdf.

52 Loan servicers were mostly automated: Adam J. Levitin and Tara Twomey, "Mortgage Servicing," *Yale Journal on Regulation* 28, no. 1 (December 15, 2010).

52 force-placed insurance: Lavalle, "Predatory 'Grizzly Bear,'" 5–6, 32–33.

53 Sometimes monthly payments were missing: Ibid., 27–34.

53 "miscellaneous advances": Ibid., 29.

53 "mortgage toxic waste dump": Ibid., 21–22.

54 So the entire transaction was an elaborate game: Ibid., 93–94.

54 Nye wondered if EMC even had custody: Ibid., 93.

54–55 "the actual owners of the note or mortgage": Lavalle, "Predatory 'Grizzly Bear,'" 104.

55 Ultimately the new judge ruled for EMC: Lavalle, "Predatory 'Grizzly Bear,'" 102–3.

56 They devised ways to digitally extract profits: National Consumer Law Center, "Why Servicers Foreclose When They Should Modify and Other Puzzles of Servicer Behavior," October 2009.

56 At one point Nye counted forty-four different schemes: Nye Lavalle, "White-Collar Mafia Uses 21st Century Loan Sharks to Prey on Americans," 25–26, http://documents.jdsupra.com/197d1b59-e33e-47e0-92b0-d61992e9ed22.pdf.

56 referred to its customers as "smucks": Ibid., 30.

56 "nothing—and I mean nothing—that a bank": Gretchen Morgenson, "A Mortgage Tornado Warning, Unheeded," *New York Times*, February 4, 2012.

56 Banks would "double-pledge" mortgages: Nye Lavalle, "You Can't Trust the Mortgage Paper Trail," 2013 ed., 23–24, http://stopforeclosurefraud.com/wp-content/uploads/2013/04/CantTrustPaperTrail_Lavalle_4-13.pdf.

57 "Predatory Grizzly 'Bear' Attacks Innocent": Lavalle, "Predatory 'Grizzly Bear,'" 1–102.

57 "to defend and protect Americans": Lavalle, "White-Collar Mafia," 1.

57 "Well-known banks and mortgage companies": Ibid., 2.

58 "to support knowledge of facts": Lavalle, "You Can't Trust," 8.

58 Nye later published an entire report in 2008: Nye Lavalle, "Sue First and Ask Questions Later: A Pew Mortgage Investigations Report on the Predatory Servicing Practice of False and Forged Signatures Employed by Ocwen & Others," 2008, www.scribd.com/doc/20955838/PMI-Ocwen-Anderson-Report-Sue-First-Ask-Questions-Later.

59 He predicted the financial crisis: Lavalle, "Predatory 'Grizzly Bear,'" 15–19.

59 A judge forced the closure of some: *Bear Stearns Companies, Inc. v. Lavalle,* U.S. District Court, Northern District of Texas, December 3, 2002, summary at www.finnegan.com/BearStearnsCompaniesIncvLavalle.

59 consumer websites like RipoffReport: "Ameriquest Mortgage Company aka AMC Complaint Review," RipoffReport, March 27, 2005.

59–60 Nye infiltrated the corporate message board for MERS: Brady Dennis and Ariana Eunjung Cha, "Reston-Based Company MERS in the Middle of Foreclosure Chaos," *Washington Post*, October 8, 2010.

61 Nye was blocked from reading a study: Morgenson, "A Mortgage Tornado Warning."

61 With the saccharine title "Report to Fannie Mae": Marc Cymrot, "Report to Fannie Mae Regarding Shareholder Complaints by Mr. Nye Lavalle," Office of Corporate Justice Case No. 5595, May 19, 2006, available at www.nytimes.com/interactive /2012/02/05/business/05fannie-doc.html.

61 "Mr. Lavalle is partial to extreme analogies": Ibid., 3.

61 "Lavalle has identified an issue": Ibid., 5–6.

61 "Mr. Lavalle's assertion that Fannie Mae faces": Ibid., 7.

62 Ford Pinto memo: Mark Dowie, "Pinto Madness," *Mother Jones*, September/ October 1977.

62 "the fraud of our lifetime": Morgenson, "A Mortgage Tornado Warning."

5. The Community

66 "So it was that in the fall of 1932": T. H. Watkins, *The Great Depression: America in the 1930s* (Boston: Little, Brown, 1993), 118–19.

66 Home Defenders campaign: Fernanda Santos, "Nationwide Effort Takes Shape to Support Families Facing Foreclosure," *New York Times*, February 18, 2009.

66 ACORN members reclaimed Donna Hanks's abandoned foreclosure: Bertha Lewis, "We Are Willing to Go to Any Means Necessary," *Huffington Post*, February 20, 2009; WJZ-TV Baltimore report, February 20, 2009, accessed at https:// willnevergiveup.wordpress.com/2009/02/23/acorn.

66–67 Another group called the Neighborhood Assistance Corporation of America: John Christoffersen, "Housing Group Stages Protests at Bank Executives' Homes," Associated Press, February 9, 2009.

67 "Bushvilles": Jesse McKinley, "Cities Deal with a Surge in Shantytowns," *New York Times*, March 25, 2009; David Neiwert, "Tent Cities: Welcome to the New Bushvilles," Crooksandliars.com, March 9, 2009, http://crooksandliars.com/david-neiwert /tent-cities-welcome-new-bushvilles.

67 a way to "foam the runway": Neil Barofsky, *Bailout: How Washington Abandoned Main Street While Rescuing Wall Street* (New York: Simon and Schuster, 2012), 156–57.

67 his administration pressured congressional leaders: Paul Kiel and Olga Pierce, "Dems: Obama Broke Pledge to Force Banks to Help Homeowners," Pro Publica, February 4, 2011. Also David Dayen, "Portrait of HAMP Failure: How HAMP Went from the Bank's Counter Offer to the Whole Enchilada," September 13, 2010,

http://shadowproof.com/2010/09/13/portrait-of-hamp-failure-how-hamp-went-from
-the-banks-counter-offer-to-the-whole-enchilada.

67 **"frankly own the place":** Ryan Grim, "Dick Durbin: Banks 'Frankly Own the Place,'" *Huffington Post*, May 30, 2009.

67 **Treasury Department bigwigs would come in afterward:** Kiel and Pierce, "Dems: Obama Broke Pledge."

67 **The banks blamed homeowners:** Pat Garofalo, "Banks Blame Borrowers for Lack of Progress on Mortgage Modifications," ThinkProgress.org, December 9, 2009.

67 **Servicers turned HAMP into a predatory lending program:** Dayen, "Portrait of HAMP Failure."

68 **Bank of America employees later testified they were given:** David Dayen, "Bank of America Whistleblower's Bombshell: We Were Told to Lie," *Salon*, June 18, 2013.

68 **Robert "Jack" Wright:** Denise Richardson, "Why We Need the Right to Receive a Monthly Mortgage Statement," GiveMeBackMyCredit.com, April 24, 2008.

68 **Fairbanks would eventually settle:** "Fairbanks Capital Settles FTC and HUD Charges," Federal Trade Commission press release, November 12, 2003. Also "Fairbanks Capital Changes to Select Portfolio Servicing, Inc.," Select Portfolio Servicing press release, July 1, 2004, PRNewswire.com.

68 **Mike Dillon:** Link to GetDShirtz.com is now dead. Mike's story can be found at the *Home Preservation Network*, http://homepreservationnetwork.com/2012-10-23 -03-10-19/stories-from-homeowners/item/2776-mike-dillon-manchester-nh.

68 **"My foreclosure was filed August 2008":** *Living Lies*, "Florida Petition Seeks Mediation of Foreclosures," March 11, 2009, comment by user bt.

68 **"Can a foreclosure, in Florida, still take place":** *Living Lies*, "Reality Check: Holder in Due Course Doctrine Is Not Some Fancy Trick to Get Out of Paying," April 5, 2009, comment by user Viper.

69 **Ana Fernandez:** Gretchen Morgenson, "Guess What Got Lost in the Loan Pool," *New York Times*, March 1, 2009.

69 **Samuel Bufford:** Ibid.

69 **Judge Walt Logan:** Mike McIntire, "Tracking Loans Through a Firm That Holds Millions," *New York Times*, April 24, 2009.

69 **"If you are going to take away someone's house":** Michael Powell, "A 'Little Judge' Who Rejects Foreclosures, Brooklyn Style," *New York Times*, August 31, 2009.

69 **Anna Ramirez:** Todd Wright, "My Bad! Woman's House Mistakenly Auctioned by Bank," NBC6 Miami, August 20, 2009.

69 **Tony Louzado:** Drew Griffin and Jessi Joseph, "Are Some Law Firms Cutting Corners on Foreclosures?" CNN.com, October 23, 2010.

70 **someone with the username "Fraud in FL" commented:** *Living Lies*, "NY Times Exposes MERS," April 24, 2009, comments by users Fraud in FL, Alina, and Lisa E.

71 **"They may sit there all day for a week":** Susan Martin, "Tampa Bay Companies Help Lenders Transfer Home Loans, Foreclose," *Tampa Bay Times*, May 1, 2009.

72 Florida Default Law Group withdrew that affidavit and then filed one: Available in Lisa's comment to the Florida Supreme Court, October 7, 2009, www.floridasupremecourt.org/pub_info/documents/foreclosure_comments/Filed_10-07-2009_Epstein.pdf.

76 "And then it started like a guilty thing": Shakespeare quoted in Lisa Epstein, "Wells Fargo: Who Are They and Why Did They Have the Power to Deny a Solution to My Mortgage?" *Foreclosure Hamlet,* October 17, 2009.

76 "This Blog is NOT to be viewed as a source": Lisa Epstein, *Foreclosure Hamlet* homepage, www.foreclosurehamlet.org.

76 "When I get those large white envelopes": Lisa Epstein, "FDLG New Filing with the Court: Plaintiff's Response to my Request for Production," *Foreclosure Hamlet,* October 6, 2009.

77 The Kansas Supreme Court decided the case of Boyd Kesler: *Landmark National Bank v. Boyd Kesler,* Kansas Supreme Court, No. 98,489, August 28, 2009. Also Neil Garfield, "Kansas Supreme Court Sets Precedent—Key Decision Confirming Living Lies' Strategies," *Living Lies,* September 23, 2009.

77 The Arkansas Supreme Court made a similar ruling: *Mortgage Electronic Registration Systems, Inc v. Southwest Homes of Arkansas,* Supreme Court of Arkansas, No. 08-1299, March 19, 2009, available at https://livinglies.wordpress.com/2009/09/30/arkansas-supreme-court-denies-mers-legal-standing.

77 Kurt Aho: Neil Garfield, "The High Cost of Losing Homes: Death by Gunshot," *Living Lies,* September 30, 2009, comments by users Lisa E and Foreclosure Fraud.

6. Mr. Anonymous

80 the Boynton Beach campus shut down: Marcia Heroux Pounds, "Motorola to Close Boynton Plant," *Orlando Sun-Sentinel,* January 23, 2004.

80 retail and residential development called Renaissance Commons: Brian Bandell, "Renaissance Commons Loses $52m Foreclosure as Auction Looms," *South Florida Business Journal,* August 16, 2013.

84 a sweetheart deal for JPMorgan Chase to purchase WaMu: Christopher Palmeri, "JPMorgan Chase to Buy Washington Mutual," *Bloomberg News,* September 26, 2008.

85 Nye's report about Ocwen employee Scott Anderson: Nye Lavalle, "Sue First and Ask Questions Later: A Pew Mortgage Investigations Report on the Predatory Servicing Practice of False & Forged Signatures Employed by Ocwen & Others," 2008, www.scribd.com/doc/20955838/PMI-Ocwen-Anderson-Report-Sue-First-Ask-Questions-Later.

86 This assignment was dated April 20, 2009: Clerk of St. Lucie County Public Records, book 3081, page 231, recorded April 20, 2009.

88 "I have researched this in my county records": Susan Martin, "Tampa Bay Companies Help Lenders Transfer Home Loans, Foreclose," *Tampa Bay Times,* May 1, 2009.

88 "Looking Up Public Records": Michael Redman, "Looking Up Public Records," 4closurefraud.org, October 18, 2009.

90 "Any feedback is welcomed, good and bad": *Living Lies*, "Double Funding, Fabrication of Documents and Forgery of Signatures Revealed," October 5, 2009, comment posted on October 11 by user Foreclosure Fraud.

90 "This is so blatant and outrageous": Karl Denninger, "A Birdie on Possible Foreclosure Frauds," Market Ticker, October 15, 2009, available at www.freedom sphoenix.com/News/59786-2009-10-15-a-birdie-on-possible-foreclosure-frauds.htm.

91 Michael started 4closurefraud.wordpress.com: Michael Redman, "Foreclosure Fraud—Guide to Looking Up Public Records for Fraud," 4closurefraud.org, October 18, 2009.

91 One of his early posts was Nye Lavalle's report on Scott Anderson: Michael Redman, "PMI Ocwen Anderson Report—Sue First Ask Questions Later," 4closurefraud.org, October 21, 2009.

91 *Living Lies* was holding a seminar: Neil Garfield, "Only One (1) Day Left to Pre-Register: Workshops Scheduled for Florida—November 1–2, 2009 Sheraton Sand Key Resort in Sunny Clearwater Beach FL," *Living Lies*, October 24, 2009.

7. When Michael Met Lisa

94 "We're not going to convert you into lawyers today": Neil Garfield, "Foreclosure Defense—What You Need to Know," Cameron/Baxter Films, uploaded October 31, 2009, https://www.youtube.com/watch?v=F9L4eRaIxLQ (part 1) and https://www.youtube.com/watch?v=nZ6lPaiKmwg (part 2).

96 "By way of introduction, I am a working mother": Lisa's first letter to the Florida Supreme Court, October 7, 2009, http://www.floridasupremecourt.org/pub _info/documents/foreclosure_comments/Filed_10-07-2009_Epstein.pdf.

97 short column in the Sarasota *Herald-Tribune* by Tom Lyons: Tom Lyons, "Foreclosure Chicanery Not a Funny Lawyer Joke," Sarasota *Herald-Tribune*, September 29, 2009.

98 The clerk said the court could accept: Lisa's second letter to the Florida Supreme Court, October 21, 2009, www.floridasupremecourt.org/pub_info/summaries /briefs/09/09-1460/Filed_10-21-2009_Epstein.pdf.

100 Isaac Dieudonné: Tony Pugh, "Child's Death Mired in Nation's Foreclosure Crisis," McClatchy Newspapers, October 29, 2010.

8. Happy Hours

104 Someone with the name Erin Cullaro was working: Michael Redman, "Scandalous—Substantiated Allegations of Foreclosure Fraud that Implicates the Florida Attorney General's Office and the Florida Default Law Group," 4closurefraud.org, March 26, 2010.

104 the almost comically titled U.S. Foreclosure Network: Erin Collins Cullaro, "Is There a Right of Redemption after a Foreclosure Sale in Florida?" U.S. Fore-

closure Network, 2006, www.usfn.org/AM/PrinterTemplate.cfm?Section=USFN_E
_Update&template=/CM/HTMLDisplay.cfm&ContentID=3885.

104 That was the former name of Florida Default Law Group: "On the Move,"
Florida Bar News, September 15, 2005.

108 According to rule 1.420(e): Florida Rules of Civil Procedure, 91, available at
http://www.floridabar.org/TFB/TFBResources.nsf/Attachments/10C69DF6FF151850
85256B29004BF823/$FILE/Civil.pdf?OpenElement.

108 *Chemrock v. Tampa Electric:* Opinion from First District Court of Appeals,
decided November 17, 2009, https://cases.justia.com/florida/first-district-court-of
-appeal/08-4895.pdf

109 "PLEASE TAKE NOTICE that it appears": *U.S. Bank NA as Trustee et al v.
Vincent Savoia et al.*, Circuit Court of the Fifteenth Judicial Circuit in and for Palm
Beach County, Florida, Case No. 50-2007-CA-008051XXXXMB.

110 "virtually all paper documents of the note and mortgage": Comments of
the Florida Bankers Association, Florida Supreme Court, Case No. 09-1460, www.florida
supremecourt.org/clerk/comments/2009/09-1460_093009_Comments%20(FBA).pdf.

110 "Typically, the plaintiff in a foreclosure action": Michael Redman, "Freddie
Mac Comments on the Final Report and Recommendations on Residential Mortgage
Foreclosure Cases, Florida Supreme Court," 4closurefraud.org, November 11, 2009.

111 Antonio Ibanez: Jenifer B. McKim, "Ruling Upheld on Sale of Property,"
Boston Globe, October 15, 2009.

111 Federal bankruptcy judge Robert Drain: Gretchen Morgenson, "If the
Lender Can't Find the Mortgage," *New York Times*, October 25, 2009.

111 Even a bankruptcy judge in Idaho: *In re Sheridan*, U.S. Bankruptcy Court,
District of Idaho, Case No. 08-20381-TLM, March 12, 2009, available at https://
livinglies.files.wordpress.com/2009/10/sheridan_decision-idaho-bkr-j-myers.pdf.

9. The Network

113 special delinquent servicing prior to foreclosure: On the Veterans Administration, see the VA Servicer Guide, 59–72, www.benefits.va.gov/homeloans/documents
/docs/va_servicer_guide.pdf. For FHA loans, see the U.S. Department of Housing
and Urban Development Loan Servicing Guidance home page, http://portal.hud.gov
/hudportal/HUD?src=/federal_housing_administration/healthcare_facilities
/residential_care/loan_servicing.

113 12 USC 1701x(c)(5): Accessed at the Legal Information Institute, Cornell
University Law School, https://www.law.cornell.edu/uscode/text/12/1701x.

114 she had to meet clients in the lobby: Mike Stuckey, "'Angel' of Foreclosure
Defense Bedevils Lenders," MSNBC, December 19, 2008, www.nbcnews.com/id
/28277420/ns/business-real_estate/t/angel-foreclosure-defense-bedevils-lenders.

115 "nothing-backed securities": Christopher Ketcham, "Stop Payment!" *Harper's*,
January 2012; April Charney, "Direct or Indirect, Mortgages Are Flawed," *New York
Times* "Room for Debate," October 16, 2012.

117 **"The Document Execution team is set up":** Dory Goebel and Chrys Houston, "Department Spotlight: Document Execution," *The Summit* (internal newsletter produced by Fidelity National Foreclosure Services) 2, issue 3 (September 2006): 16–17.

117 **Max Gardner's bankruptcy boot camp:** Prashant Gopal, "Foreclosure Lawyers Go to Max's Farm for Edge," Bloomberg, October 27, 2010. Also Max Gardner's Bankruptcy Boot Camp website at www.maxbankruptcybootcamp.com.

118 **the "show me the note" defense:** Kimberly Morrison, "Lawyer's Foreclosure Defense of 'Quiet Title' Faces Tests," *Jacksonville Business Journal*, November 20, 2009.

119 **twenty hours of pro bono work:** Stuckey, "'Angel' of Foreclosure."

119 **But an appeals court reversed the decision:** Susan Martin, "Lawyer Has Strategy to Fight Foreclosures, and Shares It," *Tampa Bay Times*, April 3, 2009.

119 **dubbed her "the Loan Ranger":** Richard Wilner, "The Loan Ranger," *New York Post*, February 22, 2009.

120–121 **Judge Logan threw out all those cases where MERS tried:** Mike McIntire, "Tracking Loans Through a Firm That Holds Millions," *New York Times*, April 24, 2009.

121 **Jurists Engaged in Defending Title Integrity, or JEDTI:** Randall O. Reder, "JEDTI," *Reder's Digest* (blog), www.redersdigest.com/jedti.html.

121 **Matt Weidner started his own, in July 2009:** Available at http://mattweidnerlaw.com/latest-news/blog.

122 **"Corruption County":** "Is Palm Beach County Ready to Retire Its 'Corruption County' Reputation?" *Palm Beach Post*, March 22, 2015. Also Hector Florin, "Palm Beach: The New Capital of Florida Corruption," *Time*, January 10, 2009.

123 **going all the way to appellate court, and Ice Legal won:** *Vidal v. SunTrust Bank*, Fourth District Court of Appeals, Florida, No. 4D09-3019, opinion issued August 4, 2010, www.4dca.org/opinions/Aug%202010/08-04-10/4D09-3019.op.pdf.

124 **She swore that she had never visited Lee County:** Kimberly Miller, "Local 'Robo-Signer' Alleges Her Signatures Were Forged," *Palm Beach Post*, April 19, 2011.

124 **made numerous paragraph 22 defenses:** Greg Stopa, "Understanding the Paragraph 22 Argument," Stopa Law Firm, January 30, 2013, www.stayinmyhome.com/understanding-the-paragraph-22-argument.

125 **Johnson-Seck turned up in a case thrown out by Brooklyn judge Arthur Schack:** *Deutsche Bank National Trust Company v. Ramash Maraj*, Supreme Court of New York, Kings County, No. 25981/07, decided January 31, 2008, accessed at http://stopforeclosurefraud.com/2010/03/26/nysc-judge-schack-takes-on-robo-signer-erica-johnson-seck-deutsche-bank-v-maraj-1.

125 **She stated that she had authority to sign for MERS:** Testimony in *IndyMac Federal Bank v. Israel A. Machado*, Case No. 50-2008-CA-037322XXXXMB, Erica Johnson-Seck deposition taken July 9, 2009, accessed at http://4closurefraud.org/2009/11/15/full-deposition-of-the-infamous-erica-johnson-seck-re-indymac-federal-bank-fsb-plaintiff-vs-israel-a-machado-50-2008-ca-037322xxxx-mb.

126 But the judge sided with Ice Legal: Robbie Whelan, "Foreclosure? Not So Fast," *Wall Street Journal*, October 4, 2010.

127 Lisa Cullaro's signatures looked off as well: Michael Redman, "Scandalous— Substantiated Allegations of Foreclosure Fraud That Implicates the Florida Attorney General's Office and Florida Default Law Group," 4closurefraud.org, March 26, 2010.

127 "in complete disregard of the truth": Michael Redman, "Full Deposition of the Infamous Erica Johnson-Seck," 4closurefraud.org, November 15, 2009.

128 Matt republished the Erica Johnson-Seck deposition on his site: Matt Weidner, "IndyMac Bank Fraud—Deposition of Employee that Proves It All!" January 5, 2010, http://mattweidnerlaw.com/indymac-bank-fraud-deposition-of-employee-that-proves-it-all.

128 "In the vast majority of cases where these documents are produced": Matt Weidner, "Part III—MERS, Foreclosure Fraud and Document Mills," January 8, 2010, available at http://wordspy.com/index.php?word=robo-signer.

128 the term "robo-signing": Shira Ovide, "Just Where Did the Term 'Robo-Signer' Come From, Anyway?" *Wall Street Journal*, October 21, 2010.

128 First FDLG denied requests for communications: Court documents available at Redman, "Scandalous."

10. The Specialist

130 Nilly Mauck: " 'Trashed Out' Las Vegas Woman Victim of Foreclosure Mistake," Channel 8 News Now, Las Vegas, December 21, 2009, available at http://4closurefraud.org/2009/12/21/trashed-out-las-vegas-woman-victim-of-foreclosure-mistake.

130 another man who claimed the same thing: "Another Person Claims Theft in Foreclosure Mistake," Channel 8 News Now, Las Vegas, December 26, 2009, available at http://4closurefraud.org/2009/12/26/trashed-out-another-person-claims-theft-in-foreclosure-mistake.

130 $5,000 as compensation for everything she owned: "Attorney Claims Woman Is Inflating Her Loss in Foreclosure Mix-Up," Channel 8 News Now, Las Vegas, December 26, 2009, available at http://4closurefraud.org/2009/12/23/trashed-out-attorney-claims-woman-is-inflating-her-loss-in-foreclosure-mix-up.

130 The Horoskis of East Patchogue: Carl McGowan, "Lender Admits Foreclosure Letter Sent in Error," *Newsday*, December 18, 2009.

131 Wells Fargo (the holder of the first mortgage) suing Wells Fargo: Al Lewis, "Wells Fargo So Big It's Suing Itself," Dow Jones Newswire, July 11, 2009. Also see Angie Moreschi, "Have the Banks Gone Crazy? Wells Fargo Sues Itself," Consumer Warning Network, July 2, 2009.

131 Before Christmas, Citigroup made a big announcement: "CitiMortgage and CitiFinancial Announce National Foreclosure Suspension Program to Help Distressed Homeowners During the Holiday Season," Citigroup press release, December 17, 2009.

131 this affected only four thousand loans: Matt Weidner, "Citi Suspends Foreclosures: Will/Should Other Lenders Follow Suit?" December 21, 2009, http://

mattweidnerlaw.com/citi-suspends-foreclosures-willshould-other-lenders-follow -suit.

131 **created a banker version of the Whack-a-Mole game:** BBC News, "Bankers 'Whacked' in Arcade Game," December 13, 2009. Also see Michael Redman, "'Whack a Bankster' Game Is a Hit," 4closurefraud.org, December 15, 2009.

131 **"I am working until the wee hours":** Lisa Epstein, "Granted? Funding Is Hard to Come By!" *Foreclosure Hamlet,* December 19, 2009.

131 **"More and more each day I stare blankly":** Lisa Epstein, "The Last Day of a Difficult Year," *Foreclosure Hamlet,* December 31, 2009.

131 **"Happy New Year Banksters!":** Michael Redman, "Happy New Year Banksters," 4closurefraud.org, January 1, 2010.

131 **"An Officer of Too Many Banks":** Lynn Szymoniak, "An Officer of Too Many Banks," January 14, 2010, www.scribd.com/doc/25266216/An-Officer-of-Too-Many -Banks.

132 **On March 8, 1971, antiwar activists:** Betty Medsger, *The Burglary: The Discovery of J. Edgar Hoover's Secret FBI* (New York: Random House, 2014).

133 **In January 2014 the perpetrators finally revealed their role:** Mark Mazzetti, "Burglars Who Took on FBI Abandon Shadows," *New York Times,* January 7, 2014.

136 **Lynn hired her ex, Mark Cullen, as her lawyer, and they attempted:** *Deutsche Bank v. Lynn Szymoniak,* Case ID 502008CA022258XXXXMB, July 22, 2008, available at http://courtcon.co.palm-beach.fl.us/pls/jiwp/ck_public_qry_doct.cp_dktrpt_frames ?backto=P&case_id=502008CA022258XXXXMB&begin_date=&end_date=.

137 **Deutsche Bank didn't yet own the loan over which they sued her:** Assignment of Mortgage for Lynn E. Szymoniak, Public Records of Palm Beach County Clerk of Circuit Court, book 22918, pages 1029–30, CFN #20080386764.

138 **American Home Mortgage Servicing acquired Option One:** "Company Overview of Option One Mortgage Corporation," Bloomberg News, www.bloomberg .com/research/stocks/private/snapshot.asp?privcapId=951370.

138 **She found that Korell Harp was charged with identity theft:** "Federal Grand Jury Criminal Indictments Announced," press release, U.S. Attorney's Office, Eastern District of Oklahoma, January 14, 2009, www.fbi.gov/oklahomacity/press -releases/2009/oc011409a.htm.

139 **Korell Harp was in state prison in Oklahoma:** *State of Oklahoma v. Harp, Korell Rashaud,* filed September 12, 2008, Pittsburg County, OK, No. CF-2008-00394, http://www1.odcr.com/detail?court=061-&casekey=061-CF++0800394. The charges were later dropped when the arresting officer was found to have made racist comments about Harp and his companions. Omer Gillham, "Racist Comments Oust Officer," *Tulsa World,* February 21, 2009.

139 **What she found there wasn't the allonge:** Palm Beach County Public Records, book 19933, page 1827, http://oris.co.palm-beach.fl.us/or_web1/details.asp?doc_id =15519163&index=0&file_num=20060092890.

140 She was vice president of at least a dozen: Lynn Szymoniak, "Who Is Linda Green?" Housing Justice Foundation, December 12, 2012, http://thjf.org/2012/12/12/who-is-linda-green; Lynn Szymoniak, "Docx Fabrications and Forgeries—Comparing Signatures and Titles on Mortgage Documents," January 19, 2010, available at 4closurefraud.org.

142 In the last week of 2009 *Fraud Digest* **featured articles:** Lynn Szymoniak, "Docx Mortgage Assignments Filed in Palm Beach County, FL (A-H)," *Fraud Digest*, n.d., available at http://thjf.org/2012/12/21/docx-mortgage-assignments-filed-in-palm-beach-county-fl-a-h.

142 in a separate *Fraud Digest* **article:** Lynn Szymoniak, "Too Many Jobs," *Fraud Digest*, January 19, 2009, available at http://4closurefraud.org/2010/01/27/too-many-jobs-linda-green-tywanna-thomas-korell-harp-and-shelly-scheffey.

142 DocX . . . was supplying felonious evidence: Szymoniak, "Who Is Linda Green?" (also provides Linda Green signature samples).

11. Black Deeds

145 "Interested person, Lisa Epstein, will appear": Notice of Hearing, *U.S. Bank NA as Trustee et al. v. Vincent Savoia et al.*, Circuit Court of the Fifteenth Judicial Circuit in and for Palm Beach County, Florida, Case No. 50-2007-CA-008051XXXXMB.

145 by this time he had cross-posted a number of her *Fraud Digest* **articles:** Lynn Szymoniak, "Docx Fabrications and Forgeries—Comparing Signatures and Titles on Mortgage Documents," January 19, 2010, 4closurefraud.org; Lynn Szymoniak, "Too Many Jobs," January 27, 2010, 4closurefraud.org.

147 the class action translated into a $4 million rate rollback: Linda Chiem, "AIG to Pay $4M in Workers' Comp Class Action Settlement," Law360.com, September 17, 2012.

147 damages were limited to $1,000 per plaintiff: 15 U.S.C. § 1692k(a)(2)(A), available at https://www.law.cornell.edu/uscode/text/15/1692k.

147 case law made it impossible to get a RICO class certified: Donald R. Frederico, "Class Certification in RICO Fraud Cases," 2004, 26, www.mwe.com/info/pubs/rico.pdf.

148 "American Home Mortgage Acceptance, whose address": Assignment of Mortgage, Nassau County Clerk of Circuit Court, book 1592, page 444, available at http://4closurefraud.org/2010/02/10/beyond-bogus-docx-assignment-of-mortgage-bogus-assignee-for-intervening-asmts.

150 the clerk of courts even entered the grantee as "BOGUS ASMTS": Michael Redman, "Beyond Bogus—DocX Assignment of Mortgage—Bogus Assignee for Intervening Asmts," 4closurefraud.org, February 10, 2010.

151 he produced a five-part series: Damian Figueroa (DinSFLA), YouTube channel, "Foreclosure Fraud," https://www.youtube.com/watch?v=LoSPTjd_PXM, https://

www.youtube.com/watch?v=SD6XUboT1JM, https://www.youtube.com/watch?v=uo1 -TKj2lMw, https://www.youtube.com/watch?v=B—b7txbiKY, and https://www.you tube.com/watch?v=hn-5KN_vvMw, uploaded February 4, 2010.

151 **"Looks like DocX's 'art department' forgot to change the wording"**: Redman, "Beyond Bogus."

151 **"Wait . . . there is more. INCREDIBLE"**: Redman, "Beyond Bogus," comment from user DinSFLA.

151 **"I am going to show you something"**: Damian Figueroa (DinSFLA), YouTube channel, "Foreclosure Fraud MERS, LPS . . . BOGUS ASSIGNMENTS . . . Are You Kidding Me DocX???" uploaded February 10, 2010, https://www.youtube.com /watch?v=hY4aRn6bWKg

152 **Michael posted a new story**: Michael Redman, "Enough Is Enough! DocX Assignment of Mortgage—Bogus Assignee for Intervening Asmts All Over the Public Records," 4closurefraud.org, February 10, 2010.

152 **Karl Denninger picked up the story**: Karl Denninger, "How Far Does It Go Before Indictments Issue?" FedUpUSA, February 10, 2010, www.fedupusa.org/2010 /02/how-far-does-it-go-before-indictments-issue.

153 **"prevent the wasting of judicial resources"**: Supreme Court of Florida, "In Re: Amendments to the Florida Rules of Civil Procedure," Case No. SC09-1460, and "In Re: Amendments to the Florida Rules of Civil Procedure—Form 1.996 (Final Judgment of Foreclosure)," Case No. SC09-1579. February 11, 2010, available at http:// 4closurefraud.org/2010/02/11/supreme-court-of-florida-in-re-amendments-to-the -florida-rules-of-civil-procedure.

153 **"well-reasoned arguments"**: Jennifer D. Bailey, "Response of the Task Force on Residential Mortgage Foreclosure Cases to Comment Accepted as Timely Filed," October 26, 2009, www.floridasupremecourt.org/pub_info/summaries/briefs/09/09 -1460/Filed_10-26-2009_Task_Force_Response_To_Epstein.pdf.

154 **Tami and Vincent Savoia could move back in**: Circuit Court of the Fifteenth Judicial Circuit in and for Palm Beach County, Florida, *U.S. Bank NA v. Vincent Savoia*, hearing before the Honorable Judge Meenu Sasser, February 12, 2010, 11:05–11:19 a.m., Case No. 50-2007-CA-008051, transcript prepared by Kristina McCollum, J. Consor and Associates.

154 **"Happy Valentines Day America!"**: Lisa Epstein, "Happy Valentines Day America! This Is for You!" *Foreclosure Hamlet*, February 12, 2010.

154 **"At first I thought it was some kind of joke"**: Michael Redman, "The Whole Country Is Bogus—Fabricated Mortgage Assignments All Over the Country," 4closurefraud.org, February 14, 2010.

154 **"Let guilty men remember"**: John Webster, "The White Devil, &c.," quoted in Lisa Epstein, "Black Deeds," *Foreclosure Hamlet*, February 14, 2010.

154 **A week later, Tom Lyons**: Tom Lyons, "Bogus Foreclosure Claim Not Isolated," Sarasota *Herald-Tribune*, February 23, 2010.

154 the *Wall Street Journal* ran a story: Amir Efrati and Carrick Mollenkamp, "U.S. Probes Foreclosure Data Provider," *Wall Street Journal*, April 3, 2010.

12. The Revolution Will Be Blogged

156 an anonymous homeowner, "Mark": Michael Redman, "Bank of America at It Again—Foreclosed on Over 40 Cents?" 4closurefraud.org, February 13, 2010. Story via WINK News, Fort Myers.

156 man facing foreclosure who decided to bulldoze his own home: Michael Redman, "Frustrated Owner Bulldozes Home Ahead of Foreclosure—'I Wasn't Going to Stand for That, So I Took It Down,'" 4closurefraud.org, February 21, 2010. Story via WLWT-5, Cincinnati, Ohio.

157 (The winner the first week . . . the line disappeared): Michael Redman, "Foreclosure Fraud of the Week—Poor Photoshop Skills," 4closurefraud.org, April 8, 2010.

157 One of the first was Sam Antar: Sam Antar, "Advice from a Fraudster—White Collar Crime and Criminals," 4closurefraud.org, November 27, 2009.

158 a cease-and-desist order on every foreclosure in America: *Paul L. Muckle v. United States of America*, United States District Court, District of Massachusetts, www.scribd.com/doc/25286279/Paul-L-Muckle-Plaintiff-vs-the-United-States-of -America-et-al

160 Michael posted the complaint: Michael Redman, "All Aboard!!! Class Action Against Deutsche Bank National Trust Company, U.S. Bank National Association, Lender Processing Services, Inc. and DocX, LLC," 4closurefraud.org, February 24, 2010.

160 the Fair Debt Collection Practices Act didn't apply to banks: *Warren v. Countrywide Home Loans*, Eleventh Circuit Court of Appeals, August 14, 2009, 342, Fed. Appx. 458.

161 "Most recently, we have learned that the U.S. Attorney's Office": Lender Processing Services, Inc., Form 10-K, February 23, 2010, Item 3, Legal Proceedings, www.getfilings.com/sec-filings/100223/Lender-Processing-Services-Inc_10-K.

162 "Here is the problem with the *qui tam*": Complaint and Demand for Jury Trial, *Figueroa v. Szymoniak*, Seventeenth Judicial Circuit, in and for Broward County, March 14, 2013, 7–8, www.scribd.com/doc/168544786/Figueroa-v-Szymoniak. See also Martin Andelman, "Some of Lynn Szymoniak's Millions May Belong to Someone Else," *Mandelman Matters* (blog), September 16, 2013, http://mandelman.ml-implode .com/2013/09/some-of-lynn-szymoniaks-millions-may-belong-to-someone-else.

164 Unbeknownst to Michael, Carol listed it as her law firm's website: Profile of Carol Cobourn Asbury, Bar No. 393665, on the Florida Bar website, www.floridabar.org.

165 He recently bought his neighbor's $8 million property: Andy Kroll, "Fannie and Freddie's Foreclosure Barons," *Mother Jones*, August 4, 2010.

166 She signed as a vice president or assistant secretary of MERS: Deposition of Cheryl Samons, testimony in *Deutsche Bank National Trust Company v. Belourdes*

Pierre, Case No. 50-2008-CA-028558XXXXMB, May 20, 2009, available at http://4closurefraud.org/2010/02/23/full-deposition-of-the-soon-to-be-infamous-cheryl-samons-re-deutsche-bank-national-trust-company-as-trustee-for-morgan-stanley-abs-capital-inc-plaintiff-vs-belourdes-pierre-50-2008-ca-028558-xx. Transcript prepared by Ruthane Machson, J. Consor and Associates.

167 Michael posted the Samons deposition, and so did Matt Weidner: Michael Redman, "Full Deposition of the Soon to be Infamous Cheryl Samons RE: *Deutsche Bank National Trust Company, as Trustee for Morgan Stanley ABS Capital Inc., Plaintiff, vs. Belourdes Pierre*—50 2008 CA 028558 XXXX MB," 4closurefraud.org, February 23, 2010; Matthew Weidner, "Widespread Assignment/Notary/Foreclosure Fraud—Deposition of David Stern Employee Cheryl Sammons," February 22, 2010, mattweidnerlaw.com.

13. The Ninth Floor

168 "It is very possible that one letter": Lynn Szymoniak, "Mortgage Assignments as Evidence of Fraud," *Fraud Digest,* February 9, 2010, available at http://4closurefraud.org/2010/03/07/mortgage-assignments-as-evidence-of-fraud-lynn-szymoniak-esq-editor-fraud-digest.

169 Judge Diana Lewis granted LPS's motion: Docket report, *Deutsche Bank v. Lynn Szymoniak,* Clerk and Comptroller, Palm Beach County, accessed at http://courtcon.co.palm-beach.fl.us/pls/jiwp/ck_public_qry_doct.cp_dktrpt_frames?backto=P&case_id=502008CA022258XXXXMB&begin_date=&end_date=.

169 He had won some of the largest awards: Reuben Guttman biography, Emory University School of Law, http://law.emory.edu/faculty-and-scholarship/adjunct-faculty-profiles/guttman-profile.html.

170 the government purchased tens of billions of dollars' worth: Federal Reserve Bank of New York, "Maiden Lane Transactions," history and overview, www.newyorkfed.org/markets/maidenlane.html.

170 And the Federal Reserve bought trillions: Press release, Board of Governors of the Federal Reserve System, November 25, 2008, www.federalreserve.gov/newsevents/press/monetary/20081125b.htm.

171 Maybe she could get a prosecution going: Lynn Szymoniak, "Why Wells Fargo Must Be Ordered to Stop Its Foreclosures," *Fraud Digest,* October 7, 2010, available at http://4closurefraud.org/2010/10/07/false-statements-americas-servicing-company-lender-processing-services-wells-fargo-bank-n-a.

171 Nettles worked on voting rights issues: Stephanie Woodrow, "Meet William N. Nettles," Main Justice, January 18, 2010.

173 "The Housing Crisis: Who to Trust and Where to Turn": Flyer for event, available at http://myfloridalegal.com/webfiles.nsf/WF/KGRG-832RQV/$file/Miami-Forum-flyer-English.pdf.

175 Tom Ice obtained Erin's "Request for Approval of Dual Employment": Michael Redman, "Scandalous—Substantiated Allegations of Foreclosure Fraud That

Implicates the Florida Attorney General's Office and The Florida Default Law Group," 4closurefraud.org, March 26, 2010.

175 Erin Cullaro managed to notarize 150,000 FDLG documents: Matt Gutman and Bradley Blackburn, "Foreclosure Crisis: 23 States Halt Foreclosure as Officials Review Bank Practices," ABC News, October 4, 2010.

175 Ice Legal also found Erin's signature in several: Michael Redman, "Scandalous—Substantiated Allegations of Foreclosure Fraud That Implicates the Florida Attorney General's Office and The Florida Default Law Group" 4closurefraud.org, March 26, 2010.

176 FDLG wanted to pretend 150,000 Cullaro affidavits never existed: *Wells Fargo Bank v. Donald Needham & Blair Bergstrom*, Memorandum in Opposition to Motion for Reconsideration/Rehearing on Non-Parties' Motion for Protective Order, Case No. 2009-20298-CINS, available at www.scribd.com/doc/28979629/Motion -Substantiated-Allegations-of-Foreclosure-Fraud-That-Implicates-the-Florida -Attorney-General-s-Office-and-The-Florida-Default-Law-Group.

178 9/9/9999: Michael Redman, "I wish that this was MY mortgage, don't you? DOCX Assignments Effective 09/09/9999," 4closurefraud.org, March 9, 2010.

178 he posted one of Ice Legal's court memos: Matthew Weidner, "Bombshell— Substantiated Allegations of Foreclosure/Affidavit Fraud That Implicates the Florida Attorney General's Office," Matthew Weidner's blog, March 26, 2010, available at https://web.archive.org/web/20100328081340/http://mattweidnerlaw.com/blog/2010 /03/bombshell-substantiated-allegations-of-foreclosureaffidavit-fraud-that-implicates -the-florida-attorney-generals-office.

178 after Weidner's release he ran with it, too: Michael Redman, "Scandalous— Substantiated Allegations of Foreclosure Fraud That Implicates the Florida Attorney General's Office and The Florida Default Law Group," 4closurefraud.org, March 26, 2010.

178 Apparently he replaced his wife as FDLG's expert witness: Michael Redman, "Guess the Money Is Too Good to Pass Up—Introducing the Cullaros New Replacement—Expert Witness for Reasonable Attorneys Fees for FDLG Florida Default Law Group," 4closurefraud.org, April 2, 2010.

179 McCollum announced that his office was investigating FDLG: Michael Redman, "Florida Attorney General Bill McCollum Launches Investigations into Florida Default Law Group and Docx, LLC a/k/a Lender Processing Services," 4closurefraud.org, April 29, 2010. Also Amir Efrati, "Florida Probing Law Firm in Foreclosures," *Wall Street Journal*, April 30, 2010.

179 The attorney general also opened: Shannon Behnken and Michael Sasso, "State AG Investigates Its Own," *Tampa Tribune*, May 1, 2010.

14. The Rally in Tally
181 legislation to make Florida a non-judicial foreclosure state: James Thorner, "Florida Bankers Move to Dramatically Speed Up the Foreclosure Process," *Tampa Bay Times*, January 28, 2010.

182 Non-Judicial Foreclosure Act for Non-Homestead Properties: SB 2270, Florida Senate, 2010, http://www.scribd.com/doc/27382056. Also see Michael Redman, "Florida Legislature—Banksters Propose Taking Foreclosures Out of Court—The Nonjudicial Foreclosure Act for Nonhomestead Properties," 4closurefraud.org, February 24, 2010.

182 Wells's arbitrary designation of abandonment could end up: Todd Ruger, "An Abrupt Eviction, Narrowly Averted," Sarasota *Herald-Tribune*, February 22, 2010.

182 Michael created a mini-site about the legislation: PigsAss.org, available through the Internet Wayback Machine, http://web.archive.org/web/20100701215705 /http://pigsass.org.

182–183 "The Bankers have thrown down the gauntlet": Michael Redman, "Florida Bankers to States Citizens: 'Bend Over!!! Your Assets Are Mine!!!'" Florida Consumer Protection and Homeowner Credit Rehabilitation Act," 4closurefraud.org, February 1, 2010.

184 Bruce Marks took a picture with the pig and the banker: Michael Redman, "Updates from 4closureFraud.org Coming Soon LPS, FIS, NACA, PigsAss, Foreclosure Fraud Lender Processing Services, Inc.—Form 10-K—EX-21.1—February 23, 2010 Legal Proceedings et al.," 4closurefraud.org, March 1, 2010. Photo available at 4closurefraud.files.wordpress.com/2010/02/the-pig-the-banker-and-the-naca-ceo.jpg.

184 Homeowner Relief and Housing Recovery Act: Matthew Weidner, "Bank's Newest Effort to Take Homes—Turn Florida into a Non-Judicial State," March 29, 2010, http://mattweidnerlaw.com/banks-newest-effort-to-take-homes-turn-florida-into-a -non-judicial-state.

184 Foreclosure Bill of Rights: HB75, Florida House of Representatives, 2010, www.myfloridahouse.gov/Sections/Documents/loaddoc.aspx?FileName=_h0075__ .docx&DocumentType=Bill&BillNumber=0075&Session=2010.

185 They set a date, April 21: Matthew Weidner, "Rally in Tally—Why It Is Absolutely Necessary for You to Come with Us—April 18, 9:00 am," April 15, 2010, http:// mattweidnerlaw.com/rally-in-tally-why-it-is-absolutely-necessary-for-you-to-come -with-usapril-21-900-am. Also Lisa Epstein, "Freedom Ride Circa 2010: A Pilgrimage," *Foreclosure Hamlet*, April 15, 2010.

186 While they were planning all this, the bills actually stalled: Florida Senate website archive for SB 2270 shows that the bill was "not considered" in the Senate Banking and Insurance Committee on April 8, 2010; http://archive.flsenate.gov/Session /index.cfm?Mode=Bills&SubMenu=1&Tab=session&BI_Mode=ViewBillInfo &BillNum=2270&Chamber=Senate&Year=2010.

187 "We gotta give credit to the consumer activists": "Foreclosure: Rally in Tallahassee Florida 2010," video shot by Cory Luttrell, https://vimeo.com/11293248.

188 "The protection of life and property": Daniel Webster, *The Speeches and Orations of Daniel Webster: With an Essay on Daniel Webster as a Master of English Style* (Boston: Little, Brown, 1914), 536.

189 "too easy to protect the consumer": Michael Redman, "Senator Michael Bennett, You Are the Pig's Ass," 4closurefraud.org, April 23, 2010.

189 all of Bennett's campaign contributions from bankers: Michael Redman, "Bennett 2008 Contributor List," posted April 23, 2010, www.scribd.com/doc/30443023 /Bennett-2008-Contributor-List.

189–190 The bill died in the Banking and Insurance Committee: Florida Senate website archive for SB 2270 shows that SB 2270 died in committee in the Senate Banking and Insurance Committee on April 30, 2010; http://archive.flsenate.gov/Session /index.cfm?Mode=Bills&SubMenu=1&Tab=session&BI_Mode=ViewBillInfo &BillNum=2270&Chamber=Senate&Year=2010.

190 Television stations from Pensacola and Tampa Bay: WEAR-TV 3 Pensacola video available at http://4closurefraud.org/2010/04/24/rally-in-tally-wear-3-news-top -stories-video-home-owners-facing-foreclosure-came-to-the-capitol-wednesday-to -drive-a-stake-in-the-heart-of-the-bill; WTSP-TV Tampa video available at www .stayinmyhome.com/media.htm.

190 local radio stations: Michael Redman, "Talk Radio Confirmation for April 23 9am ET Conquering the Stigma of Being in Foreclosure," 4closurefraud.org, April 22, 2010.

190 print outlets: Alex Tiegen, "Stop Foreclosure Fraud, Homeowners Warn," *Sunshine State News*, April 20, 2010; Shannon Behnken, "Controversial Foreclosure Bill Protest Set for Tallahassee," *Tampa Tribune*, April 20, 2010; Robert Trigaux, "Foreclosure Candidates Travel to Tallahassee to Ensure Their Day in Court," *Tampa Bay Times*, April 21, 2010.

190 "one of the most influential months we have seen": Michael Redman, "Thank You to All for One of the Best Months in the Foreclosure Fraud Fight," 4closurefraud .org, April 30, 2010.

15. By Any Means Necessary

191 Rick and Sherry Rought: John Agar, "Family Files Lawsuit Against Bank, Say Newaygo Home Was Unfairly Foreclosed," *Grand Rapids Press*, April 27, 2010. Also see Megan Stembol, "Gowen Couple Files Lawsuit Against Deutsche Bank," WOODTV .com, available at 4closurefraud.org/2010/04/26/trashed-out-deutsche-bank-acts-like -paid-off-home-is-a-foreclosure-broke-down-doors-changed-locks-stole-belongings -along-with-the-home-owners-sense-of-security.

191 Bank of America stole a woman's pet parrot: Sadie Gurman, "Woman Says Bank of America Wrongly Repossessed Home," *Pittsburgh Post-Gazette*, March 9, 2010.

191 Glazy and Jose Ruscalleda had two lenders: *Glazy Ruscalleda and Joe Ruscalleda v. HSBC*, Third District Court of Appeals, Case No. 3D09-997, opinion filed June 9, 2010, available at www.scribd.com/doc/32852281/Glazy-Ruscalleda-and-Jose -Ruscalleda-Appellants-Vs-HSBC-Bank-USA-Etc-Appellee.

191 Keith and Julie Hanover: Nathan Halverson, "Bank Didn't Admit Error," *Santa Rosa Press-Democrat*, July 18, 2010.

191 The note blamed the deaths on an imminent foreclosure: Alexander Supgul, "Police: Foreclosure Led to Murder-Suicide," MyFoxHouston, May 17, 2010, text

available at http://stopforeclosurefraud.com/2010/05/19/police-foreclosure-led-to-murder
-suicide, video available at https://www.youtube.com/watch?v=JVXMDKAHMZ0.

191 **"I don't have any confidence"**: Lynn Szymoniak, "Mass-Produced Affidavits
Filed by Foreclosure Firms," *Fraud Digest*, April 13, 2010, available at http://thjf.org
/2013/01/14/mass-produced-affidavits-filed-by-foreclosure-firms.

192 **Activists seethed that government resources were put**: "SWAT Team
Storms Keith Sadler's Home in Predawn Raid," YouTube, posted by user mmflint, May 7,
2010, https://www.youtube.com/watch?v=CfFaW2jINLo. Also see "Updated—Sadler
Taken from Foreclosed Home to Wood County Jail," WTOL News, Toledo, 2010.

192 **John Watson, a foreclosure defense attorney**: Michael Redman, "Foreclosure Mill Attorney for Marshall Watson or Foreclosure Defense Attorney for Homeowners?" 4closurefraud.org, April 14, 2010.

192 *Daily Business Review* **ran the story**: Paola Iuspa-Abbott, "Homeowners Allege Attorney Conflict of Interest," *Daily Business Review*, April 22, 2010.

192 **A** *Palm Beach Post* **writer, Kim Miller**: Kimberly Miller, "Activists Heading
to Tallahassee to Oppose Non-Judicial Foreclosures," *Palm Beach Post*, April 20, 2010.
http://www.palmbeachpost.com/money/real-estate/activists-heading-to-tallahassee
-to-oppose-non-judicial-589917.html

193 **Michael annotated the comment with a GIF**: Michael Redman, "Well Well
Well . . . Looks like Someone Is Upset—MERS Makes a Comment on 4closurefraud,"
4closurefraud.org, April 24, 2010.

193 **Michael then found a private Facebook group**: Michael Redman, "DOCX . . .
Just Might Want to Be Your Friend," 4closurefraud.org, April 12, 2010.

194 **"What about the message they will send"**: James Hagerty, "Mortgage Bankers Association Sells Headquarters at a Big Loss," *Wall Street Journal*, February 6, 2010.

194 **he characterized Garfield as an Elmer Gantry–like figure**: Steve Dibert,
"Debunking the Gospel of Garfield," Mortgage Fraud Investigations—Miami, April 7,
2010, https://web.archive.org/web/20101204015419/http://www.mfi-miami.com/2010
/04/debunking-the-gospel-of-garfield.

194 **"I won't hold it against Lisa Epstein"**: Steve Dibert, "Still No Word from the
Garfield Gang About the Garfield Challenge," Mortgage Fraud Investigations—Miami,
April 24, 2010, http://mfi-miami.com/2010/04/still-no-word-from-the-garfield-gang-to
-the-garfield-challenge; Steve Dibert, "The Groupies of Brother Neil Garfield's Traveling Salvation Show Respond," Mortgage Fraud Investigations—Miami, April 12, 2010,
http://mfi-miami.com/2010/04/the-groupies-of-brother-neil-garfields-traveling
-salvation-show-respond.

194 *Huffington Post* **blogger Richard Zombeck sided with Dibert**: Zombeck disputes that he had an editor from whom he could request a press pass or a conversation
with Lisa about press passes, or that he considered Lisa and Michael to be dilettantes.
The anecdote came from a personal email to the author from Zombeck in 2012, where
he called Lisa and Michael "screechers and extremists" and stated that he soured on
them "when they started requesting press passes and other favors" from him. Lisa

confirmed the press pass request. This passage is also based on Zombeck's relevant articles published on the *Huffington Post* website.

195 **the firm's lawyers claimed she treated them with hostility:** Polyana da Costa, "Ice Firm Claims Judge Treats Them with Hostility," *Daily Business Review,* July 7, 2010.

195 **That day Michael posted Judge Sasser's financial records:** Michael Redman, "Ouch, Thats Gotta Sting—Motion for Disqualification of PBC Judge Meenu Sasser for a $425,063.50 Conflict of Interest Involving Billions upon Billions in Assets," 4closure-fraud.org, June 13, 2010.

195 **Though Ice Legal used the equity stock holding to try:** Motion for Disqualification of Judge Meenu Sasser, *Bank of America v. Paul and Lynn Lawless,* Case No. 50-2009-CA-041333XXXX-MB, June 4, 2010, www.scribd.com/doc/32997412/Lawless-Motion-for-Disqualification-of-PBC-Judge-Meenu-Sasser.

195 **To some, particularly Steve Dibert, the charges were gratuitous:** Steve Dibert, "Florida Homeowners Are Losing the Fight but It's Not Because of the Banks," Mortgage Fraud Investigations—Miami, October 18, 2010, https://web.archive.org/web/20101104134951/http://www.mfi-miami.com/2010/10/florida-homeowners-are-losing-the-fight-but-its-not-because-of-the-banks.

195 **She started Moratorium Monday:** Lisa Epstein, "Moratorium Mondays: Monday Morning Protests at Courts, Offices of Elected Officials, and Government Buildings Across the State and the Country," *Foreclosure Hamlet,* 2011.

196 **"A BOGUS ASSIGNMENT OF MORTGAGE filed":** Brief of Amicus Curiae Lisa Epstein, Pro Se, in Support of Neither Party, *HSBC Bank v. Anabel Santiago,* Circuit Court of the Fifteenth Judicial Circuit in and for Palm Beach County, Florida, Case No. 50-2008-CA-016305.

197 **Lynn compiled dozens of examples:** Lynn Szymoniak, "Suddenly Appearing Endorsements Used by Bank-Trustees in Foreclosures," Housing Justice Foundation, June 27, 2014.

197 **"Holders of the notes are often unfamiliar with the status":** Michael Redman, "Response to the Florida Supreme Court RE: Amendments to the Florida Rules of Civil Procedure Motion for Rehearing," 4closurefraud.org, May 13, 2010.

197 **She teamed up with Nye Lavalle, writing:** Lisa Epstein and Nye Lavalle, "Comments and Response in Opposition to Shapiro-Fishman, LLP's Motion for Rehearing or Clarification," Supreme Court of Florida, Case No. SC09-1460, available athttp://api.ning.com/files/ndc8DqfBQG6hENNk8laYm3Rmu8kuMuiez2S0-Z*tgoWUZYfh OfmLacMhWQcNvz4eGIGTLnRzCoHWUUJWYC4-1KIOEk94TpIK/NyeLisa FLASCEfile.pdf.

197 **switched from robo-signers to robo-verifiers:** Michael Redman, "Florida Example—Verification of Mortgage Foreclosure Complaint," 4closurefraud.org, April 18, 2010.

198 **"It is all about awareness":** Michael Redman, "Palm Beach County Bar Association Professional Committee—Thank You for Listening!" 4closurefraud.org, May 19, 2010.

198 On June 3 the state supreme court denied: Supreme Court of Florida, "In re Amendments to the Florida Rules of Civil Procedure," Case Nos. SC09-1460 and SC09-1579, June 3, 2010, www.floridasupremecourt.org/decisions/2010/sc09-1460order.pdf.

199 The U.S. attorney told Charney they were working: Peter Coy, Paul Barrett, and Chad Terhune, "Joseph Lents Dodged Foreclosure for 8 Years, Started a Movement," *Bloomberg Business*, October 21, 2010.

199 "The defendants concealed that the notes and the assignments": *United States of America (Lynn Szymoniak, relator) v. American Home Mortgage Servicing et al.*, Second Amended Complaint, filed May 13, 2011, available at http://2zn5qz 3e2ex118kh0e3kfc7c.wpengine.netdna-cdn.com/wp-content/uploads/2013/08 /complaint-symoniak-false-claimS.C.-Second-Amended-Complaint-ECF-3.pdf.

200 "For all of the reasons set forth above, I conclude": Sample affidavit from *U.S. Bank National Association v. Shirley McFarland*, Circuit Court of Cook County, Illinois (Municipal Department—First District), Case No. 13 M1 708544, Affidavit of Lynn E. Szymoniak, Esq. as Defendant's Expert Witness in Opposition to Summary Judgment.

202 "I cannot get my group to act": Martin Andelman, "Some of Lynn Szymoniak's Millions May Belong to Someone Else," *Mandelman Matters* (blog), September 16, 2013. See also *Figueroa v. Szymoniak*, Seventeenth Judicial Circuit in and for Broward County, Florida, March 4, 2013, available at www.scribd.com/doc/168544786 /Figueroa-v-Szymoniak.

202 Kim Miller at the *Palm Beach Post* wrote a big story on it: Kimberly Miller, "Lawsuit Claims That Florida's Largest Foreclosure Firm Faked Documents," *Palm Beach Post*, August 4, 2010.

202 The bloggers were certain that would come back to haunt Sasser: Michael Redman, "I Haven't Seen Any Widespread Prob, Oh, Wait, What? Foreclosure 'Robo-Signers' Appear to Be Widespread?" 4closurefraud.org, October 12, 2010.

202 The suit was the latest in a host of setbacks for Stern: Susan Martin, "Foreclosures Bring Wealth, Rebukes for Florida Lawyer," *Tampa Bay Times*, July 17, 2010. Also Michael Redman, "Florida Bar v. David J. Stern—Complaint, Consent Judgment, Report of Referee and Judgment," 4closurefraud.org, July 19, 2010.

202 Damian's new lawyer, Trent, released a deposition of Shannon Smith: Deposition of Shannon Smith, *Citimortgage v. Dennis Brown*, Circuit Court of the Seventeenth Judicial District in and for Broward County, Florida, Case No. CACE 08-011097, available at www.scribd.com/doc/34340050/Full-Deposition-of-David-J-Stern-s-Notary -Para-Legal-Shannon-Smith.

202 A separate class action alleged that Stern refused: *Hugo San Martin and Melissa San Martin v. Law Offices of David J. Stern P.A.*, United States District Court for the Southern District of Florida, entered on docket July 29, 2010, available at www .motherjones.com/files/Port_Lt_Lucie_David_J_Stern_Consumer_Suit_July_2010.pdf.

202 "way to create a profit center": *Stan Cooper and Neeraj Mehti v. DJSP Enterprises*, United States District Court, Southern District of Florida, Fort Lauderdale Division, entered on docket July 20, 2010, available at www.scribd.com/doc/34646050

/Stan-Cooper-and-Neeraj-Methi-v-Djsp-Enterprises-Inc-David-j-Stern-and-Kumar
-Gursahaney.

203 Andy Kroll at *Mother Jones* released his story on David Stern: Andy Kroll,
"Fannie and Freddie's Foreclosure Barons," *Mother Jones*, August 4, 2010.

203 He settled that suit out of court: *Bridgette Balboni v. Law Offices of David J.
Stern, P.A.*, United States District Court, Southern District of Florida, Case No.
99-6009-Civ-Ferguson/Snow, filed July 6, 1999, available at www.motherjones.com
/files/Sexual_Harassment_Amended_Complaint.pdf.

203 new investigations of Stern and two other mills: Andy Kroll, "Florida AG
Unveils Foreclosure Mills Probe," *Mother Jones*, August 10, 2010. http://www.mother
jones.com/mojo/2010/08/florida-ag-probing-foreclosure-mills

204 A couple weeks later McCollum lost the primary: "Scott Shakes Up Florida
Governor Race with GOP Primary Win over McCollum," FoxNews.com, August 25, 2010.

204 "The plaintiff is not a proper party to the suit": *M&T Bank v. Lisa D. Smith*,
Circuit Court of the Seventh Judicial Court in and for St. Johns County, Florida, Case
No. CA09-0418, available at http://api.ning.com/files/mzeTxRs3d7j0HRsuMlUH-Zb9
jXNaO6kuX7m3hDkkSM3G3uhTEqH1ZJea1**aFugMSTbMXz*soAWvoyHPBoF0fL
BiEwg*Px8O/SmithOrderdismissalwithprej2.pdf.

204 "I want responsible attorneys who meet the basic standards": *HSBC Bank v.
Orlando Eslava*, Circuit Court of the Eleventh Judicial Circuit in and for Miami-Dade
County, Florida, Case No. 1-2008-CA-055313, transcript of hearing available at http://
api.ning.com/files/WrhLWtvQuslFmfpxKAiuxo51H8souSjcsF5L-UwzuJ1tYWkjL-Re
heX3nB3HV0iZ*EFVMkA5B1hxxVhcCIIHs5NvdFN9Co2C/JudgeBaileyOrderSanc
tionFDLG.pdf.

204 Lisa started keeping a list: Lisa Epstein, "Half-Dozen Florida Judges' Rulings Reveal the Dawning of Understanding," *Foreclosure Hamlet*, June 20, 2010.

205 "I never thought that being in Foreclosure could be so invigorating": Michael Redman, "Foreclosure Fraud—The Florida Bar Convention Strategic Defense Session," 4closurefraud.org, June 27, 2010.

16. Downfall

206 62 percent within a year: Gretchen Morgenson and Geraldine Fabrikant, "Florida's High-Speed Answer to a Foreclosure Mess," *New York Times*, September 4, 2010.

206 Orange and Osceola Counties completed 1,319 cases: Ibid.

206 "clear the foreclosure cases": Kimberly Miller, "Extra Help Hired to Pare
Caseload," *Palm Beach Post*, July 8, 2010.

206 "What is this HAMP": *Foreclosure Hamlet*, "Extra Extra Read All About It!
Calling All Retired Judges for Easy Weekly Extra Money to Sit and Deny Deny Deny!!!"
posted by user "Jen" on July 23, 2010.

206 "I know all about sickness, I know all about divorce": Rhonda Swan, "Legislature Did Not Approve $9.6 million for Judges to Listen Only to Lenders," *Palm
Beach Post*, September 23, 2010.

207 Attorney Greg Stopa saw a judge: Mark Stopa, "When Do Judges Decide Who Wins a Foreclosure Case?" August 20, 2010, www.stayinmyhome.com/blog /when-do-judges-decide-who-wins-a-foreclosure-case.

207 Other summary judgments were entered without informing: Jeff Barnes, "Florida Courts Out of Control: Summary Judgment Entered in Miami-Dade County Without a Hearing; 'Hallway Hearings' in Broward County; and 'Magistrate References' Without Consent in Lee County; Due Process Being Thrown Out the Window," Foreclosure Defense Nationwide, September 15, 2010, http:// foreclosuredefensenationwide.com/?p=282.

207 In Broward County they did it in the hallway: Ibid.

207 her job was to "dispose of cases": Morgenson and Fabrikant, "Florida's High-Speed Answer."

207 April got an email an hour later from Judge Soud: Matt Taibbi, "Invasion of the Home Snatchers," *Rolling Stone*, November 10, 2010.

208 Lisa contacted Laurence Tribe: Charlie Savage, "For an Obama Mentor, A Nebulous Legal Niche," *New York Times*, April 8, 2010.

208 4closureFraud routinely posted depositions: Michael Redman, "Bryan Bly, Is It a Lie? Robo-Signer for Nationwide Title," 4closurefraud.org, June 20, 2010; Michael Redman, "Cheryl Samons Notary Fraud? Full Deposition of David J. Stern's Notary Shannon Smith," 4closurefraud.org, July 16, 2010.

209 GMAC promised it would: Order Granting Defendant's Motion for Sanctions, *TCIF REO2, LLC v. Martin L. Leibowitz*, Circuit Court of the Fourth Judicial Circuit, in and for Duval County, Florida, Case No. 16-2004-CA-4835-XXXX-MA, May 15, 2006, available at https://www.nclc.org/images/pdf/litigation/archibald -exhibits1-4.pdf.

209 "It's too many entities for me to actually quote": Deposition of Jeffrey Stephan, *GMAC Mortgage v. Ann Michelle Perez et al.*, Circuit Court of the Fifteenth Judicial Circuit, in and for Palm Beach County, Florida, Case No. 50-2008-CA-040805XXXX-MB, December 10, 2009, available at http://api.ning.com/files/s4SMwlZXvPu4A7kq7XQUsG W9xEcYtqNMPCm0a2hISJu88PoY6ZNqanX7XK41Fyf9gV8JIHDme7KcFO 2cvHqSEMcplJ8vwnDT/091210gmacmortgagevsannmneu1.pdf.

210 "The statements appearing herein are based": Sample of Affidavit in Support of Mortgage Indebtedness, available at www.mortgage-investments.com/wp/wp -content/uploads/Sample%20Forms%20Downloads/2_affidavit-in-proof-of-claim.pdf.

210 "These depositions would be comical if it weren't for the fact": Michael Redman, "Full Deposition of Jeffrey Stephan—GMAC's Assignment/Affidavit Slave—10,000 Documents a Month," 4closurefraud.org, March 22, 2010.

211 She lived in a tiny wood-framed house across from a construction site: David Streitfeld, "From a Maine House, a National Foreclosure Freeze," *New York Times*, October 14, 2010.

212 Ice Legal got Stephan to admit that Kwiatanowski was his boss: Deposition of Jeffrey Stephan, *GMAC Mortgage v. Ann Michelle Perez et al.*

212 **"I compare the principal balance. I review the interests"**: Oral deposition of Jeffrey Stephan, *Federal National Mortgage Association v. Nicolle M. Bradbury*, Maine District Court, District Nine, Division of North Cumberland, Docket No. BRI-RE-09-65, June 7, 2010, available at http://graphics8.nytimes.com/packages/pdf/business/15mainestephandeposition.pdf.

213 **He posted the Stephan deposition on his site on June 15**: Matthew Weidner, "New Robo Signer Deposition Jeffrey Stephan," June 15, 2010, http://mattweidnerlaw.com/new-robo-signer-deposition-jeffrey-stephan.

213 **Michael Redman saw it and cross-posted it**: Redman, "2nd Deposition of Jeffrey Stephan."

213 **"When Stephan says in an affidavit"**: Martha Neil, "Humble Maine Home, Ex-Lawyer at Epicenter of Storm over Defective Docs in Foreclosure Cases," *American Bar Association Journal*, October 15, 2010

213 **"The Court is particularly troubled"**: Order on Four Pending Motions, *Federal National Mortgage Association v. Nicolle M. Bradbury*, Maine District Court, District Nine, Division of North Cumberland, Docket No. BRI-RE-09-65, September 24, 2010, available at http://graphics8.nytimes.com/packages/pdf/business/Four MotionsOrder.pdf.

213 **FDLG "has recently been notified"**: Notice in the case of *Bank of New York Mellon Trust Company v. Roberto J. Sanchez et al.*, Circuit Court of the Fifteenth Judicial Circuit, in and for Palm Beach County, Florida, Case No. 50-2008-CA-027182, September 7, 2010, available at www.scribd.com/doc/37455360/FDLG-Admits-to-Violation-of-Professional-Conduct-Code-Jeffrey-Stephan-Affidavits-GMAC. Also Michael Redman, "What, What!!! Re: Jeffrey Stephan of GMAC—Florida Default Law Group Admits to Violation of Professional Conduct Code," 4closurefraud.org, September 14, 2010.

214 **Lisa put out an APB to her network**: Lisa Epstein, "Anthology of the Works of a Prolific Robosigner: Jeffrey Stephan of GMAC (Compilation in Progress)," *Foreclosure Hamlet*, September 14, 2010.

214 **As Lynn was searching, she found a mortgage assignment**: Assignment of Mortgage, Clerk and Comptroller of Palm Beach County Public Records, book 23845, page 381, Recorded May 13, 2010.

214 **Ramsey Harris**: George Andreassi, "Neighbors Aid Disabled Veteran Ripped Off During Eviction from Rocky Point House," *Treasure Coast Palm*, September 17, 2010.

214 **Liquenda Allotey, a known robo-signer, affirmed**: Michael Redman, "Now I Am Pissed—Disabled Vet Evicted, Home Trashed Out, Property Stolen by Jack Booted Thugs," 4closurefraud.org, September 19, 2010.

214 **GMAC announced a suspension**: David Streitfeld, "GMAC Halts Foreclosures in 23 States for Review," *New York Times*, September 20, 2010.

214 **So did a reporter for the *Washington Post***: Brady Dennis, " 'Robo-Signer' Played Quiet Role in Huge Number of Foreclosures," *Washington Post*, September 22, 2010.

215 Paola Iuspa-Abbott of the *Daily Business Review*: Paola Iuspa-Abbott, "Grassroots Effort Leads to Attorney General Probe," *Daily Business Review*, September 7, 2010, available at https://web.archive.org/web/20100911083631/http://www.daily businessreview.com/news.html?news_id=65012.

215 Jeffrey Stephan's Ice Legal deposition: Michael Redman, "Full Video Deposition of Jeffrey Stephan??? Assignment/Affidavit Slave," 4closurefraud.org, September 28, 2010.

215 "an advanced-age Beavis or Butt-head": Taibbi, "Invasion of the Home Snatchers."

215 "That can't be real": Yves Smith, "Meet GMAC's Robo Signer Jeffrey Stephan," *Naked Capitalism* (blog), September 30, 2010. http://www.nakedcapitalism.com/2010 /09/meet-gmacs-robo-signer-jeffrey-stephan.html

215 "This deposition is even better than Jeffrey Stephan's depo": Michael Redman, "GMAC, You Ain't the Only One—Full Deposition of Beth Cottrell Chase Home Finance—Robo-Signer Extraordinaire," 4closurefraud.org, September 21, 2010.

216 "I have personal knowledge that my staff has personal knowledge": Michael Redman, "Full Deposition of Beth Cottrell Chase Home Finance—Robo-Signer Extraordinaire," 4closurefraud.org, May 27, 2010.

217 But most homeowners never mounted a defense: Jennifer Brunner, *Cupcakes and Courage* (Columbus, OH: Little Blue Valiant, 2012), 527.

217 When Brunner got wind of this, she asked Dettelbach: Jennifer Brunner referral letter to U.S. Attorney Steven Dettelbach re: Foreclosure Fraud, accessed at www.scribd.com/doc/38478473/Jennifer-Brunner-Ohio-Secretary-of-State-Referral -Letter-to-U-S-District-Attorney-Steven-Dettelbach-RE-Foreclosure-Fraud.   Also Jennifer Brunner, "Notarize This: The Brewing Foreclosure Storm," *Huffington Post*, October 1, 2010.

217 Chase Home Finance announced it would suspend: David Streitfeld, "JPMorgan Suspending Mortgage Foreclosures," *New York Times*, September 29, 2010.

217 the Amazing Mystico: *Monty Python's Flying Circus*, episode 35, transcript available at www.ibras.dk/montypython/episode35.htm.

218 The next day Cha wrote an article: Ariana Eunjung Cha, "Ally's Mortgage Documentation Problems Could Extend Beyond 23 States," *Washington Post*, September 23, 2010.

218 Kim Miller at the *Palm Beach Post* **published a tip:** Kimberly Miller, "More Foreclosure Affidavits Withdrawn as Another Document Signer Identified," *Palm Beach Post*, September 27, 2010.

218 documents signed by Linda Green, the infamous DocX robo-signer: Lisa Epstein, "Shaprio [sic] Fishman, 'Linda Green of DocX Had No Signing Authority on Behalf of MERS,'" *Foreclosure Hamlet*, August 26, 2010.

218 Michael Olenick found Beth Cottrell's name attached: Michael Redman, "Promiscuous Girl Beth Cottrell—Looks Like She Had Multiple Partners (Banks)," 4closurefraud.org, October 1, 2010.

218 **"The GMAC announcement was the mushroom cloud"**: Streitfeld, "JPMorgan Suspending Mortgage Foreclosures."

218 **Curing a defective mortgage would cost you $12.95**: Michael Redman, "Psst, Hey You, Yea, You. I Got Just What You Need." Lender Processing Services' DOCX Document Fabrication Price Sheet," 4closurefraud.org, October 2, 2010.

218 **As finance blogger Yves Smith of *Naked Capitalism* explained**: Yves Smith, "4closurefraud Posts DocX Mortgage Document Fabrication Price Sheet," *Naked Capitalism* (blog), October 3, 2010.

218 **"If you're right, we're fucked"**: Yves Smith, "FUBAR Mortgage Behavior: Florida Banks Destroyed Notes; Others Never Transferred Them," *Naked Capitalism* (blog), September 27, 2010.

219 **both Jason Grodensky and Fannie Mae owned the home**: Harriet Johnson Brackey, "Lauderdale Man's Home Sold Out from Under Him in Foreclosure Mistake," Fort Lauderdale *Sun-Sentinel*, September 23, 2010.

219 **Bank of America foreclosing on another house with no mortgage**: Lee Weisbecker, "Cooper: BofA Foreclosed on Homeowner Who Paid Cash," *Triangle Business Journal*, October 7, 2010.

219 **Martin and Kirsten Davis**: Teresa Dixon Murray, "Mortgage Foreclosure Uproar Sweeps Up Northeast Ohioans," *Cleveland Plain Dealer*, October 17, 2010.

219 **Nancy Jacobini**: Joel Siegel, Felicia Biberica, and David Muir, "Mortgage Bullies?: Banks Accused of Illegally Breaking into Homes Facing Foreclosure," ABC News, October 11, 2010; "Housing Crisis Reaches New Low," *Dylan Ratigan Show*, October 6, 2010; "Why Are Bailed-Out Banks Breaking into Struggling Borrowers' Homes?" *Democracy Now*, October 12, 2010.

219 **"There is no room for errors"**: Barry Ritholtz, "Why Foreclosure Fraud Is So Dangerous to Property Rights," *The Big Picture* (blog), October 12, 2010, www.ritholtz.com/blog/2010/10/why-foreclosure-fraud-is-so-dangerous-to-property-rights.

220 **"When you have people in Texas and Florida being foreclosed on"**: Barry Ritholtz, "What's the Foreclosure," *The Big Picture* (blog), October 12, 2010, www.ritholtz.com/blog/2010/10/whats-the-foreclosure; CNBC, air date October 11, 2010, 5:00 p.m. ET.

220 **And without title insurance, nobody would risk a purchase**: David Streitfeld, "Company Stops Insuring Titles in Chase Foreclosures," *New York Times*, October 2, 2010.

220 **Bank of America suspended foreclosures**: Robbie Whelan, "Bank of America Suspends Foreclosures," *Wall Street Journal*, October 2, 2010.

220 **Connecticut called a moratorium**: Ariana Eunjung Cha, "Connecticut Halts All Foreclosures for All Banks," *Washington Post*, October 1, 2010.

220 **Grayson made an easy-to-understand video**: Alan Grayson, "Fraud Factories: Rep. Alan Grayson Explains the Foreclosure Fraud Crisis," September 30, 2010, https://www.youtube.com/watch?v=AqnHLDeedVg.

220–221 **Ohio attorney general Richard Cordray announced his GMAC lawsuit**: David Dayen, "Ohio Attorney General Sues GMAC, Seeks $25,000 per False

Affidavit," FDL News Desk, October 6, 2010, http://shadowproof.com/2010/10/06/ohio
-attorney-general-sues-gmac-seeks-25000-per-false-affidavit.

221 **Federal banking regulators opened formal reviews:** Ariana Eunjung Cha,
"7 Major Lenders Ordered to Review Foreclosure Procedures," *Washington Post*, September 30, 2010.

221 **On October 8 Bank of American extended its moratorium:** Ilyce Glink,
"Bank of America, Ally Bank Extend Foreclosure Freeze to All 50 States," CBS Marketwatch, October 8, 2010.

221 **Chase, GMAC, Litton Loans, and Citi followed suit:** "Texas Mortgage
Company Halts Some Foreclosures," Associated Press, October 8, 2010. Accessed at
https://www.victoriaadvocate.com/news/2010/oct/08/bc-us-litton-foreclosures/

221 **robo-signer Xee Moua:** Suzanne Kapner, "Wells Adds to Crisis over Home
Seizures," *Financial Times*, October 14, 2010; Jia Lynn Yang, "Wells Fargo Acknowledges Problems in Foreclosure Paperwork," *Washington Post*, October 27, 2010.

221 **On October 13 the attorneys general of all fifty states:** Ray Sanchez, "Foreclosure Mess: 50 States Investigate Mortgage-Services Industry," ABC News, October 13, 2010.

17. The Big Time

222 *Good Morning America, The Daily Show,* **and nightly newscasts:** *Good
Morning America* segment on robo-signing available at http://sherriequestioningall
.blogspot.com/2010/10/good-morning-america-segment-on.html; Paul Jackson, "Jon
Stewart on Robosigners and Foreclosure-gate," Housing Wire, October 8, 2010; Matt
Gutman and Bradley Blackburn, "Foreclosure Crisis: 23 States Halt Foreclosure as Officials Review Bank Practices," ABC News, October 4, 2010.

222 **Lisa and Michael became front-page news:** Ariana Eunjung Cha, "Florida
Activists Read Between the Lines on Foreclosure Paperwork," *Washington Post*, October 21, 2010; Tony Pugh, "How 2 Civilian Sleuths Brought Foreclosure Problems to
Light," McClatchy Newspapers, October 13, 2010; Kimberly Miller, "'Deadbeat' Fights
Back Against Foreclosure Process," *Palm Beach Post*, October 20, 2010.

222 **"Funny how we have been screaming this for about a year":** Michael Redman,
"Kristine Wilson—Robo Signer Part Deux—Ally's GMAC Unit Withdraws Foreclosure
Affidavits Signed by Second Employee," 4closurefraud.org, September 25, 2010.

222 **"Preempted by a Passel of Pigs":** Lisa Epstein, "Preempted by a Passel of Pigs
Being Put in the Pen (Hopefully Foreshadowing Reality)," *Foreclosure Hamlet*, October
5, 2010.

222 **"MBS? There are no mortgages backing these securities":** Video of MSNBC
appearance available at YouTube, posted by user "Big Brother Is Watching," uploaded
October 26, 2010, https://www.youtube.com/watch?v=d6PwU4MUz9Y.

223 **"emergency happy hours":** Michael Redman, "Emergency Happy Hours—
Thurs 9/23 Tampa & Fri 9/24 St. Pete, FL: Gatherings for Combatants of Illegal Foreclosures," 4closurefraud.org, September 22, 2010.

223 They filed public records requests: "ACLU Seeks Public Records to Determine Constitutionality of Foreclosure Proceedings in Florida," ACLU press release, October 19, 2010.

223 Lisa found a flood of "replacement" mortgage assignments and affidavits: Lisa Epstein, "Shapiro Fishman File More Corrective Assignments of Mortgage," *Foreclosure Hamlet*, September 19, 2010.

224 "The mortgage follows the note": Yves Smith, "American Securitization Forum Tells Monstrous Whoppers in Senate Testimony on Mortgage Mess," *Naked Capitalism*, December 2, 2010.

224 a campaign called Where Is the Note?: David Dayen, "Democrats Continue to Pressure Lenders Toward Nationwide Foreclosure Moratorium," FDL News, October 9, 2010, http://shadowproof.com/2010/10/09/democrats-continue-to-pressure-lenders-toward-nationwide-foreclosure-moratorium.

224 "Lawyers in the field now commonly use a technique": Robbie Whelan, "Niche Lawyers Spawned Housing Fracas," *Wall Street Journal*, October 21, 2010.

224 "So we can improve the economy by throwing millions": *The Daily Show with Jon Stewart*, October 7, 2010.

224 "Fraud doesn't erase the fact that the borrower agreed": John Carney, "Let's Not Start Lionizing the Anti-Foreclosure Deadbeats," CNBC.com, October 13, 2010.

225 "recognize any lawful notarization": Text of HR 3808, 111th Congress of the United States of America, available at https://www.govtrack.us/congress/bills/111/hr3808/text.

225 States could challenge the statute, but that could take years: Jennifer Brunner, *Cupcakes and Courage* (Columbus, OH: Little Blue Valiant, 2012), 532–33, 539–45.

225 Spencer, who was still working in the West Wing, promised: Ibid., 542–43.

225 Michael reposted Brunner's email: Michael Redman, "Action Alert—Please Tell President Obama Not to Sign the Interstate Recognition of Notarizations Act," 4closurefraud.org, October 5, 2010.

226 "unintended impact of this bill": Arthur Delaney, "Obama Will Not Sign Bill Seen as Cover for Bank Foreclosures," *Huffington Post*, October 7, 2010, http://www.huffingtonpost.com/2010/10/07/obama-pocket-veto-foreclosures_n_753987.html

226 Michael published his findings: Michael Redman, "Action Alert—Is Pres Obama's Pocket Veto on H.R. 3808 Possibly Ineffective?" 4closurefraud.org, October 8, 2010.

226 "To leave no doubt that the bill is being vetoed": Barack Obama, "Presidential Memorandum—H.R. 3808," White House press release, October 8, 2010.

226 In President Obama's first six years in office he vetoed only two bills: U.S. Senate, "Vetoes by President Barack H. Obama," www.senate.gov/reference/Legislation/Vetoes/ObamaBH.htm.

227 "One person really can make a difference": Brunner, *Cupcakes and Courage*, 544.

227 **"I don't know the ins and outs of the loan":** "Robo-Signers: Mortgage Experience Not Necessary," Associated Press, October 12, 2010.

227 **Lynn was nonplussed:** Jeremy Pelofsky, "U.S. Justice Dept. Probing Foreclosure Processes," Reuters, October 6, 2010.

227 **a Bush-era assistant attorney general, Paul McNulty:** Scot J. Paltrow, "Special Report: Legal Woes Mount for a Foreclosure Kingpin," Reuters, December 6, 2010.

228 **June and Theresa took a deposition from Tammie Lou Kapusta:** Deposition of Tammie Lou Kapusta, in re: Investigation of Law Offices of David J. Stern, P.A., State of Florida Office of the Attorney General, AG #L10-3-1145, September 22, 2010, available at www.scribd.com/doc/38890568/Full-Deposition-of-Tammie-Lou-Kapusta -Law-Office-of-David-J-Stern.

229 **June and Theresa leaked the deposition:** Michael Redman, "Exclusive Bombshell of Foreclosure Fraud—Full Deposition of Tammie Lou Kapusta Law Office of David J. Stern," 4closurefraud.org, October 7, 2010.

229 **The state prosecutors sent another deposition later:** Michael Redman, "Another 4closureFraud Bombshell—Full Deposition of Kelly Scott of the Law Office of David J. Stern," 4closurefraud.org, October 18, 2010.

229 **That wiped out a large chunk of the company's business:** Andy Kroll, "Fannie, Freddie Ditch Foreclosure King," *Mother Jones*, October 13, 2010.

229 **they even formally reprimanded Erin Cullaro:** Shannon Behnken, "AG's Office Reprimands Its Attorney for 'Foreclosure Mill' Work," *Tampa Tribune*, October 19, 2010.

229 **Democrats . . . pounced on the issue:** Arthur Delaney, "Calls Mount for Foreclosure Moratorium, Investigations," *Huffington Post*, October 7, 2010.

229 **twenty pages of horrific case studies:** David Dayen, "Pelosi, California House Dems Call for Criminal Investigations of Mortgage Lenders," FDL News, October 5, 2010, http://shadowproof.com/2010/10/05/pelosi-california-house-dems-call -for-criminal-investigations-of-mortgage-lenders.

229 **Alan Grayson wanted foreclosure fraud monitored:** Yves Smith, "DC Waking Up to Escalating Foreclosure Train Wreck: Grayson Calls for FSOC to Examine Foreclosure Fraud as Systemic Risk," *Naked Capitalism*, October 7, 2010.

230 **David Axelrod told *Face the Nation* that foreclosures with proper paperwork:** Tom Cohen, "Axelrod Signals White House Opposition to Foreclosure Moratorium," CNN.com, October 10, 2010.

231 **Michael posted the Obama robo-signer story:** Michael Redman, "4closureFraud Exclusive—President Obama Falls Victim to Chase Robo-Signer," 4closurefraud .org, October 10, 2010.

231 **an irreverent Dutch blog called *GeenStijl*:** John Galt (pseudonym), "GeenStijl CrisisWatch: Foreclosure Fraud," *GeenStijl*, October 13, 2010, available at www .geenstijl.nl/mt/archieven/2010/10/crisiswatch_column_foreclosure.html.

231 **"Feel free to call or email me":** Michael Redman, "4closureFraud Exclusive Part Deux—President Obama Falls Victim to Another Robo-Signer," 4closurefraud .org, October 11, 2010.

231 **Within three weeks Bank of America pronounced themselves free of errors:** Charles Riley, "Bank of America Resumes Foreclosures in 23 States," CNNMoney .com, October 18, 2010.

231 **"10 or 25" problems in the first "several hundred":** Dan Fitzpatrick, "BofA Finds Foreclosure Document Errors," *Wall Street Journal*, October 24, 2010.

231 **4,450 errors just in the five boroughs of New York City:** Robert Gearty, "Dubious Signatures, Missing, Inaccurate Paperwork Halt 4,450 City Foreclosures," New York *Daily News*, October 24, 2010.

231 **In Cuyahoga County, Ohio, a judge ruled:** David Dayen, "Ohio Ruling: No Substitution of Foreclosure Documents in Robo-Signing Cases," FDL News, January 3, 2011, http://shadowproof.com/2011/01/03/ohio-ruling-no-substitution-of-foreclosure -documents-in-robo-signing-cases.

231 **Nobody would put themselves on the line:** "New York Courts First in Country to Institute Filing Requirement to Preserve Integrity of Foreclosure Process," press release, State of New York Unified Court System, October 20, 2010, available at www .courts.state.ny.us/press/pr2010_12.shtml; Hon. Glenn Grant, Administrative Director of the Courts of the State of New Jersey, Administrative Order Directing Submission of Information from Residential Mortgage Foreclosure Plaintiffs Concerning Their Document Execution Practices to a Special Master, Order No. 01-2010, December 20, 2010, available at https://www.judiciary.state.nj.us/notices/2010/n101220b.pdf

231 **Bank stocks sank throughout October:** David Hilzenrath, "Worries over Fast-Tracked Foreclosures Send Bank Stocks Plummeting," *Washington Post*, October 14, 2010.

232 **asked that Bank of America take back $47 billion:** Jody Shenn, "Pimco, NY-Fed Said to Seek BofA Mortgage Repurchases," *Bloomberg Business*, October 19, 2010.

232 **Analysts put the ultimate cost to the banks:** Ruth Simon, "Mortgage Losses Build Team Spirit," *Wall Street Journal*, October 27, 2010.

232 **"were never properly transferred at each step of the securitization process":** Josh Levin and Arjun Sharma, "Foreclosures Gone Wild: Takeaways from Our Conference Call," Citigroup Global Markets research document, October 12, 2010.

232 **He ended up losing by 18 points:** Mike Schneider and Bill Kaczor, "Alan Grayson Loses House Seat to Daniel Webster," Associated Press, November 2, 2010.

232 **the roster of attorneys general changed over:** Ballotpedia, "Attorney General Elections, 2010," http://ballotpedia.org/Attorney_General_elections,_2010.

233 **Jim Kowalski and Tom Cox testified:** "Foreclosed Justice: Causes and Effects of the Foreclosure Crisis," hearing before the House Judiciary Committee, December 2 and 15, 2010, www.gpo.gov/fdsys/pkg/CHRG-111hhrg62935/html/CHRG -111hhrg62935.htm.

233 Foreclosure fraud was the last stop: "Problems in Mortgage Servicing from Modification to Foreclosure," hearing before the Senate Banking Committee, November 16, 2010, www.banking.senate.gov/public/index.cfm?FuseAction=Hearings .Hearing&Hearing_ID=df8cb685-c1bf-4eea-941d-cf9d5173873a; see also Yves Smith, "Servicer-Driven Foreclosures: The Perfect Crime?" *Naked Capitalism*, November 30, 2010.

233 "Five such requests will amount to more": David Dayen, "Damon Silvers Blasts Treasury, Tries to Get Them to Wake Up on Mortgage Fraud," FDL News, October 28, 2010, http://shadowproof.com/2010/10/28/damon-silvers-blasts-treasury-tries -to-get-them-to-wake-up-on-mortgage-fraud.

233 "Just because a homeowner hasn't paid his mortgage": Testimony of Katherine Porter, Congressional Oversight Panel, hearing on the TARP Foreclosure Mitigation Program, October 27, 2010, available at http://cybercemetery.unt.edu/archive /cop/20110402015351/http://cop.senate.gov/documents/testimony-102710-porter.pdf. See also Joe Nocera, "Big Problem for Banks: Due Process," *New York Times*, October 22, 2010.

233 "The federal regulators don't want to get information": David Dayen, "Levitin Addresses Elephant in the Room: Regulators Don't Want to Fix the Foreclosure Crisis," FDL News, November 18, 2010, http://shadowproof.com/2010/11/18 /levitin-addresses-elephant-in-the-room-regulators-dont-want-to-fix-the-foreclosure -crisis; video available at http://www.cps-news.com/2010/11/22/treasury-directive -is-to-protect-the-banks.

234 "I donated my last $10": Michael Redman, "4closureFraud and Foreclosure-Hamlet are Going to Washington DC and Could Use Your Help," 4closurefraud.org, November 11, 2010.

235 provided the legal opinions that created MERS: Scot J. Paltrow, "Insight: Top Justice officials connected to mortgage banks," Reuters, January 20, 2012.

235 That guaranteed timidity: Matt Taibbi, *The Divide: American Injustice in the Age of the Wealth Gap* (New York: Spiegel and Grau, 2014), 31–38.

18. We Will Put People in Jail

236 *Kemp v. Countrywide:* *John T. Kemp v. Countrywide Home Loans*, United States Bankruptcy Court, District of New Jersey, Case No. 08-18700-JHW, ruling filed November 16, 2010, available at http://cdn.americanbanker.com/media/pdfs/kemp_v _countrywide.pdf.

236 Hilariously, most of this came out on redirect: "Word for Word: That Bank of America Exec's Testimony on Countrywide Mortgage Docs," *American Banker*, November 29, 2010.

236 Tom Adams tracked down the pooling and servicing agreement: Tom Adams, "Failure to Transfer Notes a Serious Issue for Countrywide and Its Trustee," *Naked Capitalism*, November 22, 2010.

236 "We believe the loan was sold to the trust": Gretchen Morgenson, "Flawed Mortgage Papers May Pose Economic Risk, Panel Says," *New York Times*, November 20, 2010.

237 Observing the rocket docket was the first step: "Letters Regarding Open Access to Florida State Foreclosure Proceedings," ACLU press release, November 17, 2010.

237 The reporter went to Stern's offices in Plantation: Todd Ruger, "Shortcuts on the Foreclosure Paper Trail," Sarasota *Herald-Tribune*, November 28, 2010.

237 The top foreclosure mill in Pennsylvania: Abigail Field, "Thousands of Pennsylvania Foreclosures Could Be on Shaky Ground," *Daily Finance*, December 2, 2010.

237 Brian Bly, Crystal Moore, and Dhurata Dako: Susan Martin, "On Video, Alleged 'Robo-Signers' Describe Assembly Line Work," *Tampa Bay Times*, November 12, 2010; William Alden and Ryan McCarthy, "The Most Shocking Statements from Alleged Foreclosure 'Robo-Signers,'" *Huffington Post*, November 13, 2010.

237 Michael thought Bly resembled cubicle drone Milton: Michael Redman, "Notorious Robo-signers, Bryan Bly and Crystal Moore, Still 'Working' for Nationwide Title Clearing," 4closurefraud.org, July 19, 2011.

238 You don't mess with the Scientologists: Susan Martin, "Nationwide Title Goes on Attack Against Vocal Critics," *Tampa Bay Times*, December 10, 2010; Michael Redman, "And So It Begins . . . Nationwide Title Clearing Sues Foreclosure Fraud Defense Attorney Matt Weidner," 4closurefraud.org, December 12, 2010.

238 the Massachusetts Supreme Court delivered a lightning bolt: Yves Smith, "Mass Supreme Court Rules Against Wells Fargo, Deutsche Case on Validity of Mortgage Transfers in Securitizations," *Naked Capitalism*, January 7, 2011; Tracy Alloway, "A Court Case to Challenge Securitisation Standards [Updated]," *Financial Times Alphaville*, January 7, 2011.

238 bank stocks plummeted anyway: Thom Weidlich, "Massachusetts Top Court Hands Foreclosure Loss to U.S. Bancorp," *Bloomberg Business*, January 8, 2011.

238 In Simi Valley, California, a couple broke into their foreclosed house: Emily Peck, "Evicted Family Breaks into Their Former House," *Wall Street Journal*, October 13, 2010.

238 the homeowners would move into the bank: "Families Arrested at Bank in Foreclosure Protest," People's World, December 17, 2010, http://peoplesworld.org/families-arrested-at-bank-in-foreclosure-protest; David Dayen, "22 Foreclosure Activists Arrested at Chase Bank in Downtown Los Angeles," FDL News, December 17, 2010, http://shadowproof.com/2010/12/17/22-foreclosure-activists-arrested-at-chase-bank-in-downtown-los-angeles.

238 PICO, a national faith coalition, rallied: David Dayen, "Geithner Meets with Homeowners Burned by HAMP," FDL News, November 4, 2010, http://shadowproof.com/2010/11/04/geithner-meets-with-homeowners-burned-by-hamp.

238 formed anti-foreclosure coalitions: Sean-Thomas Breitfeld and Marnie Brady, "The New Bottom Line," Building Movement Project, www.buildingmovement.org/pdf /The_New_Bottom_Line.pdf; Home Defenders League, www.homedefendersleague.org.

238 Homeless for the Holidays: Michael Redman, "Homeless for the Holidays Rally Protesting Foreclosure Fraud, West Palm Beach Courthouse | Be There or Be Homeless," 4closurefraud.org, December 8, 2010.

239 anonymous reports hyped an imminent settlement: Ariana Eunjung Cha and Brady Dennis, "States, Mortgage Lenders in Talks over Fund for Borrowers in Foreclosure Mess," *Washington Post*, November 17, 2010.

239 "Don't sit down with the banks": Michael Redman, "Action Alert—Foreclosure Fraud—Tell Your Attorney General 'Don't Sit Down with the Banks! Stand up Against Fraud!'" 4closurefraud.org, October 29, 2010.

239 "If the public gains the impression": Congressional Oversight Panel, "Examining the Consequences of Mortgage Irregularities for Financial Stability and Foreclosure Mitigation," November 16, 2010, http://cybercemetery.unt.edu/archive/cop /20110401233819/http://cop.senate.gov/reports/library/report-111610-cop.cfm.

239 "It's both": Brady Dennis, "Q and A: Head of Probe Says Victims of Wrongful Foreclosure Should Get Compensation," *Washington Post*, November 16, 2010.

239 Miller received $261,000 from banking interests: Jon Prior, "Report Spotlights Iowa AG's Campaign Contributions from Banking Industry," Housing Wire, April 22, 2011.

239 Miller acknowledged asking bank lawyers for contributions: Massimo Calabresi, "Foreclosure-Probe Chief Asked Bank Lawyers for Money," *Time*, May 9, 2011. http://swampland.time.com/2011/05/09/foreclosure-probe-chief-asked-bank-lawyers -for-money/

239 Miller told the Senate Banking Committee: "Problems in Mortgage Servicing from Modification to Foreclosure," Senate Banking Committee, November 16, 2010, transcript accessed at www.gpo.gov/fdsys/pkg/CHRG-111shrg65258/pdf/CHRG -111shrg65258.pdf, p.8

240 "we will put people in jail": Arthur Delaney, "Tom Miller: 'We Will Put People in Jail' for Foreclosure Fraud," *Huffington Post*, December 14, 2010.

240 Miller kept a low profile after that: Yves Smith, "Iowa Attorney General Tom Miller, Head of 50 State Investigation, Retreats from 'Tough With Banks' Stance," *Naked Capitalism*, January 26, 2011; David Dayen, "The Mystery of Tom Miller's Shifting Comments on Criminal Sanctions for Foreclosure Fraud," FDL News, January 6, 2011, http://shadowproof.com/2011/01/06/the-mystery-of-tom-millers-shifting -comments-on-criminal-sanctions-for-foreclosure-fraud.

240 "hundreds of investigators crawling all over the banks": Felix Salmon, "Treasury's Plan to Fix the Mortgage Mess," Reuters, November 23, 2010.

240 "global solution": David Dayen, "Bair's 'Global Solution' Doesn't Address Criminal Prosecution," FDL News Desk, October 25, 2010, http://shadowproof.com /2010/10/25/bairs-global-solution-doesnt-address-criminal-prosecution.

241 Hawaii transformed from a state with fairly lenient hurdles: Martin Andelman, "Governor Abercrombie Signs SB 651—Toughest Foreclosure Bill in Nation Now Law!" *Mandelman Matters* (blog), May 6, 2011, http://mandelman.ml-implode.com/2011/05/governor-abercrombie-signs-sb-651-toughest-foreclosure-bill-in-nation-now-law.

242 Banks restarted the Great Foreclosure Machine: David Dayen, "Banks Resume Foreclosure Sales," FDL News, December 13, 2010, http://shadowproof.com/2010/12/13/banks-resume-foreclosure-sales.

242 "We have not discovered a single instance": Testimony before the House Financial Services Committee, November 18, 2010, video at C-SPAN, www.c-span.org/video/?296661-2/mortgage-services-foreclosure-practices-bankers-panel.

243 "Unfair, Deceptive and Unconscionable Acts in Foreclosure Cases": June Clarkson, Theresa Edwards, and Rene Harrod, "Unfair, Deceptive and Unconscionable Acts in Foreclosure Cases," Office of the Attorney General, Economic Crimes Division, 2010, available at www.scribd.com/doc/46278738/Florida-Attorney-General-Fraudclosure-Report-Unfair-Deceptive-and-Unconscionable-Acts-in-Foreclosure-Cases.

243–244 That got the presentation leaked: Kimberly Miller, "State Report on Foreclosure Crisis Slams Banks, Mortgage Industry, Lawyers," *Palm Beach Post*, January 5, 2011.

244 "We object to the Florida Attorney General's characterization": Stefan Kamph, "June Clarkson and Theresa Edwards Were Fired After Revealing Widespread Foreclosure Fraud," *Broward/Palm Beach New Times*, June 21, 2012.

244 Pam Bondi . . . received thousands of dollars in campaign contributions: Michael Redman, "Pam Bondi, Lender Processing Services, Provest and Campaign Contributions from Companies Under Investigation from AG's Office," 4closurefraud, July 28, 2011.

244 Bob Julian, their supervisor, expressed frustration: Kamph, "June Clarkson and Theresa Edwards Were Fired."

246 Moratorium Monday continued and expanded: Lisa Epstein, "Announcing Moratorium Mondays: Monday Morning Protests at Courts, Offices of Elected Officials, and Government Buildings Across the State and the Country," *Foreclosure Hamlet*, February 9, 2011.

246 Dozens of protestors marched: Lisa Epstein, "Jan 13th Protest March Against Criminal Foreclosure Fraud: Goal Met!" *Foreclosure Hamlet*, January 14, 2011.

246 Lisa and Michael held Torch the Fraud: Michael Redman, "Torch the Fraud | 4closureFraud.org and ForeclosureHamlet.org Host a Bonfire on the Beach," 4closurefraud.org, February 28, 2011.

247 The sheriff ordered deputies to remove money: Michael Redman, "Deadbeat Bank | Raw Video of Sheriff Serving Writ of Possession on Bank to Seize All Property Including All Cash," 4closurefraud, February 9, 2011.

247 "Deadbeat bank" actions became more widespread: Jeff Gelles, "Phila. Homeowner Wins Judgment Against Wells Fargo over Mortgage Fees," *Philadelphia*

Inquirer, February 15, 2011; *The Daily Show with Jon Stewart,* "The Forecloser," Comedy Central, August 8, 2011.

247 second annual Rally in Tally: Michael Redman, "Continuously Updated | March 9, 2011: Second Annual Freedom Ride and Rally in Tally for Combatants of Illegal Foreclosures," 4closurefraud.org, February 23, 2011; Michael Redman, "Pictures of Our Rally in Tally," 4closurefraud, March 10, 2011.

247 Michael found the e-signature of Shapiro & Fishman lawyer Anna Malone: Kimberly Miller, "Lawyers' Name Shows Up on Foreclosure Docs Filed Months After She Resigned," *Palm Beach Post,* February 21, 2011.

247 an instruction manual on how to manufacture affidavits: Lisa Epstein, "Ben-Ezra Katz Foreclosure Mill—Internal Instructions on How to Copy/Cut/Paste, Perjury and Fraud upon the Court," *Foreclosure Hamlet,* February 19, 2011.

247 one company even taking the ashes of a woman's late husband: Andrew Martin, "Banks Accused of Illegally Breaking into Homes," *New York Times,* December 21, 2010.

247 making all their loan modification payments and still getting foreclosed: Carolyn Said, "Family Faces Foreclosure after Following the Rules," *San Francisco Chronicle,* November 25, 2010.

247 paid off her house and *then* got a default notice: Jon Yates, "Problem: Paying Off Mortgage Results in Default," *Chicago Tribune,* February 20, 2011.

247 conducting an eviction and finding a dead body: Kelli Cook, "Deputies Serving Eviction Notice Find Dead Body Inside Home," News 13 Orlando, February 17, 2011, available at https://web.archive.org/web/20110221193858/http://www.cfnews13.com/article/news/2011/february/209025/Body-found-along-with-suspicious-item-inside-Orlando-home.

247 one on children of foreclosure: Scott Pelley, "Homeless Children: The Hard Times Generation," *60 Minutes,* CBS News, June 20, 2011. Based on this post at *4closureFraud,* the story appears to have run that March: http://4closurefraud.org/2011/03/07/60-minutes-homeless-children-the-hard-times-generation.

247 and her segment, which aired on April 3: Scott Pelley, "The Next Housing Shock," *60 Minutes,* CBS News, April 3, 2011.

19. Wriggling off the Hook

250 Loeb Award for excellence in business reporting: "UCLA Anderson Announces 2012 Gerald Loeb Award Winners," press release, Anderson School of Management, UCLA, June 26, 2012.

250 Lynn got the case dismissed: Michael Redman, "Victory | Our 60 Minutes Hero, Lynn Szymoniak, had Her Foreclosure Case Dismissed," 4closurefraud.org, April 5, 2011.

250 everyone had the name Linda Green: Michael Redman, "Another Successful Foreclosure Fraud Happy Hour," 4closurefraud.org, April 22, 2011.

252 O'Brien contacted state attorney general Martha Coakley: John Carney, "The MERS Wars Heat Up in Massachusetts," CNBC, November 30, 2010; Jenifer B. McKim, "Firm May Skirt Millions in Property Fees," *Boston Globe*, December 15, 2010; "O'Brien Calls on MERS to Come Clean and Pay Up: Says Essex County Owed $22 Million Dollars," press release, February 22, 2011, available at www.foreclosurehamlet .org/profiles/blogs/deadbeat-mers-to-be-billed-22.

252 "I believe the banks' actions speak louder than words": David Dayen, "Register of Deeds John O'Brien Releases Forensic Study, Finds Mass Fraud in Foreclosure Docs," FDL News, June 30, 2011, http://shadowproof.com/2011/06/30/register-of-deeds -john-obrien-releases-forensic-study-finds-mass-fraud-in-foreclosure-docs.

253 Thigpen and O'Brien drafted an open letter: "Register of Deeds Jeff Thigpen (NC) and John O'Brien (MA) Ask 50 State Attorney General Foreclosure Work Group to Require All Past and Present MERS Assignments to Be Filed!" press release, April 7, 2011, available at http://myemail.constantcontact.com/MEDIA-RELEASE-Register-of -Deeds-Thigpen—NC—and-O-Brien—MASS—Letter-to-Iowa-AG-Miller-and-50 -State-Attorney-Generals-Foreclos.html?soid=1100673877654&aid=3bL0Fyi43yE.

253 "a betrayal of public trust": WGHP-TV, Greensboro, "Thousands of Guilford Mortgage Documents Could Be Fraudulent, County Officials Say," May 4, 2011, available at https://web.archive.org/web/20110507073044/http://www.myfox8.com/news /wghp-story-guilford-mortgage-fraud-110504,0,379574.story; David McLaughlin, "BofA, Wells Fargo Mortgage Papers Challenged in North Carolina," *Bloomberg Business*, May 4, 2011.

253 the whole thing would cost $20 billion to $30 billion: Nick Timiraos, Dan Fitzpatrick, and Ruth Simon, "U.S. Pushes Mortgage Deal," *Wall Street Journal*, February 24, 2011.

253 "a good deal of fraud": Charles Jaco, "Missouri Foreclosure Fraud: Some Say the Entire System Is Broken," KTVI-Fox2Now, March 17, 2011, available at https://web .archive.org/web/20110321075547/http://www.fox2now.com/ktvi-foreclosure-fraud -missouri-31711,0,7746033.story.

253 The proposed settlement sounded like HAMP 2.0: Marcy Wheeler, "HAMP II: The $20 Billion Get Out of Jail Free Card," Emptywheel, February 23, 2011.

253 "I really feel I shouldn't talk": Matt Stoller, "AG Tom Miller Negotiating in Secret With Banks over Whether to Put Bankers in Jail," Roosevelt Institute, February 26, 2011.

254 "settlement term sheet": David McLaughlin, "Foreclosure Settlement Terms Sent to Banks by U.S., States," *Bloomberg Business*, March 4, 2011.

254 "Without CRIMINAL INDICTMENTS, there is no settlement": Michael Redman, "50 State Attorney General 27 Page 'Settlement' on Fraudclosures," 4closure-fraud.org, March 7, 2011.

254 They described a tension between doing something quickly: David Dayen, "Democratic Attorneys General Question Unclear, Rushed Mortgage Servicer

Settlement," FDL News, March 24, 2011, http://shadowproof.com/2011/03/24/democratic -attorneys-general-question-unclear-rushed-mortgage-servicer-settlement.

254 **That vaunted interagency review . . . concluded:** Testimony of John Walsh, acting comptroller of the currency, Senate Banking Committee, February 17, 2011, 13– 17, available at www.propublica.org/documents/item/testimony-of-occs-john-walsh -feb-17-2011.

254 **2,800 loan files . . . 100 foreclosures:** Yves Smith, "Feds Reviewed Only 100 Foreclosure Files in Servicer Whitewash," *Naked Capitalism*, May 14, 2011.

254 **"critical deficiencies":** Testimony of John Walsh, 15.

255 **JPMorgan acted swiftly, firing the executive:** Dawn Kopecki, "JPMorgan Ousts Home-Lending Chief After Foreclosure Lapses," *Bloomberg Business*, June 14, 2011; Associated Press, "JPMorgan to Make Amends with Military Clients," February 15, 2011.

255 **this was "camo-washing":** David Dayen, "Camo-Washing: BofA Offers Principal Reduction Program for Service Members," FDL News, March 10, 2011, http:// shadowproof.com/2011/03/10/camo-washing-bofa-offers-principal-reduction -program-for-service-members.

255 **the Office of the Comptroller of the Currency and the Federal Reserve:** Board of Governors of the Federal Reserve System, press release, April 13, 2011, www .federalreserve.gov/newsevents/press/enforcement/20110413a.htm.

255 **guilty parties in charge of determining their own punishment:** David Dayen, "A Slap on the Wrist for Mortgage Fraud," *American Prospect*, April 15, 2011.

255 **Page 3: "The reviews showed":** Lisa Epstein, "Federal Banking Regulators Expose Massive Mortgage Backed Securities Fraud as Part of Fraudclosure Investigation?" *Foreclosure Hamlet*, April 14, 2011.

256 *In re Wilson:* Memorandum Opinion, *In re Wilson*, United States Bankruptcy Court, Eastern District of Louisiana, Case No. 07-11862, filed April 7, 2011, available at www.scribd.com/doc/52867919/In-Re-Wilson-Memorandum-Opinion-07-Apr-2011.

256 *Veal v. American Home Mortgage Servicing:* Opinion, *Veal v. American Home Mortgage Servicing et al.*, United States Bankruptcy Appellate Panel of the Ninth Circuit, BAP Nos. AZ-10-1055-MkKiJu and AZ-10-1056-MkKiJu, Appeal from the United States Bankruptcy Court for the District of Arizona, opinion filed June 10, 2011, http:// cdn.ca9.uscourts.gov/datastore/bap/2012/11/08/Veal-10-1055corr_06_10_2011.pdf.

256 *Horace v. LaSalle . . . Hendricks v. U.S. Bank:* Opinion and Order, *Phyllis Horace v. Lasalle Bank N.A.*, District Court of the United States for the Middle District of Alabama, Eastern Division, Civil Action No. 3:08cv1019-MHT, opinion filed February 17, 2009, http://law.justia.com/cases/federal/district-courts/alabama/almdce /3:2008cv01019/39791/32; Opinion and Order Denying in Part and Granting in Part Defendant's Motion for Summary Disposition and Granting Plaintiff's Motion for Summary Disposition, *James Hendricks v. U.S. Bank, N.A.*, State of Michigan, Washtenaw County Trial Court, Case No. 10-849-CH, June 6, 2011, available at www.scribd .com/doc/57374561/Hendricks-v-U-S-Bank.

256 Bank of New York v. Silverberg: Opinion of the Court, *Bank of New York v. Silverberg*, Supreme Court of the State of New York, Appellate Division, Second Judicial Department, Case No. 2010-00131, decided on June 7, 2011, www.courts.state.ny .us/Reporter/3dseries/2011/2011_05002.htm.

256 David J. Stern gave up: Letter from David J. Stern to Chief Judge, March 4, 2011, available at www.scribd.com/doc/50227529/Letter-From-David-J-Stern-to-Chief -Judge.

256 Ben-Ezra & Katz: Kimberly Miller, "Ben-Ezra and Katz to Close Foreclosure Business, Second South Florida Firm to Shut Its Foreclosure Operations," *Palm Beach Post*, April 28, 2011.

256 Stern, ultimately, was the deadbeat: Michael Redman, "Deadbeat | David J. Stern, Dethroned 'Foreclosure King' Does Not Pay His Bills," 4closurefraud.org, April 10, 2011.

256 Governor Rick Scott granted the judiciary a loan: Zach Carter, "'Awful' Florida Foreclosure Courts May Shut Down Due to GOP Budget Cuts," *Huffington Post*, May 19, 2011.

256 "too crowded": Lisa Epstein, "Foreclosure Hearings Closed to Public Despite FL Supreme Court Justice Canady's Order," *Foreclosure Hamlet*, May 6, 2011.

257 Chip Parker . . . Matt Weidner was also investigated: Julie Kay, "Lawyers Investigated for Criticizing System," *Daily Business Review*, May 18, 2011.

257 Bailiffs removed lawyer Mark Stopa: Mark Stopa, "Mark Stopa Thrown Out of Court (Literally)," *Stopa Law Blog*, April 20, 2011, www.stayinmyhome.com/blog /mark-stopa-thrown-out-of-court-literally.

257 Victor Tobin: Kimberly Miller, "Broward Chief Judge Resigns to Join So-Called 'Foreclosure Mill,'" *Palm Beach Post*, May 18, 2011.

257 140,000 foreclosure cases got cleared: Kimberly Miller, "Foreclosure Crisis: Fed-Up Judges Crack Down on Disorder in the Courts," *Palm Beach Post*, April 4, 2011.

257 Lee County judge James Thompson: Abigail Field, "The Foreclosure Mess: Florida Judges Can Do Better," *Daily Finance*, December 24, 2010; Abigail Field, "Florida Is Still Letting Banks Break the Rules in Foreclosure Cases," *Daily Finance*, January 5, 2011.

257 They filed an emergency motion to intervene: "ACLU Charges High-Speed Florida Foreclosure Courts Deprive Homeowners of Chance to Defend Homes," ACLU press release, April 7, 2011; Petition for Writ of Certiorari or Writ of Prohibition, *George E. Merrigan v. Bank of New York Mellon*, District Court of Appeal, State of Florida, Second District, Case No. 09-CA-055758, available at www.scribd.com/doc/52504270 (note that petitioner's name is Georgi Merrigan, but the circuit court erroneously referred to her as "George Merrigan").

257 denying the ACLU's request: "ACLU Calls for Immediate Reform of High-Speed Florida Foreclosure Courts," ACLU press release, June 27, 2011.

258 Citizen Warriors Radio taped Saturday mornings at eight o'clock: Michael Redman, "Warrior Lawyers | New Radio Show Saturdays from 8–10 am EDT with 4closureFraud.org and ForeclosureHamlet.org," 4closurefraud.org, May 6, 2011.

258 Federal authorities indicted Carol: Kimberly Miller, "Two More Indicted in Alleged Versailles Mortgage Fraud," *Palm Beach Post*, April 29, 2011.

259 "I find it very disturbing that the government must use": Ibid.

259 "He's just trying to save his job": Steve Dibert, "Foreclosure Attorney and Owner of 4closurefraud.org Indicted for Mortgage Fraud," Mortgage Fraud Investigations—Miami, April 30, 2011, http://mfi-miami.com/2011/04/foreclosure-attorney-owner-of-4closurefraud-org-indicted-for-mortgage-fraud.

260 The judge gave her two and a half years in prison: Martha Neil, "Lawyer Who Fought Foreclosure Fraud Takes Federal Plea in Straw-Buyer Money-Laundering Conspiracy," *American Bar Association Journal*, October 12, 2011; Kimberly Miller, "'God-Fearing' Former Lawyer Will Serve 2½ Years in Prison for Versailles Mortgage Scam," *Palm Beach Post*, November 19, 2011.

260 Attorney general Pam Bondi settled: Michael Redman, "Marshall C. Watson | Florida Attorney General Pam Bondi Settles Investigation Against One of Florida's Largest Foreclosure Firms," 4closurefraud.org, March 25, 2011.

260 fifty-state settlement without monetary penalties: Kimberly Miller, "Bondi Voices Concern over Home Loan Reductions," *Palm Beach Post*, March 23, 2011.

260 "triggering a nationwide review": Kimberly Miller, "Florida Fraud Report Key to New York Foreclosure Case," *Palm Beach Post*, July 16, 2011.

261 "It came from the top. Tallahassee didn't give me a reason": Stefan Kamph, "June Clarkson and Theresa Edwards Were Fired After Revealing Widespread Foreclosure Fraud," *Broward/Palm Beach New Times*, June 21, 2012.

261 Joe Jacquot . . . Mary Leontakianakos: Ibid.

261 But she landed with foreclosure mill Shapiro and Fishman: Michael Redman, "Erin Collins Cullaro | Fired Assistant Attorney General to Pam Bondi Joins 'Foreclosure Mill' Shapiro and Fishman," May 27, 2011, 4closurefraud.org.

261 Then her spokesperson issued a statement: Kathleen Haughney, "Florida Attorney General, Two Fired Lawyers in Public Dispute," Orlando *Sun-Sentinel*, July 21, 2011.

261 As Clarkson and Edwards found out: Letter from Andrew Spark, Assistant Attorney General, Tampa Economic Crimes, August 8, 2011, available at www.tampabay.com/specials/2011/PDFs/bondi081811/sparkletter.pdf.

261 Lisa requested a formal review: Michael Redman, "Dissecting the Pam Bondi/Jeff Atwater Inspector General Report re June Clarkson, Theresa Edwards and Lisa Epstein," 4closurefraud.org, January 9, 2012, http://4closurefraud.org/2012/01/09/dissecting-the-pam-bondi-jeff-atwater-inspector-general-report-re-june-clarkson-theresa-edwards-and-lisa-epstein/

261 Public interest group Progress Florida echoed that demand: David Dayen, "Update on the Investigators Fired by Florida's AG for Pursuing Foreclosure Fraud," FDL News, July 28, 2011, http://shadowproof.com/2011/07/28/update-on-the-investigators-fired-by-floridas-ag-for-pursuing-foreclosure-fraud.

262 including on Citizen Warriors Radio: Michael Redman, "Citizen Warriors Exclusive Part Deux | Former Bondi Assistant Attorneys General & Foreclosure Fraud Investigators June Clarkson & Theresa Edwards Live on WDJA 1420AM Saturday from 8–10 am EDT," 4closurefraud.org, August 5, 2011.

262 Bondi agreed to have the inspector general: Catherine Whittenburg, "Bondi Wants Probe on Firings," *Tampa Tribune*, August 3, 2011.

262 It was a petty tactic to harass the family into silence: Zach Carter, "Deutsche Bank Sues Foreclosure Fraud Expert's Son with No Financial Interest in Her Case," *Huffington Post*, May 13, 2011.

262 the IRS acknowledging an "active review" of REMIC practices: Scot Paltrow, "Exclusive: IRS Weighs Tax Penalties on Mortgage Securities," Reuters, April 27, 2011.

262 When Yves broached REMICs: Yves Smith, "IRS Likely to Expand Mortgage Industry Coverup by Whitewashing REMIC Violations," *Naked Capitalism*, April 28, 2011.

262 "backdoor bailout of the financial system": Paltrow, "Exclusive: IRS Weighs Tax Penalties."

20. The Final Whitewash

264 "Boy, I wish I could've done that": "Ocwen—Delivery of Modification Package and Petition by Bermuda Triangle Recovery Services," posted by Michael Redman, October 19, 2011, https://www.youtube.com/watch?v=8ZviWlPbcOE.

264 Dixie did get a modification: Michael Redman, "Victory | National Campaign Pressures Ocwen Financial to Modify Dixie Mitchell's Loan," 4closurefraud .org, October 24, 2011.

265 born from a suggestion in the Canadian magazine *Adbusters*: "#OCCU-PYWALLSTREET," *Adbusters*, July 13, 2011.

265 "We have no leverage": "AG Eric Schneiderman Opposes Foreclosure Deal," Rochester *Democrat and Chronicle*, June 28, 2011.

266 the beating heart of securitization FAIL: Gretchen Morgenson, "Two States Ask if Paperwork in Mortgage Bundling Was Complete," *New York Times*, June 12, 2011.

266 "Please everyone, we must support this man": Michael Redman, "Dismissal of NY Attorney General Schneiderman Shows Obama Administration and Iowa AG Miller Poised to Let Big Banks off the Hook for Mortgage Fraud," 4closurefraud.org, August 25, 2011.

266 "actively worked to undermine": Brady Dennis, "N.Y. Bumped from 50-State Foreclosure Committee," *Washington Post*, August 23, 2011.

266 "Wall Street is our Main Street": Gretchen Morgenson, "Attorney General of N.Y. Is Said to Face Pressure on Bank Foreclosure Deal," *New York Times*, August 21, 2011.

266 hosting tea-and-cookies settlement talks: Dina ElBoghdady, "Shaun Donovan on Confronting Hurricanes, Homelessness and Big Banks," *Washington Post*, June 11, 2014.

266 everyone would benefit from a speedy resolution: Morgenson, "Attorney General of N.Y. Is Said to Face Pressure."

266 all had active foreclosure investigations in their states: David McLaughlin, "Foreclosure-Deal Releases Draw State Resistance Amid Probes," *Bloomberg Business*, July 26, 2011; David McLaughlin, "Nevada Joins States Balking at Releases in Foreclosure Practices Deal," *Bloomberg Business*, August 16, 2011.

266 "that has not been investigated": David Dayen, "Minnesota AG Swanson Backs Schneiderman: No Settlement with the Banks Without Investigation," FDL News, September 13, 2011, http://shadowproof.com/2011/09/13/minnesota-ag-swanson-backs-schneiderman-no-settlement-with-the-banks-without-investigation.

266 "immunity against the banks": David Dayen, "Kentucky AG Conway Joins Growing Coalition Backing Schneiderman on Foreclosure Fraud," FDL News, September 22, 2011, http://shadowproof.com/2011/09/22/kentucky-ag-conway-joins-growing-coalition-backing-schneiderman-on-foreclosure-fraud.

267 Californians for a Fair Settlement: Alejandro Lazo, "Kamala Harris Pressured to Reject Bank Foreclosure Settlement," *Los Angeles Times*, September 30, 2011.

267 "inadequate for California homeowners": David Dayen, "California AG Kamala Harris Rejects Foreclosure Fraud Settlement," FDL News, September 30, 2011, http://shadowproof.com/2011/09/30/california-ag-kamala-harris-rejects-foreclosure-fraud-settlement.

267 JPMorgan Chase's headquarters has a moat: Betsy Dillner, "Storming the JPMorgan Chase Castle," Alliance for a Just Society, May 20, 2011, http://allianceforajustsociety.org/2011/05/storming-the-jp-morgan-chase-castle.

267 make it painful for banks to toss people into the street: Mike Konczal, "The Sword and the Shield: Occupy Foreclosures," *Rortybomb*, October 19, 2011, https://rortybomb.wordpress.com/2011/10/19/the-sword-and-the-shield-occupy-foreclosures.

267 a tactic they called a "live-in": Michael Redman, "Take Back the Land | Rochester Liberates Home, Moves Lennon Back into House," 4closurefraud.org, May 10, 2011.

268 Occupiers mobilized to defend those homes: Zaid Jilani, "Movers and Sheriff's Deputies Refuse Bank's Order to Evict 103-Year-Old Atlanta Woman," *ThinkProgress*, November 30, 2011; Zaid Jilani, "Occupy Cleveland Saves Woman's Home from Imminent Foreclosure," *ThinkProgress*, November 15, 2011; Micah Uetricht, "Occupy Minneapolis Occupies Second Foreclosed Home as Housing Occupations Spread," *ThinkProgress*, November 22, 2011; Kari Huus, "Homeowner Taps 'Occupy' Protest to Avoid Foreclosure," MSNBC.com, October 17, 2011.

268 "This is a shift from protesting Wall Street": Justin Elliott, "Occupy's Next Frontier: Foreclosed Homes," *Salon*, November 30, 2011.

268 Lisa organized two events: Lisa Epstein, "December 6th National Day of Action Against Foreclosures—Occupy Our Homes," *Foreclosure Hamlet*, December 5, 2011.

268 In the evening, protesters lit candles: Lisa Epstein, "Video—Occupy Our Homes National Day of Action Dec 6, 2011—Palm Beach County Fraudclosure Candlelight Vigil," *Foreclosure Hamlet*, December 7, 2011.

268 Other Occupy Our Homes groups were more aggressive: Occupy Our Homes, "National Day of Action to Stop and Reverse Foreclosures," December 6, 2011, www.occupyourhomes.org/blog/2011/dec/6/national-day-action-stop-and-reverse-foreclosures; Alain Sherter, "Occupy Wall Street, Homeowners Ally to Fight Foreclosures," CBS News, October 25, 2011; Zaid Jilani, "Occupy Atlanta Encamps in Neighborhood to Save Police Officer's Home from Foreclosure," *ThinkProgress*, November 8, 2011.

268 Rose Gudiel: Huus, "Homeowner Taps 'Occupy' Protest."

268 Beth Sommerer: Jilani, "Occupy Cleveland Saves Woman's Home."

268 Vita Lee: Jilani, "Movers and Sheriff's Deputies Refuse Bank's Order."

268 Bobby Hull: Steve Frank, "Former Marine's Home Saved from Foreclosure," MSNBC.com, February 27, 2012.

269 Rose Parade float: David Dayen, "Occupy the Rose Parade: Working Through the Next Stage of the Occupy Movement," FDL News, January 1, 2012, http://shadow proof.com/2012/01/01/occupy-the-rose-parade-working-through-the-next-stage-of -the-occupy-movement.

269 Nevada, where three out of every five homeowners: Samuel Weigley and Michael Sauter, "States with the Most Homes Underwater," NBC News, July 26, 2012.

270 he recognized the depth of the problem: J. Patrick Collican, "Housing Scam Artists Staying on the Move," *Las Vegas Sun*, September 25, 2009.

270 "Bank of America misrepresented": *Never should have represented they could*: State of Nevada's Second Amended Complaint, *State of Nevada v. Bank of America Corporation et al.*, United States District Court, District of Nevada, Case No. 3:11cv-00135-RCJ (RAM), filed August 30, 2011, available at http://graphics8.nytimes .com/packages/pdf/business/SecondAmendedComplaint.pdf.

271 employees from the Vegas LPS office, including Tracy Lawrence: Tracy Lawrence's story taken from grand jury testimony, *State of Nevada v. Gary Trafford and Gerri Sheppard*, Eighth Judicial District Court, Clark County, Nevada, Case No. 11AG3037AB, taken November 8–9, 2011, available at www.scribd.com/doc /75153635/Transcript-Day-1, www.scribd.com/doc/75153619/Transcript-Day-2.

271 "Regarding the signature of my name": Ibid., day 1 transcript, 151.

271 Trafford replied affirmatively: Ibid., day 1 transcript, 153.

272 "I didn't really think about it": Ibid., day 1 transcript, 166.

272 606 counts of signing documents: Indictment, *State of Nevada v. Gary Trafford and Gerri Sheppard*, Eighth Judicial District Court, Clark County, Nevada, November 16, 2011, available at www.scribd.com/doc/72962780/Indictment.

272 **"the signing procedures on some of these documents were flawed":** "LPS Responds to Nevada Attorney General Announcement," press release, PRNewswire, November 17, 2011.

272 **When police reached Tracy's apartment, they found her dead:** "Foreclosure Fraud Whistleblower Found Dead," MSNBC.com, November 29, 2011; Mark Ames, "Tracy Lawrence: The Foreclosure Suicide America Forgot," The eXiled, August 23, 2012, http://exiledonline.com/tracy-lawrence-the-foreclosure-suicide-america-forgot.

273 **they had other notaries from the Vegas office:** Ken Ritterthe, "Three More Nevada Notaries Charged in Foreclosure Fraud Case," Associated Press, December 5, 2011.

273 **suing LPS for document fraud:** David Dayen, "Nevada AG Masto Sues LPS for Document Fraud," FDL News, December 16, 2011, http://shadowproof.com/2011/12/16/nevada-ag-masto-sues-lps-for-document-fraud.

273 **"Sharon Bullington may lose her home":** Mark Puente, "Pasco Couple Fear Losing Home to Foreclosure for Paying Mortgage Too Early," *Tampa Bay Times*, August 19, 2011.

274 **"Love, Your Broken Home":** Tim Miller, "Love, Your Broken Home," live studio recording uploaded by Tim Miller on May 14, 2010, https://www.youtube.com/watch?v=Hm_W445bidA.

274 **"It is premature to sign an agreement":** David Dayen, "Lawmakers, 'Fair Settlement' Coalitions Pressuring AGs on Foreclosure Fraud," FDL News, December 15, 2011,http://shadowproof.com/2011/12/15/lawmakers-fair-settlement-coalitions-pressuring-ags-on-foreclosure-fraud.

274 **"conducting foreclosures when the defendants lacked the right":** Complaint, *Commonwealth of Massachusetts v. Bank of America et al.*, Suffolk County Superior Court, Docket No. 11-4363, December 1, 2011, www.mass.gov/ago/docs/press/ag-complaint-national-banks.pdf.

274 **"We are disappointed that Massachusetts":** Diana Olick, "First Major State Lawsuit Filed over 'Robo-Signing,'" CNBC, December 1, 2011.

274–275 **released his report about the firing of June Clarkson and Theresa Edwards:** Florida Department of Financial Services Office of Inspector General, "Report of Inquiry Number 12312," January 6, 2012, available at https://www.scribd.com/doc/77393414/IG-Report-1.

275 **They were unprofessional:** Letter from Barry Richard to June Clarkson, March 12, 2010, available at www.scribd.com/fullscreen/66947197.

275 **According to the report, Lisa and Lynn leveraged:** Michael Redman and Lisa Epstein, "Bondi/Atwater Inspector General Report Fail | Pointing Out a Few of the Many IG Report Deficiencies," 4closurefraud.org, January 12, 2012.

276 **"may have used a couple of slides":** Ibid.; Florida Department of Financial Services Office of Inspector General, "Report of Inquiry Number 12312," January 6, 2012, available at www.scribd.com/doc/77393414/IG-Report-1.

276 **Richard Lawson told Scott Maxwell:** Scott Maxwell, "On Foreclosure Fraud, Pam Bondi Comes Up Short," *Orlando Sentinel*, December 20, 2011.

276 Lisa obtained confidential communications: Michael Redman and Lisa Epstein, "Public Records Request from FL AG Employees to LPS," 4closurefraud.org, September 22, 2011.

276 Michigan had issued more damaging criminal subpoenas: Lisa Epstein, "LPS/DocX: MI AG Opens Criminal Investigation. Frmr Dep. FL AG Jacquot Revolving Doors into LPS," *Foreclosure Hamlet*, June 16, 2011.

276 Sue Sanford from the Michigan AG's office": Abigail Field, "Meet Pam Bondi, Foreclosure Fraudsters BFF," Reality Check, January 10, 2012, available at https://web.archive.org/web/20120113202317/http://abigailcfield.com/?p=691.

276 "It's a simple cover-up": David Dayen, "IG Report Whitewashes Firing of Foreclosure Fraud Investigators in Florida," FDL News, January 9, 2012, http://shadowproof.com/2012/01/09/ig-report-whitewashes-firing-of-foreclosure-fraud-investigators-in-florida.

277 "Tonight, I'm asking my Attorney General": Remarks by the president in State of the Union Address, January 24, 2012, www.whitehouse.gov/the-press-office/2012/01/24/remarks-president-state-union-address.

278 why would they do it now?: David Dayen, "The Schneiderman Gambit: Financial Fraud Unit Appears Designed to Fail, and Grease Skids for Foreclosure Fraud Settlement," FDL News, January 25, 2012, http://shadowproof.com/2012/01/25/the-schneiderman-gambit-financial-fraud-unit-appears-designed-to-fail-and-grease-skids-for-foreclosure-fraud-settlement.

278 he would bolt in the showiest, most public way possible: David Dayen, "How the Schneiderman Panel Could Work," FDL News, January 26, 2012, http://shadowproof.com/2012/01/26/how-the-schneiderman-panel-could-work.

278 The Campaign for a Fair Settlement front organization fell in line: Dayen, "The Schneiderman Gambit."

278 state and federal regulators announced the National Mortgage Settlement: "Federal Government and State Attorneys General Reach $25 Billion Agreement with Five Largest Mortgage Servicers to Address Mortgage Loan Servicing and Foreclosure Abuses," press release, Department of Justice, February 9, 2012.

278 Forty-nine states joined, all but Oklahoma: Richard Mize, "Oklahoma Is Lone Maverick in National Mortgage Settlement Signed by 49 States," *Oklahoman*, February 10, 2012.

278 Eric Schneiderman said at the time: "AG Eric Schneiderman Opposes Foreclosure Deal."

279 Headlines touted the largest corporate payout: Brady Dennis and Sari Horwitz, "Settlement Launches Foreclosure Reckoning," *Washington Post*, February 10, 2012.

279 one million borrowers would get mortgage balances cut: Margaret Chadbourn and Aruna Viswanatha, "One Million Homeowners May Get Mortgage Writedowns: U.S.," Reuters, January 18, 2012.

280 violations of the False Claims Act: Rick Rothacker, "Whistleblowers Reap Millions in U.S. Mortgage Suits," Reuters, March 14, 2012.

280 **she would receive $18 million of that herself:** Alexander Eichler, "Lynn Szymoniak, Mortgage Victim, Receives $18 Million for Investigating Mortgage Crisis," *Huffington Post*, March 15, 2012.

21. Lisa's Last Stand

281 **"It's very satisfying to recover this money":** Zach Carter, "Lynn Szymoniak, Foreclosure Activist, Says $18 Million Doesn't Make Up for Homeowners' Harms," *Huffington Post*, March 20, 2012

281 **Deutsche Bank removed Mark Elliot from the case:** Zach Carter, "Bank Drops Legal Pressure on Foreclosure Fraud Expert's Family," *Huffington Post*, June 13, 2011.

282 **Akerman said they wanted to depose pool maintenance staff:** Kimberly Miller, "Pool Guy, Landscaper of $18 Million Foreclosure Winner Subpoenaed," *Palm Beach Post*, March 27, 2012.

283 **"failing to maintain accurate account statements":** Complaint, *United States et al. v. Bank of America Corporation et al.*, United States District Court for the District of Columbia, Case No. 1:12-cv-00361-RMC, filed March 14, 2012, 22, available at https://d9klfgibkcquc.cloudfront.net/Complaint_Corrected_2012-03-14.pdf.

283 **thirty-five of those cases:** Office of Inspector General, U.S. Department of Housing and Urban Development, "JPMorgan Chase Bank N.A. Foreclosure and Claims Process Review, Columbus, OH," Memorandum No. 2012-CH-1801, March 12, 2012, 8, available at https://www.hudoig.gov/sites/default/files/documents/audit-reports//2012-ch-1801.pdf.

283 **"pay what you can" corporate penalties:** Aruna Viswanatha, "Government Details Mortgage Pact, Promises Tough Oversight," Reuters, March 12, 2012.

283 **nearly half the penalty—over $1 billion:** Pamela M. Prah, "States Used Mortgage Settlement Money to Balance Budgets," *USA Today*, October 8, 2013.

284 **The settlement codified predatory servicing:** Consent Judgment, *United States of America et al. v. Bank of America et al.*, United States District Court for the District of Columbia, Case No. 1:12-cv-00361-RMC, filed April 4, 2012, E-4, E-5, E-8–E-12, E1-1–E1-14. Each of the five mortgage servicers in the National Mortgage Settlement agreed to a separate consent judgment, but the language on threshold error rates in all of them is the same.

284 **folded into the settlement:** "Notice of Anticipated Settlement by Petitioner Attorney General Mike DeWine," *Ohio v. GMAC*, Supreme Court of Ohio, Case No. 2011-0890, filed February 6, 2012, available at http://www.sconet.state.oh.us/pdf_viewer/pdf_viewer.aspx?pdf=701829.pdf; "Attorney General Masto Announces Two Historic Mortgage Servicing Foreclosure Settlements," press release, Office of the Attorney General, Nevada, February 9, 2012.

284 **Eric Schneiderman filed a last-minute suit:** Ruth Simon and Nick Timiraos, "New York to Settle Some Mortgage Claims with 5 Banks," *Wall Street Journal*, March 13, 2012.

284 Martha Coakley got only $2.7 million: "Four National Banks to Pay $2.7 Million to Massachusetts over Unlawful Foreclosures," press release, Office of Attorney General, Massachusetts, January 16, 2015.

284 $350,000 settlement with Nationwide Title Clearing: Final Consent Decree, *People of the State of Illinois v. Nationwide Title Clearing*, Circuit Court of Cook County, Illinois, County Department, Chancery Division, Case No. 12-CH-03602, filed December 11, 2013, available at http://stopforeclosurefraud.com/2013/12/13/the -people-of-the-state-of-illinois-v-nationwide-title-clearing-inc-final-consent-decree -alleging-violated-the-consumer-fraud-act-and-the-uniform-deceptive-trade -practices-act.

284 Beau Biden settled with MERS for $0: "Biden Secures Reforms from National Mortgage Registry," press release, Delaware.gov, July 13, 2012. See also David Dayen, "Delaware AG Biden Settlement with MERS Promises Reforms Already Pledged," FDL News, July 13, 2012, http://shadowproof.com/2012/07/13/delaware-ag -biden-settlement-with-mers-promises-reforms-already-pledged.

284 The facts came out in an affidavit provided to the court: Affidavit of John P. Kelleher, State of Nevada, County of Clark, December 2012, available at http://nevada journal.com/assets/uploads/2013/02/affidavit-of-john-p.pdf.

284 a notice of default taped to Kelleher's door: Steven Miller, "AG Covered Up Conflict of Interest in Robo-Signing Case, Says Brief," *Nevada Journal*, November 29, 2012.

284 The judge dismissed the charges against Trafford and Sheppard entirely: Ken Ritter, "Judge Tosses Mortgage 'Robosigning' Case in Vegas," Associated Press, February 26, 2013.

284 "complete embarrassment": Kyle Gillis, "New Robo-Signing Brief: Misconduct by AG Masto's Office Could 'Seriously Damage Public Confidence' in That Office," *Nevada Journal*, February 25, 2013.

285 "When we first got involved in the case": Brian Mahoney, "How They Won It: Irell Unravels Nevada Robosigning Case," Law360, April 1, 2013.

285 Curtis Hertel, a register of deeds: *Hertel v. Bank of America N.A. et al*, Thirtieth Circuit Court, Ingham County, Michigan, Case No. 11-687-CZ, filed June 22, 2011. The case was eventually moved to U.S. District Court, Western District of Michigan, on July 22, 2011. Opinion in the U.S. District Court case available at https://scholar .google.com/scholar_case?case=2806553639914624068.

285 Thigpen had just sued MERS: Complaint and Motion for Appointment of a Special Master and for Injunctive Relief, *Guilford County ex rel. Jeff Thigpen v. Lender Processing Services et al.*, General Court of Justice, Superior Court Division, Guilford County, North Carolina, Case No. 12-CVS-4531, filed March 14, 2012, available at www.scribd.com/doc/85343328/Guilford-Complaint. Case dismissed on May 29, 2013: www.ncbusinesscourt.net/opinions/2013_NCBC_30.pdf.

286 Palm Beach County had 1.3 million residents: United States Census Bureau Quick Facts, http://quickfacts.census.gov/qfd/states/12/12099.html.

286 So she announced her intent to run: George Bennett, "Redistricting Could Pit Several Incumbent Palm Beach County State Legislators Against Each Other," *Palm Beach Post*, March 18, 2012.

287 a case management contract with a division of LPS: "Florida Court Selects LPS Case Management Software," MortgageOrb, June 26, 2009, www.mortgageorb.com/e107_plugins/content/content.php?content.3769; "LPS' Largest Implementation of ShowCase® Court Case Management System to Date in Palm Beach County, Fla.," LPS press release, PRNewswire, March 14, 2012.

287 LPS gave Sharon a maximum-level contribution: Florida Department of State, Division of Elections, Campaign Treasurer's Report Summary, Sharon R. Bock for Clerk of the Circuit Court, covering period from 1/1/2012–3/31/2012, 5, 10.

288 other activists, inspired by her run, started their own campaigns: Ryan Grim and Arthur Delaney, "Foreclosure Victims Aim to Take over County Courthouses," *Huffington Post*, May 2, 2012.

290 "our public land records have been defiled": "Lisa Epstein Clerk of Court Channel 12 Interview," WPEC-12 TV, uploaded June 14, 2012, https://www.youtube.com/watch?v=9jr8hvOfgwI.

290 "damage Lisa Epstein as the voice of the dispossessed": George Bennett, "PBC Races Are Drawn: Bock, Vana, Negron All Draw Late Challenges," *Palm Beach Post*, June 8, 2012.

290 Lynn bought a Buick: Karen Weise, "Mortgage Fraud Whistle-Blower Lynn Szymoniak Exposed Robosigning's Sins," *Bloomberg BusinessWeek*, September 12, 2013.

291 Foreclosure filings rose 85 percent: Kimberly Miller, "Foreclosures, Repos up from Last Year in South Florida," *Palm Beach Post*, April 12, 2012.

292 It was the 274th and final docket entry: Docket report, *Deutsche Bank v. Lynn Szymoniak*, Clerk and Comptroller, Palm Beach County, available at http://courtcon.co.palm-beach.fl.us/pls/jiwp/ck_public_qry_doct.cp_dktrpt_frames?backto=P&case_id=502008CA022258XXXXMB&begin_date=&end_date=.

292 Steve Dibert trashed Lisa as "a joke": Steve Dibert, "Yves Smith's Plea for Votes for Lisa Epstein Puts a Serious Bite into Her Credibility," Mortgage Fraud Investigations—Miami, August 10, 2012, http://mfi-miami.com/2012/08/is-yves-smith-at-naked-capitalism-sniffing-glue.

293 the *Palm Beach Post*, which had endorsed Sharon Bock: Rhonda Swan, "Editorial: Bock for Clerk of Court," *Palm Beach Post*, July 25, 2012.

293 Three clerks were under criminal investigation: Daphne Duret, "West Palm Beach Woman's Arrest Reveals Clerk's Office Probe Focused on 1,000-Plus Missing Oxycodone Pills," *Palm Beach Post*, August 21, 2012.

293 Michael accused the *Post* of sitting on the story: Michael Redman, "Well, Wouldn't Ya Know . . . PBC Clerk Sharon Bock's Office Criminal Arrest Reveals Probe Focused on 1,000-Plus Stolen Oxycodone Pills from Evidence Department," 4closure-fraud.org, August 21, 2012.

293 Lisa was proud to have received 27,003 votes: Palm Beach County Supervisor of Elections, primary election results, August 14, 2012, available at http://results.enr.clarityelections.com/FL/Palm_Beach/41045/96143/en/summary.html.

293 Leticia Arias was a known robo-signer: Release of Mortgage Lien, Clerk of Palm Beach County Public Records, book 26197, page 1091, recorded July 22, 2013. Sampling of Leticia Arias documents via Lisa Epstein, "Pigs Ass: A Sampler of Ocwen Documents (Leticia Arias Notary Examples)," *Foreclosure Hamlet*, November 16, 2010.

Epilogue

294 the Housing Justice Foundation: Official website at http://thjf.org.

294 SunTrust, a regional bank that paid fines: Michael Corkery and Jessica Silver-Greenberg, "SunTrust Settles with Justice Dept. over Mortgages; Talks Continue for Citigroup and Bank of America," *New York Times*, June 17, 2014.

295 Brent Bentrim: *Brent E. Bentrim v. Wells Fargo Bank*, County of Charleston, South Carolina, Court of Common Pleas, Ninth Judicial Circuit, Case No. 2011-CP-10-2946, series of filings in the case available at http://imgweb.charlestoncounty.org/CMSOBView/Service1.asmx/StreamDocAsPDF?viewertype=cms&ctagency=10002&casenumber=2011CP1002946&docseq=P2A14, case docket at http://jcmsweb.charlestoncounty.org/PublicIndex/CaseDetails.aspx?CourtAgency=10003&Casenum=2011CP1002946&CaseType=V&Org=CR&AspxAutoDetectCookieSupport=1; Yves Smith, "Repeated Foreclosures on an On-Time Borrower Demonstrate Failure to Fix Servicing and Fallacy of 'Save Banks at All Costs' Policy," *Naked Capitalism*, June 17, 2014.

295 Abby Lopez: *HSBC Bank v. Abby Lopez*, Circuit Court of the Fifteenth Judicial Circuit in and for Palm Beach County, Florida, Civil Division, Case No. 50-2009-CA-0304030XXMBAW. Emails posted at 4closurefraud.org, "Lender Processing Services (LPS) Internal Email Accidentally Leaked in a Fraudclosure Case," April 24, 2012. The Florida First Amendment Foundation filed motions to prevent the purge of the emails from the court record; its filing is available at http://floridafaf.org/files/2012/12/HSBC-v-Lopez---Motion-for-In-Camera-Hearing-attachment-2.pdf.

295 Phoenix Light v. JPMorgan Chase: Complaint, *Phoenix Light v. JPMorgan Chase*, Supreme Court of the State of New York, County of New York, September 4, 2013, available at www.scribd.com/doc/165380406/Phoenix.

295 A 2012 case against Barclays Bank: Consolidated Complaint, *HSH Nordbank et al. v. Barclays Bank*, Supreme Court of the State of New York, County of New York, Index No. 652678/2011, filed April 2, 2012, available at www.labaton.com/en/cases/upload/HSH-v-Barclays-Consolidated-Complaint.pdf.

296 "some of the least ethical behavior on Wall Street wasn't illegal": Interview with President Obama, *60 Minutes*, CBS News, December 11, 2011, transcript p. 8, www.cbsnews.com/news/interview-with-president-obama-the-full-transcript/8.

297 "This Assignment of Mortgage was inadvertently not recorded": Second Amended Complaint, *United States of America ex rel. Lynn E. Szymoniak v. American Home Mortgage Servicing et al.*, United States District Court, District of South

Carolina, Rock Hill Division, Case No. 10-cv-01465-JFA, 47, available at http://matt weidnerlaw.com/wp-content/uploads/2013/08/complaint-symoniak-false-claimS.C. -Second-Amended-Complaint-ECF-3.pdf.

297 the Justice Department declined to intervene: Jef Feeley and David McLaughlin, "Mortgage Whistleblower Stands Alone as U.S. Won't Join Lawsuit," *Bloomberg Business,* April 27, 2014.

297 Judge Joseph Anderson threw out most of the case: Order, *United States of America ex rel. Lynn E. Szymoniak v. American Home Mortgage Servicing et al.,* United States District Court, District of South Carolina, Rock Hill Division, Case No. 10-cv-01465-JFA, filed May 12, 2014, available at https://casetext.com/case/united-states-ex -rel-szymoniak-v-am-home-mortg-servicing.

297–298 Lynn kept alive a sliver of the case: Notice of Appeal, *United States of America ex rel. Lynn E. Szymoniak v. American Home Mortgage Servicing et al.,* United States District Court, District of South Carolina, Rock Hill Division, Case No. 10-cv-01465-JFA, filed June 26, 2015.

298 Damian said Lynn stole his research: Complaint and Demand for Jury Trial, *Figueroa v. Szymoniak,* Seventeenth Judicial Circuit, in and for Broward County, filed March 4, 2013, available at www.scribd.com/doc/168544786/Figueroa-v-Szymoniak; Martin Andelman, "Some of Lynn Szymoniak's Millions May Belong to Someone Else," *Mandelman Matters* (blog), September 16, 2013.

298 Damian, whose class action suits against the banks were all dismissed: Per Curiam Opinion, *Figueroa v. Merscorp, Inc.,* United States Court of Appeals for the Eleventh Circuit, Case No. 11-10984, May 11, 2012, available at https://casetext.com /case/figueroa-v-merscorp-inc.

298 That line is the essence of Damian's argument: Complaint and Demand for Jury Trial, *Figueroa v. Szymoniak,* 5.

299 just 83,000 homeowners received a first-lien principal reduction: David Dayen, "Just 83,000 Homeowners Get First-Lien Principal Reduction from National Mortgage Settlement, 90 Percent Less than Promised," *Naked Capitalism,* March 19, 2014. Total first-lien mortgage modifications (less "conditional" forgiveness, which can be withheld, and "180DPD forgiveness," which extinguishes a loan that is unrecoverable): Bank of America 30,609, JPMorgan Chase 18,114, Citi 10,296, Wells Fargo 23,428, Ally Bank (known post-bankruptcy as ResCap) 1,149, for a total of 83,596.

299 Donovan touted over $50 billion in tangible benefits: Shaun Donovan, "Mortgage Settlement Begins to Deliver," *Politico,* June 21, 2013.

299 Servicers received credit for "forgiving" debt already discharged: Shahien Nasiripour, "US Mortgage Bond Investors Take Large Hit," *Financial Times,* November 15, 2012; Gretchen Morgenson, "How to Erase a Debt That Isn't There," *New York Times,* September 29, 2012.

299 this supposed "gift" to homeowners had no material value: David Dayen, "IRS Confirms That $12 Billion in 'Mortgage Relief' in National Mortgage Settlement Completely Worthless," *Naked Capitalism,* November 18, 2013.

299 an insulting $1,480, less than two months' rent: $1,480 figure via the Joint State-Federal National Mortgage Servicing Settlement FAQ, www.national mortgagesettlement.com/faq.

299 Oklahoma . . . set up a mortgage fund: Cary Aspinwall and Casey Smith, "Facing Foreclosure: Oklahoma Goes Its Own Way in Facing the Foreclosure Mess," *Tulsa World*, October 20, 2013. It should be noted that the Oklahoma program has helped significantly fewer borrowers, as the state tried to make subjective determinations of harm, which limited payouts. But each homeowner received an average of $11,173, according to the Oklahoma attorney general.

300 The other big settlement: Yves Smith, *Whistleblowers Reveal How Bank of America Defrauded Homeowners and Paid for a Cover Up—All With the Help of "Regulators,"* self-published e-book based on an investigative series published at *Naked Capitalism*, available at http://econ4.org/wp-content/uploads/2013/04/Naked-Capitalism -Whistleblower-Report-on-Bank-of-America-Foreclosure-Reviews-12.pdf.

300 banks instead paying $3.6 billion in cash: "Amendments to Consent Orders Memorialize $9.3 Billion Foreclosure Agreement," press release, Office of the Comptroller of the Currency, February 28, 2013; Independent Foreclosure Review Payment Agreement Details, Office of the Comptroller of the Currency, www.occ.gov/news -issuances/news-releases/2013/nr-ia-2013-60a.pdf.

300 But robo-signing, document fraud, and predatory servicer abuse continue: Roger Lohse, "Couple's Paid-Off Home Foreclosed Mistakenly," WPLG-TV Miami/Fort Lauderdale, March 17, 2014; Matt Drange, Amy Julia Harris, and Elizabeth Wagner, "Error Claims Cast Doubt on Bank of America Foreclosures in Bay Area," KNTV-TV San Francisco, April 27, 2013.

300 no executive director, no offices, no phones, and no staff: Mike Gecan and Arnie Graff, "Obama's Mortgage Unit Is AWOL," New York *Daily News*, April 18, 2012.

300 "most of the investigative work": Robert Khuzami, testimony before House Financial Services Committee, May 17, 2012; David Dayen, "Waters Challenges Khuzami on Securitization Fraud Task Force, Gets Revealing Answers," FDL News, May 18, 2012, http://shadowproof.com/2012/05/18/waters-challenges-khuzami-on-securitiza tion-fraud-task-force-gets-revealing-answers.

300 the task force secured several headline-grabbing settlements: Ben Protess and Jessica Silver-Greenberg, "Tentative Deal Hands JPMorgan Chase a Record Penalty," *New York Times*, October 19, 2013; Aruna Viswanatha, "Citigroup to Pay $7 Billion to Settle U.S. Mortgage Probe," Reuters, July 14, 2014; Evan Perez, "Bank of America to Pay $16.65 Billion over Mortgages," CNNMoney, August 21, 2014.

300 a high "bullshit-to-cash" ratio: Yves Smith, "Bank Settlement Grade Inflation: High Bullshit to Cash Ratio in $17 Billion Bank of America Deal," *Naked Capitalism*, August 21, 2014.

301 the $37 billion fine looked more like $11 billion: David Dayen, "Tony West's Departure Ends Era of Pathetic Bank Settlements," *Naked Capitalism*, September 5, 2014.

301 Theresa and Joe Giudice: Karen Sudol, Todd South, and Chris Harris, "Despite Tearful Pleas, 'Real Housewives' Stars Joe, Teresa Giudice Sentenced to Prison," NorthJersey.com, October 2, 2014. Case was *United States of America v. Giuseppe & Teresa Giudice*, United States District Court, District of New Jersey, filed July 29, 2013, available at www.justice.gov/sites/default/files/usao-nj/legacy/2013/11/29/Guidice %2C%20Giuseppe%20and%20Teresa%20Indictment.pdf. "Stars of 'Real Housewives of New Jersey' Television Series Indicted on Fraud and Tax Charges," press release, U.S. Department of Justice, July 29, 2013, lists four agencies that worked on the case.

301 Lanny Breuer and Eric Holder: Katelyn Polantz, "Holder's Return to Covington Was Six Years in the Making," *National Law Journal*, July 5, 2015; Catherine Ho, "Lanny Breuer, Chief of DOJ's Criminal Division, Returns to His Old Law Firm Covington and Burling," *Washington Post*, March 28, 2013.

302 Lorraine O'Reilly Brown: *United States of America v. Lorraine Brown*, United States District Court, Middle District of Florida, Jacksonville Division, Case No. 3:12-cr-198-J-2S, filed November 20, 2012, available at www.scribd.com/doc /113917843/Brown.

302 LPS wiggled out of criminal indictments: "Florida-Based Lender Processing Services Inc. to Pay $35 Million in Agreement to Resolve Criminal Fraud Violations Following Guilty Plea from Subsidiary CEO," press release, U.S. Department of Justice, February 15, 2013.

302 the 10,567 polluted DocX land records: John O'Brien, Affidavit and Request for Restitution, *United States of America v. Lorraine Brown*, United States District Court, Middle District of Florida, Jacksonville Division, Case No. 3:12-cr-198-J-2S, filed January 11, 2013.

303 "I don't know how you fix that": Excerpt of Sentencing Hearing, *United States of America v. Lorraine Brown*, United States District Court, Middle District of Florida, Jacksonville Division, Case No. 3:12-cr-198-J-2S, April 23, 2013, 17–18.

303 Brown got five years, the maximum sentence: "Former Executive at Florida-Based Lender Processing Services Inc. Sentenced to Five Years in Prison for Role in Mortgage-Related Document Fraud Scheme," press release, U.S. Department of Justice, June 25, 2013.

305 Too many judges in Florida, and really nationwide: Allison Fitzgerald, "Homeowners Steamrolled as Florida Courts Clear Foreclosure Backlog," Center for Public Integrity, September 10, 2014.

306 the state did pass a law to speed up the foreclosure process: Drew Harwell, "'Faster Foreclosures' Law Unintentionally Slows Florida Filings," *Tampa Bay Times*, September 10, 2013.

306 One judge in Broward County closed 786 cases: Fitzgerald, "Homeowners Steamrolled."

306 Bondi threw up her hands: Kimberly Miller, "Attempt to Subpoena Foreclosure Mills Stalls," *Palm Beach Post*, February 6, 2012.

306 The Florida Bar belatedly disbarred David Stern: Andy Kroll, "Fallen Foreclosure King David J. Stern Disbarred," *Mother Jones*, January 13, 2014.

306 Marshall C. Watson agreed to a plea deal: Law Office of Evan M. Rosen, "Marshall Watson Foreclosure Mill Shut Down After Guilty Plea and Consent to Judgment, Changed Name to Choice Legal Group," January 9, 2013, www.evanmrosen.com/2013/01/09/marshall-watson-foreclosure-mill-shut-guilty-plea-consent-judgment-choice-legal.

306 They've built up significant appellate court case law: Adolfo Pesquera, "4th DCA Robo-Witnesses Ruling a Win for Former Condo Owners," *Daily Business Review*, August 29, 2012.

307 Off that deposition, Rosen won the case: Michael Redman, "Full Deposition of Lona Hunt: Robo-Verifier of Foreclosure Complaints for Seterus/Fannie Mae," 4closurefraud.org, November 12, 2014; Michael Redman, "Happy Thanksgiving from Lona Hunt—Foreclosure Case Dismissed After Taking Depo of Fannie Mae/Seterus Robo-Verifier," 4closurefraud.org, November 26, 2014.

307 the state supreme court ruled that voluntary dismissal was fine: Revised Opinion, *Roman Pino v. Bank of New York*, Supreme Court of Florida, Case No. SC11-697, issued February 7, 2013, available at www.floridasupremecourt.org/decisions/2013/sc11-697.pdf.

307 When he succeeds—and he often does—it's thrilling: Michael Redman, "Judge Has Enough, Tells Bank Lawyer She Is Referring Him to the Bar in Our Latest Trial Win!" 4closurefraud.org, February 23, 2015.

308 The case remains in limbo: *US Bank v. Mara Papasoff*, Case No. 50-2012-CA-001698XXXXMB, docket report available at http://courtcon.co.palm-beach.fl.us/pls/jiwp/ck_public_qry_doct.cp_dktrpt_frames?backto=P&case_id=502009CA005542XXXXMB&begin_date=&end_date=.

308 The house on Gazetta Way: *US Bank N.A. v. Lisa Epstein*, Case No. 50-2009-CA-005542XXXXMB, docket report at http://courtcon.co.palm-beach.fl.us/pls/jiwp/ck_public_qry_doct.cp_dktrpt_frames?backto=P&case_id=502009CA005542XXXXMB&begin_date=&end_date=.

311 the Consumer Financial Protection Bureau: Consumer Financial Protection Bureau, "2013 Real Estate Settlement Procedures Act (Regulation X) and Truth in Lending Act (Regulation Z) Mortgage Servicing Final Rules," January 17, 2013.

311 the Homeowner's Bill of Rights: "California Homeowner Bill of Rights Signed into Law," press release, California Office of the Attorney General, July 11, 2012; Jennifer Bjorhus, "Minnesota to Get Stricter Law on Home Foreclosures," *Minneapolis Star-Tribune*, May 23, 2013.

311 turn the island into a judicial foreclosure state: Robert Brown, "Hawaii Adopts Nation's 'Strongest' Foreclosure Law," *Honolulu Civil Beat*, May 4, 2011.

311 But the best estimate is close to six million: "CoreLogic Reports 38,000 Completed Foreclosures in July 2015," press release, September 8, 2015. "Since the financial crisis began in September 2008, there have been approximately 5.8 million completed foreclosures across the country." Since the housing bubble peaked at the end of 2006, the number of post-bubble foreclosures is much higher.

311 **linked high foreclosure rates with increased suicides:** Jason N. Houle and Michael T. Light, "The Home Foreclosure Crisis and Rising Suicide Rates, 2005 to 2010," *American Journal of Public Health*, April 17, 2014.

311 **"an extinction event":** Zoe Carpenter, "Five Years After Dodd-Frank, 'It's Still a Financial System That Needs Reform,'" *The Nation*, July 23, 2015.

312 **Diana Lewis lost 54 percent to 46 percent, becoming just the fourth:** Palm Beach County Supervisor of Elections, primary election results, August 26, 2014, available at http://results.enr.clarityelections.com/FL/Palm_Beach/52688/139169/en /summary.html; Jane Musgrave, "Ticktin Ousts Lewis, Goodman Tops Two Rivals in Palm Beach Judge Races," *Palm Beach Post*, August 27, 2014.

Afterword

314 **Trump selected his campaign finance chair:** Julie Hirschfeld Davis, Binyamin Appelbaum, and Maggie Haberman, "Trump Taps Hollywood's Mnuchin for Treasury and Dines with Romney," *New York Times*, November 29, 2016.

314 **purchased failed subprime lender IndyMac:** Tami Luhby, "Investors to Buy IndyMac—$13.9B," CNNMoney.com, January 2, 2009.

314 **changed the name to OneWest Bank:** William Heisel, "IndyMac's New Name: OneWest Bank," *Los Angeles Times*, March 20, 2009.

314 **sweetheart deal they struck:** Shared-Loss Agreement Between the Federal Deposit Insurance Corporation as Receiver for IndyMac Federal Bank and OneWest Bank, March 19, 2009, www.fdic.gov/about/freedom/indymacsharedlossagrmt.pdf.

314 **OneWest turned a $3 billion profit:** E. Scott Reckard, "Lender CIT to Buy OneWest Bank, Formerly IndyMac, for $3.4 Billion," *Los Angeles Times*, July 22, 2014.

314 **selling the bank to CIT:** James F. Peltz, "CIT Group Closes $3.4-Billion Purchase of OneWest Bank in Pasadena," *Los Angeles Times*, August 3, 2015.

314 **OneWest foreclosed on over 36,000 families:** "New Maps of OneWest Foreclosures in California Communities," California Reinvestment Coalition, badbankmerger.com/maps.

314 **68 percent of those evictions occurring in non-white zip codes:** Ibid.

314 **Leslie Parks of Minneapolis:** Abby Simons, "After 2-year Foreclosure Battle, She Owns Minneapolis Home," *Minneapolis Star-Tribune*, August 23, 2011.

314 **Heather McCreary of Sparks:** David Dayen, "Treasury Pick Steve Mnuchin Denies It, but Victims Describe His Bank as a Foreclosure Machine," *The Intercept*, January 19, 2017, theintercept.com/2017/01/19/treasury-pick-steve-mnuchin-denies-it -but-victims-describe-his-bank-as-a-foreclosure-machine.

314 **Tim Davis of northern Virginia:** Ibid.

314 **Myrtle Lewis, 103:** Jack Douglas Jr., "103-Year-Old North Texas Woman Fights to Keep Her House," CBS 11 News Dallas Fort Worth, November 21, 2014.

314 $89 million settlement: David Dayen, "Steve Mnuchin's Old Company Just Settled for $89 Million for Ripping Off the Government on Dodgy Loans," *The Intercept*, January 19, 2017, //theintercept.com/2017/05/16/steve-mnuchins-old-company -just-settled-for-89-million-for-ripping-off-the-government-on-dodgy-loans.

314 Teena Colebrook: Josh Boak and Jeff Horowitz, "Trump Voter Lost Home, Blames Incoming Treasury Secretary," Associated Press, December 2, 2016.

315 Senate Democrats brought four homeowners: "Senate Democrats Host Forum with Mnuchin Bank OneWest Foreclosure Victims," January 18, 2017, www. youtube.com/watch?v=kPjfVonvPkE.

315 camped out on the lawn: Kari Huus, "Homeowner Taps 'Occupy' Protest to Avoid Foreclosure," MSNBC.com, October 17, 2011.

315 led a march back: Dayen, "Treasury Pick Steve Mnuchin Denies It, but Victims Describe His Bank as a Foreclosure Machine."

315 demonstrators sat down: Sarah Jaffe, " 'The Swamp Is Goldman Sachs': How the Bank Is Rewarded for Putting Profits over People," *The Guardian*, January 18, 2017.

315 I delivered my contribution: David Dayen, "Treasury Nominee Steve Mnuchin's Bank Accused of 'Widespread Misconduct' in Leaked Memo," *The Intercept*, January 3, 2017, theintercept.com/2017/01/03/treasury-nominee-steve-mnuchins-bank -accused-of-widespread-misconduct-in-leaked-memo.

315 Harris called it: David Dayen, "Kamala Harris Fails to Explain Why She Didn't Prosecute Steven Mnuchin's Bank," *The Intercept*, January 5, 2017, theintercept. com/2017/01/05/kamala-harris-fails-to-explain-why-she-didnt-prosecute-steven -mnuchins-bank.

316 At the confirmation hearing: Treasury Secretary Confirmation Hearing, January 19, 2017, www.c-span.org/video/?421858-1/treasury-secretary-nominee-steven -mnuchin-testifies-confirmation-hearing.

316 Mnuchin grew prickly: David Dayen, "Democrats Missed an Opportunity to Expose Steve Mnuchin as a Predator," *The Nation*, January 19, 2017.

316 "trial plan offers extended": "Making Home Affordable Program Performance Report Through July 2013," Treasury Department, www.treasury.gov/initiatives /financial-stability/reports/Documents/July%202013%20MHA%20Report%20Final.pdf.

316 lying in written answers: David Dayen, "Mnuchin Lied About His Bank's History of Robo-Signing Foreclosure Documents," *The Intercept*, January 25, 2017, theintercept.com/2017/01/25/mnuchin-lied-about-his-banks-history-of-robo-signing -foreclosure-documents.

316 dozens of other clear examples: Alan Johnson and Jill Riepenhoff, "Trump Treasury Pick Mnuchin Misled Senate on Foreclosures, Ohio Cases Show," *Columbus Dispatch*, January 29, 2017.

316 Mnuchin responded by lying again: David Dayen, "Mnuchin Again Denies Robo-Signing, Despite Yet More Evidence He Is Lying," *The Intercept*, January 30, 2017, theintercept.com/2017/01/30/mnuchin-again-denies-robo-signing-despite-yet -more-evidence-he-is-lying.

316 handpicked the not-so-independent reviewers: David Dayen, "Wonder Warren," *American Prospect*, February 6, 2013.

317 Mnuchin became treasury secretary: Alan Rappeport, "Steven Mnuchin Is Confirmed as Treasury Secretary," *New York Times*, February 13, 2017.

317 he hired Craig Phillips: Matt Taibbi, "Man Trump Named to Fix Mortgage Markets Figured in Infamous Financial Crisis Episode," *Rolling Stone*, April 28, 2017.

317 Brian Brooks also got a top job: Doina Chiacu, "Fannie Mae's Brooks to Be Nominated U.S. Deputy Treasury Secretary," Reuters, June 10, 2017.

317 Trump chose Joseph Otting: Jesse Hamilton, "Trump Picks Ex-Banker Otting to Regulate Wall Street at OCC," Bloomberg, June 5, 2017.

317 Wilbur Ross, Trump's commerce secretary: Lynn Szymoniak, "Who Is Wilbur Ross?" Housing Justice Foundation, November 25, 2016.

317 A June 2017 study: John M. Griffin, Samuel A. Kruger, and Gonzalo Maturana, "Do Labor Markets Discipline? Evidence from RMBS Bankers," June 1, 2017, papers.ssrn.com/sol3/papers.cfm?abstract_id=2977741.

318 According to the files: David Dayen, "Inside the Abortive FBI Investigation of Illegal Foreclosure in Florida," Vice.com, May 31, 2016, www.vice.com/en_us/article /yvxajb/what-happened-when-the-fbi-investigated-foreclosure-fraud-in-florida.

319 sentenced in 2013: "Former Executive at Florida-Based Lender Processing Services Inc. Sentenced to Five Years in Prison for Role in Mortgage-Related Document Fraud Scheme," U.S. Department of Justice, June 25, 2013, www.fbi.gov/jacksonville /press-releases/2013/former-executive-at-florida-based-lender-processing-services-inc. -sentenced-to-five-years-in-prison-for-role-in-mortgage-related-document-fraud -scheme.

319 paroled into federal custody: David Dayen, "The Only Person Jailed for the Foreclosure Crisis Will Soon Go Free," *Vice*, August 30, 2016, www.vice.com/en_us /article/the-only-person-jailed-for-the-foreclosure-crisis-will-soon-go-free.

320 exposé of Wilbur Ross: Lynn Szymoniak, "Who Is Wilbur Ross?" Housing Justice Foundation, November 25, 2016.

320 a mortgage assignment from February 2007: Michael Redman, "MERS Assignment Fail: Mortgage Electronic Registration Sidesteps, Inc.," 4closurefraud.org, May 12, 2017.

320 Wells Fargo trying to evict: Michael Redman, "Please Help Stop Wells Fargo Foreclosure on 85 Year Old Woman with Alzheimer's Disease," 4closure fraud.org, June 4, 2016.

320 Michigan woman's property foreclosed: Michael Redman, "Michigan: Hillsdalle County Forecloses on Woman's Property Over $7 Late Fee," 4closurefraud.org, June 14, 2016.

321 a fabricated set of documents: Michael Redman, "Foreclosure Tales from the Interwebz: Forged, Fabricated, Altered Documents," 4closurefraud.org, June 19, 2016.

321 found a job description: Michael Redman, "Fraudclosure: Select Portfolio Servicing Help Wanted—Chain of Title Specialist," 4closurefraud.org, June 11, 2016.

321 April Charney sent him another one: Michael Redman, "Now Hiring! Pay Raise $22.00–$24.00/Hour: Default Breach Specialist to Complete the Chain of Title Prior to Foreclosure Referral," 4closurefraud.org, June 14, 2016.

321 *Living Lies* tracked down: Neil Garfield, "Ocwen Employee Admits She 'Creates Needed Documents,'" *Living Lies*, June 25, 2016.

321 Michael also wrote about Ocwen: Michael Redman "The Script: Ocwen Lawyer Spoon-Fed Foreclosure Questions and Answers to Robo-Witnesses," 4closurefraud.org, August 23, 2016.

321 two dozen states charged Ocwen: David Dayen, "The CFPB Just Sued a Crooked Mortgage Servicer but Indicted Itself," *The Nation*, April 21, 2017.

321 A few states actually banned the company: Ben Lane, "Massachusetts Sues Ocwen for 'Abusive' Mortgage Servicing Practices," Housing Wire, May 2, 2017.

321 CFPB fined Ocwen: *Consumer Financial Protection Bureau et al v. Ocwen Financial Corporation and Ocwen Loan Servicing*, United States District Court for the District of Columbia, consent judgment filed December 10, 2013, files.consumerfinance.gov/f/201312_cfpb_consent-order_ocwen.pdf.

322 have been dismissed in court: Stacy Cowley and Jessica Silver-Greenberg, "As Paperwork Goes Missing, Private Student Loan Debts May Be Wiped Away," *New York Times*, July 17, 2017.

322 The Capitol Forum: Lisa Epstein staff page, The Capitol Forum, thecapitolforum.com/staff/lisa-epstein.

322 rip-offs by a subprime auto lender: Lisa Epstein, "Credit Acceptance Corp: How the Machine Works," The Capitol Forum, November 17, 2016.

322 a company that offered fuel discounts for small businesses: Lisa Epstein: "FleetCor: Risk Based Pricing Raises Additional Disclosure Issues and Further Undermines the Fuel Card Value Proposition," The Capitol Forum, April 11, 2017.

323 Goldman started buying up distressed loans: David Dayen, "How Goldman Sachs Wins, and You Lose, From Its Mortgage Crisis 'Punishment,'" *Fiscal Times*, March 21, 2017.

323 Deutsche Bank's strategy was even loopier: Matt Scully, "Deutsche Bank Eyes Private Equity Help in U.S. Settlement," Bloomberg, January 4, 2017.

323 CBS MarketWatch quoted Lisa: Andrea Riquier, "How Should Deutsche Bank Repay Consumers for Its Toxic Mortgage Mess?" CBS MarketWatch, January 17, 2017.

323 deemed one of these bonfires: Michael Redman, "Torch the Fraud | 4closureFraud.org and ForeclosureHamlet.org Host a Bonfire on the Beach," 4closurefraud.org, February 28, 2011.

323 According to the freshly named Black Knight Financial Services: Mortgage Monitor, Black Knight Financial Services, March 2017 report, www.bkfs.com/Data/DataReports/BKFS_MM_Mar2017_Report.pdf.

324 wondering whether another bubble: Sean Williams, "With Home Prices Soaring, Should We Worry About Bubble 2.0?" *Newsweek*, November 13, 2016.

324 new standards from the Consumer Financial Protection Bureau: Ability-to-Repay and Qualified Mortgage Standards Under the Truth in Lending Act (Regulation Z), Consumer Financial Protection Bureau, January 30, 2013, www.federalregister.gov/documents/2013/01/30/2013-00736/ability-to-repay-and-qualified-mortgage-standards-under-the-truth-in-lending-act-regulation-z.

324 started to flow my way: David Dayen, "Sorry You Lost Your Home: Americans Deserve More Than an Apology for the Foreclosure Fraud Epidemic," *Salon*, August 9, 2016.

325 banks breaking into their homes: Marina Read, "This Crusade Ain't New," *Pro Se We Stand* (blog), May 7, 2016, www.prosewestand.org/unlegal/this-crusade-aint-new.

325 despite never missing a payment: Andy Wise, "Mortgage-Servicer Faces Allegations of Foreclosure Fraud," WMC Action News 5, September 22, 2016; and Michael Redman, "Couple Loses Foreclosure Battle Never Missing a Single Payment," 4closurefraud.org, October 24, 2016.

325 magically appearing affidavits: *HSBC Bank USA v. Joseph T. Buset et al.*, Circuit Court of the Eleventh Judicial Circuit, In and For Miami Dade County, Order Granting Defendant's Motion for Involuntary Dismissal for Unclean Hands and Lack of Substantial Competent Evidence, April 26, 2016, pdfserver.amlaw.com/dbr/Ocwen-Order.pdf.

325 signatures on mortgage documents: David Dayen, "Foreclosure Fraud Is Supposed to Be a Thing of the Past, but It Happens Every Day," *The Intercept*, May 18, 2016, theintercept.com/2016/05/18/foreclosure-fraud-is-supposed-to-be-a-thing-of-the-past-but-it-happens-every-day.

325 Erik and Renee Sundquist: David Dayen, "How a Cruel Foreclosure Drove a Couple to the Brink of Death," *Vice*, March 31, 2017.

INDEX

ABOUT THE AUTHOR

David Dayen is a contributor to *Salon* and *The Intercept*, and a weekly columnist for the *Fiscal Times* and the *New Republic*. He also writes for publications including the *American Prospect*, *The Guardian*, *Vice*, and the *Huffington Post*. He lives in Los Angeles. This is his first book.

PUBLISHING IN THE PUBLIC INTEREST

Thank you for reading this book published by The New Press. The New Press is a nonprofit, public interest publisher. New Press books and authors play a crucial role in sparking conversations about the key political and social issues of our day.

We hope you enjoyed this book and that you will stay in touch with The New Press. Here are a few ways to stay up to date with our books, events, and the issues we cover:

- Sign up at www.thenewpress.com/subscribe to receive updates on New Press authors and issues and to be notified about local events
- Like us on Facebook: www.facebook.com/newpressbooks
- Follow us on Twitter: www.twitter.com/thenewpress

Please consider buying New Press books for yourself; for friends and family; or to donate to schools, libraries, community centers, prison libraries, and other organizations involved with the issues our authors write about.

The New Press is a 501(c)(3) nonprofit organization. You can also support our work with a tax-deductible gift by visiting www.thenewpress.com/donate.

THE STUDS AND IDA TERKEL AWARD

On the occasion of his ninetieth birthday, Studs Terkel and his son, Dan, announced the creation of the Studs and Ida Terkel Author Fund. The Fund is devoted to supporting the work of promising authors in a range of fields who share Studs's fascination with the many dimensions of everyday life in America and who, like Studs, are committed to exploring aspects of America that are not adequately represented by the mainstream media. The Terkel Fund furnishes authors with the vital support they need to conduct their research and writing, providing a new generation of writers the freedom to experiment and innovate in the spirit of Studs's own work.

Studs and Ida Terkel Award Winners

David Dayen, *Chain of Title: How Three Ordinary Americans Uncovered Wall Street's Great Foreclosure Fraud*

Aaron Swartz, *The Boy Who Could Change the World: The Writings of Aaron Swartz* (awarded posthumously)

Beth Zasloff and Joshua Steckel, *Hold Fast to Dreams: A College Guidance Counselor, His Students, and the Vision of a Life Beyond Poverty*

Barbara J. Miner, *Lessons from the Heartland: A Turbulent Half-Century of Public Education in an Iconic American City*

Lynn Powell, *Framing Innocence: A Mother's Photographs, a Prosecutor's Zeal, and a Small Town's Response*

Lauri Lebo, *The Devil in Dover: An Insider's Story of Dogma v. Darwin in Small-Town America*